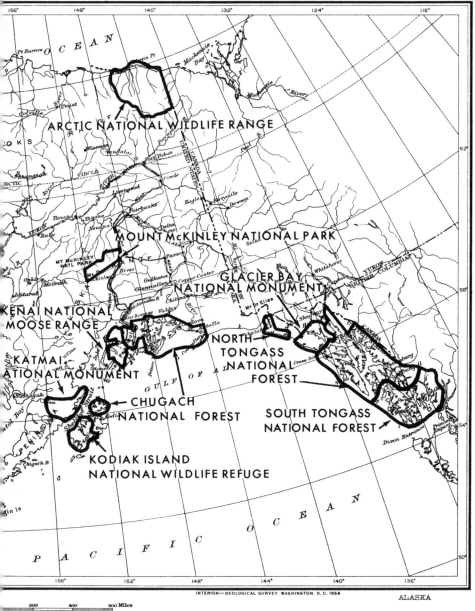

ALASKA TREES AND SHRUBS

by

Leslie A. Viereck, Principal Plant Ecologist
Institute of Northern Forestry
Pacific Northwest Forest and Range Experiment Station
U.S.D.A. Forest Service, College, Alaska

and

Elbert L. Little, Jr., Chief Dendrologist
Division of Timber Management Research
U.S.D.A. Forest Service, Washington, D.C.

Agriculture Handbook No. 410
Forest Service
United States Department of Agriculture

Washington, D.C.
1972

Reprinted by the
University of Alaska Press

Fairbanks, Alaska
1986

Library of Congress Catalog Card Number: 86-050727

ISBN 0-912006-19-6

Cover: The scratchboard cover design by William Berry is a typical white spruce—
paper birch stand in interior Alaska in early winter. The shrub layer is
alder and willow.

For sale by the   University of Alaska Press
Signers' Hall
University of Alaska
Fairbanks, Alaska 99775-1580

PREFACE TO THE 1986 PRINTING OF ALASKA TREES AND SHRUBS

It gives me great pleasure to write this new preface to "Alaska Trees and Shrubs" and to acknowledge that the University of Alaska Press will now take over publication of the book. After three printings by the U.S. Government Printing Office, the book has been out of print and unavailable for the past few years.

This series of publications first began in 1929 when the USDA Forest Service published the "Pocket Guide to Alaska Trees," written by Raymond Taylor. The small pocket guide was revised by Taylor and Dr. E.L. Little and again published by the Forest Service in 1950. In 1967, when Dr. Little and I first began work on the present volume, we decided to include all of the native Alaska woody species, thus considerably enlarging the scope of the book. Our efforts over the next eight years resulted in three publications: "Alaska Trees and Shrubs;" "Guide to Alaska Trees;" and "Atlas of United States Trees, Volume 2, Alaska Trees and Common Shrubs" (1975). Both the Guide and the Atlas are now out of print.

When I first learned of the interest of the University of Alaska Press in reprinting "Alaska Trees and Shrubs," I thought immediately of making revisions, updating distribution maps and nomenclature, and even interspersing some colored photographs into the book. However, after considerable thought and discussion with the University of Alaska Press, it was decided that it would be best at this time to reprint the book in its original form and to wait until another time for making revisions. Any revisions in the original copy would have greatly increased the cost of publication and caused delays of at least a year. Because the changes would be minor revisions in distribution and nomenclature, it was decided to delay making any revisions until a later printing; therefore, the book is essentially identical to the original "Alaska Trees and Shrubs," first published in 1972.

The land ownership in Alaska has changed considerably since the book was published in 1972; one only needs to compare a current map of Alaska's federal parks, refuges, and forests with that produced on the inside front cover of this book. In the text of the book, however, the distribution of each species is listed for the national parks, refuges, and forests that were in existence prior to the Alaska Native Claims Settlement Act and the Alaska National Interests Land Conservation Act. It was, therefore, necessary to leave in this old map of federal units, or make major revision in the text.

Although land ownership maps of Alaska have changed drastically since the early 1970s, the distributions of the trees and shrubs have changed little, if at all. As the vegetation of Alaska becomes more well known through new studies and through additional plant collections, ranges of some of the trees and shrubs have been extended beyond those indicated on the maps. In most cases the range extensions are minor and would not show on the small maps in the book. There are a few exceptions to this: Green mountain ash (*Sorbus scopulina*) was recently found in the Kobuk Valley, extending the known range by several hundred kilometers. A thorough search of new herbarium specimens and recent reports might reveal other major range extensions within Alaska, but there are none that I am aware of at this time. Under the direction of Dr. David Murray, the University of Alaska Herbarium is in the process of computerizing its entire collection plus literature citations of past Alaska plant collections. It should, therefore, be possible to use computer-generated range maps of Alaska tree and shrub species in a future revision of "Alaska Trees and Shrubs."

There have also been some nomenclature changes in some of the shrubs since the book was published. For example, a recent study of the alders (the genus *Alnus*) of the world resulted in American green alder (*Alnus crispa*) and Sitka alder (*Alnus sinuata*) being changed from separate species to subspecies of *Alnus viridis*. Under this new nomenclature, American green alder becomes *Alnus viridis* subsp. *crispa* (Ait.) Turrill and Sitka alder becomes *Alnus viridis* subsp. *sinuata* (Regel) Love & Love. In the same study, thinleaf alder is renamed from *Alnus tenuifolia* to *Alnus incana* subsp. *tenuifolia* (Nutt.) Breitung.

In the case of alder there is no change in the common names, but a recent study of the genus *Spiraea* changed the name *Spiraea beauverdiana* to *Spiraea steveni* (Schn.) Rydb., thus making the common name Beauverd spirea incorrect. The alternate common name "Alaska spirea" might now be more appropriate. Several other minor name changes will be needed in the next revision to keep up with the ever-changing plant names resulting from new taxonomic studies.

One major omission from this 1986 edition of "Alaska Trees and Shrubs" is the fold-out Vegetation Map of Alaska. Apparently the original plates for this map have been lost. There presently is no adequately scaled vegetation map of Alaska available. The "Major Ecosystems of Alaska" map produced by the Joint Federal-State Land Use Planning Commission for Alaska in 1973 is out of print, as is an earlier vegetation map (1963) by Lloyd Spetzman. Alaska is sorely in need of a new statewide vegetation map based on recent vegetation inventories and the excellent new high-altitude aerial photography.

Dr. Elbert L. Little, coauthor of the book, has retired from the Forest Service but is active in his role as the U.S. authority on both North American and tropical tree taxonomy. Dr. Little was coauthor of the 1950 edition of the "Pocket Guide to Alaska Trees" and made several field trips in Alaska, including the extensive field trips we made together during the preparation of "Alaska Trees and Shrubs." Without his support and guidance throughout the long publication process, it is likely that "Alaska Trees and Shrubs" would not have survived the many tedious and detailed steps necessary for the completion of a book of this nature. I especially appreciated his cooperation during the four months that I spent in Washington DC, when I was going through Alaskan collections in the Forest Service and National herbaria and preparing descriptions and maps for the book.

Finally, I would like to dedicate this new printing of "Alaska Trees and Shrubs" to the cover artist, William D. Berry, who was killed in Fairbanks in 1979. Bill was a personal friend who had a great appreciation for all aspects of the natural world. I believe that in the simple scratchboard drawing on the cover Bill Berry has captured the unique feeling of an interior Alaskan spruce-birch forest in winter.

Leslie A. Viereck
Principal Plant Ecologist
Institute of Northern Forestry
USDA Forest Service
Fairbanks, Alaska

May 1986

CONTENTS

LIST OF SPECIES[1]

---

[1] Size is indicated by letters: LT, large tree; MT, medium tree; ST, small tree; LS, large shrub; MS, medium shrub; SS, small shrub; PS, prostrate shrub. General distribution is given as I, interior, and C, coastal, with small letter where restricted, and R, rare. The 10 tree species producing nearly all the commercial timber are indicated by an asterisk (*). Explanation under Statistical Summary, page 6.

vi

INTRODUCTION

"Alaska Trees and Shrubs" describes and illustrates the native woody plants of the 49th State. It follows "Pocket Guide to Alaska Trees" (Taylor and Little 1950[1]) as a somewhat larger reference covering also the shrubs, their identification, distribution, and uses.

Upon the elevation of Alaska to statehood in 1959, interest in Alaska's natural resources, including management and conservation, has greatly increased. This handbook was prepared for people desiring to learn the names of native trees and shrubs and additional related information. The varied audience includes: (1) Foresters, wildlife managers, and recreation and land-use planners who need to identify woody plants in their work in land management and especially the many seasonal employees from outside; (2) Alaskan residents with a desire to know more about their natural surroundings; (3) tourists with an interest in the scenery and vegetation; (4) students and teachers studying various aspects of plant life; (5) military personnel in programs of conservation and survival; (6) scientific groups, especially those with meetings or field trips in Alaska; and (7) conservation groups concerned with the preservation and development of the State's resources; and (8) all who are interested in the environment in general and problems such as destruction of vegetation and pollution.

Trees and shrubs, classed as woody plants, have hard stems composed largely of wood tissue. These stems are perennial, in that they remain above the ground from year to year. In contrast, herbs are either soft stemmed plants that die at the end of the growing season (annuals) or are plants whose stems die down to the ground each year (perennials). The numerous species of herbs, such as wildflowers, weeds, grasses, and sedges, are not included in this handbook.

Trees are defined as woody plants having one erect perennial stem or trunk at least 3 in. (7.5 cm.) in diameter at breast height (4½ ft., 1.4 m.), a more or less definitely formed crown of foliage, and a height of at least 12 ft. (4 m.) (Little 1953). However, large willows of tree size but with several trunks from the same root and shrubby species rarely attaining these dimensions are accepted here as trees.

Shrubs are woody plants smaller than trees, commonly with several perennial stems from the base. Among these are large or high shrubs and small or low shrubs. Also included are dwarf shrubs and subshrubs, creeping or prostrate plants with erect woody stems or woody at base, even if only 1–2 in. (2.5–5 cm.) above the ground. Woody vines, or plants with climbing stems supported usually on other plants, are not native in the northernmost State.

Alaska has no woody plants poisonous to the touch or in contact with the skin. Poison-ivy and

[1] Names and dates in parentheses refer to Selected References, p. 254.

poison-oak (*Rhus* spp.), though widespread in all but 1 of the lower 48 States, are absent. However, as noted, several species (also some herbs) have fruits or foliage poisonous when eaten.

Identification of the trees and shrubs of Alaska is not difficult, because relatively few kinds of trees and shrubs grow in far northern lands. Most States contain within their boundaries at least twice as many native tree species as does Alaska. The number seems relatively less also, because some tree species generally are shrubby and many are not widely distributed within the State.

New residents and visitors will find some familiar species. Nearly all species of large woody plants native in Alaska grow wild somewhere in the lower 48 States. More than half of the Alaska tree species range as far south as some part of California.

This handbook covers all Alaska from the narrow southeastern coastal region along the Pacific Ocean west and southwest through the long chain of the Aleutian Islands, and north through the interior to the Arctic Ocean, also the many islands along the coasts. However, this reference should be useful over a larger area in northwestern Canada, including the Yukon Territory, District of Mackenzie, and northwestern British Columbia. Most native woody plants of those adjacent areas will be found here.

The species of wild woody plants recorded in the technical botanical floras of Alaska are included. No additions have been noted, but 3 more shrub species have been observed to reach tree size. Nearly all species are described and illustrated. However, 5 rare or minor species are mentioned briefly under their closest relatives. In general, the variations within a species, such as varieties and subspecies, are not distinguished, but these can be found in the botanical floras. Cultivated plants introduced from other areas, such as ornamental shrubs and fruits, are not included. Many native species, being adapted to the local climates, are grown around houses as shade trees and ornamental shrubs. One introduced ornamental tree species, European mountain-ash, merits inclusion, having spread from cultivation until established or naturalized.

Previous Work

Many botanists and foresters have studied the trees and shrubs of Alaska. Naturalists with the early exploring expeditions collected botanical specimens, which were named by European specialists. A history of the botanical exploration has been prepared by Hultén (1940a).

Information about the woody plants of the 49th State has appeared in numerous publications. Selected References (p. 254) lists many, such as floras, monographs, and lists, which have been helpful in the preparation of this handbook and which may be consulted for further details. The most comprehensive references for identification of the higher plants of Alaska are the technical floras by Hultén (1941–50, 1960, 1968) and by Anderson (1959).

Foresters have long been active in Alaska. Most of the valuable coastal forest lands were designated as forest reserves between the years 1892 and 1902. These areas became the Tongass and Chugach National Forests in 1907, 2 years after establishment of the Forest Service in the United States Department of Agriculture. Under multiple use planning, these publicly owned timberlands are managed for orderly development of the many resources so that the land remains productive.

The trees of Alaska were included in the classic, well illustrated reference published in 1908 (reprinted in 1967), "Forest Trees of the Pacific Slope," by George B. Sudworth (1864–1927), for many years dendrologist in the Forest Service. "Pocket Guide to Alaska Trees" by Raymond F. Taylor, research forester, appeared first in 1929. This compact booklet described and illustrated 28 species. A revision in 1950 by Taylor and Little contained 31 species (1 naturalized), as well as brief descriptions of 12 shrub species.

Many other publications on the forests and trees of Alaska have been issued by the Forest Service. "Alaska's Forest Resource" (Hutchison 1967) is a report of the first forest inventory of Alaska, made as part of the nationwide Forest Survey. "Characteristics of Alaska Woods" (U.S. Forest Products Laboratory 1963) compiled information relating to the characteristics, distribution, and utilization of 11 commercially important species.

Forestry research in Alaska is being conducted by the USDA Forest Service through its Institute of Northern Forestry under the Pacific Northwest Forest and Range Experiment Station, with headquarters at 809 NE. 6th Ave., P.O. Box 3141, Portland, Oreg. 97208. Following early studies in the 1920's, a project location (formerly research center) was established at Juneau in 1948. Present address is Federal Bldg., P.O. Box 909, Juneau, Alaska 99801. Another project location at the University of Alaska is the Forestry Sciences Laboratory, College, Alaska 99701.

Preparation of this Handbook

An extensive field trip in Alaska by the junior author in 1961 indicated the need for a reference for identification of woody plants and served as the start in the preparation of this handbook. As the dendrologist of the USDA Forest Service, he was co-author of the 1950 revision of "Pocket Guide to Alaska Trees" (Taylor and Little 1950) and included the 49th State in publications about the trees of the United States.

The senior author has been engaged in field work in Alaska since 1949 with various Federal and State agencies including Mt. McKinley National Park, U.S. Army, Atomic Energy Commission, University of Alaska, and Alaska Department of Fish and Game. Since 1963 he has been conducting research on the forests of interior Alaska with the Institute of Northern Forestry, of the Forest Service, at College, Alaska.

During the preparation of this handbook, the authors have collected and examined many botanical specimens of the woody plants of Alaska. Their plant collections have been deposited mostly in the Forest Service Herbaria at Fort Collins, Colorado, and Juneau, Alaska, and the University of Alaska at College. The large collections at the National Herbarium, U.S. National Museum of Natural History, Washington, D.C., have been consulted also. A set of the junior author's specimens has been deposited there.

The text of the willow genus (*Salix*), the heath family (Ericaceae), and several other families was prepared by the senior author. The junior author wrote the text of the trees (except willow), the rose family (Rosaceae), and several other families.

The range maps in this handbook were prepared by the senior author primarily from the excellent detailed distribution maps in "Flora of Alaska and Neighboring Territories" by Eric Hultén (1968). Additional information has been

3

compiled from published and unpublished sources including reports and other information from the Forest Service, Bureau of Land Management, and Alaska Department of Fish and Game, and from the authors' observations. Maps for the willows follow closely those in "The Genus *Salix* in Alaska and Yukon" by George W. Argus (1972).

There is still much to be learned about tree and shrub distribution in Alaska. In order that more detailed information can be assembled, the earlier request for additional data, particularly regarding the ranges of trees and shrubs, is repeated here. This information can be sent to the Forestry Sciences Laboratory, College, Alaska 99701.

Plan

As listed under Contents, this Introduction is followed by: Vegetation of Alaska, Keys for Identification, the descriptive text of Alaska Trees and Shrubs in the usual botanical arrangement by plant families, and an index of common and scientific names. A brief description is given for each plant family and for each genus with 2 or more species. The species are numbered in one series for ready reference to drawings and maps.

For each species there are included: (1) Common and scientific names, also other names in use; (2) nontechnical description with emphasis on identification, vegetative characters including size and habit, leaves, twigs, and buds (also bark and wood of trees), and reproductive characters, such as flowers and fruits; (3) notes including abundance, site, vegetation type, and uses, such as wood, food, and wildlife; (4) geographic distribution both within and outside Alaska; (5) distribution map of Alaska; and (6) drawing.

Common and scientific names of trees are those accepted by the Forest Service, U.S. Department of Agriculture (Little 1953). Scientific names of shrubs follow conservative usage. Other widely used names including synonyms have been added.

Descriptions and notes refer to trees and shrubs growing in Alaska. Measurements are in the English system, but equivalents in the metric system have been added in parenthesis. Basic equivalents are: $\frac{1}{8}$ inch (3 millimeters); $\frac{3}{8}$ inch (1 centimeter); 1 inch (2.54 centimeters); 1 foot (0.3048 meter); 3.28 feet (1 meter). A ruler with both inches and centimeters appears on the last page. Trunk diameters of trees are measured at breast height ($4\frac{1}{2}$ ft. or 1.4 m.). Most tree species attain larger heights and diameters southward.

Geographic distribution within Alaska, as known, is stated by place names along the corners and borders of the range. The larger areas under management by the Federal Government are listed because of special interest to residents and visitors. Those cited are South Tongass, North Tongass, and Chugach National Forests, under the Forest Service, U.S. Department of Agriculture. Mt. McKinley National Park and Glacier Bay and Katmai National Monuments are under the National Park Service, U.S. Department of the Interior. Kodiak and Aleutian Islands National Wildlife Refuges, Kenai National Moose Range, and Arctic National Wildlife Range are all under the Fish and Wildlife Service, U.S. Department of the Interior. General distribution beyond Alaska has been added. A map of Alaska showing these areas, as well as most place names mentioned, is printed on the end papers in front.

Because of space limitations, the species distribution maps are small, thus, distribution is not shown in detail. The range is mapped as continuous to the outer boundaries. Small gaps within, such as high mountains and glacier-covered areas, are not shown.

Each species is illustrated by one or more line drawings. Most show a leafy twig (or stem) with both flowers and fruits, some also winter twigs. The scales are indicated, mostly natural size or one-half natural size.

How to Use this Handbook

Most native trees and shrubs of Alaska can be identified easily by reference to the drawings, descriptions, and maps. If you know a common name, consult the Index of Common and Scientific Names for page numbers, then match your specimen with the drawings and text. The List of Species under Contents may be consulted, if the family is recognized or if the specimen resembles one previously named.

It is desirable to have flowers or fruits or both, as well as a twig or stem with leaves. However, most trees can be identified from foliage alone.

Many trees and a few shrubs are evergreen and can be identified readily at any time of the year. For those plants shedding their leaves, frequently a few old leaves and fruits can be found in winter either still attached or on the ground beneath. In winter, twig and bud characters are useful. Maps may be used to eliminate species not known to grow wild where the specimen was found.

If clues to identification are lacking, Keys for Identification (page 24) should be consulted. There are keys for both summer and winter, which are based mostly on vegetative characters.

Acknowledgments

Many persons, notably fellow workers in the Forest Service, have helped in the preparation of this handbook. Arland S. Harris, research forester, has contributed much information on the trees and shrubs of southeast Alaska including descriptions, ranges, and uses. Mrs. Joan Foote, biological technician, had aided in collecting and processing specimens, drafting the vegetation map, reviewing the keys, and checking numerous details. Mrs. Suzanne Foster Manley, assistant botanist, has drafted the species distribution maps and made a number of drawings. Other drawings were made by Carol Ann Kanter, Hazel M. Hartman, and Marion D. Shoquist.

Many drawings are from Forest Service publications. The figures in "Pocket Guide to Alaska Trees" (1950) have been retained. Most appeared originally in "Forest Trees of the Pacific Slope" (Sudworth 1908). Nine others were made for the 1950 revision by Leta Hughey. That of tamarack was by W. F. Wight (1908). Some drawings of shrubs are from "Important Western Browse Plants" (Dayton 1931) and "Key to Important Woody Plants of Eastern Oregon and Washington" (Hayes and Garrison 1960). Six drawings of willows (*Salix*), species number 25, 26, 31, 32, 33, and 43, are from "The Willows of Alaska" (Coville 1901).

Twenty-two drawings are from "Vascular Plants of the Pacific Northwest" by C. Leo Hitchcock, Arthur Cronquist, Marion Ownbey, and J. W. Thompson (1955–69). These are species number 28, 29, 35, 37, 39, 56, 57, 58, 60, 61, 62, 65, 74, 76, 79, 80, 81, 82, 83, 87, 88, and 94. Grateful acknowledgment is given the authors and the publishers, University of Washington Press, Seattle, Wash., for permission to copy these illustrations.

William Berry, Alaskan artist, has prepared the scratchboard

5

cover design of a typical white spruce—paper birch stand in interior Alaska in early winter.

Dr. George W. Argus, Canadian Forestry Service, Ottawa, Ont., authority on the extremely complex genus of willows (*Salix*) with many years of field experience in Alaska, has assisted in identifying collections and in providing an advance manuscript copy of "The systematics of the genus *Salix* in Alaska and Yukon" (Argus 1972).

Professor Eric Hultén, Naturhistoriska Riksmuseum, Stockholm, Sweden, the foremost authority on Alaska plants, sent advance copies of his detailed species distribution maps, which have been adapted here with minor additions. His floras and other publications have been indispensable references in the preparation of this handbook.

Lloyd A. Spetzman, botanist, New Crops Research Branch, Agricultural Research Service, U.S. Department of Agriculture, who has had extensive field work in Alaska, has made many valuable suggestions and has checked the species distribution maps. His detailed vegetation map of Alaska has been followed largely in the smaller map published here. (In pocket.)

STATISTICAL SUMMARY

The trees and shrubs of Alaska, described and illustrated here, number 128 species in 54 genera and 19 plant families, as summarized in the List of Species under Contents. However, one of these, European mountain-ash (*Sorbus aucuparia*), is introduced. Also, 6 additional species of shrubs, mostly rare in Alaska, are mentioned briefly as follows: sprouting willow (*Salix stolonifera*), eastern arctic willow (*S. arctophila*), wedgeleaf willow (*S. spenophylla*), Athabasca willow (*S. athabascensis*), Canada gooseberry (*Ribes oxycanthoides*), and a small cranberry (*Vaccinium palustre*). Thus, the total number of native woody plants treated is 133 species.

Most species are grouped in relatively few families. The willow, rose, and heath families together have about two-thirds of the species. Of the 19 plant families, 9 are represented by a single species each, and 2 others by 2 each. The largest are as follows:

Willow family (Salicaceae), 2 genera, 36 species

Heath family (Ericaceae), 13 genera, 30 species

Rose family (Rosaceae), 10 genera, 21 species

Pine family (Pinaceae), 5 genera, 9 species

Gooseberry family (Grossulariaceae), 1 genus, 7 species

Honeysuckle family (Caprifoliaceae), 5 genera, 5 species

The largest genera of native woody plants in Alaska are as follows: willow (*Salix*), 33 species; blueberry (*Vaccinium*), 8; currant (*Ribes*), 7; and alder (*Alnus*), raspberry (*Rubus*), and cassiope (*Cassiope*), 4 each. Of the other genera, 8 have 3 species each, 9 have 2, and 31 have only 1.

Thus, willow (*Salix*) far outnumbers all other genera having 33 species, one-fourth of all the woody species in Alaska. Obviously, the cold climate and abundant wet sites are favorable for development of willows. Likewise, the heath family (Ericaceae), having nearly one-fourth of the species, is well displayed in the numerous bogs or muskegs and other sites with acid soils.

Growth Forms

The woody-plant species of Alaska differ slightly in size and growth form or life form from those of the lower 48 States. Size

6

class is indicated in the List of Species under Contents.

The size groups, with limits and number of native species totaling 127, are listed below. A species is counted only once, under the largest size attained.

LT Large trees, more than 70 ft. (21 m.) high, 12 species

MT Medium trees, 30–70 ft. (9–21 m.) high, 5 species

ST Small trees, 12–30 ft. (4–9 m.) high, 16 species

LS Large shrubs, 6–20 ft. (2–6 m.) high, 19 species

MS Medium shrubs, 2–6 ft. (0.3–2 m.) high, 30 species

SS Small or low shrubs, 0–2 ft. (0–0.6 m.) high, 12 species

PS Prostrate or creeping shrubs, 32 species

Parasite or epiphyte, 1 species

Woody vines, none

A more detailed classification of the life forms of plants based largely upon the location of renewal or perennating buds was prepared by Raunkiaer (1934). He showed further that the percentages of the different classes varied somewhat according to climate. The simpler classification here omits herbaceous plants and combines species growing in three rather different climates of the coastal and interior forests and tundra of Alaska, each with distinct vegetation.

Several observations on growth forms may be made when the woody plants of Alaska are compared with those of the lower 48 States. First, the number of woody plant species northward in Alaska becomes smaller, both in total and in percentage of total flora. The 133 native woody plant species listed here for Alaska are only about 8 percent of the 1,559 vascular plant species accepted by Hultén (1968) for a larger area covering also Yukon Territory and other neighboring territories.

The number of native tree species in the largest State is low, only 33 species, less than in any other State. Most States have more than twice as many tree species. The average height of tree species becomes less northward in Alaska. Only 12 species are classed as large trees. Nine of these are confined to the coastal forests of southeast Alaska, and only 3 are found in the interior forests. Of the 16 species of small trees, several commonly are shrubs and infrequently reach tree size. However, a few other species classed as large shrubs in Alaska are trees southward.

Vast areas of Alaska, shown as tundra on the vegetation map, have no native trees. The tundra vegetation beyond the tree line has a climate so severe that trees are absent. In some ways it corresponds to the alpine zone above timberline on high mountains southward.

Northward the number of shrub species becomes less in Alaska, also the height is relatively lower. However, the number of species of prostrate, or creeping, or mat-forming shrubs is higher, 32 species or nearly one-fourth of the total of woody plants. These dwarf plants with slender stems and a small amount of woody tissue at the base might have been omitted. Several are so slightly woody that they are often classed as herbs, subshrubs, or half-shrubs. These small shrubs, included with some hesitation, emphasize the adaptations to the severe cold climate.

The only native species of woody epiphyte or parasite, hemlock dwarf-mistletoe (*Arceuthobium tsugense*), is confined to southeast Alaska.

There are no native species of woody vines or climbing plants in Alaska. The nearest example is trailing black currant (*Ribes lax-iflorum*), which has branches running along the ground but is sometimes vinelike and climbing on shrubs.

A conspicuous element has evergreen leaves. Of the 14 species of conifers, all except 1 are evergreen with leaves reduced to needles or scales. Some species of creeping shrubs and low shrubs, particularly in the heath family, have persistent leaves, classed as broad but relatively small and thick. These plants may be covered by winter snows.

A few genera are represented by species of different sizes and growth forms. Willows (*Salix*) range from several species with tiny prostrate or creeping stems to 7 of small trees and 1 medium-sized tree. Both shrub and tree species are found in these genera: birch (*Betula*), alder (*Alnus*), mountain-ash (*Sorbus*), and serviceberry (*Amelanchier*). Dogwood (*Cornus*) and raspberry (*Rubus*) are represented not only by shrubs but by herbaceous species, which are mentioned also for identification.

Alaska Trees

Thirty-three of the 133 species of native woody plants in Alaska described here reach tree size, although several commonly are shrubby and a few are rare. As trees make up only one-fourth of the species of this handbook and were treated separately in "Pocket Guide to Alaska Trees" (Taylor and Little 1950), a summary seems appropriate.

In the List of Species under Contents, only 12 tree species in Alaska are classed as large, that is, more than 70 ft. (21 m.) high. However, 2 conifers of the southeastern coastal forests become very large. Sitka spruce (*Picea sitchensis*) reaches a height of 225 ft. (69 m.) and a trunk diameter of

8 ft. (2.4 m.) or more. Western hemlock (*Tsuga heterophylla*) attains 190 ft. (58 m.) in height and 5 ft. (1.5 m.) or more in trunk diameter. A giant black cottonwood (*Populus trichocarpa*) near Haines has a massive trunk 32 ft. 6 in. (9.9 m.) in circumference and a broken top 101 ft. (30.8 m.) high.

Sixteen species, about half, are small trees less than 30 ft. (9 m.) high. All 8 species of tree willows, as well as 8 others, are classed as both shrubs and trees and often may be seen as shrubs, especially in unfavorable sites.

Three additions to "Pocket Guide to Alaska Trees" are accepted here as sometimes reaching tree size. Grayleaf willow (*Salix glauca*) in favorable sites may become a small clump-forming tree to 20 ft. (6 m.) high and 5 in. (12.5 cm.) in trunk diameter. Pacific red elder (*Sambucus callicarpa*) and Greene mountain-ash (*Sorbus scopulina*) have been observed to reach the same height in southeast Alaska.

The 33 species of Alaska trees belong to 17 genera in 8 plant families. However, the pine family (*Pinaceae*) contains 9 species and the willow family (*Salicaceae*) 11 tree species. Largest genera are: willow (*Salix*), 8 tree species, and spruce (*Picea*), poplar (*Populus*), and alder (*Alnus*), 3 each.

Four tree species of southeast Alaska are so rare and local that they would not likely be seen without a special trip to the places mentioned. These are Pacific yew (*Taxus brevifolia*), Pacific silver fir (*Abies amabilis*), subalpine fir (*Abies lasiocarpa*), and Hooker willow (*Salix hookeriana*).

Nearly all the commercial timber of Alaska is produced by 10 tree species, indicated by an asterisk (*) in the List of Species. Six are conifers and 4 are hardwoods. In the coastal spruce-hemlock forests of southeastern Alaska the 5 important conifers are as follows: Sitka spruce (*Picea sitchensis*), western hemlock (*Tsuga heterophylla*), mountain hemlock (*Tsuga mertensiana*), western redcedar (*Thuja plicata*), and Alaska-cedar (*Chamaecyparis nootkatensis*). The lone commercial hardwood in the southeast is black poplar (*Populus trichocarpa*). In the interior spruce-hardwood forests, the commercially important species are white spruce (*Picea glauca*) and 3 hardwoods, balsam poplar (*Populus balsamifera*), quaking aspen (*Populus tremuloides*), and paper birch (*Betula papyrifera*).

The number of tree species native in any area of Alaska is relatively small. Many localities have fewer than 10 tree species, while great expanses of tundra beyond the tree line and above the timberline of mountains have none.

The extensive spruce-hardwood forests of interior Alaska are composed of only 3 coniferous tree species, white spruce (*Picea glauca*), black spruce (*P. mariana*), and tamarack (*Larix laricina*), and 3 hardwoods, balsam poplar (*Populus balsamifera*), quaking aspen (*P. tremuloides*), and paper birch (*Betula papyrifera*), also 5 or fewer species of willow (*Salix*) and 2 of alder (*Alnus*) sometimes reaching tree size.

Geographic Distribution

Numerous species of Alaska's arctic shrubs, also herbs, are widely distributed in far northern regions around the globe, or circumpolar, across Canada, Europe, and Asia to Siberia. Other Alaskan species extend just to northern Europe, while several range west into Siberia but not beyond. Some, known as arctic-alpine species, occur southward above the timberline in the alpine zone of the Rocky Mountains and high peaks of New England. These widespread species are indicated in the text by the range outside the State given for each. Also, Hultén (1968) published a small map of each Alaska species showing the entire natural distribution as seen around the North Pole.

The only Alaska tree species native also in the Old World is Sitka alder (*Alnus sinuata*), which ranges into northeastern Asia. By some authors thinleaf alder (*Alnus tenuifolia*) has been united with an Old World species, European speckled alder (*A. incana* (L.) Moench). Also, Pacific red elder (*Sambucus callicarpa*) has been treated also as a variety of European red elder (*S. racemosa* L.) of Eurasia.

Seven tree species of the interior spruce-hardwood forest are transcontinental in range, being widely distributed in the northern coniferous forest ("north woods" or boreal forest) from Alaska across Canada east to Labrador and Newfoundland and south into the Northeastern States. Besides the 3 common conifers and 3 hardwoods mentioned under Alaska Trees, Bebb willow (*Salix bebbiana*) is a small tree with similar distribution.

Three tree species have a great north-south distribution. Lodgepole pine (*Pinus contorta*) and black cottonwood (*Populus trichocarpa*) range south in the coastal forests from Alaska to California and beyond in mountains of northern Baja California, more than 30° of latitude. Quaking aspen (*Populus tremuloides*), the tree species with the greatest geographic extent in North America, has a north-south range of about 48° from Alaska and northwestern Canada south to mountains of Mexico. Sandbar willow (*Salix interior*), a shrub along the banks of the Yukon River in central Alaska, seems equally adapted as a small tree along the Mississippi River in Mississippi and Louisiana and ranges also into northern Mexico.

The woody plant species of Alaska generally can be separated

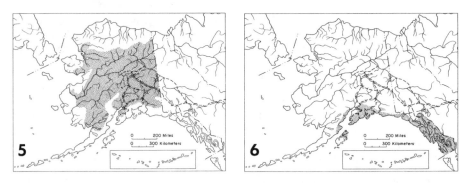

Left, map of white spruce (*Picea glauca*), showing maximum spruce-hardwood forests of the interior (I). Right, Sitka spruce (*Picea sitchensis*), showing occurrence of coastal spruce-hemlock forests (C) of southeast Alaska.

into two groups according to distribution within the State corresponding to the forest regions, as indicated in the List of Species under Contents. Many are confined to the coastal spruce-hemlock forests (C) of southeast Alaska. Others are characteristic of the spruce-hardwood forests of the interior (I) or the tundra beyond. However, some species are found in both regions or extend a short distance into the other. Of the 33 species of trees native in Alaska, 20 are confined to the coastal region, several to the southern end. The other 13 are found in the interior, but 11 of these extend at least a short distance southward to the Pacific coast also.

The two forest regions which limit the distribution of many woody plant species are shown on the vegetation map and by maps of the characteristic tree species, which are repeated here. The map of white spruce (*Picea glauca*) shows the maximum extent of the spruce-hardwood forests of the interior (I). That of Sitka spruce (*Picea sitchensis*) locates the occurrence of the coastal spruce-hemlock forests (C) of southeast Alaska.

All Alaska's tree species range southward across Canada to other States, with the exception of 3 usually shrubby species of willow (also 2 varieties of paper birch). Nineteen, or more than half, grow wild somewhere in California.

Local and Rare Species

Few of Alaska's species of native trees and shrubs are local or restricted in distribution and possibly rare or endangered at present. Nearly all woody species of local occurrence here have broader areas beyond the State's boundaries and obviously are not in danger of extinction. Most are found also eastward in adjacent Canada, but a few occur westward in nearby Asia. About 25 species of trees and shrubs have local ranges in Alaska, as shown in the maps published here. These local and rare species are mentioned below.

No species of woody plants is confined to Alaska, or endemic. One tree variety, by some authors accepted as a species, is restricted to Alaska though not rare, Kenai birch (*Betula papyrifera* var. *kenaica*). Setchell willow (*Salix setchelliana*), a distinct prostrate species, is endemic to Alaska and extreme southwestern Yukon Territory. Yakutat willow (*Salix amplifolia* Cov.), for many years regarded as a local species in the Yakutat Bay region, recently has been united as a synonym of Hooker willow (*Salix hookeriana*), of the

10

Pacific coast from British Columbia to California. A few minor variations of shrubs, named as varieties or subspecies but omitted here, may be endemic to Alaska also.

The woody species of local distribution may be grouped into the following: southeastern, interior, and extreme western. Several species of more southern range are rare at their northern limit in extreme southeast Alaska. They are:

Pacific yew *Taxus brevifolia*
Pacific silver fir *Abies amabilis*
Pacific ninebark
Physocarpus capitatus
Douglas spirea *Spiraea douglasii*
cranberry *Vaccinium palustre*

These more southern species are found both at the southern end of southeast Alaska and also northward at the northern end:

subalpine fir *Abies lasiocarpa*
black hawthorn *Crataegus douglasii*
western black raspberry
Rubus leucodermis
bearberry honeysuckle
Lonicera involucrata

A few species enter Alaska from Canada only at or near the northeast end of southeast Alaska, namely:

Hooker willow *Salix hookeriana*
pipsissewa *Chimaphila umbellata*
red mountain-heath
Phyllodoce empetriformis
snowberry *Symphoricarpos albus*

Two tree varieties cross the Rocky Mountains westward into the coastal forests at the head of Lynn Canal near Skagway and Haines: lodgepole pine (*Pinus contorta* var. *latifolia*) and western paper birch (*Betula papyrifera* var. *commutata*). Subalpine fir (*Abies lasiocarpa*) appears both here at the northern end of southeast Alaska and also at the southern end.

The following species, mostly Canadian, are local or rare in interior Alaska:

creeping juniper
Juniperus horizontalis
eastern arctic willow
Salix arctophila
Athabasca willow
Salix athabascensis
silver willow *Salix candida*
Canada gooseberry
Ribes oxycanthoides
saskatoon serviceberry
Amelanchier alnifolia
Woods rose *Rosa woodsii*
blue mountain-heath
Phyllodoce coerulea

Of special interest are a few east Asian species reaching North America only in western Alaska. Two known in Alaska only in the westernmost Aleutian Islands are Siberian mountain-ash (*Sorbus sambucifolia*) of Siberia and Miquel wintergreen (*Gaultheria miqueliana*) of Japan and adjacent Asia. Wedgeleaf willow (*Salix sphenophylla*) of Siberia has been reported from Seward Peninsula. Another Asiatic species common in the Aleutian Islands and local eastward and northward is Kamchatka rhododendron (*Rhododendrom camtschaticum*).

VEGETATION OF ALASKA

Alaska is a land of contrasts—contrasts in climate, physical geography, and vegetation. Containing 365.5 million acres (146 million hectares), Alaska has the highest mountain in North America, as well as hundreds of square miles of boggy lowlands. The climate varies from mild and wet to cold and dry. Temperatures in the interior may range over 150° F. (83° C.) in 1 year and precipitation may be less than 10 inches (250 mm.) annually in contrast to 150 inches (3,800 mm.) annual precipitation and a temperature range of 70° F. (38° C.) in the southeastern coastal area. Spanning nearly 1,300 miles (2,100 km.) of latitude and 2,200 miles (3,500 km.) of longitude, Alaska's vegetation varies from the towering fast growing forests of the southeastern coast, through the low, slow-growing boreal forests of the interior, to the treeless tundra of the north and west. Distribution of the vegetation types is shown in the folded map at the end of this handbook.

Of Alaska's great land surface, approximately 119 million acres (48 million hectares) are forested. Of these, 28 million acres (11.2 million hectares) are classified as "commercial forests." These great timber reserves provide the basis for one of the State's largest industries, and one that will continue to expand in size and importance as the timber demands of the heavily populated areas of the world increase. At present, most of the State's timber production is from the South Tongass, North Tongass, and Chugach National Forests, which contain 92 percent of commercial forests of coastal Alaska. Nearly all of the rest is from other areas within the coastal forests. But as timber demands increase, more and more use will be made of the great timber reserves of the interior boreal forests. Much of this land is presently under the jurisdiction of the Bureau of Land Management, but the State of Alaska is in the process of selecting most of the commercial forest land. Production of timber on State lands has increased annually since statehood and will continue to increase as more land is selected and the demand for timber grows.

In addition to the timber values, there are many other important uses of Alaska's forest and tundra areas. Much of Alaska is still wilderness, and the value of undisturbed wild areas may someday far outweigh the potential value for producing lumber and pulp. An increasing number of people look to Alaska for wilderness that is no longer present in the more developed areas of the world. Thus, it is important that some areas of Alaska forests be retained in their natural state. Tourism in Alaska is an important and growing industry, based primarily on scenic, wilderness, and wildlife values.

The Alaska forests provide many recreational opportunities, including hiking, camping, fishing, and canoeing. In the National Forests are extensive trails and shelter systems that can be used by the hiker, hunter, or canoeist. The National Parks and Monuments provide the visitor with an opportunity to see some of the most spectacular forest and mountain scenery, while the Wildlife Refuges and Ranges, although primarily set aside for the protection and management of wildlife species, also have campgrounds, trails, and other recreational facilities. In the interior boreal forests, the Bureau of Land Management and the State of Alaska have provided campgrounds, canoe trails, and occasional hiking trails through the forested and tundra areas. More development of recreational facilities is planned for the future.

One of the most important resources of the Alaska forests is the wildlife species that inhabit them. The Alaska forests provide a living place for large numbers of birds and mammals, most of which are dependent upon the woody plants either directly or indirectly for food and shelter. Even those big game animals, such as the mountain sheep, mountain goat, and muskox, that spend much of their lives above or beyond tree line, often use low woody plants for food during some part of the season.

Of the forest species, the moose is probably the most abundant and widespread large mammal of the interior forests; occasionally its range extends into the coastal areas. The moose survives the winter primarily by browsing on willows and other shrubs, especially in areas where the shrubs are growing thickly following forest fires, and in willow thickets along the rivers. In coastal areas, the blacktail deer feeds primarily on blueberry and other shrubs during the periods when the snow covers the lower vegetation. In the summer the deer feeds mainly on the herbaceous plants that grow in the openings in the coastal forests. Even the caribou, often considered a tundra animal, spends the winters in the open forested area adjacent to tree line, especially where lichen growth is abundant. In the summer the caribou may utilize several woody shrubs, especially resin and dwarf arctic birch and willows, as well as the herbaceous tundra vegetation. The small red squirrel, which is itself a source of food for larger furbearers, is dependent throughout the winter on seeds from spruce cones stored beneath the ground.

Several bird species survive through the Alaskan winters primarily by utilizing the woody plants as a source of food. Ptarmigan feed on willow and shrub birch buds, while ruffed and sharptailed grouse forage for berries from the past summer and feed on the buds of shrubs and trees. The spruce grouse of the interior and the blue grouse of the coastal areas live largely from the needles and buds of the spruce trees, as well as berries and buds of many shrubby species.

In the summer, insect life abounds in the forests and produces food for large numbers of small birds that nest and rear their young before migrating southward in the fall. In addition, the Alaskan forests and tundra are dotted with numerous lakes that serves as nesting places where large numbers of waterfowl rear their young during the short summer season.

Thus it can be seen that the forests of Alaska provide more than timber to the people of Alaska and the rest of the United States. They offer wilderness, a place to hike, hunt, fish, and areas to see and photograph wildlife. They are important in protecting our water resource, and they furnish a habitat for a large number of wildlife species.

The following section lists the main vegetation types of Alaska and the most important trees and shrubs found in each. Numbers 1–8 correspond to the types designated by color in the folded vegetation map in the pocket.

Coastal Forests

The dense forests of western hemlock and Sitka spruce, a continuation of similar forests along the coast of British Columbia, Washington, and Oregon, extend about 900 miles (1,440 km.) along the Alaska coast from the southeastern tip to Cook Inlet and Kodiak Island. Commercial stands occur from sea level to about 1,500 feet (460 m.) elevation, but scattered trees rise to a timberline at 2,000 to 3,000 feet (460 to 915 m.).

The coastal forests are characterized by steep rough topography. In many areas only a narrow band of trees exists between the ocean and the tundra on snowclad mountains above. The scenic grandeur of the region is unsurpassed. The narrow waterways with steep forested slopes, the rugged high mountains, and the many glaciers reaching to the coast through forested valleys along with an abundance of streams and lakes offer a wealth of recreation values to Alaskans and tourists.

The climate is cool and cloudy in summer, and the winters are mild. Snowfall may be heavy in some forested areas in the northern part, but much of the high precipitation falls as rain. Annual precipitation varies from as much as 222 inches (5,640 mm.) on the outside coast of the southeasternmost islands to 25 inches (630 mm.) at Homer on the boundary between coastal and interior forests. The mean annual temperature in the coastal forests ranges from 46° F. (8° C.) at Ketchikan to 37° F. (3° C.) at Cordova. Summer temperatures range in the upper 50's (13–16° C.) and winter temperatures for the coldest month range from the low 20's (−6° C.) to the mid 30's (+2° C.).

1. *Coastal Spruce-Hemlock Forests*

In the southern part the coastal forests are composed primarily of western hemlock and Sitka spruce with a scattering of mountain hemlock, western redcedar, and Alaska-cedar. Red alder is common along streams, beach fringes, and on soils recently disturbed by logging and landslides. Black cottonwood grows on the flood plains of major rivers and recently deglaciated areas on the mainland. Subalpine fir and Pacific silver fir occur occasionally at tree line and near sea level but are not abundant enough to be of commercial value. Blueberries, huckleberry, copperbush, devilsclub, and salal are the most important shrubs. Because of the high rainfall and resulting high humidity, mosses grow in great profusion on the ground, on fallen logs, and on the lower branches of trees, as well as in forest openings.

In poorly drained areas at low elevations, open muskegs of low shrubs, sedges, grasses, and mosses are common. These areas are tree-less or may have a few scattered shrubby trees of shore pine (lodgepole pine), western hemlock, mountain hemlock, Alaska-cedar, and Sitka spruce.

In the northern and western sections of the coastal forests, the makeup of the tree species changes. Western redcedar is not found north of Frederick Sound, and Alaska-cedar drops out at Prince William Sound. Cottonwood is extensive along some of the glacial outwash rivers and becomes commercially important in the Haines area and on the alluvial terraces to the west. Western hemlock becomes of less importance westward but is found as far as Cook Inlet. Only Sitka spruce remains as the important tree in the coastal forests west of Cook Inlet and the lone conifer on Afognak and Kodiak Islands. Douglas-fir, which is characteristic of the coastal forests of Oregon, Washington, and southern British Columbia, does not reach Alaska.

The common trees and shrubs of the coastal forests are as follows:

Trees

Sitka spruce   *Picea sitchensis*
western hemlock
    Tsuga heterophylla
mountain hemlock
    Tsuga mertensiana
Alaska-cedar
    Chamaecyparis nootkatensis
red alder   *Alnus rubra*
black cottonwood
    Populus trichocarpa

Shrubs

Sitka alder   *Alnus sinuata*
salal   *Gaultheria shallon*
rusty menziesia
    Menziesia ferruginea
devilsclub   *Oplopanax horridus*
stink currant   *Ribes bracteosum*
trailing black currant
    Ribes laxiflorum
western thimbleberry
    Rubus parviflorus

salmonberry   *Rubus spectabilis*
Barclay willow   *Salix barclayi*
Scouler willow   *Salix scouleriana*
Sitka willow   *Salix sitchensis*
Pacific red elder
                            Sambucus callicarpa
Alaska blueberry
                            Vaccinium alaskaense
dwarf blueberry
                            Vaccinium caespitosum
early blueberry
                            Vaccinium ovalifolium
red huckleberry
                            Vaccinium parvifolium
high bushcranberry
                            Viburnum edule

Interior Forests

The white spruce-paper birch forest, extending from the Kenai Peninsula to the south slopes of the Brooks Range and westward nearly to the Bering Sea, is called the boreal forest or taiga—the Russian equivalent. These forests cover about 32 percent of the area or about 106 million acres (42.4 million hectares). However, only about one-fifth or 22.5 million acres (9 million hectares) are classified as commercial forest land.

Characteristic forest stands are found in the Tanana and Yukon Valleys. Here, in contrast to the coast, climatic conditions are extreme. The mean annual temperature is 20 to 30° F. (—7° C. to —1° C.) but winter temperatures below —40° F. (—40° C.) are common and the coldest month averages —10 to —20° F. (—23° to —29° C.). In contrast, summer temperatures may reach into the 90's (above 30° C.), and the warmest month of the year has an average of 60° F. (16° C.). Permanently frozen ground is of scattered occurrence in the southern part of the interior forests and nearly continuous in the northern sections. Although precipitation is light, 6 to 12 inches (150 to 300 mm.) per year, evaporation is low and permafrost forms an impervious layer so that bogs and wet areas are common. Snowfall averages 55 inches (140 cm.) per year at Fairbanks, but snow cover usually persists from mid-October until mid- to late-April. Day length is also extreme in the boreal forest regions with nearly 24 hours of daylight available for plant growth in June, but with only a few hours of sunlight during the winter months. Forest fires have always been an important aspect of the environment of the Alaska interior forests. Even now with modern fire detecting and fighting techniques, more than 4 million acres may burn in a single dry summer.

The vegetation types in interior Alaska form a mosiac of patterns that is related in part to past fire history, to slope and aspect, and to the presence or absence of permafrost. Most forest stands are mixtures of two or more tree species but are usually classified by the dominant species.

2. Closed Spruce-Hardwood Forests

White spruce type.—In general, the best commercial stands of white spruce are found on the warm, dry, south-facing hillsides and adjacent to rivers where drainage is good and permafrost lacking. These stands are rather open under the canopy but may contain shrubs of rose, alder, and willow. The forest floor is usually carpeted with a thick moss mat. On the better sites 100 to 200 year-old spruce with diameters of 10 to 24 inches (25 to 60 cm.) may average 10,000 board feet per acre (58 cubic meters per hectare). Stands in which commercial white spruce are dominant occupy 12.8 million acres (5.1 million hectares) in interior Alaska. The most common trees and shrubs of the white spruce type are as follows:

15

Trees

white spruce	*Picea glauca*
paper birch	*Betula papyrifera*
balsam poplar	*Populus balsamifera*

Common Shrubs

red-fruit bearberry	
	Arctostaphylos rubra
crowberry	*Empetrum nigrum*
narrow-leaf Labrador-tea	
	Ledum decumbens
American red currant	*Ribes triste*
prickly rose	*Rosa acicularis*
feltleaf willow	*Salix alaxensis*
littletree willow	*Salix arbusculoides*
Bebb willow	*Salix bebbiana*
buffaloberry	*Shepherdia canadensis*
mountain-cranberry	
	Vaccinium vitis-idaea
bog blueberry	
	Vaccinium uliginosum
high bushcranberry	
	Viburnum edule

Occasional to Rare Shrubs

bearberry	*Arctostaphylos uva-ursi*
resin birch	*Betula glandulosa*
rusty menziesia	
	Menziesia ferruginea
bush cinquefoil	*Potentilla fruticosa*
grayleaf willow	*Salix glauca*
halberd willow	*Salix hastata*
Richardson willow	
Salix lanata ssp. *richardsonii*	
park willow	*Salix monticola*
tall blueberry willow	
	Salix novae-angliae
Scouler willow	*Salix scouleriana*
dwarf blueberry	
	Vaccinium caespitosum

Recent burns.—Because of extensive burns during the past 100 years, large areas of the interior are in various stages of forest succession. The succession that follows fire is varied and depends upon topography, previous vegetation, severity of burn, and available seed source at the time of burn. In general, fires are followed by a shrubby stage consisting primarily of light-seeded willows.

The most important woody plants to follow immediately after fire are:

Common Shrubs

narrow-leaf Labrador-tea	
	Ledum decumbens
Labrador-tea	
	Ledum groenlandicum
prickly rose	*Rosa acicularis*
littletree willow	*Salix arbusculoides*
Barclay willow	*Salix barclayi*
Bebb willow	*Salix bebbiana*
Scouler willow	*Salix scouleriana*
dwarf blueberry	
	Vaccinium caespitosum
mountain-cranberry	
	Vaccinium vitis-idaea

Occasional or Rare Shrubs

American green alder	*Alnus crispa*
Sitka alder	*Alnus sinuata*
thinleaf alder	*Alnus tenuifolia*
red-fruit bearberry	
	Arctostaphylos rubra
bearberry	*Arctostaphylos uva-ursi*
crowberry	*Empetrum nigrum*
bush cinquefoil	*Potentilla fruticosa*
American red currant	*Ribes triste*
buffaloberry	*Shepherdia canadensis*
Beauvered spirea	
	Spiraea beauverdiana
bog blueberry	
	Vaccinium uliginosum

Quaking aspen type.—Following fire and a willow stage, fast growing aspen stands develop in upland areas on south facing slopes. The aspen mature in 60 to 80 years and are eventually replaced by white spruce, except in excessively dry sites where they may persist. Occasionally aspen stands also follow fire on well drained lowland river terraces and, in these situations, are usually replaced by black spruce in the successional sequence. Stands with aspen dominant occupy about 2.4 million acres (960,-000 hectares) in central Alaska. Woody plants occurring in the aspen type are as follows:

16

Trees

quaking aspen *Populus tremuloides*
white spruce   *Picea glauca*
black spruce   *Picea mariana*

Common Shrubs

bearberry *Arctostaphylos uva-ursi*
prickly rose   *Rosa acicularis*
Bebb willow   *Salix bebbiana*
Scouler willow   *Salix scouleriana*
buffaloberry *Shepherdia canadensis*
mountain-cranberry
        Vaccinium vitis-idaea

Occasional to Rare Shrubs

red-fruit bearberry
        Arctostaphylos rubra
Alaska sagebrush
        Artemisia alaskana
fringed sagebrush
        Artemisia frigida
resin birch   *Betula glandulosa*
crowberry   *Empetrum nigrum*
common juniper
        Juniperus communis
Labrador-tea
        Ledum groenlandicum
American red raspberry
        Rubus idaeus var. *strigosus*
dwarf blueberry
        Vaccinium caespitosum
bog blueberry
        Vaccinium uliginosum
high bushcranberry
        Viburnum edule

Paper birch type.—Paper birch is the common invading tree after fire on east- and west-facing slopes and occasionally on north slopes and flat areas. This species occurs either in pure stands or more often mixed with white spruce, aspen, or black spruce. Shrubs may be similar to those under aspen but usually Labrador-tea and mountain-cranberry are more common. Paper birch may be 60–80 feet (18–24 m.) tall and have diameters up to 18 inches (46 cm.), but an average diameter of 8–9 inches (20–22 cm.) is more common in the interior birch stands. Stands dominated by paper birch

occupy about 5 million acres (2 million hectares) of interior forests and are especially widespread in the Susitna River Valley. Trees and shrubs occurring in the birch type are as follows:

Trees

paper birch   *Betula papyrifera*
white spruce   *Picea glauca*
black spruce   *Picea mariana*

Common Shrubs

narrow-leaf Labrador-tea
        Ledum decumbens
Labrador-tea
        Ledum groenlandicum
American red currant *Ribes triste*
prickly rose   *Rosa acicularis*
Bebb willow   *Salix bebbiana*
Scouler willow   *Salix scouleriana*
Barclay willow   *Salix barclayi*
mountain-cranberry
        Vaccinium vitis-idaea
high bushcranberry
        Viburnum edule
dwarf blueberry
        Vaccinium caespitosum

Occasional to Rare Shrubs

crowberry   *Empetrum nigrum*
rusty menziesia
        Menziesia ferruginea
devilsclub   *Oplopanax horridus*
northern black currant
        Ribes hudsonianum
American red raspberry
        Rubus idaeus var. *strigosus*
Pacific red elder
        Sambucus callicarpa
Greene mountain-ash
        Sorbus scopulina

The balsam poplar type.—Another tree species of importance within the closed spruce-hardwood forest in interior Alaska is balsam poplar, which reaches its greatest size and abundance on the floodplain of the meandering glacial rivers. It invades sandbars and grows rapidly to heights of 80–100 feet (24 to 30 m.) and diameters of 24 inches (60 cm.) before being replaced by white spruce. Balsam

17

poplar also occurs in small clumps near the altitudinal and latitudinal limit of trees in the Alaska Range and north of the Brooks Range. Commercial stands occupy 2.1 million acres (840,000 hectares), primarily along the Yukon, Tanana, Susitna, and Kuskokwim Rivers. In the Susitna Valley balsam poplar is often replaced in this type by black cottonwood or by hybrids between the two. The woody plants of this type include:

Trees

balsam poplar
               Populus balsamifera
black cottonwood
               Populus trichocarpa
white spruce   *Picea glauca*

Common Shrubs

American green alder *Alnus crispa*
Sitka alder   *Alnus sinuata*
thinleaf alder   *Alnus tenuifolia*
littletree willow *Salix arbusculoides*
feltleaf willow   *Salix alaxensis*
prickly rose   *Rosa acicularis*
high bushcranberry
               Viburnum edule

Occasional to Rare Shrubs

silverberry   *Eleagnus commutata*
bush cinquefoil *Potentilla fruticosa*
high blueberry willow
            Salix novae-angliae
Scouler willow *Salix scouleriana*
buffaloberry *Shepherdia canadensis*

3. Open, Low Growing Spruce Forests

On north-facing slopes and poorly drained lowlands, forest succession leads to open black spruce and bogs, usually underlain by permafrost. The black spruce are slow growing and seldom exceed 8 inches (20 cm.) in diameter and are usually much smaller; a tree 2 inches (5 cm.) in diameter is often 100 years in age. The black spruce comes in abundantly after fire because its persistent cones open after a fire and spread abundant seed over the burned areas. A thick moss mat, often of sphagnum mosses, sedges, grasses, and heath or ericaceous shrubs usually make up the subordinate vegetation of the open black spruce stands. Associated with black spruce in the wet bottom lands is the slow-growing tamarack. As with the black spruce, it is of little commercial value, seldom reaching a diameter of more than 6 inches (15 cm.). The woody plants of these low growing spruce forests include the following:

Trees

black spruce   *Picea mariana*
tamarack   *Larix laricina*
paper birch   *Betula papyrifera*
white spruce   *Picea glauca*

Common Shrubs

red-fruit bearberry
            Arctostaphylos rubra
crowberry   *Empetrum nigrum*
Labrador-tea
          Ledum groenlandicum
prickly rose   *Rosa acicularis*
littletree willow
           Salix arbusculoides
Bebb willow   *Salix bebbiana*
grayleaf willow   *Salix glauca*
blueberry willow
            Salix myrtillifolia
diamondleaf willow
      Salix planifolia ssp. *pulchra*
Scouler willow *Salix scouleriana*
bog blueberry
           Vaccinium uliginosum
mountain-cranberry
          Vaccinium vitis-idaea

Occasional to Rare Shrubs

resin birch   *Betula glandulosa*
dwarf arctic birch   *Betula nana*
narrow-leaf Labrador-tea
           Ledum decumbens
rusty menziesia
         Menziesia ferruginea
bush cinquefoil *Potentilla fruticosa*
dwarf blueberry
          Vaccinium caespitosum
bog cranberry *Vaccinium oxycoccos*

4. Treeless Bogs

Coastal areas.—Within the coastal forests in depressions, flat areas, and on some gentle slopes where drainage is poor, treeless areas occur. The vegetation is variable but most commonly consists of a thick sphagnum moss mat, sedges, rushes, low shrubs, and fruticose lichens. This type is locally called "muskeg." Often a few slow growing, poorly formed, shore pine, western hemlock, or Alaska-cedar are scattered on the drier sites. In more exposed situations and in the driest areas, shrubs may be dominant over the sedge and herbaceous mat. Ponds are often present in the peaty substrate. Characteristic shrubs of the coastal Alaska bogs include:

bog-rosemary *Andromeda polifolia*
crowberry   *Empetrum nigrum*
common juniper
                Juniperus communis
bog kalmia   *Kalmia polifolia*
Labrador-tea
                Ledum groenlandicum
rusty menziesia
                Menziesia ferruginea
Barclay willow   *Salix barclayi*
undergreen willow *Salix commutata*
bog cranberry *Vaccinium oxycoccos*
bog blueberry
                Vaccinium uliginosum
mountain-cranberry
                Vaccinium vitis-idaea

Interior areas.—Within the boreal forest are extensive bogs where conditions are too wet for tree growth. North of the Alaska Range in the unglaciated areas, they occur on old river terraces and outwash, in filling ponds and old sloughs and occasionally on gentle north, facing slopes. They are common south of the Alaska Range, on the fine clay soils formed in former glacial lake basins and on morainal soils within the glaciated area. They are also common on the extensive flat areas of the lower Yukon and Kuskokwim Rivers.

The vegetation of these bogs consists of varying amounts of grasses, sedges, and mosses, especially sphagnum. Often the surface is made uneven by stringlike ridges. Much of the surface of these bogs is too wet for shrubs but on the drier peat ridges are a number of heath or ericaceous shrubs, willows, and dwarf birches. The woody plants of the treeless bogs include the following:

Common Shrubs

bog-rosemary *Andromeda polifolia*
resin birch   *Betula glandulosa*
dwarf arctic birch   *Betula nana*
leatherleaf
                Chamaedaphne calyculata
narrow-leaf Labrador-tea
                Ledum decumbens
Labrador-tea
                Ledum groenlandicum
sweetgale   *Myrica gale*
Barclay willow   *Salix barclayi*
Alaska bog willow
                Salix fuscescens
low blueberry willow
                Salix myrtillifolia
diamondleaf willow
                Salix planifolia ssp. *pulchra*
bog cranberry *Vaccinium oxycoccos*
bog blueberry
                Vaccinium uliginosum
mountain-cranberry
                Vaccinium vitis-idaea

Occasional to Rare Shrubs

American green alder *Alnus crispa*
Sitka alder   *Alnus sinuata*
thinleaf alder   *Alnus tenuifolia*
red-fruit bearberry
                Arctostaphylos rubra
crowberry   *Empetrum nigrum*
bush cinquefoil *Potentilla fruticosa*
grayleaf willow   *Salix glauca*
netleaf willow   *Salix reticulata*
Beauverd spirea
                Spiraea beauverdiana

19

5. Shrub Thickets

Coastal alder thickets.—Dense thickets of shrubs occur in a number of sites in all the major vegetation zones in Alaska. In coastal Alaska there are extensive alder thickets between the beach and the forest, between the treeline and the alpine tundra meadows, and extending from treeline downward through the forest in avalanche tracks and along streams. The shrub thicket is also common in southeastern Alaska in the many clearcut areas. The alder thicket is almost impenetrable as the boles of the shrubs tend to grow horizontally as well as vertically. To travel through the thicket is even worse; the spiny devilsclub and salmonberry are frequently present. Beneath the alders there is often a well developed grass and fern layer, as well as a number of herbs and shrubs. The most common woody plants in this type are as follows:

Sitka alder	*Alnus sinuata*
luetkea	*Luetkea pectinata*
rusty menziesia	
	Menziesia ferruginea
Oregon crab apple	
	Malus diversifolia
devilsclub	*Oplopanax horridus*
stink currant	*Ribes bracteosum*
trailing black currant	
	Ribes laxiflorum
Nootka rose	*Rosa nutkana*
Western thimbleberry	
	Rubus parviflorus
salmonberry	*Rubus spectabilis*
Barclay willow	*Salix barclayi*
Scouler willow	*Salix scouleriana*
Sitka willow	*Salix sitchensis*
Pacific red elder	
	Sambucus callicarpa
Sitka mountain-ash	
	Sorbus sitchensis
Alaska blueberry	
	Vaccinium alaskaense
dwarf blueberry	
	Vaccinium caespitosum
early blueberry	
	Vaccinium ovalifolium
red huckleberry	
	Vaccinium parvifolium

Floodplain thickets.—Another major shrub type, floodplain thickets, is found on the floodplains of the rivers. Although somewhat different in species composition, the type is rather similar from the rivers of the southern coastal areas to the broad braided rivers north of the Brooks Range. This type forms on newly exposed alluvial deposits that are periodically flooded. It develops quickly and may reach heights of 15 to 20 feet (4.5–6 m.) in the south and central Alaska and 5 to 10 feet (1.5–3 m.) along the rivers north of the Brooks Range. The main dominant shrubs of this type are willows and occasionally alders with a number of lower shrubs under the canopy. The shrubs of this type include the following:

American green alder	
	Alnus crispa
thinleaf alder	*Alnus tenuifolia*
Sitka alder	*Alnus sinuata*
red-osier dogwood	
	Cornus stolonifera
silverberry	*Eleagnus commutata*
sweetgale	*Myrica gale*
prickly rose	*Rosa acicularis*
American red raspberry	
	Rubus idaeus var. *strigosus*
feltleaf willow	*Salix alaxensis*
littletree willow	*Salix arbusculoides*
Barclay willow	*Salix barclayi*
Bebb willow	*Salix bebbiana*
barren-ground willow	
	Salix brachcarpa ssp. *niphoclada*
undergreen willow	*Salix commutata*
grayleaf willow	*Salix glauca*
halberd willow	*Salix hastata*
sandbar willow	*Salix interior*
Richardson willow	
	Salix lanata ssp. *richardsonii*
Pacific willow	*Salix lasiandra*
park willow	*Salix monticola*
tall blueberry willow	
	Salix novae-angliae

diamondleaf willow
Salix planifolia ssp. *pulchra*
Setchell willow   *Salix setchelliana*
Sitka willow   *Salix sitchensis*
buffaloberry *Shepherdia canadensis*
high bushcranberry
Viburnum edule

Birch-alder-willow thickets.—A third type of shrub thicket occurs near tree line in interior Alaska and beyond tree line in extensive areas of the Alaska and Seward peninsulas. It consists of resin birch, alder, and several willow species, usually forming thickets 3 to 10 feet (1–3 m.) tall. The thickets may be extremely dense, or they may be open and interspersed with reindeer lichens, low heath type shrubs, or patches of alpine tundra. The alders tend to occupy the wetter sites, the birch the mesic sites, and the tundra openings the drier or wind exposed areas. The type extends below tree line where it is often associated with widely spaced white spruce. Shrubs of this type include the following:

American green alder *Alnus crispa*
Sitka alder   *Alnus sinuata*
alpine bearberry
Arctostaphylos alpina
resin birch   *Betula glandulosa*
dwarf arctic birch   *Betula nana*
crowberry   *Empetrum nigrum*
narrow-leaf Labrador-tea
Ledum decumbens
bush cinquefoil *Potentilla fruticosa*
Barclay willow   *Salix barclayi*
undergreen willow *Salix commutata*
Alaskan bog willow
Salix fuscescens
diamondleaf willow
Salix planifolia ssp. *pulchra*
Richardson willow
Salix lanata ssp. *richardsonii*
netleaf willow   *Salix reticulata*
Beauverd spirea
Spiraea beauverdiana
bog blueberry
Vaccinium uliginosum
mountain-cranberry
Vaccinium vitis-idaea

Tundra

The low tundra vegetation can be divided into three main types: moist tundra, wet tundra, and alpine tundra. Within each of these major types are mosaics of subtypes related to differences in topography, slope, aspect, and substrate.

6. *Moist Tundra*

Moist tundra occupies the foothills and lower elevations of the Alaska Range as well as extensive areas on the Seward and Alaska peninsulas, the Aleutian Islands, and the islands of the Bering Sea. The type varies from almost continuous and uniformly developed cottongrass (*Eriophorum*) tussocks with sparse growth of other sedges and dwarf shrubs to stands where tussocks are scarce or lacking and dwarf shrubs are dominant. Over wide areas in Arctic Alaska, the cottongrass tussock type is the most widespread of all vegetation types. In northern areas the type is often dissected by polygonal patterns created by underlying ice wedges. On the Aleutian Islands the type consists of tall grass meadows interspersed with a dense low heath shrub type. The shrubs found in this type from the Aleutian Islands to the north slope of the Brooks Range include the following:

American green alder *Alnus crispa*
alpine bearberry
Arctostaphylos alpina
resin birch   *Betula glandulosa*
dwarf arctic birch   *Betula nana*
four-angled cassiope
Cassiope tetragona
entire-leaf mountain-avens
Dryas integrifolia
white mountain-avens
Dryas octopetala
narrow-leaf Labrador-tea
Ledum decumbens

alpine-azalea
            Loiseleuria procumbens
Aleutian mountain-heath
            Phyllodoce aleutica
Kamchatka rhododendron
            Rhododendron camtschaticum
Lapland rosebay
            Rhododendron lapponicum
arctic willow   *Salix arctica*
Barclay willow   *Salix barclayi*
Barratt willow   *Salix barrattiana*
Chamisso willow *Salix chamissonis*
undergreen willow *Salix commutata*
Alaska bog willow *Salix fuscescens*
grayleaf willow   *Salix glauca*
Richardson willow
      Salix lanata ssp. *richardsonii*
diamondleaf willow
      Salix planifolia ssp. *pulchra*
ovalleaf willow   *Salix ovalifolia*
polar willow   *Salix polaris*
netleaf willow   *Salix reticulata*
least willow   *Salix rotundifolia*
Beuverd spirea
            Spiraea beauverdiana
bog cranberry *Vaccinium oxycoccos*
bog blueberry
            Vaccinium uliginosum
mountain-cranberry
            Vaccinium vitis-idaea

7. Wet Tundra

The wet tundra type as shown on the vegetation map includes also the low coastal marshes of southern Alaska. The type is most extensive along the coastal plain north of the Brooks Range, the northern part of the Seward Peninsula, and on the broad Yukon delta. It is usually found in areas with many shallow lakes and little topographic relief. Standing water is almost always present in the summer and in the northern parts permafrost is close to the surface. Microrelief is provided by peat ridges and polygonal features related to frost action and ice wedges. The vegetation is primarily a sedge and cottongrass mat, usually not formed into tus-

socks. The few woody plants occur on the driest sites where the microrelief raises them above the standing water table. The shrubs in this type include the following:

bog-rosemary *Andromeda polifolia*
resin birch   *Betula glandulosa*
dwarf arctic birch   *Betula nana*
narrow-leaf Labrador-tea
            Ledum decumbens
Alaska bog willow *Salix fuscescens*
diamondleaf willow
      Salix planifolia ssp. *pulchra*
netleaf willow   *Salix reticulata*
Richardson willow
      Salix lanata ssp. *richardsonii*
ovalleaf willow   *Salix ovalifolium*
bog cranberry *Vaccinium oxycoccos*
bog blueberry
            Vaccinium uliginosum
mountain-cranberry
            Vaccinium vitis-idaea

8. Alpine Tundra

In all the mountain ranges of Alaska and on exposed ridges in the arctic and southwestern coastal areas, there is a zone of alpine tundra. Much of this type consists of barren rocks but interspersed between the bare rocks and rubble are low mat plants, both herbaceous and shrubby. Dominant in this type in northern areas and in the Alaska Range are low mats of white mountain-avens which may cover entire ridges and slopes along with many mat forming herbs, such as moss-campion (*Silene acaulis* L.), black oxytrope (*Oxytropis nigrescens* (Pall.) Fisch.), arctic sandwort (*Minuartia arctica* (Stev.) Aschers. & Graebn.), and several grasses and sedges. In the southeastern coastal mountains and the Aleutians, the most important plants are the low heath shrubs, especially cassiopes and mountain-heaths. They are most abundant where snow accumulates in the winter and lingers into late spring. On the Aleutian Islands this type consists primarily of crowberry, bog blueberry, mountain-cranberry, alpine-azalea, and several dwarf willows. Shrubs in this type throughout its range in Alaska include the following:

alpine bearberry
    Arctostaphylos alpina
resin birch   *Betula glandulosa*
dwarf arctic birch   *Betula nana*
Alaska cassiope
    Cassiope lycopodioides
Mertens cassiope
    Cassiope mertensiana
starry cassiope *Cassiope stelleriana*
four-angled cassiope
    Cassiope tetragona
diapensia   *Diapensia lapponica*
white mountain-avens
    Dryas octopetala
entire-leaf mountain-avens
    Dryas integrifolia
crowberry   *Empetrum nigrum*
alpine-azalea
    Loiseleuria procumbens
narrow-leaf Labrador-tea
    Ledum decumbens
luetkea   *Luetkea pectinata*
Aleutian mountain-heath
    Phyllodoce aleutica
blue mountain-heath
    Phyllodoce coerulea
red mountain-heath
    Phyllodoce empetriformis
Kamchatka rhododendron
    Rhododendron camtschaticum
Lapland rosebay
    Rhododendron lapponicum
arctic willow   *Salix arctica*
Chamisso willow *Salix chamissonis*
Alaska bog willow *Salix fuscescens*
ovalleaf willow   *Salix ovalifolia*
skeletonleaf willow
    Salix phlebophylla

polar willow   *Salix polaris*
diamondleaf willow
    Salix planifolia ssp. *pulchra*
netleaf willow   *Salix reticulata*
least willow   *Salix rotundifolia*
dwarf blueberry
    Vaccinium caespitosum
bog blueberry
    Vaccinium uliginosum
mountain-cranberry
    Vaccinium vitis-idaea

Vegetation Map

The colored folded vegetation map of Alaska (in pocket), compiled by the senior author, combines some aspects of five published Alaska vegetation maps. It follows primarily the detailed, large-scale "Vegetation Map of Alaska" by Lloyd A. Spetzman (1963), compiled for the Military Geology Branch of the U.S. Geological Survey. Other maps consulted are the following: A. W. Küchler's map "Potential Natural Vegetation of Alaska" (U.S. Geological Survey, National Atlas, Sheet No. 89, 1967), "Vegetation Map of Northwestern North America" (Sigafoos 1958); Alaska Forest Regions in the revision of "Pocket Guide to Alaska Trees" (Taylor and Little 1950); and the revised, enlarged map printed in color in "Alaska's Forest Resource" (Hutchison 1967). The last, much reduced, appeared also on the map "Major Forest Types" (U.S. Geological Survey, National Atlas, Sheet No. 182, 1969). In addition, the compiler has made some changes based on his own observations and experiences.

KEYS FOR IDENTIFICATION

Keys are provided to aid identification, both in summer, when leaves, flowers, and fruits are present, and in winter, when twigs, winter buds, and bark are used. Four assembled here are as follows: Key to Alaska Trees Based Mainly on Leaves, Winter Key to Deciduous Trees of Alaska, Key to Genera of Alaska Shrubs, and Winter Key to Alaska Shrubs. Also, each genus with two or more species has a key to its Alaska species. For the willows (*Salix*), the largest genus, there are two: Key to Alaska Willows and Vegetative Key to Alaska Willows.

A key is an outline for identifying specimens or plants through the process of elimination. This device is a short cut to save time in reading every description until the one that agrees is found. The species are divided into two groups according to certain distinguishing characters, and each group is divided successively into two smaller groups down to a single species at the end. The name of a particular specimen is found through selection, one by one, of the group in which it belongs.

Like an outline, the keys are indented. The two groups forming a pair of contrasting characters are designated by the same letter, single and double, and spaced one directly below the other but usually not together. Step by step, elimination proceeds from left to right by selection of the group to which the specimen belongs until the name is reached. Species numbers are cited beside each name for reference. Then verification is made by comparison with description, illustration, and map. If agreement is lacking or doubtful, the steps followed in the key may be retraced and different steps tried. With incomplete specimens, it may be desirable to check both groups of a pair where the contrasting characters are absent or uncertain.

Emphasis is given to nontechnical and vegetative characters, which are present over longer periods than flowers or fruits, also, to the larger parts. However, a hand lens will be helpful for observing details.

The first step is to select the proper key for the specimen, whether it is a tree or shrub and in summer or winter condition. Usually, the keys based mainly on leaves and other vegetative characters are simpler and easier to use than the winter keys. The latter must depend largely upon differences in twigs and buds. Even in winter, enough old leaves, flowers, and fruits may be found for use of the main keys. Of course, keys based largely on leaves can be used throughout the year for the evergreens.

For example, a tree specimen with broad leaves would be identified with the Key to Alaska Trees Based Mainly on Leaves. First, both contrasting parts or groups of the key, beginning with the pair "A" and "AA," should be read. The specimen with broad leaves belongs under "AA," and all the trees under "A," having needlelike or scalelike leaves, are eliminated. Next, the lines "N" and "NN" are read. If the leaves and twigs are in pairs (opposite), the specimen belongs under "NN." Then, if the leaves have 3 long-pointed lobes, the specimen agrees with "j" instead of "jj" and is a Douglas maple. Confirmation is made by comparison with the description, illustration, and map.

Key to Alaska Trees Based Mainly on Leaves

A. Leaves needlelike or scalelike, evergreen (except in tamarack), trees resinous (except in yew); seeds more or less exposed and not enclosed in a fruit—conifers or softwoods (gymnosperms).

B. Leaves needlelike, flattened, abruptly pointed but not prickly, in 2 rows comblike with leafstalks extending down twig; seeds single in scarlet juicy cuplike disk; rare in extreme southeast Alaska _____ 1. Pacific yew (*Taxus brevifolia*)

BB. Leaves needlelike or scalelike, not as above; seeds borne on scales of a cone.

C. Leaves needlelike, more than ¼ in. (6 mm.) long, single, or clustered.

D. Needles shedding in fall, 12–20 in cluster on short spur twigs (also single on leading twigs)_____ _____ 3. tamarack (*Larix laricina*)

DD. Needles evergreen, single or 2 (sometimes 3) in a bundle.

E. Needles 2 (sometimes 3) in a bundle with sheath at base— 2. lodgepole pine (*Pinus contorta*)

F. Cones pointing backward, opening at maturity; generally low spreading tree of muskegs in coastal forests ____ _____ 2a. shore pine (*Pinus contorta* var. *contorta*)

FF. Cones pointing outward, mostly remaining closed many years; tree often tall and narrow of inner fiord forests at head of Lynn Canal (Skagway to Haines)_____ ____ 2b. lodgepole pine (*Pinus contorta* var. *latifolia*)

EE. Needles single, without sheath at base.

G. Older twigs roughened by projections where needles were shed.

H. Needles sharp-pointed, stiff, without leafstalks—spruce (*Picea*).

I. Needles 4-angled.

J. Twigs hairy; needles mostly less than ½ in. (12 mm.) long, resinous; cones egg-shaped or nearly round, mostly less than 1 in. (2.5 cm.) long, curved down on short stalks, remaining on tree _____ 4. black spruce (*Picea mariana*)

JJ. Twigs hairless; needles more than ½ in. (12 mm.) long, with skunklike odor when crushed; cones cylindric, 1¼–2½ in. (3–6 cm.) long, falling at maturity _____ 5. white spruce (*Picea glauca*)

II. Needles flattened but slightly keeled _____ _____ 6. Sitka spruce (*Picea sitchensis*)

HH. Needles blunt, soft and not stiff, with short leaf-stalks —hemlock (*Tsuga*)

K. Needles flat, appearing in 2 rows, shiny dark green above, with 2 whitish bands (stomata) on lower surface _____ _____ 7. western hemlock (*Tsuga heterophylla*)

KK. Needles half-round and keeled or angled beneath, crowded on all sides of short side twigs, blue green, with whitish lines (stomata) on both surfaces _____ _____ 8. mountain hemlock (*Tsuga mertensiana*)

GG. Older twigs smooth—fir (*Abies*).
　　　L. Needles shiny dark green on upper surface and silvery
　　　　　white with many lines (stomata) on lower surface
　　　　　_____ 9. Pacific silver fir (*Abies amabilis*)
　　　LL. Needles dull dark green with whitish lines (stomata)
　　　　　on both surfaces _____
　　　　　_____ 10. subalpine fir (*Abies lasiocarpa*)
　CC. Leaves scalelike, usually less than ⅛ in. (3 mm.) long, crowded,
　　　forming fanlike or flattened sprays.
　　　M. Leafy twigs flattened; leaves flattened and curved, not
　　　　　spreading _____ 11. western redcedar (*Thuja plicata*)
　　　MM. Leafy twigs 4-angled or slightly flattened; leaves pointed,
　　　　　spreading _____
　　　　　_____ 12. Alaska-cedar (*Chamaecyparis nootkatensis*)
AA. Leaves broad and flat, shedding in fall (deciduous); trees non-
　　resinous; seeds developed from a flower and enclosed in a fruit—
　　flowering plants (angiosperms).
　N. Leaves and twigs arranged singly (alternate).
　　　O. Leaves not divided into leaflets (simple).
　　　　　P. Leafstalks (petioles) mostly less than ½ in. (12 mm.) long;
　　　　　　leaves mostly more than twice as long as broad, with edges
　　　　　　finely toothed or without teeth; winter buds covered by a
　　　　　　single scale—willow (*Salix*).
　　　　　Q. Leaf edges without teeth or only sparsely and indistinctly
　　　　　　toothed.
　　　　　　R. Leaves rounded at base, broadly elliptic, becoming hairless
　　　　　　　on both sides __ 32. Hooker willow (*Salix hookeriana*)
　　　　　　RR. Leaves tapering or short-pointed at base, narrower, with
　　　　　　　hairs on lower surface.
　　　　　　S. Lower surface of leaves covered by dense hairs, appearing
　　　　　　　silvery, white, or gray.
　　　　　　　T. Leaves thick, lower surface with dense white woolly
　　　　　　　　hairs _____ 38. feltleaf willow (*Salix alaxensis*)
　　　　　　　TT. Leaves thin, lower surface with dense straight hairs.
　　　　　　　U. Lower surface of leaves silvery silky hairy, upper
　　　　　　　　surface green with scattered hairs _____
　　　　　　　　_____ 43. Sitka willow (*Salix sitchensis*)
　　　　　　　UU. Lower surface of leaves dull gray hairy, upper
　　　　　　　　surface greenish gray and hairless _____
　　　　　　　　_____ 26. grayleaf willow (*Salix glauca*)
　　　　　　SS. Lower surface of leaves visible through less dense hairs.
　　　　　　　V. Leaves thick, nearly hairless above; hairs on lower
　　　　　　　　surface short and stiff, at least some red, giving
　　　　　　　　reddish hue _____
　　　　　　　　_____ 42. Scouler willow (*Salix scouleriana*)
　　　　　　　VV. Leaves thin, hairy on both sides; hairs longer, not
　　　　　　　　reddish _____ 40. Bebb willow (*Salix bebbiana*)
　　　　　QQ. Leaf edges finely and distinctly toothed from base to apex.
　　　　　　W. Leaves 1–3 in. (2.5–7.5 cm.) long, mostly short-pointed at
　　　　　　　both ends _____
　　　　　　　_____ 44. littletree willow (*Salix arbusculoides*)
　　　　　　WW. Leaves 2–5 in. (5–12.5 cm.) long, long-pointed, mostly
　　　　　　　rounded at base __ 46. Pacific willow (*Salix lasiandra*)

PP. Leafstalks (petioles) mostly more than ½ in. (12 mm.) long (often shorter in alder); leaves less than twice as long as broad, with edges finely or coarsely toothed; winter buds with 2 or more scales exposed.

  X. Leaf edges finely toothed with curved and rounded teeth—cottonwood, poplar, aspen (*Populus*).

    Y. Leaf blades nearly round, less than 2 in. (5 cm.) long; leafstalks flattened _____ 17. quaking aspen (*Populus tremuloides*)

    YY. Leaf blades longer than broad, 2½–5 in. (6–12.5 cm.) long; leafstalks round.

      Z. Seed capsules pointed, hairless, 2-parted; leaves pale green and brownish beneath; tree of interior forests _____ 15. balsam poplar (*Populus balsamifera*)

      ZZ. Seed capsules rounded, hairy, 3-parted; leaves whitish beneath; tree of coastal forests _____ 16. black cottonwood (*Populus trichocarpa*)

  XX. Leaf edges coarsely toothed with sharp-pointed teeth.

    a. Leaf edges doubly toothed with teeth of 2 sizes.

      b. Leaf edges not lobed; bark papery and peeling off, white, brown, or pinkish—50. paper birch (*Betula papyrifera*).

        c. Leaves long-pointed, usually wedge-shaped at base; bark usually white in age; interior Alaska _____ 50b. Alaska paper birch (*Betula papyrifera* var. *humilis*)

        cc. Leaves mostly short-pointed.

          d. Leaves thin, mostly rounded at base; bark usually reddish brown; northern part of southeast Alaska _____ 50a. western paper birch (*Betula papyrifera* var. *commutata*)

          dd. Leaves thick, wedge-shaped or rounded at base, with white hairs on toothed edges; bark usually dark brown or gray; southern and southern interior Alaska _____ 50c. Kenai birch (*Betula papyrifera* var. *kenaica*)

      bb. Leaf edges wavy or shallowly lobed; bark usually gray and smooth, not papery nor peeling off—alder (*Alnus*).

        e. Leaves yellow green above, shiny on both sides and especially beneath, sticky when young, edges with relatively long-pointed teeth _____ 52. Sitka alder (*Alnus sinuata*)

        ee. Leaves dark green above, dull, not sticky when young, edges with short-pointed teeth.

          f. Leaves thick with edges curled under slightly, with rusty hairs along veins beneath _____ 53. red alder (*Alnus rubra*)

          ff. Leaves thin with edges flat, finely hairy or nearly hairless beneath _____ 54. thinleaf alder (*Alnus tenuifolia*)

    aa. Leaf edges with uniform teeth.

      g. Leaves short-pointed, sometimes 3-lobed _____ 66. Oregon crab apple (*Malus diversifolia*)

27

gg. Leaves rounded at apex _____
_____ 72. Pacific serviceberry (*Amelanchier florida*)
OO. Leaves divided into 7–17 leaflets (compound), the leaflets attached along extended leafstalk and shedding with it—
mountain-ash (*Sorbus*).
  h. Leaflets mostly 11–15, short-pointed, edges toothed nearly to
base.
    i. Leaflets becoming hairless _____
_____ 67. Greene Mountain-ash (*Sorbus scopulina*)
    ii. Leaflets white-hairy beneath; naturalized tree _____
_____ 68. European mountain-ash (*Sorbus aucuparia*)
  hh. Leaflets mostly 9 or 11, rounded or short-pointed at apex, edges
not toothed in lowest third _____
_____ 69. Sitka mountain-ash (*Sorbus sitchensis*)
NN. Leaves and usually twigs in pairs (opposite).
  j. Leaves with 3 long-pointed lobes, irregularly or doubly toothed
_____ 85. Douglas maple (*Acer glabrum* var. *douglasii*)
  jj. Leaves divided into 5 or 7 leaflets (compound), finely toothed
_____ 122. Pacific red elder (*Sambucus callicarpa*)

Winter Key to Deciduous Trees of Alaska

A. Twigs with many wartlike, blackish spur twigs about ⅛ in. (3 mm.)
long; upright brown cones usually present; trees with pointed
crown _____ 3. tamarack (*Larix laricina*)
AA. Twigs without spur twigs or with longer spurs; trees with spreading,
usually rounded crown.
  B. Winter buds, leaf-scars, and twigs arranged singly (alternate).
    C. Winter buds covered by a single scale _____ willow
(*Salix*; the species not readily distinguished in winter)
    CC. Winter buds with 2 or more scales exposed.
      D. Winter buds usually resinous or sticky, shiny, brown, long-
pointed; lowest bud-scale centered over leaf-scar—cottonwood, poplar, aspen (*Populus*).
        E. Winter buds ¼ in. (6 mm.) or less in length, slightly or not
resinous ____ 17. quaking aspen (*Populus tremuloides*)
        EE. Winter buds ⅜–1 in. (10–25 mm.) long, very resinous.
          F. Tree of interior forests _____
_____ 15. balsam poplar (*Populus balsamifera*)
          FF. Tree of coastal forests _____
_____ 16. black cottonwood (*Populus trichocarpa*)
      DD. Winter buds not resinous or sticky (slightly so in Sitka
alder); lowest bud-scale at side of bud.
        G. Winter buds mostly stalked (slightly in No. 52), with the 3
exposed scales meeting at edges (overlapping in No.
52); old, hard, blackish cones or conelike fruits usually
present—alder (*Alnus*).
          H. Cones with long stalks more than ½ in. (12 mm.) long,
mostly longer than cones _____
_____ 52. Sitka alder (*Alnus sinuata*)

HH. Cones with short stalks less than ½ in. (12 mm.) long.
  I. Cones ½–1 in. (12–25 mm.) long _____
         _____ 53. red alder (*Alnus rubra*)
  II. Cones less than ½ in. (12 mm.) long _____
       _____ 54. thinleaf alder (*Alnus tenuifolia*)
GG. Winter buds not stalked, composed of overlapping scales;
  fruits not conelike.
  J. Winter buds ¼ in. (6 mm.) or less in length; bud-scales
    with few or no hairs.
    K. Twigs with many small whitish dots (lenticels and
      resin); bark papery, peeling off _____
        _____ 50. paper birch (*Betula papyrifera*)
    KK. Twigs with few inconspicuous dots (lenticels); bark
      not papery.
      L. Winter buds blunt-pointed, dark brown; twigs coarse,
        gray or brown, often with dense gray hairs near
        tip, with short side twigs or spurs _____
        ____ 66. Oregon crab apple (*Malus diversifolia*)
      LL. Winter buds sharp-pointed, purple; twigs slender,
        reddish purple, shiny, hairless, without short side
        twigs or spurs _____
        __ 72. Pacific serviceberry (*Amelanchier florida*)
  JJ. Winter buds large, usually more than ⅜ in. (10 mm.)
    long; inner exposed bud-scales densely hairy—moun-
    tain ash (*Sorbus*).
    M. Winter buds with whitish hairs.
      N. Winter buds reddish brown, inner scales with whitish
        hairs at tip _____
        ___ 67. Greene mountain-ash (*Sorbus scopulina*)
      NN. Winter buds densely covered with whitish hairs;
        naturalized tree _____
        68. European mountain-ash (*Sorbus aucuparia*)
    MM. Winter buds with rusty brown hairs _____
      _____ 69. Sitka mountain-ash (*Sorbus sitchensis*)
BB. Winter buds, leaf-scars, and usually twigs in pairs (opposite).
  O. Twigs slender, reddish, with small dark red buds _____
    _____ 85. Douglas maple (*Acer glabrum* var. *douglasii*)
  OO. Twigs stout, gray, with large gray buds _____
    _____ 122. Pacific red elder (*Sambucus callicarpa*)

Key to Genera of Alaska Shrubs

This summer key is for use with flowering specimens and is based upon some flower and fruit characters, as well as vegetative characters of twigs and leaves. The 46 genera of shrubs are included. Identification is to species also in the 26 genera represented in Alaska by a single native shrub species. Keys to species are included in the text for the genera with 2 or more species. For incomplete specimens the winter key to Alaska shrubs is also available. It is more detailed, including species except in willow (*Salix*), as well as genera.

A. Plants parasitic on conifer twigs; leaves reduced to paired brownish scales ___ 55. hemlock dwarf-mistletoe (*Arceuthobium tsugense*)
AA. Plants growing on land; leaves green.
  B. Shrubs without true flowers; seeds in persistent berrylike resinous blue or green cones; leaves scalelike, awl-shaped, or needlelike, resinous _____ 13–14. juniper (*Juniperus*)
  BB. Shrubs with flowers; seeds enclosed in fruits; leaves mostly broad (if needlelike or scalelike, fruit a capsule or black berry).
    C. Flowers crowded in heads or catkins.
      D. Flowers in dense yellow heads; leaves finely dissected, whitish hairy, with sagebrush odor _____
      _____ 127–128. sagebrush (*Artemisia*)
      DD. Flowers in catkins, long narrow clusters, male and female separate; leaves various.
        E. Fruit a capsule with many hairy seeds; bud covered by 1 scale _____ 18–46. willow (*Salix*)
        EE. Fruit a nutlet, 1-seeded, not hairy, bud covered by 2 or more scales.
          F. Leaves aromatic, with minute resin dots, oblanceolate, rounded at tip and with several coarse teeth; male catkins erect _____ 47. sweetgale (*Myrica gale*)
          FF. Leaves not aromatic or resin dotted, elliptic or ovate, toothed along margin; male catkins drooping (birch family, Betulaceae).
            G. Leaves small, mostly less than 1 in. (2.5 cm.) long, nearly as broad as long, twigs densely glandular _____ 48–49. birch (*Betula*)
            GG. Leaves larger, mostly more than 2 inches (5 cm.) long, longer than broad, pointed at tip; twigs not glandular _____ 51–54. alder (*Alnus*)
    CC. Flowers not in heads or catkins.
      H. Leaves with minute scales; flowers with calyx but no corolla (elaeagnus family, Elaeagnaceae).
        I. Leaves opposite, with brown scales _____
        _____ 86. buffaloberry (*Shepherdia canadensis*)
        II. Leaves alternate, with silvery scales _____
        _____ 87. silverberry (*Elaeagnus commutata*)
      HH. Leaves not scaly; flowers with both calyx and corolla.
        J. Petals separate.
          K. Ovary or ovaries superior, with calyx and corolla attached below.

L. Ovaries few to many (rose family, Rosaceae).
  M. Fruits dry; stems without spines and prickles.
    N. Shrubs low or prostrate, less than 6 in. (15 cm.) high.
      O. Leaves twice divided into 3 narrow pointed segments, thin, hairless _____ _____ 65. luetkea (*Luetkea pectinata*)
      OO. Leaves oblong, leathery, densely white-hairy beneath ____ 79–81. mountain-avens (*Dryas*)
    NN. Shrubs upright, more than 12 in. (30 cm.) high.
      P. Leaves pinnately compound; petals yellow _____ __ 78. bush cinquefoil (*Potentilla fruitcosa*)
      PP. Leaves simple; petals white or pink.
        Q. Leaves 3–5 lobed, palmately veined _____ 62. Pacific ninebark (*Physocarpus capitatus*)
        QQ. Leaves not lobed, pinnately veined _____ _____ 63–64. spirea (*Spiraea*)
  MM. Fruits fleshy; stems mostly with spines or prickles.
    R. Fruit a raspberry or similar, of crowded drupelets; leaves simple or divided into 3–5 leaflets _____ 74–77. raspberry, salmonberry, thimbleberry (*Rubus*)
    RR. Fruit a rose hip, fleshy and rounded enclosing the "seeds"; leaves pinnate with 5 or more leaflets _____ 82–84. rose (*Rosa*)
LL. Ovary 1.
  S. Leaves less than ¼ in. (6 mm.) long, needlelike; fruit berrylike, blue black or purple _____ _____ 90. crowberry (*Empetrum nigrum*)
  SS. Leaves larger and broader; fruit a capsule.
    T. Leaves thin, deciduous, with straight or entire margins _____ 92. copperbrush (*Cladothamnus pyrolaeflorus*)
    TT. Leaves thick and leathery, evergreen, with rolled or toothed margins.
      U. Leaves densely woolly beneath, rolled under on margins ____ 93–94. Labrador-tea (*Ledum*)
      UU. Leaves hairless beneath, sharply toothed on margins _____ ____ 91. pipsissewa (*Chimaphila umbellata*)
KK. Ovary inferior, with petals and sepals attached above; fruits fleshy.
  V. Leaves opposite or paired _____ _____ 89. red-osier dogwood (*Cornus stolonifera*)
  VV. Leaves alternate or single.
    W. Low creeping shrubs; petals 4, red to pink, bent backward; fruit a cranberry _____ _____ 120. bog cranberry (*Vaccinium oxycoccos*)
    WW. Upright shrubs; petals 5, spreading.
      X. Leaves palmately veined and lobed.
        Y. Leaves small, not prickly; twigs slender, mostly without spines or prickles _____ _____ 56–61. currant, gooseberry (*Ribes*)

YY. Leaves large, with prickles on veins; twigs stout, very spiny _____
_____ 88. devilsclub (*Oplopanax horridus*)

XX. Leaves or leaflets pinnately veined; fruit like a small apple (pome) (rose family, Rosaceae).

Z. Leaves pinnately compound with 7–17 leaflets ____
_____ 67–70. mountain-ash (*Sorbus*)

ZZ. Leaves simple.

a. Leaves elliptic, rounded at apex, not lobed ____
_____ 71–72. serviceberry (*Amelanchier*)

aa. Leaves mostly ovate, pointed at apex, often lobed.

b. Twigs usually bearing stout spines; fruit blackish _____ 73.
black hawthorn (*Crataegus douglasii*)

bb. Twigs sometimes ending in spines; fruit yellow or red _____ 66.
Oregon crab apple (*Malus diversifolia*)

JJ. Petals united, at least partly, into a corolla tube.

c. Leaves alternate or single (heath family, Ericaceae; except No. 121).

d. Fruit a berry or berrylike.

e. Ovary superior.

f. Fruit a berrylike capsule, covered by fleshy purplish or white calyx; leaves sharply or wavy toothed on margin _____
____ 109–110. salal, wintergreen (*Gaultheria*)

ff. Fruit a drupe with 4–5 stony nutlets, red or blue-black; leaves not toothed on margin _____
_____ 111–113. bearberry (*Arctostaphylos*)

ee. Ovary inferior; berry blue or red; leaves entire or finely toothed on margin _____
___ 114–119. blueberry, huckleberry (*Vaccinium*)

dd. Fruit a dry capsule.

g. Shrubs more than 4 ft. (1.2 m.) high; leaves thin, deciduous; twigs and leaves with glandular ("sticky") hairs _____
____ 97. rusty menziesia (*Menziesia ferruginea*)

gg. Shrubs less than 4 ft. (1.2 m.) high; leaves thick, evergreen; twigs and leaves without glandular ("sticky") hairs.

h. Upright shrubs, loosely branching, not forming mats; leaves not crowded, not needlelike, more than ½ in. (12 mm.) long.

i. Leaves oblong to linear, edges rolled under.

j. Corolla purple, saucer-shaped; leaves whitish beneath with inconspicuous veins _____
_____ 99. bog kalmia (*Kalmia polifolia*)

jj. Corolla pinkish to crimson, urn-shaped; leaves greenish or whitish beneath with conspicuous veins _____
107. bog-rosemary (*Andromeda polifolia*)

ii. Leaves elliptic or oblanceolate, edges not or slightly rolled under.
    k. Flowers erect or spreading, with saucer-shaped showy pink to purple corolla _ _ _ _ _ _ 95–96. rosebay, rhododendron (*Rhododendron*)
    kk. Flowers hanging singly under twig, with bell-shaped white corolla _ _ _ _ _ _ _ _ _ _ _ _ _ 108. leatherleaf (*Chamaedaphne calyculata*)
  hh. Low shrubs forming dense mats; leaves crowded, needlelike.
    l. Flowers usually several at stem tip, corolla yellow, blue, or red _ 100–102. mountain-heath (*Phyllodoce*)
    ll. Flowers usually single, corolla pink or white.
      m. Stems partly erect, to 6 in. (15 cm.) high; flower stalk less than ½ in. (12 mm.) high _ _ _ _ 105. starry cassiope (*Cassiope stelleriana*)
      mm. Stems creeping, forming dense mats less than 2 in. (5 cm.) high; flower stalk ¾–1½ in. (2–4 cm.) long _ 121. diapensia (*Diapensia lapponica*)
cc. Leaves opposite or paired.
  n. Ovary superior, with calyx and corolla attached below (heath family, Ericaceae).
    o. Leaves scalelike, pressed against stems _ 103–106. cassiope (*Cassiope*)
    oo. Leaves larger, spreading.
      p. Stems creeping, forming dense mats to 2 in. (5 cm.) high; leaves needlelike, ¼ in. (6 mm.) long _ _ _ _ _ _ 98. alpine-azalea (*Loiseleuria procumbens*)
      pp. Stems upright, 4–20 in. (1–5 dm.) high; leaves oblong, ¾–1½ in. (2–4 cm.) long _ _ _ _ _ _ _ _ _ _ _ 99. bog kalmia (*Kalmia polifolia*)
  nn. Ovary inferior, with calyx and corolla attached above (honeysuckle family, Caprifoliaceae).
    q. Stems creeping; leaves evergreen, rounded, ¼–⅝ in. (6–15 mm.) long and wide _ 125. twin-flower (*Linnaea borealis*)
    qq. Stems upright.
      r. Leaves pinnately compound with 5–7 sharply toothed leaflets _ 122. Pacific red elder (*Sambucus callicarpa*)
      rr. Leaves simple.
        s. Leaves slightly 3-lobed above middle, with sharply toothed margin _ 123. high bushcranberry (*Viburnum edule*)
        ss. Leaves entire or slightly toothed.
          t. Twigs not angled; leaves blunt-pointed; corolla pink to white; berrylike drupes white _ _ _ _ 124. snowberry (*Symphoricarpos albus*)
          tt. Twigs 4-angled when young: leaves short-pointed; corolla yellow, sometimes tinged with red; berries black _ _ _ _ _ _ _ _ 126. bear-berry honeysuckle (*Lonicera involucrata*)

33

Winter Key to Alaska Shrubs

To find the name of a shrub in its winter condition, you must be somewhat of a detective. The first twig seen may not run down quickly in the key. Every bit of evidence will help in finally determining the name. In the field, look for old leaves and remains of flowers and fruits, also well-formed buds of foliage and flowers for the next year. Take notes on the size and general characteristics and look around the area carefully to see whether the specimen is typical.

Becoming familiar with the characters used in the key may save time. Thus, knowing that all shrubs in Alaska with winter buds covered by a single bud-scale are willows (*Salix*) will aid in learning this genus. Recognition of willows will eliminate running each willow through several steps in the key. When you finally reach a name in the key, check it with the description and range on the map. If either does not agree with your plant, go back through the key to see if alternatives might have been taken along the way. As it is only for native species, this key may not work for shrubs planted around homes.

This winter key to Alaska shrubs is to species except in the willows. Species of willow are not readily distinguished in winter. However, if old dead leaves are present, the vegetative key to willows may be used for further identification.

A. (AA on p. 37). Plants evergreen or with leaves persistent in winter.
  B. Plants parasitic on conifer twigs; leaves reduced to paired brownish scales __ 55. hemlock dwarf-mistletoe (*Arceuthobium tsugense*)
  BB. Plants growing on land; leaves green.
    C. (CC on p. 36). Low shrubs usually less than 1 ft. (30 cm.) high, mostly forming mats or clumps.
      D. Leaves scalelike, awl-shaped or needlelike, narrow.
        E. Plants resinous, with persistent berrylike resinous cones, coniferous.
          F. Leaves awl-shaped, sharp-pointed, spreading in groups of 3 _____ 13. common juniper (*Juniperus communis*)
          FF. Leaves mostly scalelike, blunt, pressed against twig, paired _____ ____ 14. creeping juniper (*Juniperus horizontalis*)
        EE. Plants not resinous, not producing berrylike cones, heatherlike.
          G. Leaves less than ¼ in. (6 mm.) long, scalelike or needlelike; twigs without peglike leaf-scars.
            H. Leaves alternate or whorled, spreading, linear or linear-lanceolate, not scalelike.
              I. Leaves mostly 4 in a whorl, sometimes alternate, linear, ⅛–¼ in. (3–6 mm.) long, rounded at tip, with groove on lower surface, hairless; black berries sometimes persistent _____ _____ 90. crowberry (*Empetrum nigrum*)
              II. Leaves alternate, linear-lanceolate, ¹⁄₁₆–³⁄₁₆ in. (2–5 mm.) long, pointed, without groove on lower surface, often with long hairs on margin; dried capsule often persistent at tip of twig _____ ____ 105. starry cassiope (*Cassiope stelleriana*)

HH. Leaves paired or opposite, scalelike, pressed against twig.
  J. Leaves deeply grooved on lower surface, $\frac{1}{8}$–$\frac{3}{16}$ in. (3–5 mm.) long _____
    _ _ 103. four-angled cassiope (*Cassiope tetragona*)
  JJ. Leaves not deeply grooved on lower surface, $\frac{1}{16}$– $\frac{5}{32}$ in. (1.5–4 mm.) long.
    K. Twigs with leaves about $\frac{1}{16}$ in. (1.5 mm.) in diameter _____
      106. Alaska cassiope (*Cassiope lycopodioides*)
    KK. Twigs with leaves $\frac{1}{8}$ in. (3 mm.) in diameter ____
      104. Mertens cassiope (*Cassiope mertensiana*)
GG. Leaves more than $\frac{1}{4}$ in. (6 mm.) long, needlelike.
  L. Twigs smooth; leaves tightly rolled under, with dense brownish hairs beneath _____
    93. narrow-leaf Labrador-tea (*Ledum decumbens*)
  LL. Twigs with peglike leaf-scars; leaves flat—mountain-heath (*Phyllodoce*). (The 3 species below are not readily distinguished by leaves.)
    M. Leaves short, $\frac{3}{16}$–$\frac{5}{16}$ in. (5–8 mm.) long and about $\frac{1}{16}$ in. (1.4–1.8 mm.) wide _____
    101. blue mountain-heath (*Phyllodoce coerulea*)
    MM. Leaves longer, more than $\frac{5}{16}$ in. (8 mm.) long, and narrower. about $\frac{1}{32}$ in. (1–1.2 mm.) wide.
      N. Lower surface of leaves with white hairs _____ 102. Aleutian mountain-heath (*Phyllodoce aleutica*)
      NN. Lower surface of leaves with reddish resin glands or hairless _____ 100. red mountain-heath (*Phyllodoce empetriformis*)
DD. Leaves relatively broader.
  O. Leaves with brown resin dots on both surfaces _____ ____ 95. Lapland rosebay (*Rhododendron lapponicum*)
  OO. Leaves without brown resin glands.
    P. Leaves mostly less than $\frac{3}{8}$ in. (10 mm.) long.
      Q. Leaves crowded, spatula-shaped, appearing as a whorl at tip of stem _ _ 121. diapensia (*Diapensia lapponica*)
      QQ. Leaves scattered, rounded or linear.
        R. Leaves elliptic, rounded at tip, lower surface with dense hairs; stems coarse, much branched; plants of dry alpine and arctic tundra _____ ____ 98. alpine-azalea (*Loiseleuria procumbens*)
        RR. Leaves oval to lance-shaped, short-pointed, lower surface hairless; stems very fine, creeping in peatmoss; plants usually in bogs _____ ____ 120. bog cranberry (*Vaccinium oxycoccos*)
    PP. Leaves more than $\frac{3}{8}$ in. (10 mm.) long.
      S. Leaves oblong, leathery, with wavy-toothed or straight edges, densely white hairy beneath, with 2 narrow long-pointed stipules.
        T. Leaves wedge-shaped at base; plants mainly pioneers on gravel and sand _____ 79. Drummond mountain-avens (*Dryas drummondii*)

35

TT. Leaves notched (heart-shaped) at base; plants of
    alpine tundra or open spruce and shrubs near
    tree line.
  U. Leaves with straight or slightly wavy edges, not or
      slightly rough above, without glands and scales
      on midvein beneath _____ 81.
      entire-leaf mountain-avens (*Dryas integrifolia*)
  UU. Leaves with wavy-toothed edges, very rough above,
      with glands and scales on midvein beneath __
      80. white mountain-avens (*Dryas octopetala*)
SS. Leaves oval or spatula-shaped, not densely white hairy
    beneath, with stipules.
  V. Leaves spatula-shaped, broadest at tip and tapering
      toward base.
    W. Leaves whorled, edges with sharp teeth _____
        _____ 91. pipsissewa (*Chimaphila umbellata*)
    WW. Leaves alternate, edges not toothed.
      X. Leaves without petiole, with conspicuous stiff
        hairs on edges and lower surface; upright
        shrub of alpine tundra of southwest Alaska
        _____ 96. Kamchatka rho-
        dodendron (*Rhododendron camtschaticum*)
      XX. Leaves with petiole ⅛ in. (3 mm.) long, hairless
        on lower surface; reddish berries often per-
        sistent; creeping shrub, usually of dry
        forested area _____
        __ 111. bearberry (*Arctostaphylos uva-ursi*)
  VV. Leaves oval, broadest at middle.
    Y. Leaves not toothed, with edges slightly rolled under
      _____ 114.
      mountain-cranberry (*Vaccinium vitis-idaea*)
    YY. Leaves toothed, flat.
      Z. Leaves toothed at tip; delicate creeping herbaceous
        shrub __ 125. twin-flower (*Linnaea borealis*)
      ZZ. Leaves finely wavy-toothed; dwarf shrub of
        Kiska Island in eastern Aleutians _____ 110.
        Miquel wintergreen (*Gaultheria miqueliana*)
CC. (C on p. 34). Shrubs usually more than 1 ft. (30 cm.) high (less
    in tundra), not forming mats.
  a. Leaves 2–4 in. (5–10 cm.) long, broad, shiny, sharply toothed
    on edges _____ 109. salal (*Gaultheria shallon*)
  aa. Leaves less than 2 in. (5 cm.) long, narrow, dull, not toothed
    on edges.
    b. Leaves with dense brownish red curly hairs beneath.
      c. Leaves oblong, 1–2 in. (2.5–5 cm.) long, ³⁄₁₆–½ in. (5–12
        mm.) wide, curled downward slightly on edges; fruit
        stalk bent or curved throughout its length _____
        _____ 94. Labrador-tea (*Ledum groenlandicum*)
      cc. Leaves linear, ⁵⁄₁₆–⅝ in. (8–15 mm.) long, ¹⁄₆₄–⅛ in. (0.5–
        3 mm.) wide, tightly rolled under, curled edges
        covering lower surface; fruit stalk abruptly bent
        near capsule _____
        __ 93. narrow-leaf Labrador-tea (*Ledum decumbens*)

bb. Leaves hairless or nearly so beneath.
    d. Leaves flat or only slightly rolled under, with scurfy scales often appearing as white dots; young twigs with fine short white hairs _____
    _____ 108. leatherleaf (*Chamaedaphne calyculata*)
  dd. Leaves rolled under, without scurfy scales; twigs hairless.
    e. Leaves elliptic, ⅛–½ in. (3–12 mm.) wide, slightly rolled under, whitish beneath, veins inconspicuous; southeast Alaska ____ 99. bog kalmia (*Kalmia polifolia*)
    ee. Leaves slightly narrower, ¹⁄₁₆–¼ in. (2–6 mm.) wide, tightly rolled under and partly concealing greenish or whitish lower surface with conspicuous veins; throughout Alaska _____
    _____ 107. bog rosemary (*Andromeda polifolia*)
AA (A on p. 34). Plants deciduous, leafless in winter, dead leaves sometimes persistent.
  f. Leaves (or leaf-scars) and twigs opposite or paired.
    g. Twigs and buds covered with minute brown shield-shaped scales _____ 86. buffaloberry (*Shepherdia canadensis*)
    gg. Twigs not scaly.
      h. Buds large, more than ⅜ in. (10 mm.) long and nearly as broad, stalked; twig stout, dying back at tip; pith broad _____
      _____ 122. Pacific red elder (*Sambucus callicarpa*)
      hh. Buds small, mostly less than ⅜ in. (10 mm.) long, if longer then less than ³⁄₁₆ in. (5 mm.) wide, stalked or stalkless; twig slender, usually not dying back; pith narrow.
        i. Twigs 4-angled or squarrish _____
        ____ 126. bearberry honeysuckle (*Lonicera involucrata*)
        ii. Twigs round.
          j. Leaf-scars raised, often torn or indistinct, with 1 bundle-scar; twigs very slender with bark becoming shreddy _____ 124. snowberry (*Symphoricarpos albus*)
          jj. Leaf-scars not raised or torn, with 3 or more bundle-scars; twigs less slender, with bark not shreddy.
            k. Twigs gray, hairless, buds red.
              l. Buds long, narrow, pointed, dark brownish red, outer bud-scales united at edges, inner bud-scales hairless; loose straggling shrubs often with persistent red berries or fruit stalks _____
              ____ 123. high bushcranberry (*Viburnum edule*)
              ll. Buds rounded, blunt, bright red, outer bud-scales often spreading and exposing hairy inner bud-scales; erect shrub or small tree with maple key fruits often persistent _____
              85. Douglas maple (*Acer glabrum* var. *douglasii*)
            kk. Twigs red, shiny, densely gray hairy near tip; buds gray brown _____
            ____ 89. red-osier dogwood (*Cornus stolonifera*)
ff. Leaves (or leaf-scars) and twigs alternate or single.
  m. Twigs with spines, thorns, or prickles (often absent on young plants and new shoots, especially in No. 75).
    n. Twigs very stout, light brown, densely covered with slender sharp spines _____ 88. devilsclub (*Oplopanax horridus*)

nn. Twigs slender, of various colors, with spines less dense or partly enlarged at base.
    o. Spines stout, ⅜–1 in. (10–25 mm.) long, few on shiny red brown twigs; purplish black berries often persistent _____ 73. black hawthorn (*Crataegus douglasii*)
    oo. Spines less than ½ in. (12 mm.) long.
      p. Spines 3–9 at nodes and smaller single spines between; pith with spongelike cavities; shrubs usually trailing ____ _____ 56. swamp gooseberry (*Ribes lacustre*)
      pp. Spines single; pith not spongelike; erect shrubs.
        q. Twigs light brown or whitish, soft and easily broken, bark usually shreddy, pith occupying more than ⅔; old raspberries often present—raspberry (*Rubus*).
          r. Twigs brown.
            s. Twigs straight, covered with bristles and prickles _____ 74. American red raspberry (*Rubus idaeus* var. *strigosus*)
            ss. Twigs zigzag, with weak straight rounded prickles _____ 75. salmonberry (*Rubus spectabilis*)
          rr. Twigs whitish, with stout hooked flattened prickles or spines _____ 76. western black raspberry (*Rubus leucodermis*)
        qq. Twigs dark red, hard, bark not shreddy, pith occupying less than ⅔; old rose hips often present—rose (*Rosa*).
          t. Twigs with prickles or spines round or partly so, many to few.
            u. Prickles or spines many _____ _____ 82. prickly rose (*Rosa acicularis*)
            uu. Prickles or spines few, scattered _____ _____ 83. Woods rose (*Rosa woodsii*)
          tt. Twigs with few flattened prickles or spines usually paired at nodes _____ _____ 84. Nookta rose (*Rosa nutkana*)
mm. Twigs without spines, thorns, or prickles.
    v. Shrubs low, less than 6 in. (15 cm.) high or dying back to woody base.
      w. Shrubs creeping.
        x. Buds covered by a single bud-scale _____ _____ 18–25. dwarf willows (*Salix* spp.) (If old dead leaves are present, the vegetative key to willows may be used for identification to species.)
        xx. Buds with 2 or more bud-scales.
          y. Red or brown leaves or skeletonized leaves persisting, black berries often persistent _____ ____ 112. alpine bearberry (*Arctostaphylos alpina*)
          yy. Leaves shedding first year; red berries often persistent ___ 113. red-fruit bearberry (*Arctostaphylos rubra*)
      ww. Shrubs herbaceous, dying back to woody base; dead leaves often persistent, divided into narrow segments.
        z. Leaves twice 3-forked, hairless, without odor _____ _____ 65. luetkea (*Luetkea pectinata*)

38

zz. Leaves finely dissected, whitish hairy, with sagebrush odor persisting.

A. Basal leaves ¼–½ in. (6–12 mm.) long, 2–3 times divided into narrow segments 1/32 in. (1 mm.) wide ------------ 127. fringed sagebrush (*Artemisia frigida*)

AA. Basal leaves 1–2 in. (2.5–5 cm.) long, 2–3 times divided into spatula-shaped segments 1/16–⅛ in. (2–3 mm.) wide -- 128. Alaska sagebrush (*Artemisia alaskana*)

vv. Shrubs usually upright and more than 6 in. (15 cm.) high.

B. Twigs with expanded buds of next year's catkins, remains of last year's catkins, and conspicuous dots (lenticels or resin glands).

C. Twigs resinous, buds of next year's catkins small, ¼ in. (6 mm.) long and stalkless, covered by several white-bordered bud-scales; remains of last year's catkin spikelike; winter buds not stalked, of overlapping bud-scales.

D. Remains of last year's catkin a stalkless straight stout spike ⅜ in. (10 mm.) long, 1/16 in. (1.5 mm.) wide, with conspicuous concave bud-scars; resin dots inconspicuous, on young twigs only -------------------------------- 47. sweetgale (*Myrica gale*)

DD. Remains of last year's catkin very narrow, ⅜–⅝ in. (10–15 mm.) long, 1/64 in. (0.5 mm.) wide, long stalked; twigs covered with resin glands—birch (*Betula*).

E. Shrubs usually less than 2 ft. (0.6 m.) high, in bogs and tundra; catkin scale without resiniferous dot or hump, glandless; broad wing around nutlet ---------- 48. dwarf arctic birch (*Betula nana*)

EE. Shrub to 5 ft. (1.5 m.) high, near tree line; catkin scale with resinous dot or hump, often glandular; wing of nutlet narrow, often broader toward apex ---------- 49. resin birch (*Betula glandulosa*)

CC. Twigs not resinous, buds of next year's catkins ⅜–⅝ in. (10–15 mm.) long on stalks of 3/16–⅜ in. (5–10 mm.), bud-scales not white-bordered; old, hard blackish cones or conelike fruits usually present—alder (*Alnus*).

F. Winter buds of overlapping scales.

G. Cones ⅜–⅝ in. (10–15 mm.) long, on stalks ¼–½ in. (6–12 mm.); shrub of interior Alaska -------------- 51. American green alder (*Alnus crispa*)

GG. Cones ½–¾ in. (12–20 mm.) long, on stalks ⅜–¾ in. (10–20 mm.); shrub or small tree of southern and southeast Alaska -------------------------------------- 52. Sitka alder (*Alnus sinuata*)

FF. Winter buds with 3 exposed scales meeting at edges.

H. Cones ½–1 in. (12–25 mm.) long ----------------------------------- 53. red alder (*Alnus rubra*)

HH. Cones less than ½ in. (12 mm.) long ------------------------ 54. thinleaf alder (*Alnus tenuifolia*)

BB. Twigs without catkins.

I. Stipules and bases or stumps of petioles persistent, partly covering buds.

    J. Stipules narrow, bent or twisted; twigs soft, canelike, dying back from tip _____
        ____ 77. western thimbleberry (*Rubus parviflorus*)

    JJ. Stipules broad, papery, spreading; twigs hard, not dying back _____
        _____ 78. bush cinquefoil (*Potentilla fruticosa*)

II. Stipules and bases of petioles absent.

    K. Fruits persistent in conspicuous clusters.

        L. Fruits fleshy, like a small apple, red; winter buds large, mostly more than ⅜ in. (10 mm.) long, with densely hairy inner bud-scales; large shrubs and small trees—mountain-ash (*Sorbus*).

            M. Winter buds with whitish hairs.

                N. Winter buds reddish brown, inner bud-scales with whitish hairs at tip _____
                67. Greene mountain-ash (*Sorbus scopulina*)

                NN. Winter buds densely covered with whitish hairs; naturalized tree _____ 68. European mountain-ash (*Sorbus aucuparia*)

            MM. Winter buds with rusty brown hairs.

                O. Winter buds dull reddish brown, densely rusty hairy _____
                69. Sitka mountain-ash (*Sorbus sitchensis*)

                OO. Winter buds shiny reddish brown, slightly rusty hairy; only in westernmost Aleutian Islands _____ 70. Siberian mountain-ash (*Sorbus sambucifolia*)

        LL. Fruits dry, 3–5 from a flower, egg-shaped, podlike, splitting open, brown; winter buds less than ⅜ in. (10 mm.) long.

            P. Fruits ¼–⅜ in. (6–10 mm.) long; bark peeling and shedding in long strips _____
            62. Pacific ninebark (*Physocarpus capitatus*)

            PP. Fruits less than ⅛ in. (3 mm.) long; bark not shedding.

                Q. Fruit clusters flat-topped to half round _____
                63. Beauverd spirea (*Spiraea beauverdiana*)

                QQ. Fruit clusters conic, much longer than broad __
            ____ 64. Douglas spirea (*Spiraea douglasii*)

    KK. Fruits absent or borne singly.

        R. Winter buds covered by a single scale _____
        _____ 15–46. willow (*Salix*)
(Species not readily distinguished in winter. Old leaves and catkins sometimes can be found for identification to species in the Vegetative Key to Alaska Willows. Descriptions, size of plants, and range maps may be helpful.)

        RR. Winter buds with 2 or more scales exposed.

            S. Twigs with rusty brown scales when young, becoming silvery; silvery berries often persistent ___
            _____ 87. silverberry (*Elaeagnus commutata*)

SS. Twigs and fruits not as above.

    T. Twigs without end buds; side buds with 2 bud-scales meeting at edges (except in No. 119); fruit a blue or red berry, seldom persistent—blueberries and huckleberries (*Vaccinium*).

      U. Shrubs mostly less than 16 in. (40 cm.) high; twigs round or sometimes slightly angled.

        V. Bud-scales 2, meeting at edges ____ 115. dwarf blueberry (*Vaccinium caespitosum*)

        VV. Bud-scales several, overlapping _____ 119. bog blueberry (*Vaccinium uliginosum*)

      UU. Shrubs mostly more than 2 ft. (60 cm.) high; twigs angled.

        W. Twigs green, strongly angled; fruit red ____ _____ 116. red huckleberry (*Vaccinium parvifolium*)

        WW. Twigs brown or reddish, weakly angled; fruit blue or black.

          X. Fruit stalks usually less than ⅜ in. (1 cm.) long, curved, not enlarged below fruit _____ 117. early blueberry (*Vaccinium ovalifolium*)

          XX. Fruit stalks often more than ⅜ in. (1 cm.) long, straight or nearly so, enlarged just below fruit __ 118. Alaska blueberry (*Vaccinium alaskaense*)

  TT. Twigs with true end buds covered by 3 or more bud-scales.

    Y. Shrubs spreading; twigs angled, with papery shedding or shredded bark, often with unpleasant odor when crushed; pits porous or spongy—currants (*Ribes*).

      Z. Twigs stout, ¼ in. (6 mm.) in diameter; leaf-scars heart-shaped, large, gray _____ ___ 57. stink currant (*Ribes bracteosum*)

      ZZ. Twigs slender, less than 3/16 in. (5 mm.) in diameter; leaf-scars V-shaped, narrow and inconspicuous.

        a. Twigs with black gland dots.

          b. Buds hairless; twigs 1/16 in. (2 mm.) in diameter _____ 58. northern black currant (*Ribes hudsonianum*)

          bb. Buds with white hairs; twigs about ⅛ in. (3 mm.) in diameter _____ 59. skunk currant (*Ribes glandulosum*)

        aa. Twigs without gland dots.

          c. Twigs hairy, yellow brown, becoming dark brown, about 3/16 in. (5 mm.) in diameter _____ 60. trailing black currant (*Ribes laxiflorum*)

          cc. Twigs hairless, light brown, becoming reddish brown and shredded, about

⅛ in. (3 mm.) in diameter ____ 61.
American red currant (*Ribes triste*)

YY. Shrubs erect (or becoming small trees) ; twigs rounded, with bark not shedding (except in No. 92) ; pith hard, solid.

  d. Twigs paired or whorled, widely forking, with gland hairs, odorous when crushed __ 97. rusty menziesia (*Menziesia ferruginea*)

  dd. Twigs not paired, without gland hairs.

    e. Winter buds orange _____ 92. copperbush (*Cladothamnus pyrolaeflorus*)

    ee. Winter buds darker.

      f. Winter buds blunt-pointed, dark brown; twigs coarse, gray or brown, often with dense gray hairs near tip, with short side twigs or spurs __ 66. Oregon crab apple (*Malus diversifolia*)

      ff. Winter buds sharp-pointed, purple; twigs slender, reddish purple, shiny, hairless, without short side twigs or spurs.

        g. Shrub rare in central and southern Alaska _____ 71. saskatoon serviceberry (*Amelanchier alnifolia*)

        gg. Shrub or small tree of southern and southeast Alaska _____ _____ 72. Pacific serviceberry (*Amelanchier florida*)

ALASKA TREES AND SHRUBS

YEW FAMILY
(Taxaceae)

The seed plants with seeds partly exposed (gymnosperms), not enclosed in fruits, are represented in Alaska by 3 families of conifers or softwoods, the yew family (Taxaceae), the pine family (Pinaceae), and the cypress family (Cupressaceae). The Alaska examples are evergreen (with 1 exception) trees and shrubs with narrow or small leaves resembling needles or scales. Pacific yew (*Taxus brevifolia* Nutt.), the Alaska member of the yew family, is distinguished by the brown seeds borne singly in a scarlet, juicy, cuplike or berrylike disk, by the flat, pointed, nonresinous needles in 2 rows, and by the twisted leafstalks extending down the twig.

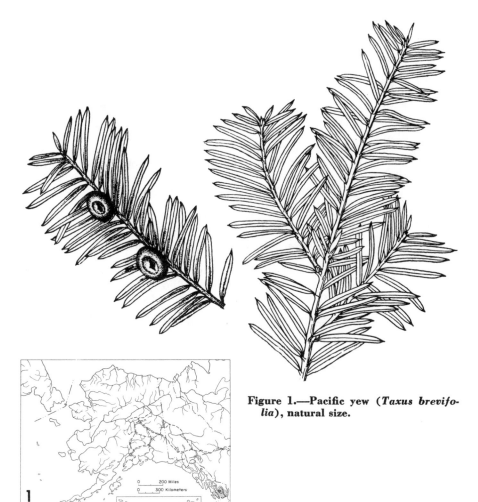

Figure 1.—Pacific yew (*Taxus brevifolia*), natural size.

43

1. PACIFIC YEW

(*Taxus brevifolia* Nutt.)

Other name: western yew.

Small tree or large shrub of extreme south end of southeast Alaska, to 20–30 ft. (6–9 m.) tall, with straight conical trunk 2–6 in. (5–15 cm.) or rarely 12 in. (30 cm.) in diameter at breast height, with open crown or horizontal or drooping branches. **Leaves** (needles) in 2 rows, ¼–¾ in. (12–20 mm.) long, flat, slightly curved, stiff or soft, abruptly pointed but not prickly, shiny yellow green above, pale green beneath, not resinous. Petioles yellow, extending down the slender twigs, twisting to produce an even, comblike arrangement of needles. **Bark** purplish brown, thin, scaly, ridged, and fluted. **Wood** bright red with thin light yellow sapwood, fine-textured, heavy, hard, elastic.

Pollen and seeds on different trees (dioecious). **Seeds** single, ⅜ in. (1 cm.) long, brown, exposed at apex but partly surrounded by a thick scarlet, juicy, cuplike disk or "berry."

Southward, the strong, durable wood is used for poles, bows, canoe paddles, and cabinet work. However, in Alaska the trees are too scarce to be commercially important. The plants could serve as ornamentals.

The seeds are poisonous when eaten, causing vomiting, diarrhea, and inflammation of urinary ducts and the uterus. Also, yew foliage is poisonous when browsed by livestock. However, the juicy scarlet "berries" around the seeds are not toxic.

Pacific yew is rare and local in the extreme south end of southeast Alaska, near sea level on poor sites and in canyons. It is scattered in understory of the coast forest of western redcedar, western and mountain hemlocks, and Sitka spruce. The irregular distribution may be related to dispersal of the seeds by birds. Growth is slow. Another species of yew has been introduced in southeast Alaska as an ornamental shrub and hedge plant.

Pacific yew has been found in Alaska only on a few islands near Ketchikan. These include Annette, Dog, Cat, Mary, Bold, and Gravina Islands. Also southern end of Prince of Wales Island north to Kasaan Island in Kasaan Bay. Probably rare in nearby areas. South Tongass National Forest. Pacific coast region from Alaska and British Columbia south through western Washington to central California and in mountains to Idaho and northwestern Montana.

PINE FAMILY

(Pinaceae)

Conifers, or softwoods, are economically the most important group of trees in Alaska. Many have tall straight trunks and narrow crowns, except where dwarfed near the limits of tree growth. However, the 2 native species of juniper are low shrubs. These narrowleaf evergreens make up nearly all the trees of the coastal forests of southeast Alaska and most of the timber of the interior forests. They furnish nearly all the State's lumber, pulpwood, building logs, and other wood products.

These cone-bearing trees are resinous softwoods with needlelike or scalelike evergreen leaves with seeds exposed in cones, usually hard and woody. Pollen is borne in small male cones usually on the same plant, and true flowers and fruits are lacking. Alaska's conifers are classified in 3 plant families, yew family (Taxaceae), pine family (Pinaceae) with needlelike leaves, and cypress family (Cupressaceae) with scalelike leaves. Members of the yew family have seeds borne singly in a scarlet juicy cuplike disk, rather than in a cone, and may not be true conifers.

The pine family (Pinaceae) is well represented in Alaska by 5 genera and 9 species of trees with narrow, mostly long needles. The cones have many cone-scales, each bearing 2 long-winged seeds at its base. Characters of the 5 genera and names of their Alaska species are summarized here for ready identification.

Larch (*Larix*), the only Alaska conifer shedding its leaves in fall and leafless in winter. One species, tamarack (*L. laricina* (Du Roi) K. Koch), with slender flexible needles borne 12–20 in a cluster on short stout spur twigs (or single on leading twigs).

Pine (*Pinus*), 1 species, lodgepole pine (*P. contorta* Dougl.), with 2 varieties. Needles 2 in a bundle or cluster with sheath at base, relatively long and stiff. Cones one-sided, with many prickly cone scales.

Spruce (*Picea*), 3 species, black, white, and Sitka spruce. Needles sharp-pointed and stiff, either 4-angled or flattened and slightly keeled, extending out on all sides of twig. There is no leafstalk, but each leaf is attached on a small stalklike or peglike projection of the twig. Older twigs without needles are rough because of these projections. Cut branches of spruce and hemlock shed their needles promptly upon drying. The cones hang down. (In the preparation of botanical specimens, immersion of freshly cut twigs in boiling water for a few minutes before pressing reduces shedding of needles.)

Hemlock (*Tsuga*), 2 species, western and mountain hemlock. Needles short, blunt, soft and not stiff, flat or slightly keeled, with short leafstalks, spreading in 2 rows or curved upward. As in spruce, the older twigs are slightly rough

from the peglike projections. The cones hang down.

Fir (*Abies*), 2 species, Pacific silver fir and subalpine fir. Needles flat and without leafstalks, often spreading in 2 rows or curving upward. Older twigs smooth with round leaf-scars. Cones upright in highest branches of the narrow pointed crowns. As the cone-scales fall from the axis at maturity, old cones are not found on or under the trees.

2. LODGEPOLE PINE
(*Pinus contorta* Dougl.)

Other names: scrub pine, tamarack pine.

The general description and range of this species are followed by similar notes for the 2 varieties in Alaska. Small to large evergreen, resinous tree of southeast Alaska, 20–75 ft. (6–23 m.) tall and 8–32 in. (20–81 cm.) in trunk diameter, with crown rounded spreading or narrow pointed. **Leaves** (needles) 2 in a bundle with sheath at base, 1–2¼ in. (2.5–6 cm.) long, relatively long and stiff, often twisted, yellow green to dark green with whitish lines (stomata). **Twigs** stout, orange when young, becoming gray brown and rough. **Winter buds** short-pointed, of many narrow red brown scales. **Bark** gray to dark brown, scaly, thin or becoming thick. **Wood** resinous or pitchy, coarse-textured, straight-grained (scrubby trees with spiral grain), moderately lightweight, moderately soft. Heartwood light yellow to yellow brown, sapwood narrow and whitish.

Cones 1 to few, almost stalkless, egg-shaped, one-sided, 1¼–2 in. (3–5 cm.) long, light yellow brown, with many prickly cone scales, maturing in 2 years, persistent, opening or remaining closed many years. **Seeds** brown, about ⅝ in. (15 mm.) long, including the long broad wing.

45

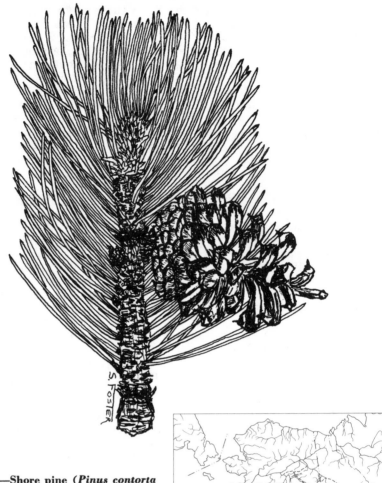

Figure 2a.—Shore pine (*Pinus contorta var. contorta*), natural size.

Alaska's only native species of pine is not important for lumber because of its mostly small size and limited occurrence. The wood is used for poles and fuel. The sweet orange-flavored sap served the Indians as a delicacy, fresh or dried. In the vicinity of Fairbanks, the inland variety has been introduced as a fast growing hardy shade tree.

Wood of lodgepole pine of the Rocky Mountain region is suitable for pulping for papers and fiberboard. Other uses are lumber, railroad ties, mine timbers, and poles, posts, and fuelwood. The lumber is mostly for rough construction, occasionally for boxes, siding, finish, and flooring.

This species including 3 geographic varieties has a broad range from southeast Alaska, central Yukon, and southwestern Mackenzie, south in mountains and along coast to Colorado, Utah, and California; also local in northern Baja California.

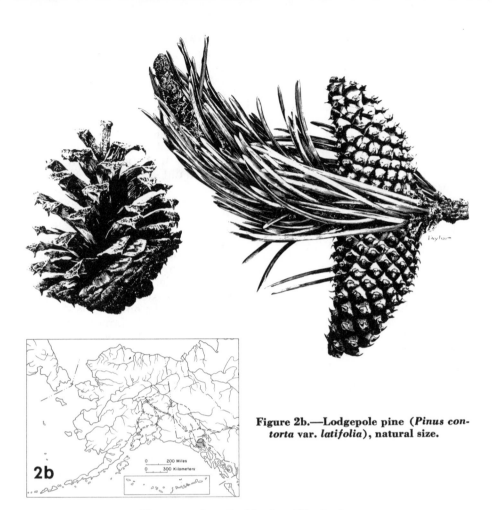

Figure 2b.—Lodgepole pine (*Pinus contorta* var. *latifolia*), natural size.

2b

Key to the 2 Alaska Varieties

Cones pointing backward, opening at maturity; generally low spreading tree of muskegs in coastal forests _____
_____ 2a. shore pine (*Pinus contorta* var. *contorta*)
Cones pointing outward, mostly remaining closed many years; tree often tall and narrow of inner fiord forests at head of Lynn Canal (Skagway to Haines) ___ 2b. lodgepole pine (*Pinus contorta* var. *latifolia*)

2a. SHORE PINE
(*Pinus contorta* Dougl. var. *contorta*)

Other names: lodgepole pine, scrub pine, tamarack pine.

Shore pine, the common pine through southeast Alaska, is often a low spreading or scrubby tree 20–40 ft. (6–12 m.) high and 8–12 in. (20–30 cm.) in trunk diameter. However, it sometimes becomes 75 ft. (23 m.) tall and 18–32 in. (45–81 cm.) in diameter. Cones pointing backward on twig, opening at maturity in October–November but remaining attached.

47

The dwarf coastal form is common in open muskegs of peat moss and on benches near lakes. Intolerant of shade, it grows in open stands as a scrub pine, straight when young but gnarled in age, with large branches extending almost to the ground. On the poorest sites, it is often like a prostrate shrub. It is best developed and largest in the better-drained borders between muskeg and hemlock or hemlock-redcedar stands. Occasionally the trees are pioneers of rapid growth after infrequent fires or logging or on outwash sand and gravel.

This coastal variety ranges throughout southeast Alaska north to the head of Lynn Canal at Haines and to Glacier Bay and Dixon Harbor. The northwestern outlier is an area of several square miles on rolling muskegs about 15 miles (24 km.) east of Yakutat, where the trees of poor form reach 40 ft. (12 m.) in height and 1 ft. (30 cm.) in trunk diameter. South Tongass and North Tongass National Forests, Glacier Bay National Monument. Pacific coast from southeast Alaska through western British Columbia to northwestern California.

2b. LODGEPOLE PINE

(*Pinus contorta* var. *latifolia* Engelm.)

Other names: Rocky Mountain lodgepole pine, *Pinus contorta* ssp. *latifolia* (Engelm.) Critchfield.

The Rocky Mountain or inland variety of lodgepole pine reaches the State only in the vicinity of Skagway and Haines. This mostly tall form with narrow crown becomes 50–75 ft. (15–23 m.) high and 8–12 in. (20–30 cm.) in trunk diameter here and somewhat larger

southward. Cones hard, heavy, pointing outward, mostly remaining closed many years, opening after a forest fire to release seeds. However, in Alaska some cones open at maturity.

The Rocky Mountain variety of lodgepole pine can be added to the list of Alaska trees, though not mentioned in botanical references. This inland variety differs from shore pine in being generally a taller tree with narrow crown and thinner scaly bark, in having slightly longer needles, and in the slightly larger, heavier, closed cones which point outward on the twig rather than backward.

This variety of lodgepole pine crosses the Coast Range from Canada into Alaska only in the vicinity of Skagway and Haines and Chilkot River at the head of Lynn Canal near the northernmost end of southeast Alaska. It forms stands in the mixed forest with Sitka spruce, western paper birch, and subalpine fir (also from the Rocky Mountains) and in the inner fiords down to sea level. North Tongass National Forest. Also northward in Yukon Territory along Yukon River and tributaries near Dawson to within about 50 miles (80 km.) of the Alaska border. East to southwestern Mackenzie and south through western Alberta and British Columbia and in Rocky Mountains to Colorado and Utah.

3. TAMARACK

(*Larix laricina* (Du Roi) K. Koch)

Other names: Alaska larch, eastern larch, hackmatack; *Larix alaskensis* W. F. Wight, *L. laricina* var. *alaskensis* (W. F. Wight) Raup.

Figure 3.—Tamarack (*Larix laricina*), natural size. Winter twigs at bottom.

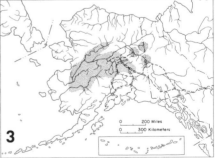

Small to medium-sized deciduous tree 30–60 ft. (9–18 m.) high, with straight tapering trunk 4–10 in. (10–25 cm.) in diameter, occasionally to 75 ft. (24 m.) tall and 13 in. (33 cm.) in diameter, horizontal branches extending nearly to ground, and thin pointed crown of blue green foliage. **Leaves** (needles) shedding in fall (deciduous), in crowded clusters of 12–20 on short stout spur twigs or branches or single on leading twigs, 3/8–1 in. (1–2.5 cm.) long, very narrow, slender and flexible, 3-angled, blue green, turning yellow before falling in early autumn. **Twigs** long, stout, dull tan, hairless, with many short stout spur twigs to 1/4 in. (6 mm.) long, bearing crowded raised leaf-scars, becoming blackish and rough. **Winter buds** small, round, about 1/16 in. (2 mm.) long, covered by many short-pointed overlapping scales. **Bark** dark gray, smoothish, thin, becoming scaly and exposing brown beneath. **Wood** light brown, hard, heavy, elastic.

49

Cones curved upright on short stalks along horizontal twigs, rounded, ⅜–⅝ in. (1–1.5 cm.) long, dark brown, composed of about 20 rounded, finely toothed cone-scales, opening in early autumn and remaining attached in winter. **Seeds** light brown, ½ in. (12 mm.) long, including long broad wing.

Tamarack is the only Alaska conifer shedding its leaves in winter. It is scattered in muskegs and various moist soils of the interior in open stands with paper birch, black spruce, alders, and willows. Occasionally it forms dense stands on flood plains with black spruce and white spruce. Where it does occur naturally on upland well drained sites, its growth rate may be equal to that of white spruce; one stand in the Tanana Valley has produced trees 13 in. (33 cm.) in diameter in 100 years.

The durable, strong wood is used to some extent for poles, railroad ties, and fenceposts.

Interior Alaska tamarack is restricted to drainages between Brooks Range on the north and Alaska Range on the south. Locally abundant along Tanana River but scattered along Yukon and Kuskokwim Rivers and up Koyukuk River to Allakaket but not north to the limit of trees. West to Unala-kleet River, which drains into Norton Sound, and to Napaimiut on the lower Kuskokwim River. Mt. McKinley National Park. There are broad gaps separating the Alaska trees from the main range from Yukon Territory eastward, except for 2 records from near the Alaska-Yukon Border. From Alaska, Yukon Territory, and District of Mackenzie east across Canada along northern limit of trees to Hudson Bay, Labrador, and Newfoundland, south in Northeastern United States to New Jersey, Illinois, and Minnesota (local in Maryland and West Virginia), and northwest to northeastern British Columbia.

The Alaska tree were named as a separate species, afterwards reduced to a variety and to synonymy. The slight differences in cone-scales and their bracts seem insufficient for retention of a separate name.

SPRUCE (*Picea*)

Spruce trees have short leaves (needles) spreading on all sides of twig, mostly 4-sided or slightly flattened, sharp-pointed and stiff, shedding promptly on drying. Twigs become rough from peglike bases of leaves. The cones hang down.

Key to the 3 Alaska Species

Leaves (needles) 4-angled, with whitish lines (stomata) on all sides.
  Twigs hairy; needles mostly less than ½ in. (12 mm.) long, resinous; cones egg-shaped or nearly round, mostly less than 1 in. (2.5 cm.) long, curved down on short stalks, remaining on tree _____
  _____ 4. black spruce (*Picea mariana*)
  Twigs hairless; needles more than ½ in. (12 mm.) long, with skunk-like odor when crushed; cones cylindric, 1¼–2½ in. (3–6 cm.) long, falling at maturity _____ 5. white spruce (*Picea glauca*)
Leaves (needles) flattened but slightly keeled, with 2 whitish bands (stomata) on lower surface; twigs hairless; cones cylindric, 2–3½ in. (5–9 cm.) long, falling at maturity _____
  _____ 6. Sitka spruce (*Picea sitchensis*)

Figure 4.—Black spruce (*Picea mari-ana*), natural size.

4. BLACK SPRUCE

(*Picea mariana* (Mill.) B.S.P.)

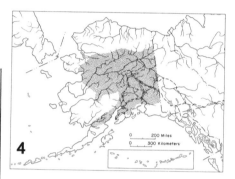

Other names: bog spruce, swamp spruce.

Evergreen resinous tree of interior forests, usually small and 15–30 ft. (4.5–9 m.) high, and 3–6 in. (7.5–15 cm.) in trunk diameter, with narrow pointed crown. Often a shrub 10 ft. (3 m.) or less in height. Sometimes a medium-sized tree to 50–60 ft. (15–18 m.) tall and 9 in. (23 cm.) in trunk diameter, the maximum height measured 72 ft. (22 m.). The branches are short, sparse, and often slightly drooping at ends. **Leaves** (needles) short-stalked, spreading on all sides of twig, ¼–⅝ in. (6–15 mm.) long, 4-angled, pointed, stiff, ashy blue green, with whitish lines (stomata) on all sides. **Twigs** slender, hairy, covered with very short reddish hairs, becoming brown and rough from peglike bases of leaves. **Bark** thin, composed of gray or blackish scales, brown beneath, the cut surface of inner bark yellowish. **Wood** yellowish white, light-weight, soft, fine-textured, with growth rings very narrow to almost microscopic.

Cones curved downward on short stalks, small and short, egg-shaped or nearly round, ⅝–1¼ in. (1.5–3 cm.) long, dull gray or blackish, remaining on tree several years and often conspicuously clustered in tree tops; cone-scales rigid and brittle, rounded, and slightly toothed. **Seeds** brown, about ½ in. (12 mm.) long including large wing.

Black spruce is characteristic of cold wet flats, muskegs, north-facing slopes, silty valley terraces, and lake margins in the spruce-birch interior forests up to an altitude of 2,000 ft. (610 m.), locally to 2,700 ft. (823 m.). Extending to tree line on gentle damp slopes, such as northern side of Alaska Range. Dense pure stands are frequently on wet area burns. Clusters of black spruce are common, because the lower branches take root to form a ring of small trees around the central parent tree.

51

Besides its usually different habitat and smaller size with more compact branching, black spruce is distinguished from white spruce by the shorter and blunter needles, hairy twigs, and smaller cones with brittle, slightly toothed cone-scales curved down on short stalks and remaining attached several years. The twigs of black spruce are reported to be tougher and gummier also. These 2 species of the interior forests can be distinguished also in the seedling stage by the finely toothed leaf margins in white spruce and absence of teeth in black spruce. Logs and tree trunks can be identified by inner bark color, yellowish in black spruce and whitish in white spruce. Annual growth rings of black spruce wood are narrower also.

The wood is of slight importance for lumber because of the small size of the trees. Occasionally the logs are cut along with white spruce for cabins. The trees are important as fuel, especially in stands killed by fire, remaining standing and well preserved for several decades. Southward black spruce is a popular Christmas tree.

Interior Alaska north to southern slopes of Brooks Range but at lower elevations and not as far north as white spruce. West to upper Kobuk River and to Elim at base of Seward Peninsula; reported only to Kaltag on Yukon River and the Stoney River on Kuskokwim River. Southwest at base of Alaska Peninsula to Bristol Bay at Naknek. South of Alaska Range in Susitna Valley, Cook Inlet and Kenai Peninsula south to Homer, and Copper River basin south to Tonsina. Not in southeast Alaska. Chugach National Forest, Mt. McKinley National Park, Kenai National Moose Range. East across Canada near northern limit of trees to Hudson Bay, Labrador, and Newfoundland, south to New Jersey, Minnesota, Manitoba, and British Columbia.

5. WHITE SPRUCE

(*Picea glauca* (Moench) Voss)

Other names: western white spruce, Canadian spruce, Alberta spruce, *Picea glauca* var. *albertiana* (S. Brown) Sarg.; Porsild spruce, *P. glauca* var. *porsildii* Raup.

White spruce, the most important tree of the spruce-birch interior forest, is a medium-sized to large tree 40–70 ft. (12–21 m.) high and 6–18 in. (15–46 cm.) in trunk diameter. On the best sites it reaches 80–115 ft. (24–35 m.) and 30 in. (76 cm.), but at timberline it becomes a prostrate shrub with a broad base below the snow-cover line. Crown pointed and usually very narrow and spirelike, sometimes broad and conical, composed of slightly drooping branches with upturned ends and many small drooping side twigs. **Leaves** (needles) short-stalked, spreading on all sides of twig but massing on top near ends, ½–¾ in. (12–20 mm.) long, 4-angled, sharp-pointed, stiff, blue green, with whitish lines on all sides; leaves and twigs with skunklike odor when crushed. **Twigs** slender, hairless, orange brown, becoming rough from peglike bases of leaves. **Bark** thin, gray, smoothish or in scaly plates, the cut surface of inner bark whitish. **Wood** almost white, the sapwood not easily distinguished, moderately lightweight, moderately soft, of fine and moderately uneven texture, with growth rings easily seen in cross-sections. **Cones** nearly stalkless, hanging down, cylindric, 1¼–2½ in. (3–6 cm.) long, shiny light brown, falling at maturity; cone-scales thin and flexible, margins nearly straight and without teeth. **Seeds** brown, about ⅜ in. (10 mm.) long, including large wing.

White spruce is the commonest tree of interior Alaska, occuring from near sea level to tree line at

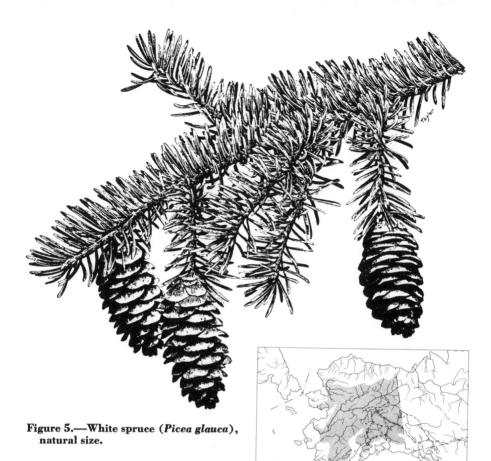

Figure 5.—White spruce (*Picea glauca*), natural size.

about 1,000–3,500 ft. (305–1,607 m.). The tree line is lowest in the north and west and on north-facing slopes and highest in the southeast interior and on south-facing slopes. This species is found in mostly open forests, usually with paper birch or in pure stands. In a few places, such as the Chugach National Forest, it extends to tidewater. Although not exacting as to site, this species grows best on well drained soils on south-facing gentle slopes and sandy soils along the edges of lakes and rivers. It forms the tallest forests along the large rivers, where running water thaws the soil. It is seldom found where permafrost is close to the surface. White spruce often replaces balsam poplar along the river floodplains and also in-

vades the open forests of birch and aspen that follow fire. The trees have average growth rate, attaining an age of 100–200 years at maturity.

Alaska trees commonly have very narrow crowns and short broad cones and have been referred to a western variety (western white spruce, var. *albertiana* (S. Brown) Sarg.). In contrast the trees of the typical variety, for example, in the Lakes States and Northeast, have broader conical crowns. Another western variation scattered in Alaska has smooth bark with resin blisters (as in fir) and relatively broad crown (Porsild spruce, var. *porsildii* Raup).

53

On Kenai Peninsula, where this species meets Sitka spruce, hybrids or intermediate trees occur, as noted under that species. Natural hybrids between white spruce and black spruce apparently are very rare in interior Alaska. One intermediate tree identified as a hybrid was discovered among trees of these two species on the north edge of Tanana Valley about 250 miles (400 km.) east-southeast of Fairbanks, at about 1,800 feet (550 m.) elevation.

White spruce is used extensively in interior Alaska for cabin logs, peeled and in natural form, sawed flat on 3 sides, or milled on lathes into uniformly round logs having diameters of 6, 8, or 10 inches (15, 20, or 25 cm.). Large numbers of pilings and rough timbers from interior Alaska have been transported to the North Slope for construction of oil drilling platforms. Timbers for bridges and corduroy roads are other uses. A small quantity is cut for fuel also. This species supplies much of the lumber sawed in interior Alaska, also dimension material for buildings in light and medium construction. Early uses included flumes, sluice boxes, and boats.

In Canada, white spruce is the most important commercial tree species and the foremost pulpwood. Uses include scaffolding planks, paddles and oars, sounding boards in musical instruments, shop fittings, agricultural implements, kitchen cabinets, boxes, cooperage, shelving, veneer, and plywood. The seasoned wood is almost tasteless and odorless and well suited for food containers.

The range of white spruce through interior Alaska corresponds to that mapped for the spruce-birch interior forests, north and west to the limit of tree growth but not in the southeast. In the northeast to Firth River and its tributary Joe Creek on the Arctic slope and north to south slopes of Brooks Range and northwest to Noatak River near Chukchi Sea. West to upper Fish River on Seward Peninsula, Unalakleet, Mountain Village on Yukon River, Holitna River on Kuskokwim River, and reaching Bristol Bay coast at Dillingham on Nuskagak Bay. Also south of Alaska Range from Susitna Valley to Cook Inlet and northern Kenai Peninsula and east to Copper River basin. Chugach National Forest, Mt. McKinley National Park, Katmai National Monument, Kenai National Moose Range, Arctic National Wildlife Range. East across Canada near northern limit of trees to Hudson Bay, Labrador, and Newfoundland, south to New York, Minnesota, Montana, and British Columbia, also local in Black Hills.

6. SITKA SPRUCE
(*Picea sitchensis* (Bong.) Carr.)

Other names: tideland spruce, yellow spruce, western spruce, silver spruce, coast spruce.

Sitka spruce is the largest and one of the most valuable trees in Alaska, also the State tree. Large to very large evergreen tree to 160 ft. (49 m.) in height and 3–5 ft. (0.9–1.5 m.) in trunk diameter, infrequently to 200–225 ft. (61–69 m.) and 7–8 ft. (2.1–2.4 m.) or more. From the much enlarged or buttressed base, the tall straight evenly tapering trunk rises to an open pointed broad conical crown with horizontal branches. **Leaves** (needles) standing out on all sides of twig, flattened and slightly keeled, ⅝–1 in. (15–25 mm.) long, sharp-pointed, dark green, the upper surface slightly keeled or angled and with 2 whitish bands (stomata), lower surface rounded or slightly keeled and sometimes with few whitish lines. **Twigs** stout, stiff, hairless, light brown to dark brown,

Figure 6.—Sitka spruce (*Picea sitchensis*), three-fourths natural size.

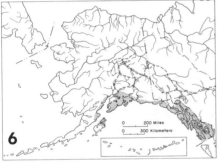

6

becoming rough from peglike bases of leaves. **Bark** gray and smoothish on small trunks, thin, becoming dark purplish brown with scaly plates, the inner bark whitish with brown dots. **Wood** moderately lightweight, moderately soft, of fine and moderately even texture, and usually very straight grained. Sapwood nearly white and heartwood light reddish brown.

Cones short-stalked, hanging down, cylindric, 2–3½ in. (5–9 cm.) long, light orange brown, falling at maturity; cone-scales long, stiff, thin, rounded and irregularly toothed. **Seeds** brown, about ½ in. (12 mm.) long, including large wing.

Sitka spruce forms more than 20 percent of the hemlock-spruce coastal forests of Alaska and also occurs in pure stands. It grows more rapidly and to larger size than western hemlock and is more light-requiring. The largest old growth trees in southeast Alaska have trunk diameters exceeding 8 ft.

55

(2.4 m.) and ages of 500–750 years or more. Many years ago there was reported a giant 14½ ft. (4.4 m.) in trunk diameter measured 6 ft. (1.8 m.) above the ground, but further information including the locality is lacking. (The national champion Sitka spruce, at Forks, Wash., is somewhat larger, approximately 17.9 ft. (5.4 m.) in trunk diameter and 248 ft. (75.6 m.) in height.) Westward on the Chugach National Forest, the trees are smaller, averaging 80 ft. (24 m.) in height, 1½ ft. (45 cm.) in diameter, and about 200 years in age. At Afognak and Kodiak Islands there are pure stands of Sitka spruce, the only conifer. On Kodiak Island near the southwestern limit, this tree is reported to be migrating westward during the past few centuries.

This species extends from sea level to the timberline up to about 3,000 ft. (914 m.) in the coastal mountains but grows mainly at altitudes below 1,500 ft. (457 m.). However, dwarf plants have been seen as high as 3,500–3,900 ft. (1067–1189 m.) on unglaciated rocky outcrops (nunataks) projecting above the Juneau Ice Field.

In bare or open areas, such as at Glacier Bay, the bushy trees often propagate by layering. The lowest branches touch the ground, become partly covered up, develop roots, and then turn upward to form separate trees. Sprouts from stumps have been observed also.

Small groves of Sitka spruce trees were planted as early as 1805 by Russians at Unalaska, near the eastern end of the treeless Aleutian Islands and far outside the tree limits. These trees are still growing and have produced cones. Younger trees are absent, perhaps because of grazing. Several plantings have been made also on other Aleutians. Both the common and scientific names honor Sitka Island, now Baranof Island, where the southeast Alaska town of Sitka is located.

Sitka spruce produces high-grade wood pulp, the best on the Pacific coast. The wood with that of western hemlock is extensively used in manufacture of newsprint. This species is also the principal sawtimber tree of southeast Alaska and is made into all the usual forms of lumber. The high-grade lumber from the large clear trunks has many uses. It is the most important wood for airplane and glider construction, and in World War II was utilized especially in British mosquito bombers. Other important uses are oars, ladders and scaffolding, and boats, particularly racing sculls. Resonant qualities, large size, and uniformity make the wood valuable for piano sounding boards. Much low-grade lumber is made into packing boxes for the Alaska salmon industry. Other uses are general construction, food containers, shelving, and kitchen furnishings. Alaska has about two-fifths of the total supply of this species and seven-eighths of the United States supply.

The range of Sitka spruce is the same as the hemlock-spruce coastal forests of southeast and southern Alaska. Throughout southeast Alaska north to head of Lynn Canal at Skagway, Glacier Bay, and Yakutat Bay. West along coast of southern Alaska to Prince William Sound, Kenai Peninsula, and west side of Cook Inlet. Along southern coast of Alaska Peninsula southwest to its westernmost limit at Cape Kubagakli near southern boundary of Katmai National Monument. Also Afognak Island and eastern half of Kodiak Island, where it is the only conifer. South Tongass, North Tongass, and Chugach National Forests, Glacier Bay National Monument, Kenai National Moose Range, Kodiak Island National Wildlife Refuge. From Kodiak Island and southern Alaska

Figure 7.—Western hemlock (*Tsuga heterophylla*), natural size.

southeast along Pacific coast to northwestern California.

On Kenai Peninsula there are natural hybrids between white spruce and Sitka spruce (*Picea glauca* × *sitchensis*; Lutz spruce, *Picea* ×*lutzii* Little). The hybrid is a tree 55–70 ft. (17–21 m.) high and 1–1½ ft. (30–45 cm.) in trunk diameter. Hybrid trees are recognized by their leaves and cones intermediate between those of the parent species. The leaves are slightly 4-angled, less so than in white spruce and are near Sitka spruce in the whitish upper surfaces. The cones are intermediate in size or small as in white spruce.

Cone-scales are short as in white spruce but like Sitka spruce in being thin, light brown, and irregularly toothed. These hybrids are found on Kenai Peninsula where the ranges of the two species meet and overlap slightly and may be sought elsewhere along the border between the coastal and interior forest types.

HEMLOCK (*Tsuga*)

Hemlock trees have very slender leading twigs or leaders which are curved down or nodding. The leaves are short needles, flat or half-round, blunt, soft, and not stiff, with short leaf-stalks, shedding promptly on drying. Twigs are very slender, becoming roughened by peglike bases after leaves fall. The cones are stalkless and usually hang down.

Key to the 2 Alaska species

Leaves (needles) flat, appearing in 2 rows, shiny dark green above, with 2 whitish bands (stomata) on lower surface; 5/8–1 in. (1.5–2.5 cm.) long ------------------ 7. western hemlock (*Tsuga heterophylla*)
Leaves (needles) half-round and keeled or angled beneath, crowded on all sides of short side twigs, blue green, with whitish lines (stomata) on both surfaces; cones cylindric, 1–2½ in. (2.5–6 cm.) long ------ --------------------- 8. mountain hemlock (*Tsuga mertensiana*)

7. WESTERN HEMLOCK

(*Tsuga heterophylla* (Raf.) Sarg.)

Other names: west coast hemlock (lumber), Pacific hemlock; formerly *Tsuga mertensiana* auth.

Large evergreen tree becoming 100–150 ft. (30–46 m.) tall and 2–4 ft. (0.6–1.2 m.) in trunk diameter, with long slender trunk often becoming fluted when large, and short narrow crown of horizontal or slightly drooping branches, the very slender leading twig curved down or nodding. The largest trees are as much as 190 ft. (58 m.) in height and 5 ft. (1.5 m.) or more in diameter. **Leaves** (needles) short-stalked, spreading in 2 rows, ¼–⅞ in. (6–22 mm.) long, flat, rounded at tip, flexible, shiny dark green above, and with 2 whitish bands (stomata) on lower surface. **Twigs** slender, dark reddish brown, finely hairy, roughened by peglike bases after leaves fall. **Bark** reddish brown to gray brown, becoming thick and furrowed into scaly plates; a pocketknife will disclose the red inner bark not found in spruce. **Wood** moderately light-weight, moderately hard, of moderately fine and even textured, non-resinous. Heartwood pale reddish brown, sapwood similar or whitish.

Cones stalkless and hanging down at end of twig, small, elliptic, 5/8–1 in. (1.5–2.5 cm.) long, brown, with many thin papery scales.

Seeds about ½ in. (12 mm.) long including large wing.

Western hemlock is the most abundant and one of the most important tree species in southeast Alaska and forms more than 70 percent of the dense hemlock-spruce coastal forests. This species attains its largest size on moist flats and lower slopes, but with abundant moisture, both atmospheric and soil, it grows well on shallow soils. It is very tolerant of shade.

This species is one of the best pulpwoods for paper and paperboard and products such as rayon. Other important uses are lumber for general construction, railway ties, mine timbers, and marine piling. The wood is suited also for interior finish, boxes and crates, kitchen cabinets, flooring and ceiling, gutter stock, and veneer for plywood. The outer bark contains a high percentage of tannin and is a potential source of this product. Alaska Indians made coarse bread from the inner bark of this tree and shore pine. Western hemlock is the State tree of Washington.

Western hemlock has the distribution of the hemlock-spruce coastal forests of southeast and southern Alaska but does not go as far west as Sitka spruce, not reaching Afognak and Kodiak Islands or the west side of Cook Inlet. It extends throughout southeast Alaska north to head of Lynn Canal at Skagway, Glacier Bay, and Yakutat Bay, west to Prince William Sound and east side of Cook Inlet to Portlock at southwest end of Kenai Peninsula and northwest to

Figure 8.—Mountain hemlock (*Tsuga mertensiana*), natural size.

8

hills around Anchorage. South Tongass, North Tongass, and Chugach National Forests, Glacier Bay National Monument, and Kenai National Moose Range. Southeast along Pacific coast to northwestern California and east in mountains to southeastern British Columbia, northwestern Montana, and northern Idaho.

8. MOUNTAIN HEMLOCK

(*Tsuga mertensiana* (Bong.) Carr.)

Other names: alpine hemlock, black hemlock.

Small to large evergreen tree becoming 50–100 ft. (15–30 m.) high and 10–30 in. (25–76 cm.) in trunk diameter, maximum about 125 ft. (38 m.) and 40 in. (1 m.), with marked taper when open grown, narrow crown of horizontal or drooping branches, and very slender leading twig curved down or nodding; a shrub near timber line. **Leaves** (needles) mostly crowded on all sides of short side twigs and curved upward, short-stalked, ¼–1 in. (6–25 mm.) long, flattened above and rounded, keeled, or angled beneath (half-round in section), stout and blunt, blue green and with whitish lines (stomata) on both surfaces. **Twigs** mostly short, slender, light reddish brown, finely hairy, roughened by peglike bases after leaves fall. **Bark** gray to dark brown, thick, and deeply furrowed into scaly plates. **Wood** moderately heavy, moderately hard, and moderately fine and even textured. Heartwood pale reddish brown, sapwood thin and similar or whitish.

Cones stalkless and usually hanging down, cylindric, 1–2½ in. (2.5–6 cm.) long and ¾ in. (2 cm.) wide, purplish but turning brown, with

59

many thin papery scales. **Seeds** light brown, about ½ in. (12 mm.) long including large wing.

Mountain hemlock extends from sea level to an altitude of 3,000–3,500 ft. (914–1067 m.), growing in an altitude higher than other trees. On upland sites, it is well formed and resembles western hemlock. Toward the timberline, it replaces the latter and becomes a prostrate shrub. It grows with shore pine in muskegs of deep peat as well as on subalpine slopes on the ocean side of the Coast Range in southeast Alaska. In the Prince William Sound and Cook Inlet regions, mountain hemlock is found on better drained slopes and near tidewater, reaching its maximum height.

The wood is marketed with western hemlock, being similar but somewhat more dense, and has the same uses. Nearly pure stands of mountain hemlock on Prince of Wales Island have been logged for pulp. The wood has been used for railroad ties. However, in the higher altitudes where commonly found, mountain hemlock is largely inaccessible and unimportant commercially.

Southeast and southern Alaska. Through southeast Alaska north to head of Lynn Canal at Skagway, Glacier Bay, and Yakutat Bay, west to Prince William Sound, Kenai Peninsula, and east side of Cook Inlet. Also local at Lake Iliamna on Alaska Peninsula. South Tongass, North Tongass, and Chugach National Forests, Glacier Bay National Monument, Kenai National Moose Range. Southeast along Pacific Coast of British Columbia and in mountains to western Montana and central California.

This species honors the German naturalist Karl Heinrich Mertens (1796–1830), who discovered it near Sitka, Alaska, in 1827.

Douglas-fir (*Pseudotsuga menziesii* (Mirb.) Franco; *Ps. taxifolia* (Poir.) Britton) though not native is sometimes planted in southeast Alaska as an ornamental and in forestry tests. Growth is rapid. The flat leaves (needles) ⅝–1¼ in. (1.5–3 cm.) long resemble those of fir but are narrowed into stalks at base and have an elliptic leaf-scar. Winter buds are distinctive, pointed, red brown, and not resinous. The elliptic, light brown cones 2–3½ in. (5–9 cm.) hang down and have thin rounded cone-scales and prominent 3-toothed bracts. Douglas-fir, one of the world's most valuable timber trees, is widespread in the Pacific coast and Rocky Mountain regions north in British Columbia nearly to Alaska. On the coast it extends almost to the north end of Vancouver Island and slightly inland north to Gardner Canal. In the interior it ranges north to Fort McLeod and Tacla Lake at latitude 55°, north of the southern tip of Alaska.

FIR (*Abies*)

Fir trees have narrow pointed crowns with mostly horizontal branches. The leaves are flat needles without leafstalks, those on lower branches often spreading in 2 rows along the twig, others mostly curving upward. Older twigs are smooth with round leaf-scars. Cones are upright and stalkless in the highest branches. At maturity the cone-scales and seeds are shed, but the narrow upright axis persists on the twig. No old cones remain on the trees or on the ground.

Two species of fir are present in southeastern Alaska, both rare and local. They are not likely to be seen without a special trip to one of the places mentioned.

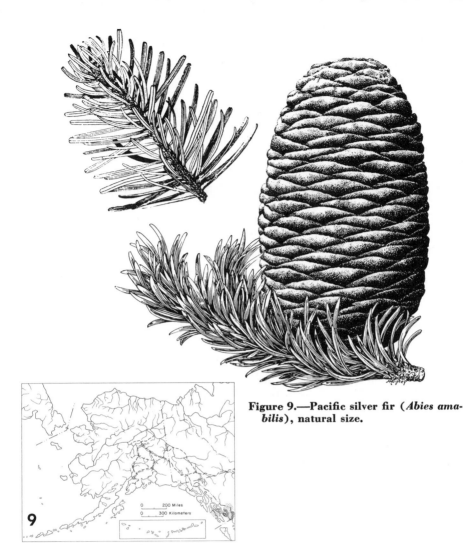

Figure 9.—Pacific silver fir (*Abies amabilis*), natural size.

Key to the 2 Alaska Species

Leaves (needles) shiny dark green on upper surface and silvery white with many lines (stomata) on lower surface _ 9. Pacific silver fir (*Abies amabilis*)
Leaves (needles) dull dark green with whitish lines (stomata) on both surfaces _ _ _ _ _ _ _ _ _ _ _ _ _ _ _ _ _ _ 10. subalpine fir (*Abies lasiocarpa*)

9. PACIFIC SILVER FIR (*Abies amabilis* (Dougl.) Forbes)

Other names: silver fir, white fir (lumber).

Medium-sized resinous and aromatic tree rare and local in extreme southeast Alaska, becoming 80 ft. (24 m.) tall and 24 in. (60 cm.) in trunk diameter, maximum 149 ft. (45 m.) tall and 49 in. (1.24 m.) in diameter. **Leaves** (needles) crowded and spreading, stalkless, ¾–1¼ in. (2–3 cm.) long, flat, deeply grooved

61

and shiny dark green above, beneath silvery white with whitish lines (stomata), those on lower branches notched or rounded at tips and spreading in 2 rows, those toward top of tree shorter and sharp-pointed, twisted in brushlike mass on upper side of twig. **Twigs** slender, finely hairy. **Bark** smooth, gray, splotched with white. **Wood** with whitish sapwood and pale brown heartwood, fine-textured, lightweight, soft.

Cones in highest branches, upright, 4–5 in. (10–12.5 cm.) long, 2–2½ in. (5–6 cm.) in diameter, purplish, finely hairy or nearly hairless; many fan-shaped rounded overlapping scales, falling from axis in autumn. **Seeds** light brown, about 1 in. (2.5 cm.) long, including broad wing.

The trees are logged with other conifers. Fir logs are sawed into lumber with Sitka spruce, if large and clear, or chipped with hemlock and used for pulp. Southward, where more abundant, the wood is used for interior finish.

Pacific silver fir is rare and local in extreme southeast Alaska. It has been recorded from well-drained lower slopes of canyons, benches, and flats from sea level to 1,000 ft. (305 m.) altitude. In the Salmon River valley near Hyder, it is common in the coastal forest of Sitka spruce and eastern hemlock, being very shade tolerant. Large trees were found on forest survey plots east of Ketchikan in mountains near Marten Arm of Boca de Quadra, Smeaton Bay of Behm Canal, and near Thorne Arm. Northeast of Ketchikan, trees have been observed in Carroll Inlet and George Inlet. However, earlier reports from Kosciusko Island and near northern end of Prince of Wales Island remain unverified. South Tongass National Forest. South through Pacific coast region of British Columbia and in mountains to Oregon and northwestern California.

10. SUBALPINE FIR

(*Abies lasiocarpa* (Hook.) Nutt.)

Other names: alpine fir, white fir (lumber).

Small to medium-sized evergreen tree, rare and local in southeast Alaska, commonly 20–60 ft. (6–18 m.) high and 4–12 in. (10–30 cm.) in trunk diameter, with long, narrow, sharp-pointed or spirelike crown and branches extending nearly to base, resinous and aromatic. However, larger trees to 95 ft. (29 m.) tall and 27 in. (69 cm.) in diameter have been observed. **Leaves** (needles) crowded and spreading, stalkless, ¾–1½ in. (2–4 cm.) long, flat, dark blue green and with whitish lines (stomata) on both sides, grooved above, those on lower branches rounded or occasionally notched at tip and in 2 rows, those near top of tree shorter, pointed, stiff, and twisted upward and curved on upper side of twig. **Twigs** gray, rusty hairy. **Bark** ash gray, smooth, thin. **Wood** pale brown, fine-textured, lightweight, soft, usually knotty because of the many persistent branches.

Cones in highest branches, upright, cylindric, 2½–4 in. (6–10 cm.) long and 1¼–1½ in. (3–4 cm.) in diameter, dark purple, finely hairy; many fan-shaped, rounded, overlapping scales, falling from axis in autumn. **Seeds** light brown, ⅝ in. (1.5 cm.) long, including broad wing.

Subalpine fir is of rare, local occurrence in mountains of southeast Alaska. This inland tree grows in cool, moist subalpine slopes near timberline, becoming shrubby or prostrate, and is found on the valley floors as well. It appears to be very shade tolerant.

Figure 10.—Subalpine fir (*Abies lasio-carpa*), natural size.

10

0   200 Miles
0   300 Kilometers

Near the southernmost tip of Alaska, subalpine fir is known from several localities. At Hyder it is reported to be common mostly at higher altitudes near the timberline at 2,500 ft. (762 m.) and accessible on the Texas Creek road. It grows with Pacific silver fir in the forest of Sitka spruce and hemlock. Southeast of Ketchikan, subalpine fir has been recorded from Very Inlet, Boca de Quadra, and Thorne Arm. Another stand is found at 3,000 ft. (914 m.) altitude on Har-ris Ridge near Hollis on Prince of Wales Island, associated with mountain hemlock and Sitka spruce.

At the northern end of southeast Alaska, subalpine fir from the interior of British Columbia crosses over the divide of the Coast Range. In Taku River valley northeast of Juneau, this species extends from the Canadian border down to sea level on outwash of Norris Glacier. It is common, scattered with Sitka spruce, hemlock, and black cottonwood. Near Skagway at head of Lynn Canal, subalpine fir descends from timberline at 3,000 ft. (914 m.) to sea level.

Northeastward in Yukon Territory, this species occurs within 125 miles (200 km.) of the Alaska border along Stewart River, a tributary of Yukon River. South Tongass and North Tongass National Forests. Southeast Alaska, central Yukon Territory, and southwestern District of Mackenzie, south through British Columbia and southwestern Alberta and in mountains to New Mexico, Arizona, and Oregon.

Subalpine fir has been reported from 3 localities in south central Alaska: Copper River basin, Mentasta Pass on Glenn Highway, and mountains northeast of Anchorage. Specimens are needed before those unverified range extensions should be accepted.

CYPRESS FAMILY
(Cupressaceae)

The cypress family (Cupressaceae) has 2 genera and species of trees in Alaska, also a third genus with 2 species of low shrubs, junipers. This family formerly included in the pine family is characterized by small scalelike leaves paired or in 3's. The cones are small with few cone-scales bearing mostly few seeds with short side wings. However, junipers have berrylike cones and wingless seeds.

Characteristics of the 3 genera and names of their Alaska species are summarized here for ready identification.

Western redcedar (*Thuja plicata* Donn), the only Alaska species of thuja. Leaves scalelike, flattened and curved, on flattened twigs in fanlike sprays. Small cones clustered near ends of twigs and becoming turned up.

Alaska-cedar (*Chamaecyparis nootkatensis* (D. Don) Spach), the only species of white-cedar. Leaves scalelike, pointed and spreading. Leafy twigs 4-angled or slightly flattened. Cones small, hard, nearly round.

Juniper (*Juniperus*), 2 species, common juniper and creeping juniper. Dwarf shrubs with scalelike or awl-shaped leaves, small round berrylike cones, and few wingless seeds.

11. WESTERN REDCEDAR
(*Thuja plicata* Donn)

Other names: giant arborvitae, canoe cedar, shinglewood, Pacific redcedar, arborvitae.

Large evergreen tree 70–100 ft. (21–30 m.) tall, sometimes 130 ft. (40 m.), with tapering trunk 2–4 ft. (0.6–1.2 m.) in diameter, sometimes to 6 ft. (1.8 m.), swollen or buttressed base, pointed conical crown, and horizontal branches curving upward at tips. **Leaves** scalelike, flattened, 1/16–1/8 in. (1.5–3 mm.) long, on leader twigs to 1/4 in. (6 mm.) long and pointed, shiny yellow green above and dull green below. Leafy **twigs** flattened, in fanlike sprays, slightly drooping, older twigs gray and smooth. **Bark** gray or brown, thin, fibrous and stringy or shreddy, becoming thick and furrowed into long ridges. **Wood** with the distinctive odor of cedars, fine-textured, straight-grained, lightweight, moderately soft, and brittle. Heartwood reddish brown, the narrow sapwood white.

Cones clustered near ends of twigs and becoming turned up on short stalks, elliptic, 1/2 in. (12 mm.) long, light brown, composed of several paired elliptic leathery cone-scales. **Seeds** 3 or fewer under a cone-scale, 3/16 in. (5 mm.) long, light brown, with 2 narrow wings.

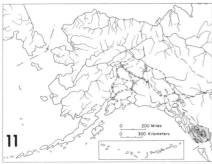

Figure 11.—Western redcedar (*Thuja plicata*), natural size.

Western redcedar is native in the southern half of southeast Alaska from sea level to 3,000 ft. (915 m.) altitude on the west slopes of the Coast Range, attaining its largest size below 500 ft. (150 m.). Although sometimes in pure stands, it is also dominant in the redcedar-hemlock forest and scattered in the hemlock-spruce forest. It is of moderately slow growth and long-lived.

Western redcedar is well suited for boat and canoe construction. It is the most widely used wood for shingles. Other uses of this very durable lightweight wood are utility poles, fenceposts, light construction, pulp, clothes closets and chests, conduits, piling, and fish-trap floats. The Indians employed the wood for totem poles, dugout canoes, and houses and made mats, baskets, and ropes from the stringy bark. This is an important timber tree of the coast region of British Columbia. Western redcedar is exported to Japan in log form, though some is used locally.

Southern half of southeast Alaska north to Wrangell and vicinity of Petersburg on southern parts of Mitkof, Kupreanof, and Kuiu Islands. On Kupreanof Island north to Duncan Canal (collected on Woewodski Island) but not found at Portage Bay on north end where formerly reported. South Tongass National Forest and south end of North Tongass National Forest. Pacific coast region of southeast Alaska south to northwestern California, also east in Rocky Mountains to eastern Montana and southeastern British Columbia.

12. ALASKA-CEDAR

(*Chamaecyparis nootkatensis* (D. Don) Spach)

Other names: Alaska yellow-cedar, Nootka false-cypress, yellow-cedar, Alaska cypress, Sitka cypress, yellow cypress.

Medium sized evergreen tree 40–80 ft. (12–24 m.) high and 1–2 ft. (30–60 cm.) in trunk diameter, sometimes a large tree to 100 ft. (30 m.) tall and 4 ft. (1.2 m.) in diameter, with narrow crown of slightly drooping branches. **Leaves** scalelike, $\frac{1}{16}$–$\frac{1}{8}$ in. (1.5–3 mm.) long, pointed and spreading, yellow green, with slightly spreading, pointed tips; leaves on leader twigs to $\frac{1}{4}$ in. (6 mm.) long and sharp-pointed. Leafy **twigs** 4-angled or slightly flattened, in flat, spreading sprays on drooping slightly branches, becoming reddish brown. **Bark** shreddy, with long narrow shreds and fissures, ash gray or purplish brown. **Wood** with distinctive odor, fine-textured, relatively straight-grained, moderately heavy, moderately hard. Heartwood bright yellow with narrow band of lighter sapwood.

Cones scattered, short-stalked, nearly round, less than $\frac{1}{2}$ in. (12 mm.) in diameter, hard, ashy gray, often covered with whitish bloom, of 4 or 6 paired rounded hard cone-scales each with a central pointed projection, maturing in 2 years. **Seeds** 2–4 under a cone-scale, $\frac{3}{16}$ in. (4 mm.) long, brown, with 2 broad wings.

Alaska-cedar extends along the coast of southeast Alaska from sea level to timberline but is best developed at 500–1,200 ft. (150–365 m.) altitude. It is scattered with western redcedar, in pure stands, in forests of Sitka spruce and western hemlock, and, on higher slopes or muskegs, with mountain hemlock. The trees are slow-growing, those 15–20 in. (38–51 cm.) in trunk diameter being 200–300 years old.

The very durable aromatic wood is easily worked and takes a beautiful finish. It is valuable for window frames and exterior doors, boat construction, and similar purposes. It is used also for utility poles, piles, interior finish, furniture, cabinet work, patterns, and novelties. Indians of southeast Alaska made their canoe paddles from this wood. Much Alaska-cedar is exported to Japan in log form, though some is used locally.

Through southeast Alaska north to Lynn Canal and Yakutat and west in southern Alaska to Glacier Island and Wells Bay in Prince William Sound. South Tongass, North Tongass, and Chugach National Forests. Pacific coast region from southern Alaska southeast through British Columbia and in mountains to Oregon and northwestern California.

Figure 12.—Alaska-cedar (*Chamaecy-paris nootkatensis*), natural size.

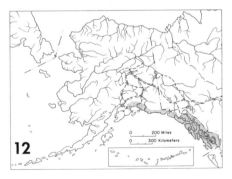

12

JUNIPER (*Juniperus*)

Low or prostrate aromatic evergreen shrubs (elsewhere also trees). **Leaves** opposite in 4 rows or in 3's, crowded, scalelike, blunt, and closely pressed against twig or awl-shaped, sharp-pointed, and spreading. Male and female cones mostly on different plants. **Cones** small, berrylike, fleshy, round, ¼–⅜ in. (6–10 mm.) in diameter, mostly blue, fleshy, resinous, not opening, containing usually 1–4 wingless seeds.

Key to the 2 Alaska Species

Leaves awl-shaped, sharp-pointed, spreading in groups of 3 _____ _____ 13. common juniper (*Juniperus communis*)
Leaves mostly scalelike, blunt, pressed against twig, paired _____ _____ 14. creeping juniper (*Juniperus horizontalis*)

13. COMMON JUNIPER

(*Juniperus communis* L.)

Other names: low juniper, mountain common juniper; *Juniperus communis* var. *saxatilis* Pall., var. *montana* Ait., var. *depressa* Pursh, ssp. *nana* (Willd.) Syme; *J. sibirica* Burgsd., *J. nana* Willd.
Low or prostrate spreading evergreen shrub to 2 ft. (0.6 m.) high, forming mats or clumps to 10 ft. (3 m.) in diameter. **Leaves** in groups of 3 (whorled), spreading at right angles or curved slightly downward, awl-shaped, ¼–½ in. (6–12 mm.) long, less than 1⁄16 in. (1.5 mm.) wide, stiff, very sharp-pointed, jointed at base, whitish and grooved above, shiny yellow green beneath. **Twigs** slender, 3-angled, light yellow, hairless. **Bark** gray or dark reddish brown, rough, scaly and thin.
Cones lateral on very short scaly stalks, berrylike, round, ¼–⅜ in. (6–10 mm.) in diameter, blue and covered with a bloom, hard, mealy, resinous and sweetish, maturing in 2 or 3 years and persistent. **Seeds** 3 or fewer, light brown, more than ⅛ in. (3 mm.) long, pointed.

Common juniper becomes a small tree rarely in New England and frequently in Europe. Including a few geographic varieties, this species is the most widely distributed conifer in the world and the most widespread tree species in the north temperate zone. In northern Europe the fruits have been used to flavor gin. Juniper is planted as an ornamental in Alaska, mostly as a ground cover in dry and rocky locations.
Scattered to rare in rocky tundra, sunny slopes, sandy areas, and forest openings. Throughout most of Alaska except extreme northwest, Alaska Peninsula, and Aleutian Islands. From southeast Alaska north in central Alaska to Porcupine, Yukon and Koyukuk Rivers and north of Brooks Range to Chandler, Canning, and Shaviovik Rivers and west to Bering Sea (Elim) and west side of Cook Inlet. South Tongass and North Tongass National Forests, Mt. McKinley National Park. Alaska, east across Canada to Labrador, Newfoundland, and Greenland, south mostly in mountains to Georgia, Illinois, New Mexico, and California. Also across northern Europe and Asia.

Figure 13.—Common juniper (*Juniperus communis*), natural size.

14. CREEPING JUNIPER

(*Juniperus horizontalis* Moench)

Other name: creeping savin.

Prostrate or trailing evergreen shrub with long horizontal stems often rooting and with short erect twigs 2–6 in. (5–15 cm.) high. **Leaves** paired in 4 rows, mostly scalelike, ¹⁄₁₆ in. (1.5 mm.) long, blunt and short-pointed with gland dot, blue green, shedding with

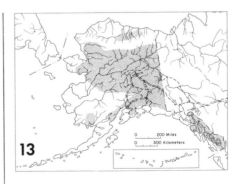

13

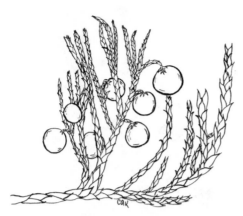

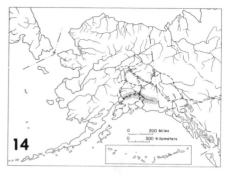

Figure 14.—Creeping juniper (*Juniperus horizontalis*), natural size.

twigs, on young plants and leaders awl-shaped, sharp-pointed, $\frac{3}{16}$–$\frac{1}{4}$ in. long (5–6 mm.) long. **Twigs** less than $\frac{1}{16}$ in. (1.5 mm.) broad, 4-angled, covered with scale leaves. **Cones** terminal and curved down on short stalks, berrylike, round, $\frac{1}{4}$–$\frac{5}{16}$ in. (6–8 mm.) in diameter, light blue and covered with a bloom, fleshy, resinous. **Seeds** 4 or fewer, brown, $\frac{1}{8}$ in. (3 mm.) long.

Rare and local on dry rocky slopes and sunny sands. Southeast interior Alaska along Chitina and Copper Rivers and west to Hicks Creek (east of Palmer). Alaska, Mackenzie, and Yukon, east to Great Slave Lake, Hudson Bay, Labrador, and Newfoundland, south to New York, Michigan, Iowa, and Colorado.

Used as an ornamental ground cover in interior and south central Alaska.

WILLOW FAMILY

(Salicaceae)

The willow family (Salicaceae) contains the cottonwoods, poplars, and aspens (all in the genus *Populus* with 3 tree species in Alaska), and the willows (*Salix*), a large genus of 30 or more native species ranging in size from creeping or dwarf shrubs to large shrubs and small trees (8 species). Distin-

guishing characters are as follows: (1) leaves borne singly (alternate), with margins evenly toothed or without teeth (entire) but not lobed; (2) flower clusters (catkins) composed of an axis bearing many small flowers each above a scale, in early spring before or with the leaves; (3) flowers without sepals or petals, of 2 kinds on different plants, male flowers with pollen and on other plants the female flowers with seeds; and (4) the tiny seeds with long white cottony hairs, borne in small seed capsules mostly 2-parted.

Cottonwoods, poplars, and aspens usually have broad leaves with petiole nearly as long as blade, stout twigs, and large winter buds with several scales exposed, resinous (except in aspen), an end (terminal) bud present. Willows usually have narrow leaves with very short petioles, slender or wiry twigs, and small winter buds covered by a single scale, without an end bud. Catkins in the genus of cottonwoods hang down, while those of willows are upright or slightly spreading. Flowers of cottonwoods have deeply lobed scales soon shedding, a broad or cup-shaped disk, and 10 to many stamens. Willow flowers have scales without or with teeth, persistent or late shedding, disk reduced usually to 1 small gland, and 2–8 stamens.

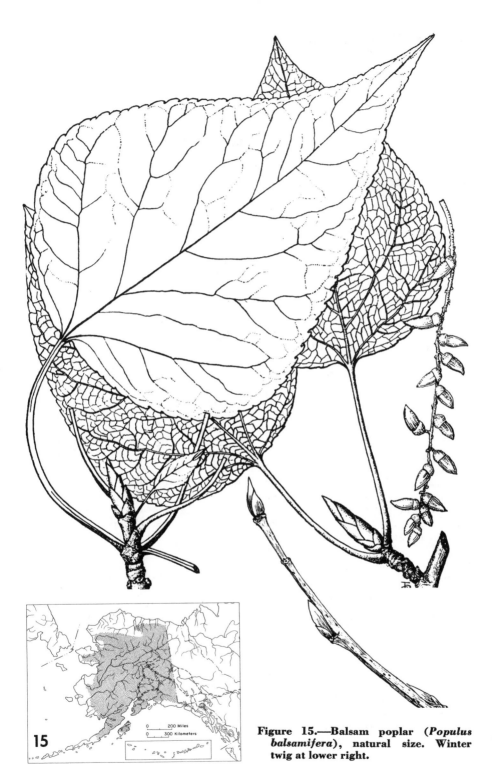

15

Figure 15.—Balsam poplar (*Populus balsamifera*), natural size. Winter twig at lower right.

COTTONWOOD, POPLAR, ASPEN (*Populus*)

This genus has no single English common name. The 3 Alaska species of the cottonwood genus, all common trees, are balsam poplar, black cottonwood, and quaking aspen.

Key to the 3 Alaska Species

Leaf blades longer than broad, 2½–5 in. (6–12.5 cm.) long; leafstalks round.
    Seed capsules pointed, hairless, 2-parted; leaves pale green and brownish beneath; tree of interior forests _____ _____ 15. balsam poplar (*Populus balsamifera*)
    Seed capsules rounded, hairy, 3-parted; leaves whitish beneath; tree of coastal forests ___ 16. black cottonwood (*Populus trichocarpa*)
Leaf blades nearly round, less than 2 in. (5 cm.) long; leafstalks flattened
    _____ 17. quaking aspen (*Populus tremuloides*)

15. BALSAM POPLAR

(*Populus balsamifera* L.)

Other names: tacamahac, tacamahac poplar, cottonwood; *Populus tacamahaca* Mill.

Medium-sized deciduous tree usually 30–50 ft. (9–15 m.) high, with straight trunk 4–12 in. (10–30 cm.) in diameter and long thin open crown, sometimes a large tree 80–100 ft. (24–30 m.) tall and 2 ft. (60 cm.) in trunk diameter. **Leaves** with slender petioles 1–2 in. (2.5–5 cm.) long, round, finely hairy. Leaf blades ovate or broadly lance-shaped, 2½–4½ in. (6–11 cm.) long, 1½–3 in. (4–7.5 cm.) wide, mostly long-pointed at apex and rounded at base, with many small rounded teeth, hairless or nearly so, shiny dark green above, pale green and rusty brown beneath. **Twigs** red brown and hairy when young, with orange dots (lenticels), becoming gray, with raised leaf scars showing 3 dots. **Winter buds** large, to 1 in. (2.5 cm.) long, long-pointed, sticky or resinous, covered with shiny brown scales, with pungent balsam odor which permeates the air in spring. **Bark** light gray to gray, smooth, becoming rough, thick, and deeply furrowed. **Wood** with thick whitish sapwood and light brown heartwood, fine-textured, lightweight, soft.

Flower clusters (catkins) 2–3½ in. (5–9 cm.) long, narrow, drooping, with many small flowers about ⅛ in. (3 mm.) long, each with disk and above a light brown hairy lobed scale, male and female on different trees (dioecious). Male **flowers** with 20–30 reddish purple stamens; female flowers with conic slightly 2-lobed hairless ovary and 2 broad wavy stigmas. **Seed capsules** in catkins to 6 in. (15 cm.) long, short-stalked, egg-shaped, ¼–⁵⁄₁₆ in. (6–8 mm.) long, long-pointed, light brown, hairless but warty, 2-parted, with many tiny cottony seeds. Flowering in May–June before the leaves, fruit maturing in June.

Balsam poplar, sometimes erroneously called balm-of-Gilead, is a rapidly growing tree. It is common in river valleys including sandy bottoms and gravelly flood plains, terraces, and coarse alluvial fans throughout the interior except near the coasts. In forests, especially in openings and clearings, it is associated with white spruce, birch, and

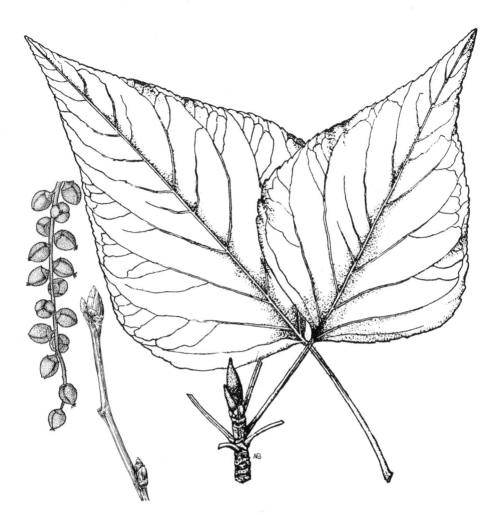

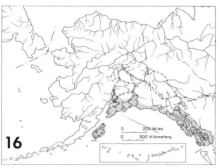

16

aspen. It is often common with willows and alders in flood plain thickets and along river banks.

In the mountains balsam poplar extends to somewhat higher altitudes than white spruce, to 3,500 ft. (1067 m.) altitude or more on north and west slopes of the Alaska Range. Also, it projects farther north to the Arctic slope in a few places. At Firth River near the northeast corner of Alaska and north of the treeline, balsam poplar, white spruce, and feltleaf willow are the only tree species.

The wood is used chiefly for boxes, crates, and pulpwood southward. A small amount is sawed for use in the Anchorage area and efforts are being made to broaden the market.

Interior Alaska, north and west to limits of trees, south to Kodiak Island and northern end of southeast Alaska. On south slopes of Brooks Range in drainages of Porcupine, Koyukuk, Kobuk, and Noatak Rivers; north of Brooks Range in small isolated stands along many of the rivers draining into Arctic Ocean but best developed and most extensive along Canning River. West to Igloo near western tip of Seward Peninsula; southward, at Unalakleet, and reaching coast of Bristol Bay near Dillingham; on Alaska Peninsula as far west as Chignik, and on Kodiak Island. South of Alaska Range in Cook Inlet and Copper River drainages and in extreme northern part of southeastern Alaska near Haines and Skagway and Taku Inlet near Juneau. North Tongass and Chugach National Forests, Mt. McKinley National Park, Katmai National Monument, Kenai National Moose Range, Kodiak National Wildlife Refuge, Arctic National Wildlife Range.

East across Canada to Labrador and Newfoundland, south in eastern United States to West Virginia, Indiana, and Iowa and in western mountains locally as far south as Colorado.

Balsam poplar intergrades or hybridizes with black poplar in southern Alaska where ranges of the two overlap, as mentioned under the latter. Rare hybrids with quaking aspen, which has smaller, rounded leaves and flattened petioles, have been recorded also.

16. BLACK COTTONWOOD
(*Populus trichocarpa* Torr. & Gray)

Other names: cottonwood, balsam cottonwood, northern black cottonwood, Pacific poplar; *Populus trichocarpa* var. *hastata* (Dode) Henry; *P. balsamifera* L. ssp. *trichocarpa* (Torr. & Gray) Brayshaw, var. *californica* S. Wats.

Large deciduous tree to 80–100 ft. (24–30 m.) tall, with straight trunk 3 ft. (1 m.) in diameter, with narrow pointed crown; in age larger and developing a tall massive trunk and small flat-topped crown. **Leaves** with slender petioles 1½–2 in. (4–5 cm.) long, round, finely hairy. Leaf blades broadly ovate, 2½–5 in. (6–12.5 cm.) long, 1½–3 in. (4–7.5 cm.) wide, mostly long-pointed at apex, rounded or slightly notched at base, with many small rounded teeth, hairless or nearly so, shiny dark green above, beneath whitish and often with rusty specks. **Twigs** red brown and hairy when young, with orange dots (lenticels), becoming dark gray, sometimes angled, with raised leaf scars showing 3 dots. **Winter buds** large, to ¾ in. (2 cm.) long, long-pointed, sticky or resinous, covered with shiny brown scales. **Bark** gray to dark gray, smooth, becoming rough, thick, deeply furrowed with flat ridges. **Wood** with thin whitish sapwood and light brown heartwood, fine-textured, lightweight, soft.

Flower clusters (catkins) 1½–3 in. (4–7.5 cm.) long, narrow, drooping, with many small flowers about ⅛ in. (3 mm.) long, each with disk and above a light brown hairy lobed scale, male and female on different trees (dioecious). Male **flowers** with 40–60 reddish purple stamens; female flowers with rounded densely hairy ovary and 3 broad lobed stigmas. **Seed capsules** in catkins to 6 in. (15 cm.) long, short-stalked, rounded, ³⁄₁₆ in. (5 mm.) in diameter, white hairy, 3-parted, with many tiny cottony seeds. Flowering in May before the leaves, fruit maturing in June–July.

Black cottonwood is the largest broadleaf tree in Alaska, growing rapidly to a height of 80–100 ft.

(24–30 m.) at maturity. It is also the hardwood or broadleaf tree of greatest size in northwestern North America, reaching a height of 125 ft. (38 m.) on the best sites at age 35 years.

A champion of this species, the largest then known, was discovered in Alaska in 1965 by foresters on the State timber inventory project. Measurements of this giant are as follows: circumference of trunk at breast height, 32 ft. 6 in. (9.9 m.), total height, 101 ft. (30.8 m.), and estimated spread of crown, 60 ft. (18.3 m.). It is located on State land about 25 miles (40 km.) northwest of Haines on a gravel flat 300 ft. (91 m.) from Klehini River about 5 miles (8 km.) west of the village of Klukwan. This ancient tree had its main stem broken off many years ago but has several large branches forming the top. The trunk is deeply grooved and hollow. In 1969 a larger black cottonwood was found near Salem, Oreg., thus replacing the northern rival as the national champion. Though with a broken top and not as tall, the Klukwan giant has a slightly broader trunk than the Oregon winner, which measures 30 ft. 2 in. (9.2 m.) in circumference.

This species is found in lowlands of the coastal forests of southeast and southern Alaska. It is best developed at lower levels on river bottoms and sandbars, forming pure stands with undergrowth of willows and alders. It is common on the valley floors of a few large streams, such as Stikine and Taku Rivers. Very rare on islands.

Trees are planted for shade in towns of southeast Alaska. Southward, the wood is used for boxes and crates, pulpwood, and excelsior. The small supply in Alaska is a possible source of paper pulp, veneer, and lumber. Square cut logs have been used for cabins.

Black cottonwood is not easily distinguished from its close relative, balsam poplar. Both have much the same general appearance and similar habitats. The chief differences are in the seed capsules, which in black cottonwood are nearly round, densely hairy, and split into 3 parts and which in balsam poplar are longer than broad and long-pointed, hairless but warty, and split into 2 parts. Also, there are minor differences in flowers. The pistil of black cottonwood has 3 carpels and 3 stigmas, while that of balsam poplar has 2 carpels and 2 stigmas. The number of stamens is reported to be greater in black cottonwood. Leaves of black cottonwood generally are broader in proportion to length and seem to be whiter beneath. As the ranges of the two species are separate except at their narrow borders, most trees or specimens without seed capsules can be identified by locality.

Black cottonwood hybridizes extensively with balsam poplar where the ranges meet and overlap slightly, for example, in the Cook Inlet and Lynn Canal areas. Hybrids or intermediate trees are recognized by the seed capsules, which may be 3-parted and hairless or 2-parted and hairy.

Pacific coast of southeastern Alaska, rare toward southern end and reported from only a few islands; commoner from Stikine River north to head of Lynn Canal along the Dyea, Chilkat, and Klehini Rivers, Glacier Bay, and Yakutat Bay; west to Prince William Sound, Cook Inlet, Susitna Valley, and Kodiak Island. South Tongass, North Tongass, and Chugach National Forests, Glacier Bay National Monument, Kenai National Moose Range, Kodiak National Wildlife Refuge. Southern Alaska and southern Yukon Territory south through British Columbia to Montana, Idaho, and California and in mountains to Utah and Baja California.

Black cottonwood and balsam poplar have long been regarded as separate species. The two have geographic ranges mostly far apart and grow under somewhat different climates with different associated tree species. Recently black poplar has been united by a few botanists as a subspecies of balsam poplar, because of the slight differences and the intermediate trees where the ranges meet. However, foresters treat the two as separate species in forest management.

17. QUAKING ASPEN
(*Populus tremuloides* Michx.)

Other names: American aspen, trembling aspen, popple, squawstongue; *Populus tremuloides* var. *aurea* (Tidestr.) Daniels.

Small to medium-sized deciduous tree commonly 20–40 ft. (6–12 m.) tall, maximum 80 ft. (24 m.), with straight trunk 3–12 in. (7.5–30 cm.) in diameter, maximum 18 in. (46 cm.), and short, irregularly bent limbs making a narrow domelike crown. **Leaves** with slender flattened petioles 1–2.5 in. (2.5–6 cm.) long. Leaf blades nearly round, 1–2 in. (2.5–5 cm.) long and broad, short-pointed at apex, rounded at base, with many small rounded teeth, hairless, shiny green above, pale beneath, which tremble in the slightest breeze, turning bright yellow (sometimes reddish) in autumn. **Twigs** slender, reddish and slightly hairy when young, becoming gray, with raised leaf scars showing 3 dots. **Winter buds** conic, ¼ in. (6 mm.) long, long-pointed, of shiny red brown hairless scales, not resinous or flower buds slightly so. **Bark** whitish or greenish gray, smooth, thin, with characteristic curved scars and black knots. **Wood** of broad whitish sapwood and light brown heartwood, fine-textured, lightweight, soft, and brittle.

Flower clusters (catkins) 1–2½ in. (2.5–6 cm.) long, narrow, drooping, with many small flowers ⅛ in. (3 mm.) long, each with saucer-shaped disk and above a brown hairy lobed scale, male and female on different trees (dioecious). Male **flowers** with 6–12 stamens; female flowers with conic ovary, short style, and 2 stigmas each 2-lobed. **Seed capsules** in catkins 3–4½ in. (7.5–11 cm.) long, nearly stalkless, less than ¼ in. (6 mm.) long, conic, hairless, 2-parted, with many tiny cottony seeds. Flowering in May before the leaves, fruit maturing in May–June.

Quaking aspen is a fast-growing tree common on south slopes, well-drained benches, and creek bottoms throughout the interior of Alaska to about 3,000 ft. (914 m.) altitude. It often occurs in dense pure stands, especially following forest fires. Aspen frequently propagates by suckers from roots. Growth will continue for 80–100 years before the stands begin to deteriorate. Also in forests with white spruce and birch. Rare hybrids with balsam poplar have been noted.

The wood has not yet been utilized commercially in quantity in Alaska. Elsewhere it is used for pulpwood, boxes and crates, and excelsior.

Interior Alaska as far north as the south slopes of Brooks Range but not as far north or as high in mountains as white spruce; westward to Koyukuk and Kobuk Rivers; south on Yukon River to Holy Cross and on Kuskokwim to Bethel and to base of Alaska Peninsula at Lake Iliamna; south of Alaska Range in Susitna Valley, Cook Inlet, Kenai Peninsula, and Copper River areas. Southeast Alaska only in extreme northern part near Haines and Skagway at head of Lynn Canal. Chugach National Forest, Mt. McKinley National Park, Kenai National Moose Range.

Figure 17.—Quaking aspen (*Populus tremuloides*), natural size. Winter twig at right.

The most widely distributed tree species in North America, ranging from Alaska east across Canada to Labrador and Newfoundland, south in the Northeastern United States to New Jersey, Virginia, and Missouri, and south in western mountains to Trans-Pecos Texas, California, and Mexico.

WILLOW (*Salix*)

Willows are well represented in Alaska, as in other far northern lands. In habit they vary from prostrate or creeping dwarf shrubs to erect bushes 2–6 ft. (0.6–2 m.)

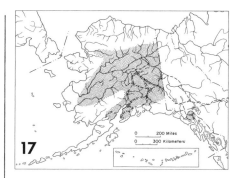

tall and large shrubs or small trees, usually with many stems. As 8 of the 33 Alaska species are known to attain the size and habit of small trees, willows (*Salix*) are the largest genus of trees here. Numerous

77

variations occur, and some species seem to intergrade or hybridize, often making identification difficult. Some botanists distinguish by name many additional varieties or subspecies of Alaska willows.

Although field identification is difficult, especially in winter, the willows as a group can be distinguished by the usually slender or wiry twigs, the winter buds covered by a single bud-scale, and by the bitter quininelike taste of the bark. The short-stalked leaves generally are long and narrow, with smooth or finely toothed edges. The yellowish or greenish male and female flowers are borne in hairy, narrow catkins 1–3 in. (2.5–7.5 cm.) long, on separate trees or shrubs in early spring before or with the leaves.

The fruits in tassellike catkins are pointed, thin-walled seed capsules about ¼ in. (6 mm.) long, which split open in spring and summer to release the numerous tiny seeds with tufts of cottony hairs.

Shrubby willows are widely distributed almost throughout Alaska, extending beyond the limits of trees to the Arctic coast, Bering Sea, and Aleutian Islands. They are the undergrowth of the open spruce-birch forest of interior Alaska and form thickets on sandbars and other porous soils along streams. Although not suitable for lumber because of their small size, shrubby willows provide important summer and winter food for many game animals, especially moose and ptarmigan.

The great variation in willows and their tendency to hybridize make it difficult to construct a completely workable key. Two keys are provided. For using the first key to Alaska willows, it is best to have material grown under normal conditions (not sprouts from stumps of fast-growing roadside shoots) and to have both mature catkins and leaves. Because the catkins often develop before the leaves, it may be desirable to tag the shrub and return to it at different times during the growing season. In addition, unusual growth forms resulting from differences in site cannot always be included in the key. For example, a high-growing shrub becoming occasionally a low prostrate one near its range limits is included only under the section of the key for upright tall willows. The second key, for specimens without catkins, is a vegetative key based on leaves, twigs, and growth form.

With considerable field experience, one can learn to distinguish many willows. It is best to start with the more common and distinctive willows, such as Sitka willow and Scouler willow in southeastern Alaska, and feltleaf willow, diamondleaf willow, and Bebb willow in central Alaska. Once the characteristics of these become familiar, it is easier to recognize the less common and less easily identified willows.

Key to Alaska Willows

A. Low, prostrate shrubs less than 3 ft. (1 m.) tall, usually only a few inches in height, with branches frequently rooting at nodes (see also AA for several normally upright shrubs, such as *Salix brachycarpa* ssp. *niphoclada* and *S. pulchra*, which may be prostrate in the tundra).
  B. Ovaries and seed capsules hairy (sometimes with few scattered hairs in age).
    C. Creeping shrubs with long branches rooting at nodes, 4–12 in. (10–30 cm.) high; leaves more than ¾ in. (20 mm.) long; catkins usually more than 1½ in. (4 cm.) long.

D. Leaves round, strong net-veined, dark green above and grayish white below; catkins at ends of long leafless twigs; female flowers with 2 glands at base of pedicel _____ _____ 18. netleaf willow (*Salix reticulata*)
DD. Leaves ovate or obovate, light green above and below, not strongly veined; catkins on leafy side twigs; flowers with only 1 gland at the base of the pedicel.
   E. Leaves finely toothed around margin; catkins about 1½ in. (4 cm.) long _____ _____ 34. Chamisso willow (*Salix chamissonis*)
   EE. Leaves entire on margin; catkins 1½–3 in. (4–7.5 cm.) long _____ 23. arctic willow (*Salix arctica*)
CC. Matted or creeping shrubs, usually less than 4 in. (10 mm.) tall; leaves less than ¾ in. (2 cm.) long; catkins less than 1½ in. (4 cm.) long.
   F. Plants densely matted, from central taproot, with abundant brown skeletonized leaves persistent in mat; leaves green on both surfaces _____ _____ 21. skeletonleaf willow (*Salix phlebophylla*)
   FF. Plants not mat-forming; creeping and rooting at nodes, with few dead leaves; leaves pale beneath _____ _____ 20. polar willow (*Salix polaris* ssp. *pseudopolaris*)
BB. Seed capsules hairless, ovaries usually hairless, sometimes with few scattered hairs.
   G. Leaves distinctly toothed on all or part of margin; shrubs trailing to semierect, to 3 ft. (1 m.).
   H. Leaves obovate or oblanceolate, tapering gradually at base, thick and fleshy, light blue green and shiny on upper surface; seed capsule stout, light green, fleshy; scales light green with hairs on margins; on silt and gravel bars or gravel and sandy beaches _____ _____ 19. Setchell willow (*Salix setchelliana*)
   HH. Leaves not tapering gradually at base, not thick and fleshy; seed capsule elongate, not fleshy; bogs and other wet habitats.
      I. Leaves regularly toothed around margin, green on both surfaces, net-veined pattern conspicuous on underside; to 3 ft. (1 m.) high _____ _____ 29. blueberry willow (*Salix myrtillifolia*)
      II. Leaves with irregular minute glandular teeth around lower edges; 6–24 in. (15–61 cm.) tall _____ _____ 24. Alaska bog willow (*Salix fuscescens*)
GG. Leaves with entire margins; prostrate or matted shrubs less than 6 in. (15 cm.) high.
   J. Creeping shrubs with elongate, prostrate branches; leaves usually more than ¾ in. (2 cm.) long; catkins many-flowered, ¾ in. (2 cm.) or longer _____ __ 25. ovalleaf willow (*Salix ovalifolia* and *S. stolonifera*)
   JJ. Densely matted shrubs usually from central taproot; leaves less than ¾ in. (2 cm.) long, crowded; catkins short, less than ½ in (12 mm.) long, few-flowered (6–12) ____ _____ 22. least willow (*Salix rotundifolia*)

79

AA. Erect shrubs or small trees, usually more than 3 ft. (1 m.) tall (or prostrate in exposed sites near range limits).
  K. Pedicels, ovaries, and seed capsules hairless (young ovaries in some species with few hairs, especially near tip).
    L. Leaves long and narrow (linear) to 4 in. (10 cm.) long and only ¼–⅜ in. (6–10 mm.) wide, usually with scattered glandular teeth; silt and sandbars of interior Alaska ____ _____ 45. sandbar willow (*Salix interior*)
    LL. Leaves much wider in proportion to their length, toothed or entire.
      M. Catkins stalkless (occasionally with a few small leaves in park willow, *S. monticola*).
        N. Young twigs densely hairy; stipules long, narrow, glandular margined, persisting on twig several years; leaves entire or with few teeth _____ 36. Richardson willow (*Salix lanata* ssp. *richardsonii*)
        NN. Young twigs glabrous; stipules broad, shedding; leaves toothed on margin, reddish when young _____ _____ 35. park willow (*Salix monticola*)
      MM. Catkins on leafy twigs.
        O. Leaf margins distinctly toothed.
          P. Leaves hairless or with scattered hairs near midvein (or young developing leaves with dense long hairs).
            Q. Leaves lance-shaped, 4–5 times as long as broad, with long narrow tip, shiny above; scales of catkin yellow, soon shedding _____ _____ 46. Pacific willow (*Salix lasiandra*)
            QQ. Leaves rounded or blunt at tip, not lance-shaped; scales of catkin not yellow or deciduous.
              R. Leaves whitish (glaucous) beneath, ovate to obovate, toothed or entire on margins, hairless or with few hairs on veins of upper surface (or both surfaces with long silky hairs when young); pedicels short, about ¹⁄₃₂ in. (1 mm.) _____ _____ 31. Barclay willow (*Salix barclayi*)
              RR. Leaves light green beneath, dark green above, regularly toothed, hairless; pedicels ¹⁄₁₆–⅛ in. (1.5–3 mm.) _____ 30. tall blueberry willow (*Salix novae-angliae*)
          PP. Leaves with scattered hairs on both surfaces, even in age, light green on both surfaces _____ _____ 33. undergreen willow (*Salix commutata*)
        OO. Leaf margins entire or with few small teeth near base.
          S. Twigs with dense long hairs when young; catkins large and thick, to ¾ in. (2 cm.) in diameter; styles ⅛ in. (3 mm.) long, small tree _____ _____ 32. Hooker willow (*Salix hookeriana*)
          SS. Twigs hairless or with scattered hairs, never densely hairy; catkins usually less than ⅝ in. (15 mm.) in diameter; styles less than ¹⁄₁₆ in. (1.5 mm.) long; shrub.
            T. Leaves hairless or hairy only on midvein.

U. Leaves broadly lance-shaped, completely hairless; pedicels $\frac{1}{32}$–$\frac{1}{16}$ in. (1–1.5 mm.) long; style $\frac{1}{64}$ in. (0.5 mm.) long _____
_____ 28. halberd willow (*Salix hastata*)
UU. Leaves ovate to obovate, usually hairy on midvein; pedicels $\frac{1}{64}$ in. (0.5 mm.) long; style $\frac{1}{16}$ in. (1.5 mm.) long _____
_____ 31. Barclay willow (*Salix barclayi*)
TT. Leaves hairy and light green on both surfaces _____
_____ 33. undergreen willow (*Salix commutata*)
KK. Ovaries hairy (mature seed capsules sometimes with few hairs near tip).
V. Pedicels of flower and seed capsule $\frac{1}{8}$–$\frac{3}{16}$ in. (3–5 mm.) long, conspicuous, exceeding scales _____
_____ 40. Bebb willow (*Salix bebbiana*)
VV. Pedicels shorter, less than $\frac{1}{8}$ in. (3 mm.) long, not exceeding scales.
W. Leaves distinctly glandular toothed around margin _____
_____ 44. littletree willow (*Salix arbusculoides*)
WW. Leaves irregularly or indistinctly toothed or entire.
X. Leaves without hairs on lower surface, except occasionally on midvein, upper surface shiny green; stipules long and narrow, glandular margined, persistent several years _____
41. diamondleaf willow (*Salix planifolia* ssp. *pulchra*)
XX. Leaves distinctly hairy on lower surface, upper surface not shiny green; stipules shedding.
Y. Leaves hairless above, lower surface with dense woolly hairs _____ 38. feltleaf willow (*Salix alaxensis*)
YY. Leaves hairy on both surfaces, sometimes with scattered hairs.
Z. Leaves linear or lance-shaped, 5–7 times longer than broad; whole plant silvery from dense woolly hairs on lower surfaces of leaves and on twigs, upper surface with scattered hairs _____
_____ 39. silver willow (*Salix candida*)
ZZ. Leaves broader, 3–4 times as long as broad.
a. Lower surface of leaves shiny, silky from straight appressed silvery hairs _____
_____ 43. Sitka willow (*Salix sitchensis*)
aa. Lower surface of leaves wihout silky sheen.
b. Lower surface of leaves with scattered, short, stiff hairs at least partly red, giving a reddish hue; catkins without leafy stalks, developing before leaves; pedicels $\frac{1}{8}$ in. (3 mm.) long__
_____ 42. Scouler willow (*Salix scouleriana*)
bb. Lower surface of leaves densely hairy, with woolly hairs, never red. Catkins either stalkless on leafy twigs or developing before or with the leaves; pedicels short or lacking.
c. Leaves densely hairy on both surfaces, regularly glandular on margin, stipules broad, hairless; catkins stalkless, developing before

81

the leaves; bud-scales giving off a waxy substance when twig is dried or pressed; low compact shrub with coarse branches __ ____ 37. Barratt willow (*Salix barrattiana*)

   cc. Leaves less densely hairy, especially on upper surface, without glands on margins; catkins on leafy stalks, developing with or after the leaves; usually upright shrub with slender branches.

      d. Petioles ⅛–⅜ in. (3–10 mm.) long, yellow; leaves obovate to oblong, short-pointed to blunt; catkins cylindrical, densely flowered; pedicel 1/32 in. (0.5–1 mm.) long__ ____ 26. grayleaf willow (*Salix glauca*)

      dd. Petioles shorter, less than ⅛ in. (3 mm.) long, reddish; leaves strap-shaped, rounded or blunt; catkins narrowly cylindrical, loosely flowered ___ 27. barren-ground willow (*Salix brachycarpa* ssp. *niphoclada*)

Vegetative Key to Alaska Willows

Because leaf, twig, and growth form characteristics of some willows are extremely variable, a vegetative key cannot account for all the variability. The key must deal primarily with the typical specimen in a typical location. Perhaps the following key will serve for three-fourths of the Alaskan willow specimens. However, many will not key out or will key to a wrong species. Usually, it should be possible to narrow the choice to 2 or 3 species. The species descriptions, drawings, and maps will then be of aid in further determination.

A. Low prostrate shrubs less than 12 in. (30 cm.) high.

  B. Creeping shrubs with long prostrate branches, often rooting at nodes, but with branches ascending from 4–12 in. (10–30 cm.); leaves more than 1 in. (2.5 cm.) long.

    C. Leaves toothed around margin, green on both surfaces or sometimes lighter green beneath.

      D. Leaves bluish green, leathery or fleshy, 3–4 times as long as wide, tapering gradually to base _____ _____ 19. Setchell willow (*Salix setchelliana*)

      DD. Leaves not bluish green, oval, not tapering to base, thin.

        E. Leaves nearly as wide as long, elliptic, ¾–2 in. (2–5 cm.) long; branches prostrate _____ _____ 34. Chamisso willow (*Salix chamissonis*)

        EE. Leaves 2–3 times as long as wide, ⅜–1½ in. (1–4 cm.) long, branches ascending _____ _____ 29. low blueberry willow (*Salix myrtillifolia*)

    CC. Leaves entire or toothed only on basal half, green above, whitish (glaucous) beneath.

F. Leaves dark green above, conspicuously net-veined, round, with long red petiole _____
_____ 18. netleaf willow (*Salix reticulata*)
FF. Leaves not conspicuously netveined, more than 2 times as long as broad, petiole green.
G. Leaves fleshy, 3–4 times as long as wide, tapering to base, bluish green; on dry gravel sites _____
_____ 19. Setchell willow (*Salix setchelliana*)
GG. Leaves not fleshy or bluish green, 2 times as long as broad, not tapering to base; in bogs or on arctic and alpine tundra.
H. Trailing shrub with long branches rooting at nodes, leaves finely glandular toothed on basal half; usually in boggy sites _____
_____ 24. Alaska bog willow (*Salix fuscescens*)
HH. Leaves entire, forming dense mats from short branches; mostly in dry alpine and arctic sites _____
_____ 23. arctic willow (*Salix arctica*)
BB. Matted or creeping shrubs, usually less than 4 in. (10 cm.) tall, usually in compact mats without long creeping branches; leaves less than 1 in. (2.5 cm.) long, entire.
I. Leaves green on both surfaces.
J. Shrubs densely matted, often from a central taproot; leaves less than ¾ in. (2 cm.) long; stems brown to reddish brown.
K. Shrub mat with abundant dead leaves persistent; leaves ⅜–¾ in. (1–2 cm.) long _____
_____ 21. skeletonleaf willow (*Salix phlebophylla*)
KK. Shrubs with few or no dead leaves; leaves ⅛–⅜ in. (4–10 mm.) long _____
_____ 2. least willow (*Salix rotundifolia*)
JJ. Shrubs forming loose mats, usually with long trailing buried branches; stems pale yellow, thin; leaves to 1 in. (2.5 cm.) long, usually smaller _____
____ 20. polar willow (*Salix polaris* ssp. *pseudopolaris*)
II. Leaves green above, whitish (glaucous) beneath _____
____ 25. ovalleaf willow (*Salix ovalifolia* and *S. stolonifera*)
AA. Erect shrubs or trees, more than 1 ft. (30 cm.) high.
L. Upright shrubs usually less than 3 ft. (1 m.) high.
M. Leaves with hairs on lower surface, gray or silvery.
N. Leaves linear to lanceolate, 5–7 times longer than broad, with dense woolly hairs beneath; rare shrub of interior bogs _____ 39. silver willow (*Salix candida*)
NN. Leaves broader, not densely woolly beneath.
O. Leaves with dense straight hairs, often oriented in vertical plane; petioles green, yellow, or brown; low compact shrub with thick branches; bud scales giving off yellow waxy substance when plant is dried _____
_____ 37. Barratt willow (*Salix barrattiana*)
OO. Leaves with scattered hairs; petioles reddish; upright shrub with slender branches; buds not giving off waxy substance _____ 27. barren-ground willow (*Salix brachycarpa* ssp. *niphoclada*)

MM. Leaves without conspicuous hairs.
  P. Leaves fleshy, bluish green, 3–4 times as long as broad, taper-
    ing gradually to base _____
    _____ 19. Setchell willow (*Salix setchelliana*)
  PP. Leaves thin, green, oval.
    Q. Stipules, if present, persisting less than 1 year.
      R. Leaves toothed around margin, lower surface light green,
        not whitish (glaucous) _____
        ____ 29. low blueberry willow (*Salix myrtillifolia*)
      RR. Leaves toothed only on basal half with fine glandular
        teeth, lower surface whitish (glaucous) _____
        _____ 24. Alaska bog willow (*Salix fuscescens*)
    QQ. Stipules persistent several years.
      S. Stipules broad at base and glandular toothed along mar-
        gins; twigs coarse, brown to black, with dense hairs
        persistent several years _____ 36. Rich-
        ardson willow (*Salix lanata* ssp. *richardsonii*)
      SS. Stipules linear, narrow at base, without glandular
        teeth; twigs fine, usually reddish brown and shiny,
        without dense hairs after 1 year _____ 41. dia-
        mondleaf willow (*Salix planifolia* ssp. *pulchra*)
LL. Tall shrubs or trees 3–25 ft. (1–7.5 m.) or more in height.
  T. Leaves linear, 1½–4 in. (4–10 cm.) long, and ¼ in. (6 mm.) wide,
    with scattered small teeth; usually growing on river
    alluvium _____ 45. sandbar willow (*Salix interior*)
  TT. Leaves broader.
    U. Adult leaves with hairs on lower surface.
      V. Lower surface of leaves with dense hairs, appearing silvery,
        white, or gray.
        W. Lower surface of leaves with dense white *woolly* hairs.
          X. Leaves long and narrow, lance-shaped, 2–4 in. (5–10
          cm.) long and only ¼–⅝ in. (6–15 mm.) wide;
          low shrubs seldom exceeding 4 ft. (1.2 m.) in
          height; rare in boggy sites in interior Alaska ____
          _____ 39. silvery willow (*Salix candida*)
          XX. Leaves broader, 2–4 in. (5–10 cm.) long, and ½–1½
          in. (12–40 mm.) wide; tall shrub or tree to 30 ft.
          (9 m.), common in many sites over most of Alaska
          _____ 38. feltleaf willow (*Salix alaxensis*)
        WW. Lower surface of leaves with dense *straight* hairs.
          Y. Lower surface silky hairy, upper surface green, with
          scattered hairs; tall shrub or tree to 20 ft. (6 m.)
          high _____ 43. Sitka willow (*Salix sitchensis*)
          YY. Lower surface dull gray hairy, upper surface greenish
          gray, without hairs; shrub usually less than 10
          ft. (3 m.) high _____
          _____26. grayleaf willow (*Salix glauca*)
      VV. Lower surface of leaves visible through less dense hairs.
        Z. Margins of leaves distinctly toothed.
          a. Leaves light green on both surfaces, not shiny, oval,
          about 2 times as long as broad; shrub 3–6 ft. (1–2
          m.) high _____
          _____ 33. undergreen willow (*Salix commutata*)

aa. Leaves dark green and shiny above, whitish (glaucous) beneath, 3–4 times as long as broad; shrub 10–15 ft. (3–4.5 m.) tall, with slender branches ____ _____ 44. littletree willow (*Salix arbusculoides*)

ZZ. Margins of leaves not toothed or with a few teeth on basal half.

   b. Hairs on lower surface short and stiff, at least some red, giving a reddish hue _____ _____ 42. Scouler willow (*Salix scouleriana*)

   bb. Hairs denser, longer, not reddish.

      c. Tall shrubs or trees 10–25 ft. (3–7.5 m.) tall; twigs diverging at nearly right angles from the main stem _____ 40. Bebb willow (*Salix bebbiana*)

      cc. Medium shrubs, usually under 10 ft. (3 m.) high; twigs usually branching at 45° angle or less.

         d. Petioles ⅛–⅜ in. (3–10 mm.) long, yellow, leaves obovate to oblong, acute to obtuse _____ _____ 26. grayleaf willow (*Salix glauca*)

         dd. Petioles less than ⅛ in. (3 mm.) long, reddish, leaves strap-shaped, rounded or blunt _____ _____ 27. barren-ground willow (*Salix brachycarpa* ssp. *niphoclada*)

UU. Adult leaves without hairs on lower surface.

   e. Stipules persistent on the twigs several years.

      f. Stipules broad at the base and glandular toothed along margins; twigs coarse, brown to black, densely hairy, even after several years _____ 36. Richardson willow (*Salix lanata* ssp. *richardsonii*)

      ff. Stipules linear, narrow at base, without glandular teeth; twigs, fine, usually reddish brown, shiny, without dense hairs at 1 year _____ 41. diamondleaf willow (*Salix planifolia* ssp. *pulchra*)

   ee. Stipules not persisting more than 1 year.

      g. Leaves with teeth around margin.

         h. Leaves 3–4 times as long as broad; tall shrubs or trees.

            i. Leaves large, 3–4 in. (7.5–10 cm.) long, lance-shaped, with long tapering tip; young twigs woolly ___ _____ 46. Pacific willow (*Salix lasiandra*)

            ii. Leaves smaller, 2–3 in. (5–8 cm.) long, not lance-shaped, shortpointed; young twigs not woolly__ ____ 44. littletree willow (*Salix arbusculoides*)

         hh. Leaves less than 3 times as long as broad.

            j. Leaves whitish (glaucous) beneath.

               k. Leaves broadly lance-shaped to oval, usually narrowing to small projection at tip (apiculate), often reddish when young; well drained alluvial soils and upland forests _____ _____ 35. park willow (*Salix monticola*)

               kk. Leaves ovate, blunt at tip; not reddish when young; moist habitats in open and forested areas and near treeline _____ _____ 31. Barclay willow (*Salix barclayi*)

            jj. Leaves light green, not whitish (glaucous) beneath ___ 30. tall blueberry willow (*Salix novae-angliae*)

85

gg. Leaves entire or with teeth only on lower part.
  l. Tall shrubs or trees, 10–25 ft. (3–7.5 m.) tall.
    m. Leaves large at maturity, to 3 in. (7.5 cm.) long, obovate; in Yakutat Bay area _____ _____ 32. Hooker willow (*Salix hookeriana*)
    mm. Leaves smaller, 1½–2½ in. (4–6 cm.) long, dull grayish green above, elliptic to ovate; widely distributed in most of Alaska except southeast _____ 40. Bebb willow (*Salix bebbiana*)
  ll. Smaller shrubs, to 10 ft. (3 m.) tall, occasionally taller.
    n. Leaves strap-shaped, grayish; petioles reddish, stipules absent _____ 27. barren-ground willow (*Salix brachycarpa* ssp. *niphoclada*)
    nn. Leaves oval, green, petioles green or yellow, stipules usually present.
      o. Upper leaf surface light green, not shiny; typically on river alluvium, interior and northern Alaska __ 28. halberd willow (*Salix hastata*)
      oo. Upper leaf surface dark green, usually shiny; typically in moist sites, open and forested areas in coastal Alaska _____ _____ 31. Barclay willow (*Salix barclayi*)

18. NETLEAF WILLOW

(*Salix reticulata* L.)

Other names: thickleaf willow, reticulate willow.

Prostrate creeping shrub, rooting along branches and ascending only a few inches; not a dense mat former. **Leaves** nearly round to oval, to 1½ in. (4 cm.) long, thick and leathery, prominently net-veined on both surfaces but more conspicuously beneath; margins entire, upper surface green and roughened, lower surface whitish (glaucous) with scattered hairs along veins, petioles slender, red, ¼–¾ in. (6–20 mm.) long. **Twigs** coarse, purplish when young, becoming reddish brown with age.

Catkins erect, long and slender, to 2 in. (5 cm.) long, on long leafless stalks; scales rounded, with long hairs on inner surface and nearly hairless on outer. **Seed capsules** stout, reddish, with short white hairs. Flowering in June, seeds dispersing July to August.

Netleaf willow is easily recognized by its thick round leaves with the net-veined pattern and by its long slender reddish catkins. It is common in a wide variety of vegetation types throughout most of Alaska, although it is more common in tundra than in forests. It grows on both dry and wet sites in the arctic and alpine tundra. In the boreal forest, it is most common around the edges of bogs and on hummocks within the bogs, but it sometimes grows in open stands of black and white spruce, usually near timberline.

From Juneau area in southeast northward across the State. To 5,000 ft. (1,524 m.) altitude on rocky cliffs or nunataks of Juneau Ice Field. On the Aleutians there is a gap in the range between Carlisle Island and Attu Island. North Tongass and Chugach National Forests, Glacier Bay and Katmai National Monuments, Mt. McKinley National Park, Kenai National Moose Range, Aleutian Islands National Wildlife Refuge, Arctic Na-

Figure 18.—Netleaf willow (*Salix reticulata*), natural size. Male catkin at left; seed capsules at right.

tional Wildlife Range. Eastward across northern Canada to Newfoundland, south to Great Slave Lake and northern Hudson Bay.

19. SETCHELL WILLOW
(*Salix setchelliana* Ball)

A semi-prostrate loose shrub with branches sometimes ascending to 12 in. (30 cm.). **Leaves** obovate or oblanceolate, 1–2½ in. (2.5–6 cm.) long, ⅜–¾ in. (1–2 cm.) wide, thick and fleshy, tapering to a petiole ⅛–¼ in. (3–6 mm.) long, rounded at tip, margins entire or irregularly glandular-toothed. Upper surface greenish blue and shiny, lower surface pale green to whitish (glaucous), with long silky hairs when young but becoming hairless. **Twigs** waxy, with dense long hairs when young but becoming smooth and gray, coarse.

Catkins thick and fleshy, ¾–1¼ in. (2–3 cm.) long and ½ in. (12 mm.) thick; scales large and conspicuous greenish yellow, with hairs on margins. **Seed capsules** thick and large, to ⅜ in. (10 mm.) long, greenish yellow, turning brown with age.

Setchell willow is unique in Alaska because of its thick fleshy leaves and catkins. It does not seem to be closely related to any other willow. In habitat it is also

87

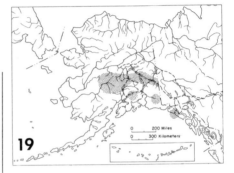

Figure 19.—Setchell willow (*Salix setchelliana*), natural size. Female catkin at upper left; seed capsules at right.

19

unusual, being nearly totally restricted to the gravel outwash of the glacial rivers of the Alaska Range and adjacent mountain ranges.

Gravel bars of the rivers of north slope of Alaska Range as far west as Tonzona River and south, to Matanuska River in Cook Inlet region. An isolated collection on terraces of Alsek River near Yakutat. North Tongass National Forest, Mt. McKinley National Park. Also in southwestern Yukon Territory, Canada, on silt and gravel outwash of the Donjek and Alsek Rivers and beaches of Lake Kluane.

Named for William Albert Setchell (1864–1943), California botanist who made a collection of Alaska willows.

20. POLAR WILLOW

(*Salix polaris* Wahlenb. ssp. *pseudopolaris* (Flod.) Hult.)

Other names: *Salix pseudopolaris* Flod., *S. polaris* var. *selwynensis* Raup.

A small prostrate shrub forming loose to sometimes dense mats, 1–2 in. tall (2.5–5 cm.), with branches often buried in moss or soil. **Leaves** oval to rounded, ¼–¾ in. (6–20 mm.) long and ⅔ as wide, on short petioles; bright green on both surfaces to slightly paler beneath, margins entire, sparsely hairy beneath when young but becoming hairless with age. **Twigs** slender, rooted at nodes, often buried, smooth and reddish.

Catkins erect on leafy stalk ¾–1½ in. (2–4 cm.) long, developing with the leaves; scales broad and rounded at tip, brown to black and slightly lighter at base, with dense long hairs. **Seed capsule** broad, flask-shaped, ¼ in. (6 mm.) long, on short stalks, reddish-purple, densely hairy when young but becoming nearly hairless with some hairs remaining near tip.

Polar willow is common to abundant in the arctic and alpine tundra of central and western Alaska. It forms loose mats in snow beds and along small streams where it is often imbedded in the

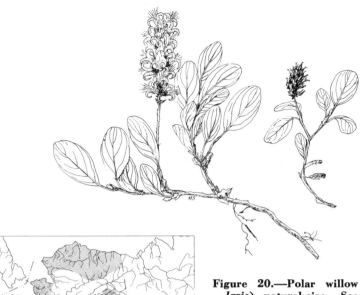

Figure 20.—Polar willow (*Salix polaris*), natural size. Seed capsules at left; female catkin at right.

20

21. SKELETONLEAF WILLOW

(*Salix phlebophylla* Anderss.)

moss and sedge mats. It characteristically forms a much looser mat than least willow and skeletonleaf willow and is usually found in wetter sites.

In alpine and arctic tundra of most of central, northern, and western Alaska but lacking along the southern coast except for one location at Atka Island in the central Aleutians. To 5,400 ft. (1,646 m.) altitude on rocky cliffs of Juneau Ice Field. Mt. McKinley National Park, Aleutian Island National Wildlife Refuge, Arctic National Wildlife Range. West along the Arctic coast to Banks and Victoria Islands, and south in the Rocky Mountains to the Peace River in northern British Columbia. The typical subspecies in northern Europe and Asia.

A tiny densely matted prostrate shrub ½–1½ in. (1–4 cm.) tall, usually with a thick central taproot. **Leaves** oblanceolate to obovate, ⁵⁄₁₆–¾ in. (8–20 mm.) long and ³⁄₁₆–⅜ in. (5–10 mm.) wide, entire on edges, shiny green on both surfaces, with scattered hairs when young but becoming hairless with age. Veins 3–5 pairs from midrib and rather prominent beneath. New leaves crowded near tips of twigs, old leaves persisting at base one or more years, brown and partially skeletonized. **Twigs** radiating from central taproot, much branched and rooting sparingly. **Catkins** erect, ½–1 in. (12–25 mm.) long, on short leafy shoots, developing with the leaves; scales broad, blunt, and black at tip, dark red at base, with long silky hairs. **Seed capsules** ¼ in. (6 mm.) long,

89

Figure 21.—Skeletonleaf willow (*Salix phlebophylla*), natural size. Female catkin at left; seed capsules at right.

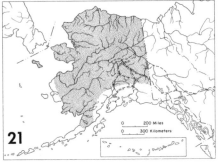

22. LEAST WILLOW
(*Salix rotundifolia* Trautv.)

Includes *Salix rotundifolia* ssp. *dodgeana* Argus.

A densely matted prostrate shrub, usually from a central taproot, forming mats about 1 in. (2.5 cm.) high. **Leaves** ovate, less than ½ in. (12 mm.) long, and ¾ to ⅘ as wide, entire, shiny green on both surfaces, 2–3 pairs of veins prominent beneath; some dry leaves persistent about 1 year. **Twigs** radiating from a central taproot, slender, much branched, and rooting at nodes.

Catkins short and few-flowered, ½ in. (12 mm.) long, with 6–10 flowers; scales dark brown to black, thinly hairy. **Seed capsules** hairless, to ¼ in. (6 mm.) long.

Least willow is found in the arctic and alpine tundra in a variety of vegetation types from dry scree to wet snow bed slopes. For differences between this willow and the closely related skeletonleaf willow (*Salix phleobophylla*), see the latter.

Arctic and alpine tundra of central and western Alaska, but not in

on short stalk, densely silvery hairy when young but becoming nearly hairless at maturity.

Skeletonleaf willow is common on dry usually exposed sites in the arctic and alpine tundra. It forms small dense mats along with a large number of mat-forming plants, especially mountain-avens. Closely related to least willow (*Salix rotundifolia*) but differs in having large, slightly hairy capsules, abundant skeletonized leaves, and 3–5 pairs of veins on leaves instead of 2–3 pairs in least willow. As numerous specimens are intermediate, possibly the two should be combined in one species.

Most of the mountains and arctic tundra of central and western Alaska. Mt. McKinley National Park, Katmai National Monument, Arctic National Wildlife Range, Aleutian Islands National Wildlife Refuge. West to the Mackenzie Mountains, and in eastern Asia.

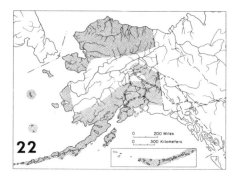

22

Figure 22.—Least willow (*Salix rotundifolia*), natural size.

Twigs reddish, coarse, and much branched, rooting at nodes.

Catkins relatively large, to 4 in. (10 cm.) long and ⅝ in. (15 mm.) thick, erect on stalks that may be leafless or with 2 or 3 leaves; scales brown to black with long silky hairs. **Seed capsules** broad, ⁵⁄₁₆ in. (8 mm.) long, with scattered hairs, reddish to pale brown. Flowering in June and July, fruits ripening in July and August.

Arctic willow is extremely variable in growth form and in the size and the shape of the leaves. It has been subdivided into several species, which by some botanists have been treated as subspecies and varieties.

In the arctic and alpine tundra it may occur as a loose trailing shrub or compact low mats. It is found in both dry and wet sites and in protected and exposed situations. In southeast Alaska although primarily in the alpine tundra, it may occur at sea level on glacial outwash and moraines.

Through the tundra and mountainous areas of Alaska. South Tongass, North Tongass, and Chugach National Forests, Mt. McKinley National Park, Glacier Bay and Katmai National Monuments, Kenai National Moose Range, Aleutian Islands National Wildlife Refuge, Arctic National Wildlife Range. East across northern Canada, south in the mountains to Quebec and California. Northern Europe and Asia.

southeast Alaska. Along the southern coast from the Aleutians to Prince William Sound. Chugach National Forest, Mt. McKinley National Park, Katmai National Monument, Kenai National Moose Range, Aleutian Island National Wildlife Refuge, Arctic National Wildlife Range. In North America only in Alaska and adjacent Canada. Eastern Asia.

23. ARCTIC WILLOW
(*Salix arctica* Pall.)

Other names: *Salix torulosa* Trautv., *S. crassijulis* Trautv., *S. angolorum* Cham.

A trailing low shrub frequently forming dense mats to 8–10 in. (20–25.5 cm.) high, commonly lower. **Leaves** variable in shape but generally obovate to elliptic ¾–3 in. (2–7.5 cm.) long and ⅜–1¼ in. (1–3 cm.) wide, blunt or short-pointed at tip. Upper surface dark green and often shiny, under surface pale green, margins entire. Petiole ³⁄₁₆–⅝ in. (5–15 mm.) long.

91

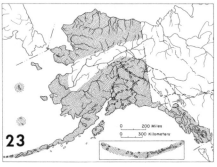

Figure 23.—Arctic willow (*Salix arctica*), natural size. Female catkin at left; seed capsules at right.

Another closely related species, **wedgeleaf willow (*Salix sphenophylla* A. Skvortz.),** of northeastern Asia, has been reported from Seward Peninsula and the extreme northeast corner of Alaska.

24. ALASKA BOG WILLOW (*Salix fuscescens* Anderss.)

Other name: *Salix arbutifolia* Pall.

Trailing shrubs only 4–12 in. (10–30 cm.) high. **Leaves** typically obovate and rounded at tip, occasionally elliptic and pointed, 3/8–1½ in. (1–4 cm.) long, margins entire or toothed near base, upper sur-

The closely related **eastern arctic willow (*Salix arctophila* Cock.)** of eastern Canada has been collected in several locations in the eastern Brooks Range including Jago Lake and along Firth River. It resembles arctic willow (*S. arctica*) in appearance but has darker, more shiny upper leaf surfaces.

24

Figure 24.—Alaska bog willow (*Salix fuscescens*), natural size. Female catkin at upper left; seed capsules at right.

face shiny dark green, lower surface whitish (glaucous). Petioles ⅛–¼ in. (3–6 mm.) long. **Twigs** dark brown and smooth when young, becoming lighter with age. **Catkins** ¾–1½ in. (2–4 cm.) long, on leafy shoots developing with leaves, loose-flowered, dark purple; scales hairy, dark colored toward the tip. **Seed capsules** long and thin, on stalk ¹⁄₁₆–⅛ in. (1.5–3 mm.) long, dark purple and with scattered hairs when young but becoming brown and hairless with age. Flowering in June, fruits ripening in July.

Alaska bog willow occurs commonly in wet tundra and small bogs beyond treeline and in open black spruce and bogs throughout most of the Alaskan boreal forest. On the southern coast of Alaska at Kodiak Island, the Alaska Peninsula, and the Cook Inlet region, one collection from Chichagof Island in southeastern Alaska; northward to Arctic Ocean at Pt. Barrow. Eastward to Alaska-Yukon border in upper Tanana and Yukon River valleys and on north slope of Brooks Range. North Tongass and Chugach National Forests, Mt. McKinley National Park, Katmai National Monument, Kenai National Moose Range, Arctic National Wildlife Range. Eastward in a narrow band across northern Canada to Hudson Bay. Throughout northern Siberia.

93

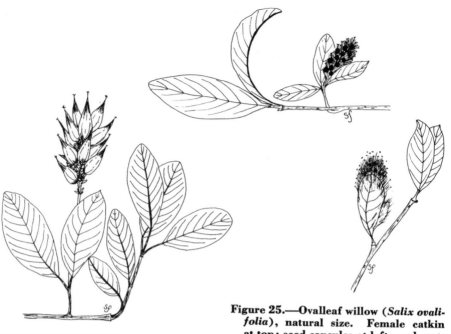

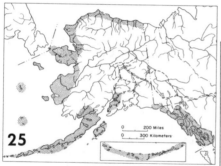

Figure 25.—Ovalleaf willow (*Salix ovalifolia*), natural size. Female catkin at top; seed capsules at left; male catkin at right.

25. OVALLEAF WILLOW

(*Salix ovalifolia* Trautv. and *Salix stolonifera* Cov.)

Other names: sprouting willow, *Salix arctolitoralis* Hult., *S. flagellaris* Hult., *S. cyclophylla* Rydb., *S. ovalifolia* var. *arctolitoralis* Argus, *S. ovalifolia* var. *glacialis* Argus, *S. ovalifolia* var. *cyclophylla* (Rydb.) Ball.

Ovalleaf willow includes two closely related prostrate creeping willows of coastal Alaska, distinguished with difficulty. It has been suggested that they probably represent variation within one species. **Leaves** elliptic to round, ⅜–1 in. (1–2.5 cm.) long and ½–⅘ as wide, on slender petioles, upper surface green, lower surface pale green to whitish (glaucous), margins entire, **Twigs** slender, orange to dark reddish brown, creeping and rooting at nodes.

Catkins ¾–1½ in. (2–4 cm.) cm.) long, on leafy shoots with scattered hairs when young, soon becoming hairless; scales reddish brown, hairy. **Seed capsule** smooth and greenish, whitish (glaucous) or reddish purple, becoming brown with age.

Willows of the ovalleaf group occur primarily in tundra along the Arctic and western coast and in alpine tundra in southeastern Alaska. In the Arctic they occur most commonly along beaches and in saline meadows and more rarely in wet sites along rivers on inland sites, although never far from the sea.

94

Figure 25.1—Sprouting willow (*Salix stolonifera*), natural size. Male catkins at top; female catkin at lower left; seed capsules at lower right.

In southeastern Alaska they grow primarily in wet sites in the alpine tundra.

Range of ovalleaf willow, *Salix ovalifolia*, north coast of Alaska southward to the Aleutians and westward to Attu Island and all islands off the west coast of Alaska. Range of sprouting willow, *Salix stolonifera*, southern Alaska from Prince of Wales Island westward to Aleutian Islands. To 5,600 ft. (1,707 m.) altitude on rocky cliffs of Juneau Ice Field. Both species, South Tongass and North Tongass National Forests, Glacier Bay National Monument, Aleutian Islands National Wildlife Refuge, Arctic National Wildlife Range. Known only from Alaska and adjacent Canada.

26. GRAYLEAF WILLOW

(*Salix glauca* L.)

Other names: *Salix cordifolia* Pursh, *S. desertorum* Richards., *S. glauca* ssp. *acutifolia* (Hook.) Hult., ssp. *callicarpaea* (Trautv.) Böcher, ssp. *desertorum* (Richards.) Anderss., ssp. *glabrescens* (Anderss.) Hult.

An erect to spreading shrub with a dull gray appearance, commonly 3–4 ft. (1–1.2 m.) tall but in exposed sites may be depressed and in favorable sites may become a small tree to 20 ft. (6 m.) high and 5 in. (12.5 cm.) in trunk diameter. **Leaves** variable in size, shape, and hairiness, oval to lanceolate, 1½– 3½ in. (4–9 cm.) long and ⅜–1½

95

Figure 26.—Grayleaf willow (*Salix glauca*), natural size. Female catkin at
upper left; male catkins at lower left;
seed capsules at right.

in. (1–4 cm.) wide, short-pointed to
rounded at tip, margins usually entire but occasionally with small
glandular teeth on the lower part.
Upper surface green, densely hairy
to nearly hairless; lower surface
whitish (glaucous) with scattered
hairs. Petiole ⅛–⅜ in. (3–10 mm.)
long. Stipules minute, glandular
margined, ¹⁄₃₂–⁵⁄₁₆ in. (1–8 mm.)
long. **Twigs** reddish brown to

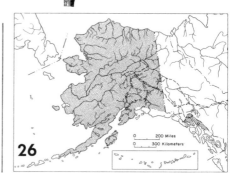

96

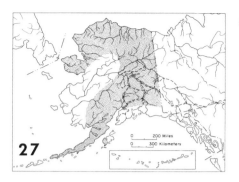

Figure 27.—Barren-ground willow (*Salix brachycarpa* ssp. *niphoclada*), natural size. Seed capsules at left; female catkin at right.

grayish, hairy or hairless, with dense white hairs when young. **Winter buds** reddish brown with scattered hairs. **Bark** gray, smooth, becoming rough and furrowed.

Catkins ¾–2 in. (2–5 cm.) long, on leafy shoots, usually several inches back from end of branches developing with the leaves, persistent during most of the summer and often after leaves have fallen; scales light brown to yellow, rounded on tip, hairy on both surfaces. **Seed capsule** hairy, gray when young and turning light brown with age; on short stalk $\frac{1}{32}$–$\frac{1}{16}$ in. (1–1.5 mm.) long. Flowering in June, fruits ripe in July and August.

Grayleaf willow is common after fire and as a pioneer species along rivers and roads and on glacial outwash, mine tailings, and abandoned fields in interior Alaska, in thickets with other willows. It also occurs as an individual open shrub in most forest types in the boreal forest. In the Arctic and western parts of Alaska, it grows on the floodplain and cutbanks of rivers, as well as protected sites in tundra habitats. Because it is such a common species and seldom grows too tall to be reached by moose, it is an important browse species.

Throughout Alaska except Aleutian Islands and southeast coast. In southeast Alaska it occurs only at Glacier Bay, the Haines-Skagway area and mountains above Juneau to 5,000 ft. (1,524 m.) altitude. North Tongass and Chugach National Forests, Glacier Bay and Katmai National Monuments, Mt. McKinley National Park, Kenai National Moose Range, Arctic National Wildlife Range. East across North America to Labrador and Newfoundland, south to southern British Columbia, and in the Rocky Mountains to northern New Mexico, Northern Europe and Asia.

Though generally shrubby, grayleaf willow in Alaska reaches the size of small, clump-forming trees. This species is added here to the list of Alaska trees, the eighth native tree willow.

The closely related species **Athabasca willow** (*Salix athabascensis* Raup) has been collected in two locations in the upper Tanana River valley.

27. BARREN-GROUND WILLOW

(*Salix brachycarpa* Nutt. ssp. *niphoclada* (Rydb.) Argus)

Other names: *Salix niphoclada* Rydb., *S. brachycarpa* var. *mexiae* Ball, *S. muriei* Hult., *S. niphoclada* var. *muriei* (Hult.) Raup, *S. glauca* ssp. *niphoclada* (Rydb.) Wiggins.

A low shrub with gray appearance, prostrate to erect, usually 1–3 ft. (3–10 dm.) tall but occasionally to 6 ft. (2 m.) in lowland and protected sites. **Leaves** variable, obovate to lanceolate, short-pointed, 1–1½ in. (25–40 mm.) long, $\frac{3}{16}$–$\frac{3}{8}$ in. (5–10 mm.) wide, upper surface green, thinly hairy, lower surface whitish (glaucous), more thickly hairy. Petioles $\frac{1}{32}$–$\frac{1}{8}$ in. (1–3 mm.) long, reddish to yellow. Stipules glandular along edge, $\frac{1}{16}$–$\frac{1}{8}$ in. (1.5–3 mm.) long. **Twigs** thin, reddish brown to yellowish brown, densely hairy when young, becoming hairless. **Winter buds** reddish brown, hairy.

Catkins 1–2½ in. (25–60 mm.) long, on ends of leafy twigs, narrowly cylindrical, appearing gray from the dense hairs on flowers and scales; scales yellowish to dark brown, rounded, hairy on both surfaces. Catkins developing with the leaves, catkins persisting throughout the summer and often through the following winter. **Seed capsule** grayish green when young but becoming brown with age, thinly hairy on short stalk $\frac{1}{32}$ in. (1 mm.) long. Flowering in June and July, seeds dispersed in July and August.

Barren ground willow is most common in arctic and alpine areas as a low shrub on talus slopes, in upland mountain-avens (*Dryas*) tundra, and in moist meadows and along stream margins. It occurs as a taller shrub, usually with other willows in the boreal forest as a pioneer on well drained alluvium and glacial outwash and moraine. Through central and northern Alaska but not found in the Yukon-Kuskokwim delta, the extreme western part of the Alaska Peninsula, Aleutian Islands, or southeast Alaska. Chugach National Forest, Mt. McKinley National Park, Katmai National Monument, Kenai National Moose Range, Arctic National Wildlife Range. Eastward to the Mackenzie River and Hudson Bay, and southward to northern British Columbia.

28. HALBERD WILLOW
(*Salix hastata* L.)

Other names: Farr willow, *Salix walpolei* (Cov. & Ball) Ball, *S. farrae* Ball var. *walpolei* Cov. & Ball, *S. hastata* var. *farrae* (Ball) Hult.

A much branched spreading shrub 3–6 ft. (1–2 m.) high. **Leaves** elliptic, lanceolate to oblanceolate, 1–2 in. (2.5–5 cm.) long and about $\frac{1}{3}$ as wide, short-pointed, hairless, edges entire or with shallow teeth, upper surface yellow green to green, lower surface whitish (glaucous). Petiole slender, $\frac{1}{16}$–$\frac{5}{16}$ in. (1.5–8 mm.) long. **Twigs** reddish brown to brown, shiny, with dense white hairs when young.

Catkins $\frac{3}{4}$–1½ in. (2–4 cm.) long, on leafy stalks, usually scattered along twig 2–4 in. (5–10 cm.) from end, with the leaves; scales yellow at base and brown at apex, hairless or thinly hairy. **Seed capsules** $\frac{1}{8}$–$\frac{1}{4}$ in. (3–6 mm.) long on short stalks, light brown to reddish brown when mature; flowering in late June, seeds dispersed during late July and early August.

Halberd willow occurs occasionally in the boreal forest of interior Alaska, primarily in willow thickets along small streams, but also as a pioneer species on river sandbars and on glacial moraines. It also occurs occasionally in alpine sedge bogs but does not seem to be abundant anywhere. From north slope of Brooks Range at Umiat south to Alaska Range and Matanuska Valley and eastward to MacKenzie Mountains. Chugach National Forest, Mt. McKinley National Park, Arctic National Wildlife Range.

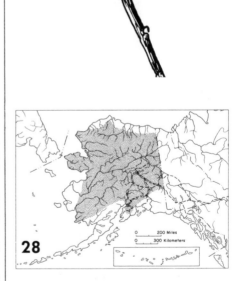

In isolated areas in central Canada as far east as Hudson Bay and in the mountains as far south as western Wyoming. Across northern Europe and Asia and south in the mountains of both continents.

29. LOW BLUEBERRY WILLOW

(*Salix myrtillifolia* Anderss.)

Low shrubs usually 8–24 in. (20–61 cm.) tall, much branched and often prostrate. **Leaves** elliptic, ovate, to obovate, ¾–1½ in. (2–4 cm.) long and ⅜–¾ in. (1–2 cm.) wide, blunt or short-pointed at tip, margins toothed, upper surface dark green and shiny, lower surface slightly lighter, conspicuously net-veined. Petioles short, stipules small and inconspicuous and soon shedding. **Twigs** brown to gray, hairless, finely hairy when young.

Catkins usually ¾–1¼ in. (2–3 cm.) long but occasionally to 2 in.

28

Figure 28.—Halberd willow (*Salix hastata*), natural size. Male catkin at upper left; seed capsules at right.

99

Figure 29.—**Low blueberry willow (*Salix myrtillifolia*), natural size. Seed capsules at left; male catkins at right.**

(5 cm.) long on leafy stalks appearing after the leaves have started to develop; scales brown to gray with long gray hairs. **Seed capsules** green to brown, hairless, $\frac{1}{4}$–$\frac{5}{16}$ in. (6–8 mm.) long on stalks $\frac{1}{16}$–$\frac{1}{8}$ in. (1.5–3 mm.) long.

Occasional in black spruce stands and bogs in the interior of Alaska. Locally abundant as a successional species following burning of low-lying black spruce stands. It also occurs occasionally in bogs below and just above treeline. From

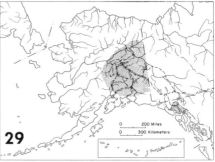

29

Umiat on north slope of Brooks Range southward in interior Alaska to upper Kuskokwim River, Matanuska Valley, and Copper River. Mt. McKinley National Park. Eastward to southern Hudson Bay and Labrador, south to St. Lawrence River and southern British Columbia.

100

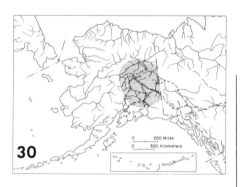

30. TALL BLUEBERRY WILLOW

(*Salix novae-angliae* Anderss.)

Other names: *Salix pseudocordata* Anderss., *S. myrtillifolia* Anderss. var. *pseudo-myrsinites* (Anderss.) Ball, *S. pseudo-myrsinites* Anderss.

A tall erect shrub usually 6–8 ft. (2–2.5 m.) tall, occasionally to 20 ft. (6 m.) and treelike. **Leaves** elliptic to obovate, 1–3 in. (2.5–7.5

Figure 30.—Tall blueberry willow (*Salix novae-angliae*), natural size. Seed capsules at upper left; male catkin at lower left; female catkin at lower right.

cm.) long and about ⅓ as wide, blunt to short-pointed at tip; margins with teeth often glandular tipped, upper surface dark green, lower surface lighter but not whitish (glaucous), prominently net-veined, with long silky hairs when young, soon becoming hairless. Petioles 1/16–¼ in. (1.5–6 mm.) long. Stipules variable, small and inconspicuous to 3/16 in. (5 mm.), broad, and glandular toothed. **Twigs** brown, usually straight, coarse, with dense white silky hairs when young.

Catkins ¾–2½ in. (2–6 cm.) long on leafy stalks, appearing after the leaves have started to develop; scales short, brown, with long gray hairs. **Seed capsule** green to brown, hairless ¼–5/16 in. (6–8 mm.) long on stalks 1/16–⅛ in. (1.5–3 mm.) long. Flowering

101

in early to mid-June, seeds maturing in late June to mid-July, catkins falling in late July.

This is a common willow on the silt and sandbars of the Tanana and Yukon Rivers, where it occurs as a pioneer with other willows. It is also common in willow thickets along small streams and roadsides. Closely related to blueberry willow and often included as a subspecies. However, the two appear to be quite distinct in ecology, size, and growth form.

Central Alaska from Yukon River southward to Copper River basin. Mt. McKinley National Park. East to British Columbia and southward in mountains to northern California and southern Utah.

31. BARCLAY WILLOW
(*Salix barclayi* Anderss.)

Spreading, much branched shrubs tending to form dense thickets 3–6 ft. (1–2 m.) high, sometimes to 10–20 ft. (3–6 m.) and treelike, variable in growth form, leaf structure, color, and habitat. **Leaves** broadly elliptic to obovate, ¾–3 in. (2–7.5 cm.) long and ⅜–1¼ in. (1–3 cm.) wide, short-pointed tip and wedge-shaped to rounded at base, margins toothed, serrate to entire; upper surface shiny yellow green thinly hairy when young but becoming hairless, sometimes with short reddish hairs along midrib; lower surface whitish (glaucous), thinly hairy but soon becoming hairless; usually turning black in drying. Petioles ¹⁄₁₆–¼ in. (1.5–6 mm.) long. Stipules inconspicuous and soon dropping. **Twigs** blackish and densely hairy when young, becoming reddish brown and hairless with blackish buds. **Bark** gray or greenish brown, smooth.

Catkins 2–3 in. (5–7.5 cm.) long, on stalks with 2–3 leaves, appearing with the leaves, scales about ¹⁄₃₂ in. (1 mm.) long, black, with long hairs. **Seed capsules** short and stout, on short stalk, hairy when young but soon becoming hairless, green to reddish. Flowering in June, seeds ripening in July, most catkins falling by August.

Barclay willow is the most common thicket-forming shrub along the southern coast of central Alaska in forest openings, along small streams, and in wet alluvial sites. On the Kenai Peninsula it forms extensive thickets at treeline in areas where it is protected by winter snow deposits.

Closely related to and easily confused with low blueberry willow and undergreen willow, but these latter willows have leaves green to pale beneath but never whitish (glaucous).

Along coast of Alaska from southeastern tip to Aleutian Islands. Occasional to rare in Alaska Range and in the interior lowlands. South Tongass, North Tongass, and Chugach National Forests, Mt. McKinley National Park, Glacier Bay and Katmai National Monuments, Kenai National Moose Range, Aleutian Islands National Wildlife Refuge. South along the coast to Washington and eastward to Alberta and Montana.

Twigs of Barclay willow often end in rounded galls, composed of deformed leaves and caused by insects. Presence of these galls often called "willow roses" may aid identification.

This species honors George Barclay, English botanical collector with the surveying expedition of the ship *Sulphur* along the western coast of America in 1835–41.

Where the range of Barclay willow overlaps that of Hooker willow and undergreen willow, there is considerable difficulty in separating the three species. The following key provided by George W. Argus should help in identification.

Figure 31.—Barclay willow (*Salix barclayi*), natural size. Male catkins at left; female catkins at bottom; seed capsules at right.

0   200 Miles
0   300 Kilometers

31

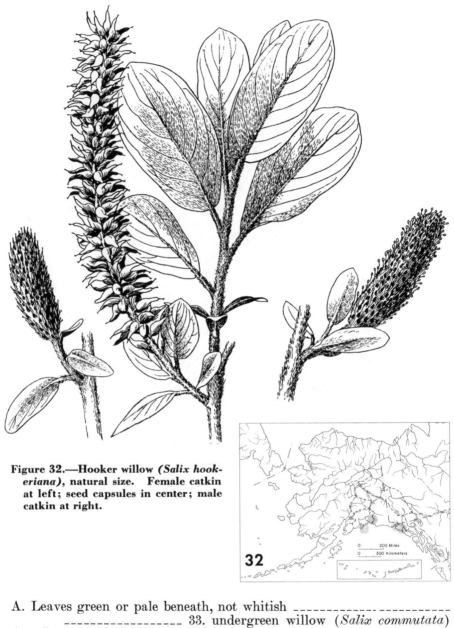

Figure 32.—Hooker willow *(Salix hook-eriana)*, natural size. Female catkin at left; seed capsules in center; male catkin at right.

32

A. Leaves green or pale beneath, not whitish _____
_____ 33. undergreen willow *(Salix commutata)*
AA. Leaves whitish (glaucous) beneath.
  B. Stipules present; leaves without hairs beneath; lacking long silky
    hairs at the base of twigs; styles greenish _____
    _____ 31. Barclay willow *(Salix barclayi)*
  BB. Stipules absent (sometimes very small on vigorous shoots); leaves
    long silky hairy beneath, at least along midrib; long silky hairs
    persistent at the base of twigs; styles red in life, drying dark
    _____ 32. Hooker willow *(Salix hookeriana)*

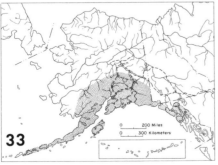

Figure 33.—Undergreen willow (*Salix commutata*), natural size. Male catkin at upper left; female catkin at lower left; seed capsules at right.

105

32. HOOKER WILLOW

(*Salix hookeriana* Barratt)

Other names: bigleaf willow, Yakutat willow, *Salix amplifolia* Cov.

A shrub or small tree, usually about 10–16 ft. (3–5 m.) tall but occasionally attaining a height of 25 ft. (7.5 m.) and a trunk diameter of 8–15 in. (20–38 cm.). **Leaves** oval to broadly obovate or rarely the uppermost ovate, 1½–3 in. (4–7.5 cm.) long and ¾–2 in. (2–5 cm.) wide, broadly pointed to rounded at apex, mostly rounded at base, edges without teeth or sparsely wavy-toothed, pale green above, whitish beneath, more or less hairy on both sides while unfolding but becoming hairless. **Twigs** stoutish, dark brown, densely white- or gray-woolly for 2 or 3 years. **Buds** dark reddish brown, hairy. **Bark** gray, smooth.

Catkins on leafy stalks, appearing before or with the leaves, 3–4 in. (7.5–10 cm.) long and ½–⅝ in. (12–15 mm.) wide at maturity; scales brownish to blackish, covered with long whitish hairs. **Seed capsules** long, hairless. Flowering in mid-May to early June, seeds ripening mid-June to July.

In Alaska, Hooker willow grows in a variety of sites including beach ridges, stabilized sand dunes, and coastal meadows. Rare in Alaska, except in the Yakutat Bay region where it has been known for many years as a local species, Yakutat willow (*Salix amplifolia* Cov.). Collected recently from a few other coastal areas including Middleton Island. At Yakutat the plants are browsed by moose.

Coastal Alaska in the vicinity of Prince William Sound and Yakutat Bay. North Tongass National Forest. Also coastal dunes, Pacific Coast from Queen Charlotte Islands (Moresby Island) and extreme southwestern British Columbia, Vancouver Island, and Puget Sound region of western Washington south to northwestern California. Reported also from eastern Siberia.

This species honors William Jackson Hooker (1785–1865), English botanist, in whose work the description was published.

33. UNDERGREEN WILLOW

(*Salix commutata* Bebb)

A much branched dense shrub 3–6 ft. (1–2 m.) tall, with an overall light green appearance. **Leaves** elliptic to obovate, to 2½ in. (6 cm.) long and about ⅓ to ½ as wide; entire or glandular toothed on margins, dense gray hairy on both surfaces when young but only thinly hairy with age, light green on both surfaces. Petioles ⅛–¼ in. (3–6 mm.) long. Stipules well developed and leaflike with glandular margins to ⅜ in. (1 cm.) long, persistent or deciduous. **Twigs** densely gray hairy when young but becoming hairless with age, dark brown. **Buds** of next season's catkins are often large and red by mid to late summer.

Catkins ¾–1½ in. (2–4 cm.) long on leafy shoots, developing with or after the leaves; scales brown with dense woolly hairs. **Seed capsules** ¼ in. (6 mm.) long, hairless, reddish but becoming brown with age. Flowering mid-June to July, seeds ripening late July and August.

Undergreen willow forms thickets in the mountains of south central Alaska at and just above treeline along small streams and in areas protected by winter snow accumulation, usually with several other willows. It also occurs occasionally along the coast in wet

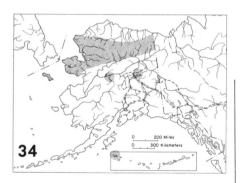

Figure 34.—Chamisso willow (*Salix chamissonis*), natural size.

34

From the mountains in the northern part of southeast Alaska westward in the coastal mountains to Kodiak Island and the Alaska Peninsula to the eastern Aleutian Islands, north to the south slopes of Alaska Range. North Tongass and Chugach National Forests, Kenai National Moose Range, Aleutian Islands National Wildlife Refuge. East to southern Yukon Territory and Saskatchewan, south to Washington, western Montana, and northern Wyoming.

open habitats. It is quite similar in appearance and often grows with Barclay willow but the soft green color resulting from the dense woolly hairs on the new leaves help to distinguish it.

107

34. CHAMISSO WILLOW

(*Salix chamissonis* Anderss.)

Prostrate loosely branched creeping shrub rooting along the branches and 4–6 in. (10–15 cm.) high at the ends. **Leaves** broadly obovate, rounded at tip and wedge-shaped at base, ¾–2 in. (2–5 cm.) long and ⅔–¾ as wide, glandular toothed on margin; green on both surfaces but slightly paler beneath. Petioles long and slender, ⅜–⅝ in. (10–15 mm.) long. **Twigs** gray or brown, coarse, often buried in mosses and rooting at nodes. **Catkins** erect on leafy twigs, about 1½ in. (4 cm.) long, developing with the leaves; scales black with grayish hairs. **Seed capsules** long and slender with gray hairs, stalkless or on a very short stalk. Flowering from late June through July, seeds ripening July and August.

Chamisso willow is a rare shrub of the Arctic tundra of northern and western Alaska and the alpine tundra of interior Alaska. In the Arctic it grows as a very loose creeping shrub in wet meadows, seepage areas, and adjacent to snow fields. It is abundant in the Eagle Summit area north of Fairbanks where it forms loose mats in similar habitats. Readily distinguished from the other creeping willows by its glandular toothed leaves and the slender gray hairy capsules.

The Eagle Summit area north of Fairbanks, western Arctic coast from Nome northward to Cape Thompson, St. Lawrence Island, the north slope of the Brooks Range; also on Attu Island in the Aleutians. Aleutian Island National Wildlife Refuge, Arctic National Wildlife Range. Eastward to Richardson Mts. in northwestern District of Mackenzie, Canada, also in northeastern Asia.

Named for Ludolf Adalbert von Chamisso (1781–1838), German botanist who visited Alaska in 1816 and 1817 on the ship *Rurik*.

35. PARK WILLOW

(*Salix monticola* Bebb)

Other names: cherry willow, serviceberry willow; *Salix padophylla* Rydb., *S. pseudomonticola* Ball, *S. pseudomonticola* var. *padophylla* (Rydb.) Ball.

An erect shrub, 3–12 ft. (1–3.5 m.) tall in Alaska but becoming a small tree southward in western Canada and northwestern contiguous United States. **Leaves** oval to elliptic, 1–4 in. (2.5–10 cm.) long, ½–⅗ as broad, usually abruptly pointed to rounded at tip, glandular toothed on margins, purple to reddish yellow when young but soon turning green, shiny green and hairless above, whitish (glaucous) beneath, with prominent veins. Petioles ¼–⅜ in. (6–10 mm.) long. Stipules small and inconspicuous or on fast growing shoots larger and leaflike with glandular teeth. **Twigs** yellow to reddish brown, shiny, hairy when young but becoming hairless. **Bark** gray, smooth. **Catkins** short, 1¼–2½ in. (3–6 cm.) long, stalkless twigs, appearing in May and early June before the leaves and usually shedding by end of June; scales 1/16 in. (1.5 mm.) long, brown with long hairs. **Seed capsules** short and stout, ⅛–3/16 in. (3–5 mm.) long, hairless, short-stalked, seeds ripening in June.

A common pioneer willow on the braided rivers of interior Alaska and along other rivers and lake shores, forming thickets with other willows. Occasional in floodplain balsam poplar and spruce stands and in upland black spruce. In early summer the reddish color of

35

Figure 35.—Park willow (*Salix monticola*), natural size. Seed capsules at left; male catkins at right.

109

the new leaves stand out from the other willows. Along the rivers it is utilized as a browse species by snowshoe hares and moose.

Central interior Alaska along Yukon and Tanana Rivers, southeast to the Susitna and Copper Rivers and at Haines and Skagway near northern end of southeast Alaska. Mt. McKinley National Park. East to Hudson Bay and south to Ontario, Colorado, and Oregon.

36. RICHARDSON WILLOW

(*Salix lanata* L. ssp. *richardsonii* (Hook.) A. Skwortz.)

Other names: woolly willow, *Salix richardsonii* Hook.

Erect much-branched shrubs usually forming dense clumps 3–6 ft. (1–2 m.) tall, sometimes to 15 ft. (4.5 m.). **Leaves** elliptic to obovate, ¾–2½ in. (2–6 cm.) long, about ½ to ¾ as wide, short-pointed or rounded at apex, entire or toothed on margins, both surfaces with long thin hairs when young but becoming hairless with age, dark green above, whitish (glaucous) beneath. Petioles stout, ⅛–⅜ in. (3–10 mm.) long. Stipules conspicuous, long and narrow, with glandular teeth on the edges, persistent on the twig for several years. Young **twigs** stout and densely hairy, dark brown to black; older twigs hairless, orange-red to red-brown and characterized by persistent stipules. **Bark** gray, smooth.

Catkins 1½–2½ in. (4–6 cm.) long on leafless peduncles, developing early in spring before the leaves; scales dark brown to black with dense silky hairs. **Seed capsules** stout, green to light brown, hairless, on short stalks. Flowering

in May and early June, seeds ripening in July, catkins shedding by August.

Richardson willow is a common thicket-forming shrub of stream banks and moist slopes in the Arctic and above timberline where it is often associated with alders and shrub birch, also in open spruce stands and old burns at lower elevations.

From the Arctic coast southward through most of central and south central Alaska but not reaching to western Alaska Peninsula or Kenai Peninsula. In southeastern Alaska only in mountains in area from Juneau to Haines. North Tongass National Forest, Glacier Bay National Monument, Mt. McKinley National Park, Arctic National Wildlife Range. This subspecies occurs across northern Canada to Baffin and Southampton Islands, south to Northwestern Hudson Bay and British Columbia; northeastern Asia. The species occurs across northern North America, Europe, and Asia and south in mountains of Asia.

37. BARRATT WILLOW

(*Salix barrattiana* Hook.)

A low upright shrub, usually 1–2 ft. (30–60 cm.) tall, commonly forming loose clumps several yards (meters) across. **Leaves** tending to have a vertical orientation, elliptic to obovate, 1½–2½ in. (4–6 cm.) long and ¼ to ⅓ as wide, short-pointed apex, both surfaces grayish from long silky hairs. Petioles to ⅝ in. (15 mm.) largest on upper leaves. **Twigs** stout, densely hairy when young and remaining so for many years, older twigs reddish brown to dark brown.

Catkins 1¼–2 in. (3–5 cm.) long, sessile on twigs, erect in habit, appearing in spring before the leaves;

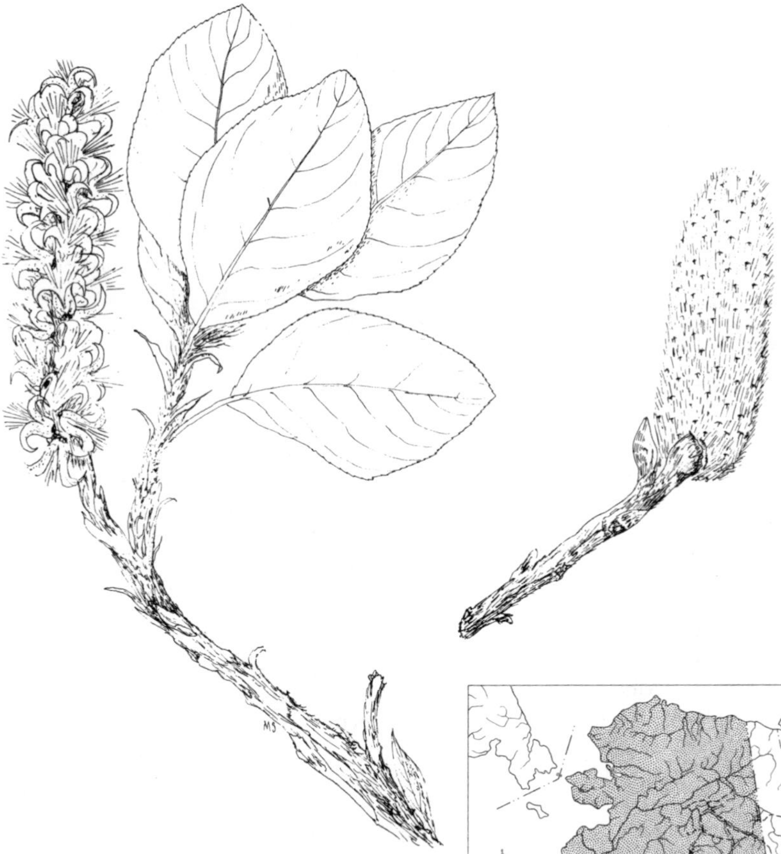

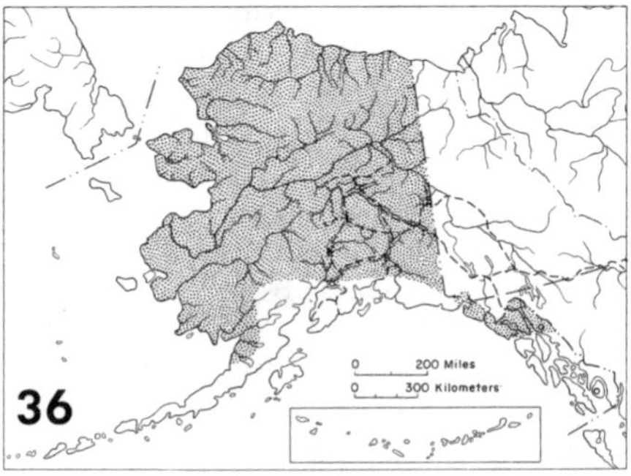

Figure 36.—Richardson willow (*Salix lanata* ssp. *richardsonii*), natural size. Seed capsules at left; female catkin at right.

36

scales black, pointed at tip, with long silky hairs. **Seed capsule** stout, about ¼ in. (6 mm.) long, with silky white hairs on pedicels ¹⁄₁₆ in. (1.5 mm.) long.

Barratt willow is a rare shrub in Alaska although it may be locally abundant above treeline on gravel terraces of some rivers in the Alaska Range where it may reach altitudes of 4,600 ft. (1,400 m.). It also occurs occasionally in wet alpine meadows. It is conspicuous among Alaskan willows and easily determined at a distance by its silvery appearance, its low growth

form into dense thickets, and its upright leaves and twigs. When collected and pressed, the scales, stipules, and young twigs exude a yellowish oily substance that stains the paper yellow. Young twigs are browsed by moose.

From the head of the Chitina River in the Copper River drainage north to the north slopes of the Alaska Range as far west as eastern end of Alaska Peninsula. On the south slopes of the Brooks Range at Wiseman and on the north slope from the Canning River eastward to the border. Mt. McKinley Na-

111

tional Park, Arctic National Wildlife Range. South and east to Yukon Territory, southern British Columbia, Montana and Colorado.

Named for Joseph Barratt (1796–1882), American student of willows.

38. FELTLEAF WILLOW

(*Salix alaxensis* (Anderss.) Cov.)

Other names: *Salix longistylis* Rydb., *S. alaxensis* var. *longistylis* (Rydb.) Schneid., ssp. *longistylis* (Rydb.) Hult.

A shrub or small tree to 20–30 ft. (6–9 m.) high with a trunk 4–7 in. (10–18 cm.) in diameter, occasionally dwarfed and nearly prostrate in exposed places. **Leaves** elliptic or oblanceolate (reverse lance-shaped), 2–4 in. (5–10 cm.) long and ½–1½ in. (1.2–4 cm.) wide, short-pointed, usually tapering to base, edges without teeth or nearly so, above dull green and hairless or sometimes somewhat short-hairy, beneath covered with a dense white or creamy-white felt; midrib yellowish. One-year and 2-year **twigs** stoutish, usually white-woolly. In a common variety (var. *longistylis* (Rydb.) Schneid. or ssp. *longistylis* (Rydb.) Hult.) the young twigs and buds without hairs and often with a bluish white bloom. **Bark** gray, smooth, becoming rough and furrowed into scaly plates.

Catkins stoutish, not stalked, appearing before the leaves, 2–4 in. (5–10 cm.) long at maturity; scales blackish. **Seed capsules** long, pointed, white-woolly. Flowering May and June, seeds ripening in June and July.

Feltleaf willow is widely distributed in valleys almost throughout Alaska. Extending beyond the limits of the spruce-birch interior forest, it is the only tree willow in many areas, such as north and west of Kodiak Island and at Firth River on the northeast Arctic slope. In many places in northern Alaska, this willow is important as the only wood available for fuel. Though not the common "diamond willow" from which ornamental canes are made, the trunks sometimes have this pattern of diamond-shaped scars where the lower twigs have died. Feltleaf willow is a preferred browse species of moose which pull down and break branches and trunks up to 1½ in. (4 cm.) in diameter. Eventually the shrub grows above the reach of the moose and becomes too thick for the moose to break. It is reported that the inner bark has served as food for humans.

Widely distributed and common almost throughout Alaska from northern part of southeast Alaska to Arctic Ocean. Southeast Alaska from Wrangell to head of Lynn Canal at Skagway, Glacier Bay, and Yakutat Bay; north through the interior to the Arctic coast and northwest to Cape Lisburne; west to Bering Sea; southwest on Alaska Peninsula and Aleutian Islands to Unalaska Island; and south to Kodiak Island, Cook Inlet, and Prince William Sound. North Tongass, South Tongass, and Chugach National Forests, Glacier Bay and Katmai National Monuments, Mt. McKinley National Park, Kenai National Moose Range, Kodiak National Wildlife Refuge, Arctic National Wildlife Range. East to northwest shore of Hudson Bay and south to central British Columbia, but not reaching contiguous United States. Also in eastern Asia.

This willow was first collected at Kotzebue Sound beyond Bering Strait. The specific name *alaxensis* means Alaskan but is from an old spelling.

Figure 37.—Barratt willow (*Salix bar-rattiana*), natural size. Female catkins at right.

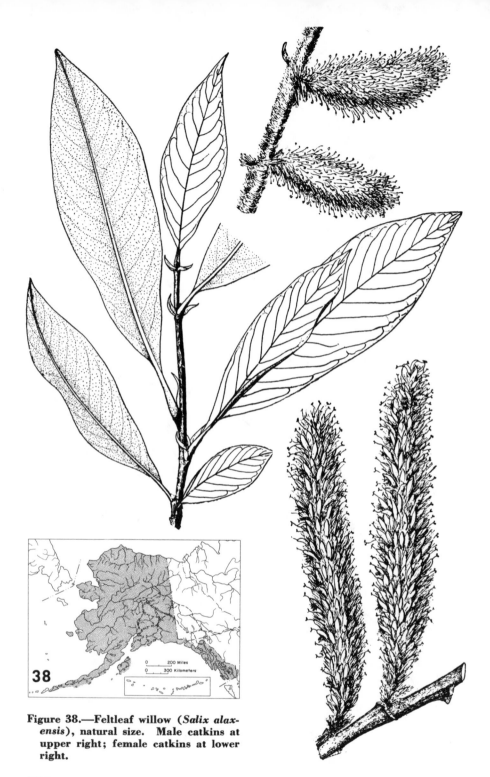

38

Figure 38.—Feltleaf willow (*Salix alaxensis*), natural size. Male catkins at
upper right; female catkins at lower
right.

114

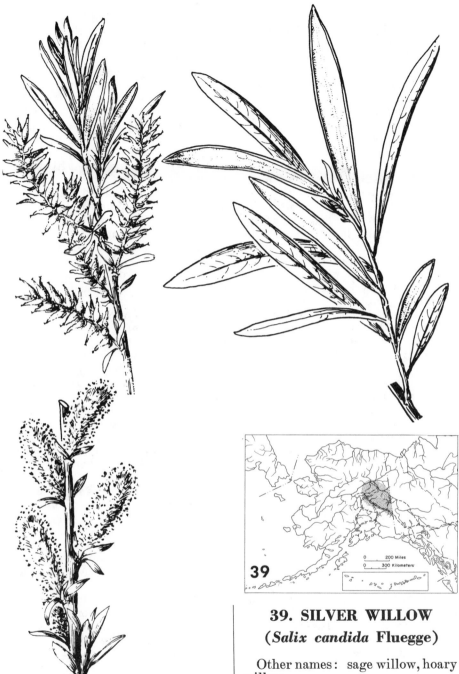

Figure 39.—Silver willow (*Salix candida*), natural size. Seed capsules at upper left; male catkins at lower left.

39. SILVER WILLOW
(*Salix candida* Fluegge)

Other names: sage willow, hoary willow.

An erect shrub usually 6 ft. (2 m.) or less in height, with an over-all silvery appearance. **Leaves** oblong to lanceolate, short-pointed at

115

both ends, 2–4 in. (5–10 cm.) long and only ¼–⅝ in. (6–15 mm.) wide, edges entire or wavy and commonly rolled toward lower surface; upper surface silvery from dense woolly hairs when young but becoming hairless and dark green with age; lower surface remaining silvery with dense woolly hairs. **Twigs** covered with white woolly hairs when young but becoming smooth and reddish with age.

Catkins ¾–2 in. (2–5 cm.) long, narrowly cylindrical, stalkless on twigs, in early spring before the leaves; scales brown, rounded at tip, with long white hairs. **Seed capsules** stout, ¼ in. (6 mm.) long, covered with short dense woolly hairs.

Silver willow is a rare shrub in Alaska, having been collected only a few times in bogs and other wet sites along the Tanana and Yukon Rivers. The silvery appearance of leaves, twigs, and catkins, and the narrow leaf shape give it a characteristic appearance.

Along Tanana and Yukon Rivers from Canadian border west to Fairbanks and Fort Yukon. East across Canada to Labrador, south to New Jersey, Colorado, and British Columbia.

40. BEBB WILLOW

(*Salix bebbiana* Sarg.)

Other names: diamond willow, beak willow, *S. rostrata* Richards., *S. depressa* L. ssp. *rostrata* (Anderss.) Hiitonen.

A large shrub 10 ft. (3 m.) tall or a small, bushy tree 15–25 ft. (4.5–7.5 m.), rarely 35 ft. (10.5 m.) with trunk diameter of 6–9 in. (15–23 cm.). **Leaves** elliptic and pointed at both ends to broadly oblanceolate or obovate-oval and very short-pointed at apex and broad at base, 1–3½ in. (2.5–9 cm.)

long and ⅜–1 in. (10–25 mm.) wide, edges without teeth or somewhat wavy, dull green above, gray or whitish and roughly net-veined beneath, more or less hairy on both sides but becoming less hairy with age. In an uncommon variety, the smaller leaves are hairless or nearly so beneath and often less rough. **Twigs** slender, branching at wide angles, yellowish to brown, gray hairy when young but afterward becoming hairless. **Bark** gray to dark gray, smooth, becoming rough and furrowed. **Wood** lightweight, brittle.

Catkins on short leafy stalks, before or with the leaves, at maturity 1–3 in. (2.5–7.5 cm.) long and loose, scales narrow, yellowish with reddish tips, hairy. **Seed capsules** long, very slender, with short hairs ⅛–³⁄₁₆ in. (3–5 mm.) long, on slender, sparsely hairy stalks. Flowering mid-May through mid-June, seeds ripening by mid- to late June, catkins shed by mid-July.

Bebb willow is the most common upland willow in interior Alaska, occurring as scattered individuals in most forest types. It is also the most common species in the willow stands that follow forest fires on upland sites and in thickets adjacent to streams, swamps, and lakes. In open meadows it forms large spreading shrubs. It is an important browse species for moose throughout interior Alaska. In winter heavy snows tend to bend the branches down so that they are in reach of both moose and snowshoe hares.

Bebb willow is the most important producer of "diamond willow." This term applies to several species with diamond-shaped patterns on their trunks. When the stems are carved they result in a striking pattern of diamond-shaped cavities with a sharp contrast between the white or cream sapwood and the reddish brown heartwood. Diamond willow is carved into canes,

Figure 40.—Bebb willow (*Salix bebbiana*), natural size. Seed capsules at left; male catkin at upper right.

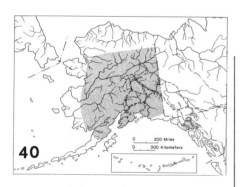

40

lamp posts, furniture and candle holders. In the old roadhouse at Copper Center, the newel posts and balusters of the whole staircase have been carved from diamond willow.

The depressions or "diamonds" are caused by one or more fungi which attack the willow at the junction of a branch with the main trunk. The "diamond willows" occur most commonly under shade of trees or where the site is poor. They are most abundant in the Copper River basin area but occur in Alaska throughout the boreal forest from the Kenai Peninsula northward. In addition to the Bebb, the following also form "diamonds" although usually to a lesser degree: Park willow, feltleaf willow, littletree willow, and Scouler willow.

In other areas of the United States, Bebb willow formerly was used for baseball bats, charcoal, gunpowder, and withes for furniture and baskets.

Widely distributed in interior Alaska, south to the Pacific Coast. In the northern part of southeastern Alaska at Glacier Bay and the head of Lynn Canal. In central Alaska from Prince William Sound north to the south slopes of the Brooks Range, west on the Yukon River to Holy Cross, and south to Katmai, Kodiak Island, and the Kenai

117

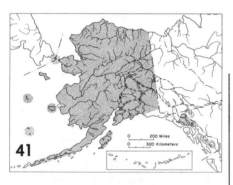

Figure 41.—Diamondleaf willow (*Salix planifolia* ssp. *pulchra*), natural size. Female catkin at left; seed capsules at right.

This species commemorates Michael Schuck Bebb (1833–95), American specialist on willows.

41. DIAMONDLEAF WILLOW

(*Salix planifolia* Pursh ssp. *pulchra* (Cham.) Argus)

Other names: *Salix pulchra* Cham., *S. pulchra* var. *yukonensis* Schneid.

An upright much branched shrub 3–6 ft. (1–2 m.) tall, rarely to 15 ft. (4.5 m.), often forming loose thickets in wet habitats but becoming a prostrate creeping shrub in

Peninsula. North Tongass and Chugach National Forests, Mt. McKinley National Park, Katmai National Monument, Kenai National Moose Range, Kodiak National Wildlife Refuge. East across Canada to Hudson Bay, Labrador, and Newfoundland, and south to New Jersey, Nebraska, New Mexico, and central California. Also in eastern Asia.

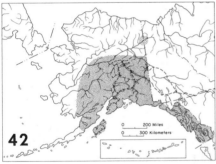

42

Figure 42.—Scouler willow (*Salix scouleriana*), natural size. Seed capsules at upper left; female catkin at upper right; male catkin at lower right.

exposed sites in arctic and alpine tundra. **Leaves** elliptic to oblanceolate, pointed at both ends and often diamond-shaped, as stated in the name, 1–2½ in. (2.5–6 cm.) long and about ⅓–½ as wide, hairless and shiny green above and pale to whitish (glaucous) beneath, entire on edges or with a few small teeth near base. Petioles ⅛–⅜ in. (4–10 mm.) long, slender. Stipules ¼–½ in. (6–12 mm.) long, linear,

glandular-toothed, persisting on twigs 2–3 years. A few brown leaves usually remain on the twigs through the following winter and into the next summer. **Twigs** shiny dark brown, reddish or purple, hairy when young but becoming hairless in age. **Bark** dark gray, smooth.
Catkins ¾–1½ in. (2–4 cm.) long stalkless on the branches, developing in early spring before the leaves; scales blackish in upper part and hairy. **Seed capsules** ⁵⁄₁₆

119

in. (8 mm.) long, stout, hairy, greenish gray when young but becoming brown with age, on a short stalk. Flowering in late May and early June, seeds ripening in late June and July; catkins shedding by August.

A common shrub in bogs and other wet sites in the boreal forest of Alaska, forming thickets usually 3–5 ft. (1–1.5 m.) tall. It is a more upright, often isolated shrub in black spruce stands. It also occurs in the arctic and alpine treeless regions along streams and in the tundra where it may become a prostrate shrub. Indians and Eskimos eat the young leaves as a green, both raw and cooked. The leaves must be picked when young, or they have a bitter taste.

In winter the twigs are browsed by moose and snowshoe hare, and the persistent leaves are often eaten by Dall sheep. Diamondleaf willow is one of the few willows that can usually be identified in the winter condition; the shiny red twigs, the persistent stipules, and the persistent brown leaves are characteristic.

Almost all of Alaska except the western Aleutians and the coastal forests of southeastern Alaska. Along the south coast from Unalaska Island to Prince William Sound. In southeastern Alaska only in the extreme northern part in mountains above Haines and Skagway. Chugach National Forest, Katmai National Monument, Mt. McKinley National Park, Kenai National Moose Range, Arctic National Wildlife Range. East to Yukon and south to British Columbia. In Asia from Novaya Zemlya to Chukchi Peninsula.

The closely related planeleaf willow (*Salix planifolia* Pursh ssp. *planifolia*; *S. phylicifolia* L. ssp. *planifolia* (Pursh) Hiitonen) has been reported from south-central Alaska.

42. SCOULER WILLOW

(*Salix scouleriana* Barratt)

Other names: mountain willow, black willow, fire willow.

A shrub or tree with compact rounded crown usually 15 ft. (4.5 m.) tall and 4 in. (10 cm.) in trunk diameter but in some localities in Alaska becoming a tree 50–60 ft. (15–18 m.) tall and 16–20 in. (40.5–51 cm.) in trunk diameter.

Leaves variable, mostly oblanceolate to narrowly obovate or sometimes oblong or elliptic, 2–5 in. (5–12.5 cm.) long and ½–1½ in. wide (12–40 mm.), mostly very short-pointed at apex and tapering to base, edges without teeth to sparsely wavy-toothed, dark green and nearly hairless above, beneath whitish to white and more or less gray hairy or becoming rusty hairy when older. **Twigs** stoutish, yellowish or greenish brown and densely hairy when young, reddish to dark brown and nearly hairless when older; buds red. **Bark** gray smooth, thin, becoming dark brown, divided into broad flat ridges. **Wood** light brown tinged with red and with thick whitish sapwood, fine-textured, lightweight, soft.

Catkins stout, stalkless or on short leafless stalks, appearing in great abundance before the leaves, at maturity 1–2 in. (2.5–5 cm.) long and nearly ½ in. (12 mm.) thick; scales obovate, black, long hairy. **Seed capsules** long, slender, gray-woolly. One of the earliest flowering of the willows, its catkins developing as pussy willows even before the snow has melted; flowering in May, seeds dispersing in June, catkins shedding by July.

Scouler willow is the most common willow of southeastern and south central Alaska where it occurs over a wide range of habitats and vegetation types. It is especially

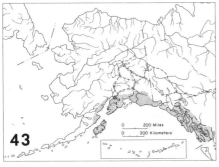

Figure 43.—Sitka willow (*Salix sitchensis*), natural size. Seed capsules at left; female catkin at right; male catkins at lower right.

fires. It is often called "fire willow" because of its rapid occupation of burned areas, forming blue-green thickets. In southeastern Alaska it comes in abundantly after logging and also occurs along streams and roadsides and occasionally in the more open spruce and hemlock stands. Over all of southeastern and south central Alaska, it commonly reaches tree size. In south central Alaska where it is an important moose browse

abundant in the vicinity of Anchorage and Kenai Peninsula where it has become widespread in the uplands following past widespread

species, most trees have been barked by moose. In the interior of Alaska, Scouler willow occurs in spruce, birch, and aspen stands, and occasionally in bogs, but is most common in areas that have been burned. It is one of several used for "diamond willow" carvings.

Southern end of southeastern Alaska north and west along the coast to Kodiak and Katmai, north to the Tanana River. Also in the upper and central Yukon River district around Dawson. South Tongass, North Tongass, and Chugach National Forests, Mt. McKinley National Park, Glacier Bay and Katmai National Monuments, Kenai National Moose Range, Kodiak National Wildlife Refuge. Eastward to Saskatchewan and south to New Mexico and California.

This species honors its discoverer, John Scouler (1804–71), Scotch naturalist who made plant collections on the northwest coast of North America in 1825–27.

43. SITKA WILLOW

(*Salix sitchensis* Sanson)

Other names: silky willow, *Salix coulteri* Anderss.

A large shrub or small tree 10–20 ft. (3–6 m.) high with trunk 4–6 in. (10–15 cm.) in diameter or rarely 30 ft. (9 m.) tall and 12 in. (30 cm.) in diameter. In exposed places, becoming a low, nearly prostrate shrub. **Leaves** oblanceolate or narrowly obovate or sometimes elliptic, 2–4 in. (5–10 cm.) long, usually short-pointed at apex, mostly tapering to a narrow base, edges without teeth or sparsely and inconspicuously wavy-toothed, above dark green and with sparse short hairs when young, beneath paler and with short silvery, silky hairs. **Twigs** slender, sometimes thinly hairy when young but when older hairless and dark reddish brown. **Bark** gray, smooth, becoming slightly furrowed and scaly. **Wood** pale red, fine-textured, lightweight, soft.

Catkins slender, tightly flowered on short leafy stalks, appearing with the leaves, 2–4 in. (5–10 cm.) long at maturity; scales small, brown, densely hairy. **Seed capsules** short, silvery hairy. Flowering in May, seeds ripening in early to mid-June, catkins shedding by July or early August.

Sitka willow is common in the coastal forest region of southeast Alaska, growing in sunny locations along streams and beaches or in the upland where the forest is open or absent. The satiny sheen on the lower surface of the leaves serves to distinguish it from other willows. The wood is not used commercially though the Indians burn it in drying fish, as the smoke has no bad odor. The supple twigs have been used by the Indians in basketmaking and for stretching skins, and the pounded bark has also been applied to heal wounds.

Pacific coast region of southeast and southern Alaska. Throughout southeast Alaska from Ketchikan northwest to head of Lynn Canal at Skagway, Glacier Bay, and Yakutat Bay, and west to Prince William Sound, Cook Inlet, and Kodiak Island, north as far as Anchorage and the Chitna River. South Tongass and North Tongass National Forests, Glacier Bay National Monument, Kenai National Moose Range, Kodiak National Wildlife Refuge. Alaska and British Columbia south along the coast to southern California and east to New Mexico and Black Hills. Also in eastern Asia.

Sitka willow was named for Sitka, Alaska, near which it was discovered by Karl Heinrich Mertens in 1827.

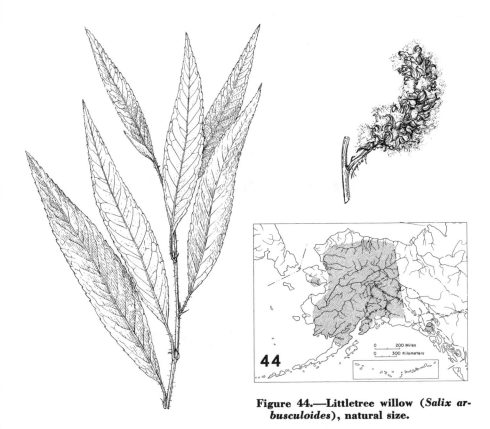

Figure 44.—Littletree willow (*Salix arbusculoides*), natural size.

44. LITTLETREE WILLOW

(*Salix arbusculoides* Anderss.)

An erect shrub 10–15 ft. (3–4.5 m.) tall or commonly a small tree 25–30 feet (7.5–9 m.) tall and 5–6 in. (12–15 cm.) in trunk diameter. **Leaves** narrowly elliptic-lanceolate, often oblanceolate while unfolding, 1–3 in. (2.5–7.5 cm.) long, ⅜–¾ in. (10–20 mm.) wide, usually short-pointed at both ends, with edges finely but shallowly toothed, green and hairless above, beneath whitish to white and finely silvery-hairy or in an uncommon variety hairless; veins closely parallel. **Twigs** slender, much branched, the younger yellowish brown and sometimes thinly short-hairy, the older reddish brown, hairless, and shiny. **Bark** gray to reddish brown, smooth.

Catkins small and slender on very short stalks, appearing slightly before or with the leaves, 1–2 in. (2.5–5 cm.) long at maturity; scales blackish. **Seed capsules** small, thinly silvery-hairy. Flowering mid-May to early June, seeds ripening mid- to late June.

Littletree willow is one of the most common willows, forming dense thickets along streams and rivers in interior Alaska. It also grows in the upland along streams and is a common successional species following the burning of open stands of black spruce in wet sites. It is less commonly found as a shrub in stands of white spruce and birch. On the north slope of

123

Figure 45.—Sandbar willow (*Salix interior*), natural size.

the Brooks Range, it grows on streambanks and gravel bars in association with several other willow species. It is one of several species that form "diamond willow" patterns.

Widely distributed in interior Alaska from the Copper River basin northward to the northern foothills of the Brooks Range, westward to the Kobuk River and Yukon Delta. Mt. McKinley National Park, Kenai National Moose Range, Arctic National Wildlife Range. East to Hudson Bay and south to British Columbia and central Quebec.

124

Figure 46.—Pacific willow (*Salix lasiandra*), natural size.

46

0	200 Miles	
0	300 Kilometers	

125

45. SANDBAR WILLOW

(*Salix interior* Rowlee)

Other names: *Salix longifolia* Muhl., *Salix exigua* ssp. *interior* (Rowlee) **Cronq.**

An upright shrub, 10–12 ft. (3–3.5 m.) tall in Alaska, but becoming a small tree 20 ft. (6 m.) high in contiguous United States. **Leaves** long and very narrow, 1½–4 in. (4–10 cm.) long, usually ¼ in. (6 mm.) wide, light green on both surfaces, edge sometimes entire but usually with sharp rather widely spaced teeth; petiole short. **Twigs** long, thin, unbranched, brown, and smooth. **Catkins** 1–2½ in. (2.5–6 cm.) long on leafy stalks, appearing with the leaves; scales long, pale yellow, with thin hairs, and dropping soon after the catkin opens. **Seed capsule** long and slender, to ⅜ in. (10 mm.) long on a short stalk. Flowering in June, seeds ripening in late June and July.

Sandbar willow is an occasional pioneer on the sand and silt bars of the rivers of interior Alaska, where it is often the first willow to invade a newly exposed bar, primarily by the development of shoots from its widely divergent root system. It seems to be unable to compete with other shrubs and trees, for it is seldom found in the older successional stages along the river and seldom reaches a height of more than 6–8 ft. (2–2.5 m.) in these localities. It is utilized as browse by moose, which often winter on the young islands and sandbars of the Tanana and Yukon Rivers.

Central Alaska in the Yukon, Porcupine, and Tanana River valleys and on the north slope of the Brooks Range along the Colville River at Umiat. East across Canada and south to Virginia, Louisiana, New Mexico, and northern Mexico.

46. PACIFIC WILLOW

(*Salix lasiandra* Benth.)

Other names: western black willow, yellow willow.

A tall shrub or small tree to 20 ft. (6 m.) high. Farther south in contiguous United States, it is a small tree 20–30 ft. (6–9 m.) tall but occasionally a larger tree 50–60 ft. (15–18 m.) tall with a trunk 2–3 ft. (60–90 cm.) in diameter. **Leaves** lance-shaped, 2–5 in. (5–12.5 cm.) long and ½–1 in. (12–25 mm.) wide, long pointed, mostly rounded at the base, with edges finely toothed, shiny green above, glaucous and more or less hairy beneath. **Twigs** hairy when young, stoutish, chestnut to reddish, shiny, hairless with age. **Bark** gray, smooth, becoming rough and deeply furrowed. **Wood** pale brown, brittle. **Catkins** on leafy stalks, appearing with the leaves, 2–4 in. long (5–10 cm.) at maturity; scales yellowish, hairy toward the base. **Seed capsules** without hairs.

Pacific willow is an occasional pioneer species on the sand and silt bars of the rivers of interior Alaska, usually with other willows but occasionally forming pure stands. It is occasional to rare in the uplands in willow thickets along streams and roadsides.

Interior and southeast Alaska. In southeast Alaska only in the vicinity of Yakutat, Haines, and Skagway and in British Columbia adjacent to the boundary along the Stikine and Chilkat Rivers. In interior Alaska from Palmer north to the central Yukon River district and Wiseman and west to Holy Cross on the lower Yukon River. North Tongass National Forest. East to Saskatchewan and south to southern California and New Mexico.

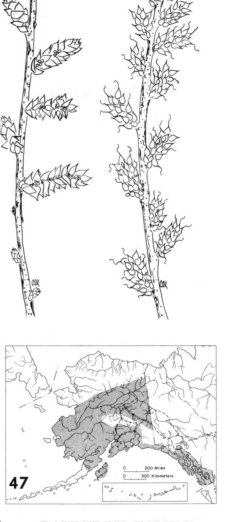

Figure 47.—Sweetgale (*Myrica gale*), natural size. Leafy twig at upper left; male catkins at upper center; fruits at upper right; winter twigs at lower left.

BAYBERRY FAMILY

(Myricaceae)

Fragrant shrubs in Alaska (elsewhere also small trees). **Leaves** alternate, simple with entire or toothed margins, and with small aromatic yellow resin dots on both surfaces. **Flowers** small, yellowish,

127

without sepals or petals, unisexual, male and female on separate plants in short scaly spikes (aments), stamens usually 4–8, ovary 1-celled. **Fruit,** tiny nutlike, with whitish waxy coat, 1-seeded. Includes bayberry and sweetfern of eastern United States. In Alaska only 1 species.

47. SWEETGALE

(*Myrica gale* L.)

Other name: *Myrica gale* L. var. *tomentosa* C. DC.
Low shrub 1–4 ft. (3–12 dm.) tall, of low wet habitats, usually branching loosely at base. **Leaves** oblanceolate, 1–2 in. (25–50 mm.) long and ⅜–½ in. (10–12 mm.) wide, rounded at tip with several coarse teeth, tapering at base to short petiole ⅛ in. (3–5 mm.) long, thinly hairy on both surfaces and dotted with yellow waxy glands. **Twigs** slender, finely hairy when young, dark brown to gray with yellow resin dots and white dots (lenticels), resembling birch and alder. **Buds** ⅛ in. (3 mm.) long, pointed, dark reddish brown, hairless.

Flowers male and female on separate plants (dioecious), small, inconspicuous, yellowish, in spikes in early spring before the leaves. Male (staminate) spikes ⅜–⅝ in. (10–15 mm.) long, female (pistillate) spikes ¼–⅜ in. (6–10 mm.), both dotted with yellow waxy glands. **Fruit** a green 2-winged nutlet ⅛ in. (3 mm.) long, resinous waxy.

Sweetgale is one of Alaska's earliest blooming plants, flowering from mid-May to the first week in June, depending on locality. It is a common shrub of low wet areas, especially bogs in interior Alaska and tidal flats along the coast. The following year's flower spikes form in late summer and the stalks of previous summer's spikes often remain throughout the winter, giving the winter twigs a distinct appearance.

Along the Yukon and Tanana Rivers to the western coast but not in intervening hills and mountains. Common along the coast from Alaska Peninsula southeastward. South Tongass, North Tongass, and Chugach National Forests, Glacier Bay and Katmai National Monuments, Kenai National Moose Range, Kodiak Island National Wildlife Refuge. Across Canada to southern end of Hudson Bay, Labrador, and Newfoundland, south in mountains to North Carolina and Tennessee and to northwest Oregon. Also in northern Europe and eastern Asia and Japan.

BIRCH FAMILY

(Betulaceae)

The birch family (Betulaceae) is represented in Alaska by 2 genera, birch (*Betula*) and alder (*Alnus*), and 7 species, also intergrading varietes and hybrids. Distinguishing characters are as follows: (1) Leaves borne singly (alternate), broad, margins sharply and usually doubly toothed with teeth of 2 sizes, and in alders often slightly wavy lobed; (2) flower clusters (catkins) composed of an axis bearing many minute greenish flowers 2–3 above a scale, in early spring before the leaves, from buds partly formed the preceding summer; (3) flowers with minute calyx, of 2 kinds on the same plant (monoecious); (4) male flowers with pollen in long, narrow catkins at end of twig and female flowers in short catkins on sides of twig; and (5) fruits conelike, ½–2 in. (1.2–5 cm.) long, of many nutlets ("seeds") and scales.

The tree birches of Alaska are

easily recognized by their smooth, thin, white, pinkish, coppery brown, or purplish brown bark, which peels off in papery strips; the soft cone-like fruits shed, leaving slender axis. Alders generally have smooth gray bark, which is not papery, and usually have at all seasons some old dead, hard, blackish or dark grown conelike fruits remaining on the twigs. Birch twigs commonly have raised gland dots and have winter buds not stalked, composed of overlapping scales. Alder twigs lack glands and have usually stalked winter buds with 3 exposed scales usually meeting at their edges or overlapping.

BIRCH (*Betula*)

Alaska has 2 species of dwarf, shrubby birches both widely distributed, and 3 kinds of tree birches. These are variable and intergrade and hybridize wherever their ranges meet. The dwarf birches have round, rounded-toothed leaves less than ¾ in. (2 cm.) long, while the tree birches have larger, ovate leaves 1½–3½ in. (4–9 cm.) long.

The tree birches of Alaska are treated as 3 geographical varieties of a single transcontinental species, paper birch (*Betula papyrifera* Marsh.). Western paper birch (var. *commutata* (Reg.) Fern.), of the northern part of southeast Alaska, has leaves mostly rounded at base and usually reddish brown bark. Alaska paper birch (var. *humilis* (Reg.) Fern. & Raup), common through the interior forests, has rather long-pointed leaves usually wedge-shaped at base and usually white bark in age (or reddish brown when young or in dense stands). Kenai birch (var. *kenaica* (W. H. Evans) Henry), of southern and southern interior Alaska and treated by some authors as a distinct species, has relatively thick, usually short-pointed leaves and usually dark brown or gray bark.

Key to Alaska Birches

A. Leaf blades rounded or elliptic, thick, less than 1¼ in. (3 cm.) long, rounded teeth on edges; shrubs or sometimes small trees with smooth bark not peeling.
  B. Leaf blades less than ¾ in. (2 cm.) long; low shrubs less than 5 ft. (1.5 m.) high.
    C. Leaf blades often broader than long, ³⁄₁₆–½ in. (5–12 mm.) long, straight or notched at base _____
    _____ 48. dwarf arctic birch (*Betula nana*)
    CC. Leaf blades longer than broad, mostly ⅜–¾ in. (10–20 mm.) long, wedge-shaped at base _____
    _____ 49. resin birch (*Betula glandulosa*)
  BB. Leaf blades 1–1¼ in. (2.5–3 cm.) long; large shrubs or trees becoming more than 10 ft. (3 m.) high _____
  _____ 49.1. hybrid birches (*Betula* hybrids)
AA. Leaf blades ovate, 1½–3½ in. (4–9 cm.) long, mostly thin, with pointed teeth on edges; trees with thin papery bark, peeling off __ 50. paper birch (*Betula papyrifera*), 3 varieties in Alaska.

D. Leaves long-pointed, usually wedge-shaped at base; bark usually white in age (or reddish brown when young or in dense stands); interior Alaska _____
_____ 50b. Alaska paper birch (*Betula papyrifera* var. *humilis*)

DD. Leaves mostly short-pointed; bark brown or pinkish; southern and southeast Alaska.

  E. Leaves thin, mostly rounded at base; bark usually reddish brown; northern part of southeast Alaska _____ 50a. western paper birch (*Betula papyrifera* var. *commutata*)

  EE. Leaves thick, wedge-shaped or rounded at base, with white hairs on toothed edges; bark usually dark brown or gray; southern and southern interior Alaska _____
_____ 50c. Kenai birch (*Betula papyrifera* var. *kenaica*)

48. DWARF ARCTIC BIRCH

(*Betula nana* L.)

Other names: dwarf birch, dwarf alpine birch, *Betula nana* subsp. *exilis* (Sukatch.) Hult., *B. glandulosa* var. *sibirica* (Ledeb.) Blake.

Low spreading deciduous shrub commonly ½–3 ft. (1.5–9 dm.) high. **Leaves** alternate, almost stalkless, with slender petioles ⅟₁₆ in. (2 mm.) long. Blades round or kidney-shaped, often broader than long, ³⁄₁₆–½ in. (5–12 mm.) long, ³⁄₁₆–⅝ in. (5–16 mm.) wide, rounded at apex, finely wavy toothed to straight or notched base, thick, hairless, above green, beneath pale green, turning cooper red in autumn. **Twigs** slightly resinous and slightly hairy, with few minute warty glands.

Male flower clusters ⅜–1 in. (1–2.5 cm.) long, with brown scales. Female flower clusters ¼–⅜ in. (6–10 mm.) long, green. **Fruits** conelike, elliptic, ³⁄₁₆–½ in. (5–12 mm.) long, ³⁄₁₆–¼ in. (5–6 mm.) wide, light brown, with many 3-lobed bracts or scales without resinous dot or hump on back. Nutlets many, elliptic, with 2 narrow wings of equal width from base to apex. Flowering June, fruits maturing July–August.

Moist soil, muskegs or bogs, rocky alpine slopes, and hummocks on tundra. Very widespread nearly throughout Alaska over the coasts and in mountains of interior from northern part of southeast Alaska to western end of Alaska Peninsula and Bering Sea, north to Arctic Coast. North Tongass and Chugach National Forests, Mt. McKinley National Park, Katmai National Monument, Kenai National Moose Range, Kodiak Island Wildlife Refuge, Arctic National Wildlife Range. Alaska, across northern Canada to Labrador and Greenland. Not in contiguous United States. Also across northern Eurasia.

49. RESIN BIRCH

(*Betula glandulosa* Michx.)

Other names: shrub birch, glandular scrub birch, bog birch, ground birch, dwarf birch.

Deciduous shrub mostly low and spreading to erect, 1–5 ft. (0.3–1.5 m.) high or taller, forming clumps. **Leaves** with short hairy petioles

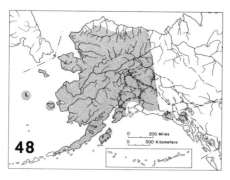

Figure 48.—Dwarf arctic birch (*Betula nana*), slightly enlarged.

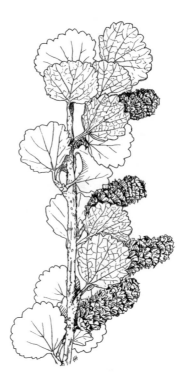

³⁄₁₆–¼ in. (5–6 mm.) long. Blades elliptic to broadly obovate, mostly ⅜–¾ in. (1–2 cm.) long, rounded but longer than broad, rounded at apex, finely wavy-toothed except near wedge-shaped base, thick and leathery, often with gland dots on both surfaces (visible only with high magnification), above shiny dark green and usually hairless, beneath yellow green and often finely hairy. **Twigs** often finely hairy when young, densely resinous with warty glands, with a gray layer of wax. **Bark** reddish brown, becoming dark gray, smooth, not peeling.

Male flower clusters (catkins) several near base of twigs, ½–1 in. (12–25 mm.) long, ³⁄₁₆–¼ in. (5–6 mm.) wide, of light brown scales and numerous stamens. Female flower clusters several to many on older twigs ¼–½ in. (6–12 mm.) long, ¹⁄₁₆ in. (2 mm.) wide, greenish. **Fruits** conelike, ⅜–1 in. (10–25 mm.) long, ⅛–¼ in. (3–6 mm.) wide, mostly erect, with many 3-lobed bracts or scales with resinous dot or hump on back. Nutlets elliptic, flattened, reddish brown, more than ¹⁄₁₆ in. (2 mm.) long, with 2 very narrow wings narrowest at base. Flowering May–June, fruits maturing July–August, persistent in winter.

The leaves and young twigs are browsed by caribou and reindeer. In winter the buds and twigs are clipped by ptarmigan.

Moist soil, especially in muskegs or boggy areas, hummocks on tundra, and boarders of lakes and streams. Forming extensive thickets at treeline in the Alaska and Brooks Ranges. Widely distributed in interior Alaska from northern Brooks Range and Firth River southward. Mt. McKinley National Park, Arctic National Wildlife Range. Alaska, across northern Canada to Labrador and Greenland, south in Northeastern United States to Maine, New York, Michigan, and Minnesota, and in western mountains to Colorado and California.

This species hybridizes with dwarf arctic birch and the tree birches.

131

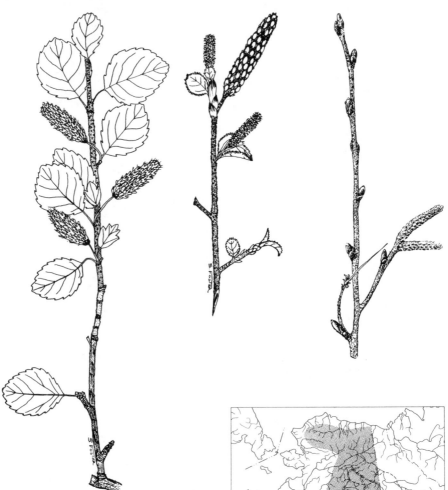

Figure 49.—Resin birch (*Betula gland-ulosa*), natural size. Leafy twig with fruits at left; male and female catkins in center; winter twig at right.

49

49.1. HYBRID BIRCHES

(*Betula* hybrids)

Many plants have characters intermediate between those of the tree and shrub birches described and illustrated here. These hybrid birches can be recognized by their characters between those of their parents growing nearby. In size, the hybrids between a tree and a shrub species are large shrubs or small trees. Bark is like that of the tree parent but does not peel off. Leaves are intermediate in size and vary in shape and margin. The shrubby species hybridize with one another as do the varieties of paper birch, the tree species.

Yukon birch, the hybrid between resin birch and paper birch (***Betula glandulosa*** × ***papyrifera*;** *Betula*

132

Figure 49.1—Yukon birch (*Betula glandulosa* ✕ *papyrifera*), natural size. Leafy twig with female catkins and fruits at upper left; leafy twig with male and female catkins at lower left; winter twig at right.

133

$\times$*eastwoodiae* Sarg., *B.* $\times$*commixta* Sarg., *B. occidentalis* auth.), is the common hybrid birch through interior Alaska, for example, at Fairbanks. Often found near tree-line, where birch trees below meet a band of resin birch shrubs above. Large, spreading clump-forming shrub 10–12 ft. (3–3.7 m.) high, with many stems 1 in. (2.5 cm.) in diameter, sometimes becoming a small tree 15–20 ft. (4.5–6 m.) high and 3–6 in. (7.5–15 cm.) in diameter. **Leaves** with slender petioles ¼–⅜ in. (6–10 mm.) long. Leaf blades elliptic to diamond-shaped, 1–1¼ in. (2.5–3 cm.) long, ¾–1¼ in. (2–3 cm.) wide, short-pointed or rounded at both ends, with rounded teeth on edges, thick, becoming hairless. **Twigs** often densely covered with gland dots. **Bark** reddish black, smooth and not peeling. **Fruits** conelike ¾ in. (2 cm.) long. Alaska, Yukon Territory, and Alberta.

The hybrid between dwarf arctic birch and paper birch has been named **Horne birch** (*Betula nana* $\times$ *papyrifera*; *Betula* $\times$*hornei* Butler, *B.* $\times$*beeniana* A. Nels.). The tree parent in central Alaska is Alaska paper birch and in southern Alaska, Kenai birch.

50. PAPER BIRCH

(*Betula papyrifera* Marsh.)

Other names: white birch, canoe birch.

The general description and range of this species are summarized here, followed by similar notes for the three varieties in Alaska. Small to medium-sized deciduous tree usually 20–60 ft. (6–18 m.) high and 4–12 in. (10–30 cm.) in trunk diameter, becoming 80 ft. (24 m.) tall and 24 in. (60 cm.) in diameter. **Leaves** with slender petioles ½–1 in. (1.2–2.5 cm.) long. Leaf blades ovate, 1½–3½ in. (4–9 cm.) long, 1–2½ in. (2.5–6 cm.) wide, long-pointed or short-pointed at apex, wedge-shaped or rounded at base, coarsely and usually doubly toothed, mostly dull dark green and hairless above, light yellow green and hairless or slightly hairy beneath. **Twigs** slender, hairless, reddish brown with many small whitish dots, with short side twigs (spur shoots) covered by many raised half-rounded leaf-scars, becoming reddish black. **Winter buds** conic, ¼ in. (6 mm.) long, long-pointed, dark brown, slightly resinous, covered by 3 overlapping scales. **Bark** smooth, with long horizontal lines (lenticels), thin, separating into papery strips and peeling off, from white to pinkish, coppery brown, or purplish brown in the different varieties; inner bark orange. **Wood** of wide white sapwood and light reddish brown heartwood, fine-textured, moderately hard, and moderately heavy (the densest of Alaska commercial woods).

Flowers male and female on same twig, tiny, in groups of 3 above a scale (bract). Male flowers in narrow catkins partly developed the preceding summer, 1–4 in. (2.5–10 cm.) long composed of calyx and 2 stamens; female flowers in shorter clusters ⅜–1 in. (1–2.5 cm.) long, composed of ovary and 2 styles. **Fruits** conelike, cylindric, 1–2 in. (2.5–5 cm.) long and ⅜ in. (1 cm.) wide, slender-stalked and hanging down. Nutlets ("seeds") many, 1/16 in. (1.5 mm.) long, brown, with 2 broad wings. Flowering in May–June, before the leaves, fruit shedding gradually into winter.

Paper birch is one of the most widespread tree species in northern North America and is composed of 6 or fewer intergrading geographical varieties. Widely distributed

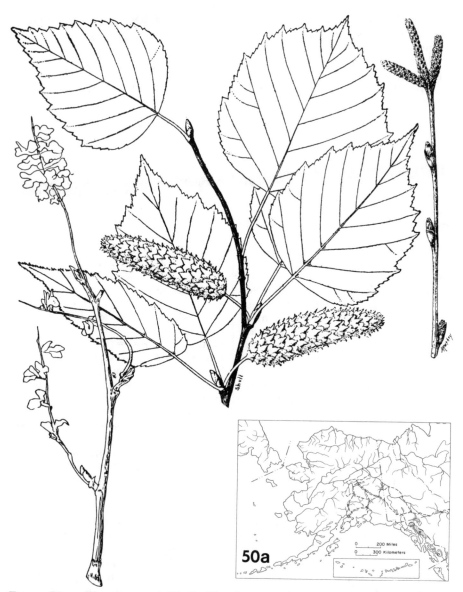

Figure 50a.—Western paper birch (*Betula papyrifera* var. *commutata*), natural size. Winter twig with old fruits at left; leafy twig with fruits in center; winter twig with buds of male catkins at right.

from northwestern Alaska east across Canada to Labrador and Newfoundland, south in Northeastern States to Pennsylvania and Iowa and in Western States to Montana and northeastern Oregon (locally south to Nebraska and in mountains to North Carolina, South Dakota (Black Hills), and Colorado).

Paper birch is a characteristic species of the interior forests of

135

Alaska, designated as spruce-birch forests, and is associated with white spruce and aspen. In the upper Cook Inlet area, extensive paper birch forests occupy the rolling benchland above the bottoms and extend up the slopes of the foothills to about 800 ft. (244 m.). Growth is moderate to fast. On the more favorable sites, trees 80 to 100 years old attain a height of 60–70 ft. (18–21 m.) and a trunk diameter of 12–14 in. (30–35 cm.) Average diameter is 8–10 in. (20–25 cm.) and maximum about 29 in. (73 cm.). Maximum age recorded is about 230 years.

Near cities and villages in Interior Alaska, paper birch has been used primarily for fuel, mainly fireplace wood. It has served locally for mine props. A small amount of lumber is cut and marketed locally in Interior Alaska. However, attempts to develop export markets have not yet been successful because of high costs and transportation problems. The wood has been made into cabinets and wall paneling.

The wood of paper birch varieties growing in Alaska is suitable for pulping and papermaking by several processes. It is satisfactory also for furniture, cabinetmaking, veneer and plywood, handles, boxes and crates, clothes pins, spools, and bobpins. Other uses of paper birch southward are turned and carved articles, toothpicks, and toys. The wood works easily and takes finishes and stains satisfactorily. The uniformity of grain is a distinct advantage in the manufacture of veneers and plywoods.

Northern Indians made canoes and various small articles from the smooth thin bark. Because of its durability and ease of working, bark was used as sheeting under sod on cabin roofs. Birch trees are planted also as ornamentals to display their attractive bark.

50a. WESTERN PAPER BIRCH

(*Betula papyrifera* var. *commutata* (Reg.) Fern.)

Other names: paper birch; *Betula papyrifera* var. *occidentalis* auth. and ssp. *occidentalis* auth., not B. *occidentalis* Hook.

Small to medium-sized tree 20–60 ft. (6–18 m.) high and 4–16 in. (10–40 cm.) in trunk diameter. Trunks often clustered, having originated from sprouts at base of old trees. **Leaf blades** ovate, 1½–3½ in. (4–9 cm.) long, 1–2½ in. (2.5–6 cm.) wide, mostly long-pointed or short-pointed at apex, rounded at base, coarsely doubly toothed, dark green and hairless above, beneath slightly hairy, especially in angles of veins; petioles slightly hairy and glandular. **Twigs** orange brown, with few hairs and whitish dots when young. **Bark** on small trunks smooth and usually reddish (coppery or purplish) brown, sometimes blackish, on larger trunks becoming papery and pinkish brown, pinkish, or sometimes whitish.

Male **flower** catkins 3–4 in. (7.5–10 cm.) long, narrow. **Fruits** cone-like, 1–1½ in. (2.5–5 cm.) long, finely hairy, spreading; nutlets with wings broader than body; bracts with long middle lobe and 2 short lobes, hairy on edges.

Western paper birch is local and uncommon along the mainland coastal river drainages and lakes in the northern part of southeast Alaska, separated from the other Alaska tree birches. It occurs on thin, rocky soils, usually below 1500 feet (457 m.) elevation, often with lodgepole pine, following fire and on poor sites. The wood is not used locally.

Vicinity of Lynn Canal, from

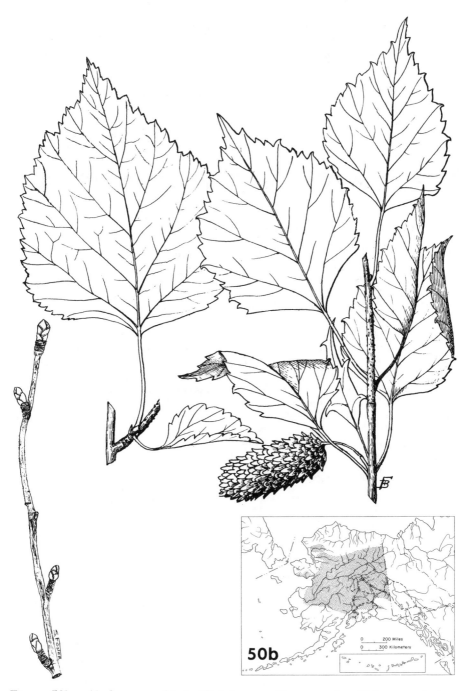

Figure 50b.—Alaska paper birch (*Betula papyrifera* var. *humilis*), natural size. Winter twig at lower left.

137

Taku River and Juneau to Skagway. North Tongass National Forest. Southern Yukon Territory east to District of Mackenzie and Saskatchewan and south to Montana and Washington. Also in northern Ontario and in Northeast from Labrador and Quebec south to northern New York and Massachusetts.

50b. ALASKA PAPER BIRCH

(*Betula papyrifera* var. *humilis* (Reg.) Fern. & Raup)

Other names: Alaska white birch, Alaska birch, canoe birch, paper birch, white birch; *Betula papyrifera* ssp. *humilis* (Reg.) Hult., *B. papyrifera* var. *neoalaskana* (Sarg.) Raup, *B. alaskana* Sarg., *B. neoalaskana* Sarg., *B. resinifera* auth., not (Reg.) Britton. Small to medium-sized tree 20–80 ft. (6–24 m.) high and 4–24 in. (10–61 cm.) in trunk diameter. **Leaf blades** ovate, 1½–3 in. (4–7.5 cm.) long, 1–2 in. (2.5–5 cm.) wide, rather long-pointed, sharply to broadly wedge-shaped at base, coarsely toothed, dark green or yellow green and hairless above, beneath pale yellow green, dotted with glands and usually with angles of lower veins hairy; petioles becoming hairless. **Twigs** with many raised resinous dots. **Bark** white, or pinkish white, sometimes grayish white or yellowish white, papery.

Male **flower** catkin short, 1–1½ in. (2.5–4 cm.) long, thick, greenish brown. **Fruits** conelike, 1–1⅜ in. (2.5–3.5 cm.) long, hairless, hanging down or spreading. Nutlets with wings broader than body; bracts with middle lobe usually longer than the blunt, diamond-shaped lateral lobes, hairy on edges.

Alaska paper birch is the variety common through the interior up to tree line. It is best developed on warm slopes with moist porous soils but is also common on cold north slopes and poorly drained lowlands following fires. Birch is generally in a mixture with white or black spruce, which replace it in the successional sequence after fire. At Cook Inlet there are important birch forests. Here paper birch has its best development on the rolling benchlands and lower foothill slopes up to an altitude of about 800 ft. (244 m.).

Common in spruce-birch forests throughout most of interior Alaska but not in southeast. North to south slopes of Brooks Range and northwest to Kobuk and Noatak Rivers and to coast along south side of Seward Peninsula; south to Unalakleet and Russian Mission on Yukon River. South of Alaska Range in Susitna Valley, Kenai Peninsula, and Copper River valley. Chugach National Forest, Mt. McKinley National Park. East to Yukon Territory and District of Mackenzie and south to Saskatchewan and British Columbia.

50c. KENAI BIRCH

(*Betula papyrifera* var. *kenaica* (W. H. Evans) Henry)

Other names: Kenai paper birch, black birch, red birch; *Betula kenaica* W. H. Evans, *B. kamtschatica* var. *kenaica* (W. H. Evans) Jansson.

Small to medium-sized tree 20–80 ft. (6–24 m.) high and 4–12 in. (10–30 cm.) in trunk diameter, rarely 18 in. (46 cm.). **Leaf blades** ovate or nearly triangular, 1½–2 in. (4–5 cm.) long, 1–1¾ in. (2.5–4.5 cm.) wide, relatively thick, usually short-pointed, broadly wedge-shaped or rounded at base, margin coarsely and often doubly toothed with white hairs, dull dark green

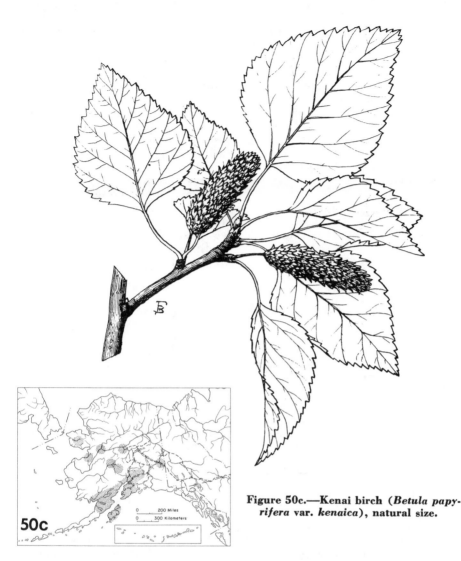

Figure 50c.—Kenai birch (*Betula papy-rifera* var. *kenaica*), natural size.

and often slightly hairy above, beneath pale yellow green and dotted with glands and hairy on veins; petioles usually hairless. **Twigs** reddish brown hairy, and often with resin dots when young, becoming blackish and hairless. **Bark** usually dark brown, often blackish or reddish brown, sometimes becoming pinkish or grayish white, papery.

Male **flower** catkins short, about 1 in. (2.5 cm.) long, narrow, dark brown. **Fruits** conelike, about 1 in.

(2.5 cm.) long, erect or spreading. Nutlets with wings slightly narrower than body; bracts, with lobes of about equal length, rounded at apex, side bracts slightly diamond-shaped.

Kenai birch, named from Kenai Peninsula and known only from Alaska, is found in the southern part of the spruce-birch interior forests but not southeast. Cook Inlet, Kenai Peninsula area, and west to Kodiak Island and base of Alaska Peninsula at Kaguyak and

139

Brooks River. Chugach National Forest, Katmai National Monument, Kenai National Moose Range, Kodiak National Wildlife Refuge.

Northward this variety intergrades or hybridizes with Alaska paper birch. Specimens apparently nearer Kenai birch have been reported from interior Alaska along the Tanana, Yukon, and Kuskokwim Rivers, at Unalakleet, and on Seward Peninsula.

ALDER (*Alnus*)

Alaska has 4 kinds of alders, 3 of which reach tree size. All are treated here as separate species, though 2 intergrade and have been united as varieties of same species. Alders are easily recognized by their smooth gray bark with horizontal lines (lenticels) and the clusters of 3–9 slender-stalked old dead, hard, blackish or dark brown conelike elliptic fruits generally present. Male flowers in narrow catkins, 3 above a scale, composed of 4 sepals and usually 4 stamens. Female catkins short, about ½ in. (12 mm.) long; flowers 2 above a scale, composed of ovary and 2 styles. Alder roots, like those of legumes, often have root nodules, swellings that fix nitrogen from the air and enrich the soil.

Key to the 4 Alaska Species

Leaves yellow green above, shiny on both sides and especially beneath, sticky when young, edges with relatively long-pointed teeth; stalks about as long as conelike fruits; nutlets with 2 broad wings; winter buds of overlapping scales.
Leaves not lobed on edges; conelike fruits ⅜–⅝ in. (10–15 mm.) long; shrub of interior Alaska _____ _____ 51. American green alder (*Alnus crispa*)
Leaves wavy lobed on edges; conelike fruits ½–¾ in. (12–20 mm.) long; shrub or small tree of southern and southeast Alaska _____ _____ 52. Sitka alder (*Alnus sinuata*)
Leaves dark green above, dull, not sticky when young, edges with short-pointed teeth; stalks shorter than conelike fruits; nutlets with 2 narrow wings or none; winter buds of 3 exposed scales meeting at edges.
Leaves thick with edges curled under slightly, with rusty hairs along veins beneath; conelike fruits ½–1 in. (12–25 mm.) long; nutlets with 2 narrow wings _____ 53. red alder (*Alnus rubra*)
Leaves thin with edges flat, finely hairy or nearly hairless beneath; conelike fruits ⅜–⅝ in. (10–15 mm.) long; nutlets almost wingless _____ 54. thinleaf alder (*Alnus tenuifolia*)

51. AMERICAN GREEN ALDER

(*Alnus crispa* (Ait.) Pursh)

Other names: green alder, mountain alder; *Alnus viridis* Vill. ssp. *crispa* (Ait.) Löve & Löve.

Spreading shrub 3–13 ft. (1–4 m.) tall. **Leaves** with short slender dark red brown petioles ¼–½ in. (6–12 mm.) long. Blades ovate or broadly elliptic, mostly 1½–3 in. (4–7.5 cm.) long, 1–2 in. (2.5–5 cm.) wide, sometimes larger, relatively thick, short-pointed at apex, rounded or broadly wedge-shaped

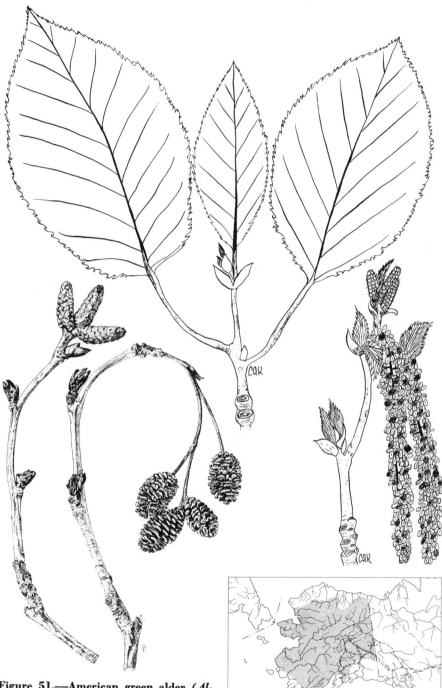

Figure 51.—American green alder (*Alnus crispa*), natural size. Winter twigs with buds of male catkins and old fruits at lower left; female and male catkins at lower right.

51

| | 200 Miles |
| 0 | 300 Kilometers |

at base, edges sharply and finely toothed with long-pointed nearly equal or even teeth and not lobed, slightly sticky resinous on both surfaces, above shiny yellow green and hairless, beneath pale green and with tufts of whitish hairs in vein angles. **Twigs** hairless, smooth, dark brownish red, with many light dots (lenticels), becoming dark gray. **Buds** long-pointed, ¼–⅜ in. (6–10 mm.) long, red-brown, with scales hairy on edges.

Male flower clusters (catkins) ¾–3 in. (2–7.5 cm.) long, about ⅜ in. (1 cm.) wide, of many reddish brown sticky scales and many yellow stamens. Female flower clusters 1–7, ¼–⅜ in. (6–10 mm.) long. **Fruits** conelike, ⅜–⅝ in. (10–15 mm.) long, ⁵⁄₁₆–⅜ in. (8–10 mm.) wide, brown to dark brown with slender stalk ¼–½ in. (6–12 mm.) long. Nutlets elliptic, flattened, almost ⅛ in. (3 mm.) long, with 2 broad wings. Flowering May–June, fruit maturing in July.

Alder twigs and buds make up an important part of the winter food of the white-tailed ptarmigan. In the fall and winter the "seeds" (nutlets) are eaten by many songbirds.

Common, often forming thickets on gravelly slopes and flood plains. Widely distributed in interior of central and northern Alaska north to Colville River, north slopes of Brooks Range, Firth River, Porcupine, Yukon, and Koyukuk Rivers, and west to Bering Strait. Mt. McKinley National Park, Katmai National Monument, Kenai National Moose Range, Arctic National Wildlife Range. Alaska and Yukon Territory across Canada to Labrador, Newfoundland, and Greenland, south to New York, North Carolina (high mountains), Michigan, and Oregon. Also across northern Asia.

Toward the southern coast this species intergrades with Sitka alder, which is regarded by some authors as a variety or subspecies.

52. SITKA ALDER
(*Alnus sinuata* (Reg.) Rydb.)

Other names: *Alnus crispa* (Ait.) Pursh ssp. *sinuata* (Reg.) Hult., *A. fruticosa* Rupr. var. *sinuata* (Reg.) Hult., *A. sitchensis* (Reg.) Sarg.

Deciduous shrub 5–15 ft. (1.5–4.5 m.) high or a small tree to 30 ft. (9 m.) tall and 8 in. (20 cm.) in trunk diameter. **Leaf blades** ovate, 2½–5 in. (6–12.5 cm.) long, 1½–3 in. (4–7.5 cm.) wide, short-pointed, rounded at base, shallowly wavy lobed and doubly toothed with long-pointed teeth of 2 sizes, sticky when young, speckled yellow green and shiny above, beneath lighter, shiny, and hairless or nearly so; petioles ½–¾ in. (12–20 mm.) long. **Twigs** sticky, finely hairy, and orange brown when young, becoming light gray. **Winter buds** short-stalked to stalkless on young twigs, to ½ in. (12 mm.) long, of overlapping scales. **Bark** gray to light gray, smooth and thin.

Male **flowers** in narrow catkins 3–5 in. (7.5–12.5 cm.) long. **Fruits** ½–¾ in. (12–20 mm.) long, on long slender spreading stalks ⅜–¾ in. (10–20 mm.) long, nutlets elliptic, with 2 broad wings. Flowering in May–June.

Sitka alder often is a spreading shrub, common to abundant, with many stems, forming thickets in marshes, along streams, on landslides, and in clearings, from sea level to the alpine zone above the timberline. It also becomes a small tree, often with many trunks.

This pioneer species follows disturbances such as landslides, logging, or glacial retreat. It requires mineral soil seedbed and develops rapidly on moist sites but grows on soils too sterile for other trees. Sitka spruce often becomes established at the same time. Alder acts as a nurse tree, improving soil conditions, and adding organic matter and nitrogen. It thrives with

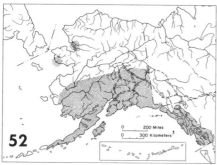

52

Figure 52.—Sitka alder (*Alnus sinuata*), natural size. Winter twig with buds of male catkins at right.

143

overhead light but is intolerant of shade and disappears from the stand when overtopped by Sitka spruce. Being smaller and hence more quickly overtopped, Sitka alder is probably not such a serious competitor as red alder on logged areas. The wood produces good fuel and is used for smoking fish.

Southeast and southern Alaska along the Pacific coast. Throughout southeast Alaska northwest to head of Lynn Canal at Skagway and Yakutat Bay, west along coast to Afognak and Kodiak Islands, Alaska Peninsula, and eastern Aleutian Islands. Also local in western Alaska on Bering Sea (Nushagak and Nome). South Tongass, North Tongass, and Chugach National Forests, Glacier Bay and Katmai National Monuments, Kenai National Moose Range, Kodiak Island and Aleutian Islands National Wildlife Refuges. Alaska and Yukon Territory southeast to southwestern Alberta, western Montana, and northern California. Also in northeastern Asia.

Intergrades with American green alder (*Alnus crispa* (Ait.) Pursh), especially northward in interior, and often treated as a variety or subspecies of that species. Sitka alder reaches larger size than American green alder, becoming a small tree, and has mostly larger leaves with margins wavy lobed as well as toothed, also larger, longer stalked cones.

53. RED ALDER

(*Alnus rubra* Bong.)

Other names: western alder; *Alnus oregona* Nutt.

Small to medium-sized deciduous tree 20–40 ft. (6–12 m.) tall, with straight trunk 4–16 in. (10–40 cm.) in diameter. **Leaf blades** ovate or elliptic, 3–5 in. (7.5–12.5 cm.) long, 1¾–3 in. (4.5–7.5 cm.) wide, short

pointed at both ends, shallowly wavy lobed and doubly toothed with both large and small teeth, thick, edges curled under slightly, dark green and nearly hairless above, beneath pale with rusty hairs along veins; petioles ¼–¾ in. (6–20 mm.) long. **Twigs** hairy when young, becoming dark red with light dots. **Winter buds** stalked, to ⅜ in. (1 cm.) long, dark red. **Bark** gray, splotched with white, smooth or becoming slightly scaly, thin. **Wood** nearly white when freshly cut, soon turning to light reddish brown, fine-textured, moderately lightweight, soft.

Male **flowers** in narrow catkins 3–6 in. (7.5–15 cm.) long. **Fruits** on short stalks ¼–½ in. (6–12 mm.) conelike, ½–1 in. (12–25 mm.) long; nutlets elliptic, with 2 narrow wings. Flowering in April–May.

Red alder is common throughout southeast Alaska on stream bottoms with rich, rocky, moist soils and along beaches where creeks enter the sea. On landslides it forms almost impenetrable thickets, often with Sitka alder.

Red alder is a pioneer species on mineral soil, thriving on moist sites. It is common below 1,000 feet elevation and absent at higher elevations, where Sitka alder is frequent. Being larger, red alder is more competitive and requires more time for overtopping. Both species come in along roadsides and where ground is disturbed after logging. They are a problem in road maintenance, requiring continual clearing of shoulders and side slopes. Seeds of both species are produced within five years and being tiny are blown great distances.

Of little economic importance in Alaska at present, red alder is the leading hardwood southward in the Pacific Northwest, where it is a larger tree and is made into furniture. The wood is used also in smoking meat and fish and for wood carving.

Throughout southeast Alaska northwest to Yakutat Bay. South Tongass and North Tongass National Forests, Glacier Bay National Monument. Pacific coast region from southeast Alaska southeast to southern California; also locally east to northern Idaho.

53

Figure 53.—Red alder (*Alnus rubra*), natural size. Male and female catkins at upper right.

0   200 Miles
0   300 Kilometers

145

54. THINLEAF ALDER

(*Alnus tenuifolia* Nutt.)

Other names: *Alnus incana* (L.) Moench ssp. *tenufolia* (Nutt.) Breitung, *A. incana* ssp. *rugosa* var. *occidentalis* (Dippel) C. L. Hitchc.

Deciduous large shrub or small tree 15–30 ft. (4.5–9 m.) high, commonly forming clumps with trunks to 8 in. (20 cm.) in diameter. **Leaf blades** ovate or elliptic, 2–6 in. (5–15 cm.) long, 1¼–2½ in. (3–6 cm.) wide, short-pointed, rounded at base, shallowly wavy lobed and doubly toothed with both large and small teeth, thin, dark green and becoming hairless above, beneath pale green and hairy or nearly hairless; petioles ¼–1 in. (6–25 mm.) long. **Twigs** reddish and hairy when young, becoming gray. **Bark** gray to dark gray, smooth, becoming reddish gray, thin and scaly. **Wood** light brown.

Male **flowers** in narrow catkins 1½–3 in. (4–7.5 cm.) long. **Fruits** on short stalks less than ¼ in. (6 mm.) long, conelike ⅜–⅝ in. (1–1.5 cm.) long; nutlets elliptic, almost wingless. Flowering in May–June.

Large trunks have been cut for poles. The wood is used for smoking salmon. Thinleaf alder with the larger willows commonly forms thickets along streams in central and southern Alaska. Interior Alaska from Yukon River valley south to base of Alaska Peninsula at Katmai, Kenai Peninsula, and Copper River valley. Also north end of southeast Alaska from vicinity of Juneau to Glacier Bay. North Tongass and Chugach National Forests. Glacier Bay and Katmai National Monuments. Alaska and Yukon Territory southeast to southwestern Saskatchewan and south in mountains to New Mexico and California.

By some authors this alder of western North America is treated as a variety or subspecies of European speckled alder (*Alnus incana* (L.) Moench), of Eurasia. It is closely related also to speckled alder (*A. rugosa* (Du Roi) Spreng.), of eastern Canada and Northeastern United States, which also has been united with the Old World species.

MISTLETOE FAMILY

(Loranthaceae)

Parasitic dwarf shrubs on woody plants, with jointed brittle stems, brown, yellow, or green. Leaves opposite, small or reduced to scales. Flowers small, male and female on different plants (dioecious), calyx 2–6-parted, corolla none, stamens as many as parts of calyx, pistil with 1-celled inferior ovary and stigma. Fruit a berry, often sticky. Only 1 species in Alaska.

55. HEMLOCK DWARF-MISTLETOE

(*Arceuthobium tsugense* (Rosend.) G. N. Jones)

Other names: dwarf-mistletoe; *Arceuthobium campylopodum* Engelm. f. *tsugense* (Rosend.) Gill.

Parasitic dwarf shrub on twigs, lower branches, and trunks of hemlock trees, greenish to reddish or brownish, usually inconspicuous, hairless. **Stems** slightly fleshy, of short thick angled joints enlarged at nodes, brittle. Male plants 1½–4 in. (4–10 cm.) high, much branched; female plants smaller, less branched. **Leaves** reduced to paired brownish scales ¹⁄₁₆ in. (1.5 mm.) long, joined at base in ring around twig.

Flowers minute, paired and stalkless or nearly so at sides of twig; male flowers less than ⅛ in. (3 mm.) broad, yellowish, with 3–4

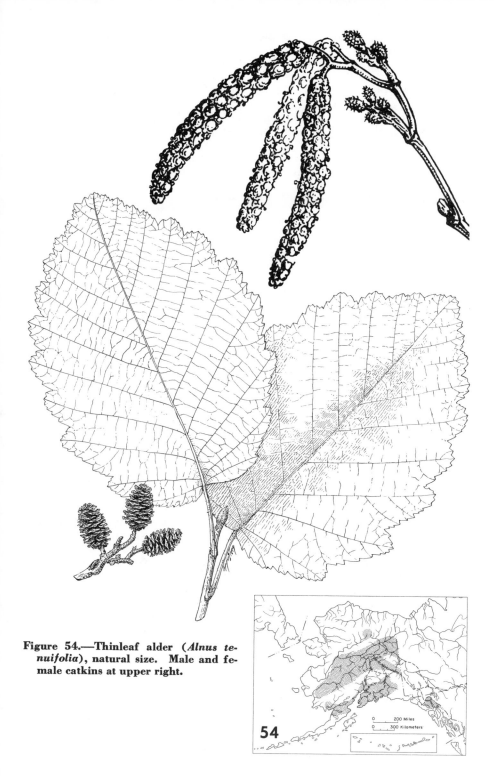

Figure 54.—Thinleaf alder (*Alnus te-nuifolia*), natural size. Male and fe-male catkins at upper right.

147

sepals and 3–4 stamens; female flowers about $\frac{1}{16}$ in. (1.5 mm.) broad, with 2 persistent sepals and pistil with inferior ovary and style. **Fruit** an elliptic flattened bluish berry $\frac{1}{8}$–$\frac{3}{16}$ in. (3–5 mm.) long on curved stalk, with mucilaginous or sticky flesh, discharging or shooting the sticky seed suddenly with force to about 20 ft. (6 m.) distance. Flowering in August–September, fruit maturing the following September.

The deformed branches of infected trees, including witches-brooms (dense broomlike masses), swollen limbs, and swollen twigs, aid in recognition. However, these symptoms may have other causes. Also, there are cup scars after the limbs die back. Large burls or swellings are formed by trunk infections.

Hemlock dwarf-mistletoe is Alaska's only parasitic woody plant and sole example of the mistletoe family. Largely confined to hemlocks, as the scientific name suggests. Western hemlock (*Tsuga heterophylla*) is the commonest host. However, this species occurs also on mountain hemlock (*Tsuga mertensiana*) and very rarely on Sitka spruce (*Picea sitchensis*). Southward it has been found on pines, firs, and other kinds of spruces.

This parasite is of considerable economic importance in southeast Alaska, though estimates of the damage are not available. Growth of hemlocks is slowed somewhat, but the trees are not killed. Many old-growth stands are infected, while others are not. Control measures have been undertaken on the National Forests. Practical control is by clearcutting infected stands. To remove the seed source of the parasite and to be effective, the infected understory plants down to about 6 ft. (2 m.) high must be cut. Elsewhere, the slash is sometimes burned.

Generally distributed through coastal forests of southeast Alaska, common but seldom noticed or collected. On mainland and islands north to Juneau and Haines at altitudes up to about 500 ft. (152 m.), to 1,100 ft. (335 m.) on Chichagof Island. South Tongass and North Tongass National Forests. Southeast Alaska south in coastal forests to Oregon and to Sierra Nevada in central California. Haines (latitude 59° 13′ N.) is the northernmost known locality of the mistletoe family not only in North America but apparently in the world.

GOOSEBERRY FAMILY

(Grossulariaceae)

One genus, *Ribes*, occurs in Alaska, containing both gooseberries (2 species) and currants (5 species). Shrubs with erect, spreading, or prostrate branches. **Leaves** alternate, palmately veined and palmately lobed, frequently with glandular hairs. **Twigs** with or without prickles and spines, angled, with papery shedding bark; pith porous or spongy. **Flowers** usually in racemes, but occasionally solitary, borne on side shoots with 1 or 2 leaves at base, small; tubular base with 5 sepals larger and more conspicuous than the 5 scalelike petals; stamens 5; pistil with inferior 1-celled ovary and 2 styles. **Fruit** a many-seeded berry with dried remains of flower at tip.

Species with spines or prickles on their stems are usually called gooseberries and those with unarmed branches, currants. Both groups are utilized for making jams and jellies. The gooseberry family is sometimes included in the closely related saxifrage family (Saxifragaceae).

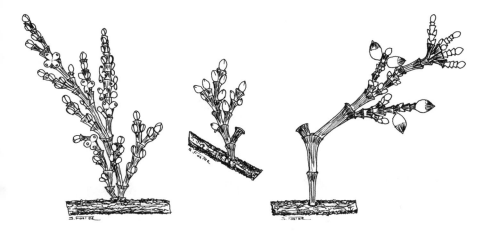

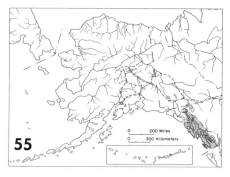

Figure 55.—Hemlock dwarf-mistletoe (*Arceuthobium tsugense*), natural size. Plant with male flowers at left; plant with female flowers in center; plant with fruits at right.

55

Key to the Alaska Species

A. Stems armed with spines and prickles; leaves small, less than 2 in. (5 cm.) long _____ 56. swamp gooseberry (*Ribes lacustre*)
AA. Stems unarmed; leaves larger, more than 2 in. (5 cm.) long.
  B. Ovary and fruit with resin dots.
    C. Racemes 6–12 in. (15–30 cm.) long, with 20–40 flowers; sepals greenish, fruit with white to bluish bloom; twigs coarse, ⅛–¼ in. (3–6 mm.) in diameter, brownish, shedding bark; leaves longer than broad, underside with resin glands ____ _____ 57. stink currant. (*Ribes bracteosum*)
    CC. Racemes 3 in. (8 cm.) long, 6–12 flowered; sepals whitish; fruit black without bluish bloom; twigs slender, ¼ in. (6 mm.) or less in diameter, gray with black spots, smooth; leaves broader than long, underside without resin glands _____ _____ 58. northern black currant. (*Ribes hudsonianum*)
  BB. Ovary and fruit without resin dots, often with stalked glands.
    D. Berries with stalked glands, red or black to dark blue; sepals green, white, or light pink; flower racemes ascending; leaves 5-lobed, divided to middle.

149

E. Berries red, sepals white to pink, without hairs; twigs fine, less than ⅛ in. (3 mm.) in diameter _____ _____ 59. skunk currant (*Ribes glandulosum*)

EE. Berries black to dark blue; sepals green to white, with hairs on back; twigs coarse, more than ⅛ in. (3 mm.) in diameter ___ 60. trailing black currant (*Ribes laxiflorum*)

DD. Berries smooth, without stalked glands, red; sepals reddish; flower racemes dropping, leaves mostly 3-lobed, occasionally with pair of smaller lobes at base, not divided to middle _____ 61. American red currant (*Ribes triste*)

56. SWAMP GOOSEBERRY
(*Ribes lacustre* (Pers.) Poir.)

Other names: prickly currant, swamp currant, swamp black currant, bristly black currant, *Ribes oxycanthoides* var. *lacustre* Pers., *R. echinatum* Dougl.

Usually a spreading shrub sometimes erect, 2–4 ft. (3–12 dm.) tall, with spiny twigs and deeply dissected **leaves** with skunklike odor. Blades 1½–2 in. (3.5–5 cm.) long and 1½–2 in. (4–5 cm.) wide, 5-lobed and divided ⅔–¾ to midrib, the lower pair of lobes smaller, each lobe again dissected into several rounded teeth. Petioles ¾–1½ in. (2–4 cm.) long, with bristly hairs. **Twigs** yellowish brown, densely to sparsely covered with sharp spines, ⅛–³⁄₁₆ in. (3–5 mm.) long with a few larger spines at nodes.

Flowers 6–15 on a drooping raceme, sepals light green to purplish, oval, ⅛ in. (2.5–3 mm.) long, covered with gland-tipped hairs. **Fruit** a berry ¼–⁵⁄₁₆ in. (6–8 mm.) in diameter, black to dark purple, bristly with gland tipped hairs. Flowering in June, fruit ripening in August.

Swamp gooseberry is an occasional shrub with white spruce and Sitka spruce in the interior and coastal forests. Because of the occurrence in isolated clumps and commonly low production and the skunklike odor, the bristly berries are infrequently used for making jellies and jams.

Along rivers of the interior, in the Cook Inlet-Kenai Peninsula area as far west as Naknek Lake in Katmai National Monument, and along the coast of southeastern Alaska. South Tongass, North Tongass, and Chugach National Forests, Glacier Bay and Katmai National Monuments. Alaska, eastward to James Bay, southern Labrador, and Newfoundland, south to Pennsylvania, Tennessee, Minnesota, Colorado, and California. Also in isolated locations in eastern Asia and northern Japan.

Canada gooseberry (*Ribes oxycanthoides* L.) has been recorded from 2 localities in south-central Alaska. This spiny shrub resembles swamp gooseberry somewhat but has flowers and fruits single or paired along the stem. The berries are edible but sour. Also from Yukon Territory to Hudson Bay, south to Michigan and Montana.

57. STINK CURRANT
(*Ribes bracteosum* Dougl.)

Other name: blue currant.

Erect to spreading shrub, 3–8 ft. (1–2.5 m.) tall, with large leaves and long racemes of flowers and fruits, and sweet, rather disagreeable odor. **Leaf** blades 3–8 in. (7.5–20 cm.) long and slightly broader, 5–7 lobed, lobes toothed at edge and short-pointed at tip, underside dotted with tiny resin

150

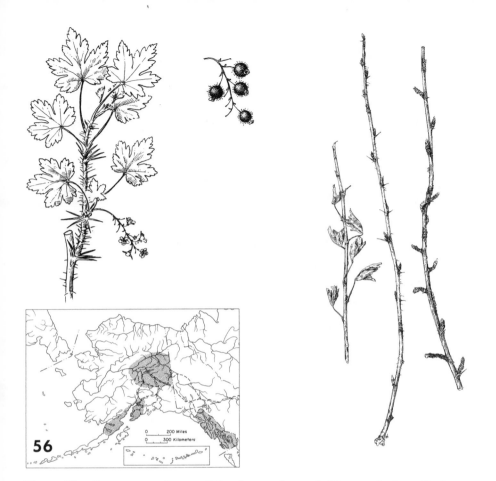

Figure 56.—Swamp gooseberry (*Ribes lacustre*), one-half natural size. Fruits at center; winter twigs at right.

glands. Petioles variable in length, from shorter to much longer than blade. **Twigs** coarse, those of previous year to ¼ in. (6 mm.) in diameter, brown to grayish, often with shredded bark; **buds** large and red.

Flowers in long erect to ascending racemes 6–12 in. (15–30 cm.) long with 20–40 flowers; stalks slender, to ⅜ in. (1 cm.) long, with leaflike bract at base often exceeding the stalk, sepals white or greenish, often with purple tinge, spreading, ⅛ in. (3–4 mm.) long;

ovary conspicuously glandular. **Fruit** a spherical berry ⅜ in. (1 cm.) in diameter, glandular, with white to bluish bloom and fetid odor. Flowering in May and June, fruit ripening in late July and August.

Stink currant occurs commonly with alder in openings in coastal spruce hemlock forests and in disturbed wet places along roadsides. In spite of the strong odor, Indians along the coast consume the fruits after mixing with salmon roe and storing for the winter.

151

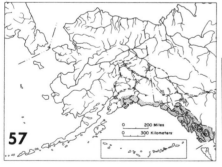

Figure 57.—Stink currant (*Ribes bracteosum*), one-half natural size.

Coastal Alaska as far north as Prince William Sound. South Tongass, North Tongass, and Chugach National Forests, Glacier Bay National Monument. From Alaska south along the coast to northwestern California.

58. NORTHERN BLACK CURRANT

(*Ribes hudsonianum* Richards.)

Other name: Hudson Bay currant.

Usually an erect shrub 3–6 ft. (1–2 m.) tall but northward often prostrate and spreading, 1–3 ft. (3–9 dm.) tall, with strong, rather unpleasant odor when leaves or berries are crushed. **Leaf** blades 3–4 in. (8–10 cm.) wide and 2–3

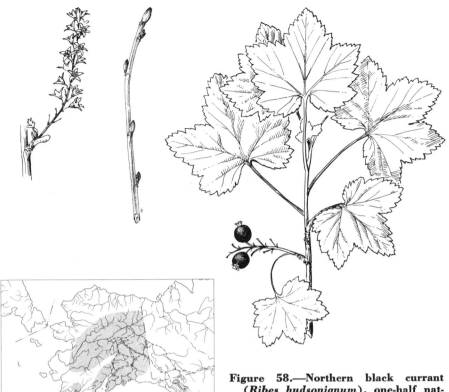

58

Figure 58.—Northern black currant (*Ribes hudsonianum*), one-half natural size. Flowers at upper left; winter twig center.

in. (5–8 cm.) long, broadly 3-lobed about ⅓ to midvein, lobes sharply toothed at edge, with resin dots and scattered hairs on lower surface; petioles about ⅔ as long as blade. **Twigs** gray and shiny, scattered with small black glands or short black hairs. **Buds** red, ⅛–¼ in. (3–6 mm.) long hairless, on short stalks.

Flowers 6–12 in short racemes 2–3 in. (5–8 cm.) long; sepals white, triangular, elongate, ⅛–³⁄₁₆ in. (3–5 mm.) long; ovary resin dotted. **Fruit** an oval berry, black, usually with resin dots but without bloom, bitter. Flowering in June and July, fruits ripening in July and August.

Northern black currant is a common shrub of boreal forests in spruce, birch, and aspen types. Near treeline it grows with alders. The berries are not utilized because of their bitter taste.

Primarily an interior species but reaching the coast at Seward, Prince William Sound, and in the vicinity of Haines and Juneau. One collection has been made at Hyder, an inland location in extreme southeastern Alaska. North to south slopes of the Brooks Range and west to lower Yukon and Kuskokwim Rivers. North Tongass, South Tongass, and Chugach National Forests, Mt. McKinley National Park, Kenai National Moose Range. Alaska east to Hudson Bay, south to Minnesota, Utah, and Oregon. A closely related species occurs in eastern Asia.

153

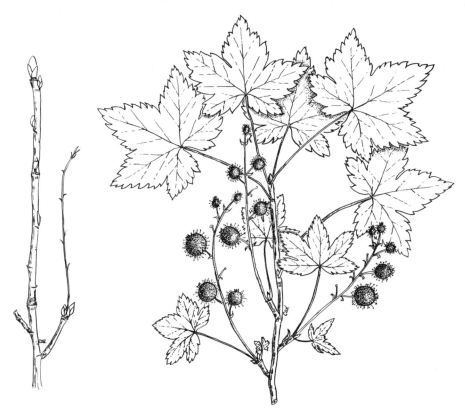

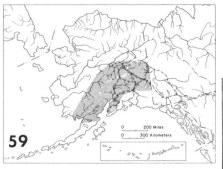

59. SKUNK CURRANT

(*Ribes glandulosum* Grauer)

Other names: fetid currant, *Ribes prostratum* L'Her.

Low shrub 2–3 ft. (0.6–0.9 m.) high with sprawling or reclining branches and strong fetid odor. **Leaf** blades 1–3 in. (2.5–7 cm.) long and slightly broader, divided nearly to middle into 5 lobes, the lower pair smaller. Petioles about equal to blade, with a few bristle-like hairs near base. **Twigs** smooth and grayish, becoming brown and with shredded bark with age. **Buds** ¼–⅜ in. (6–10 mm.) long, reddish, with fine white hairs at tip of scales.

Flowers 10–20 in erect racemes, 3–4 in. (7.5–10 cm.) long that droop when the fruit ripens, individual flower and fruit stalks (pedicels) 3/16–5/16 in. (5–8 mm.) long with gland-tipped hairs; sepals spreading, white to pinkish, rounded, 1/16 in. (2 mm.) long; ovary with gland-tipped hairs. **Fruits** bristly red berries ¼ in. (6 mm.) in diam-

154

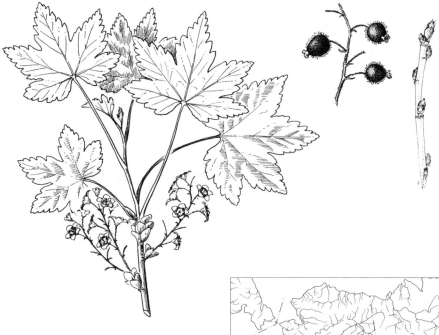

Figure 60.—Trailing black currant (*Ribes laxiflorum*), one-half natural size. Fruits and winter twig at upper right.

60

eter, with gland-tipped hairs. Flowering in June, berries ripening in late July and early August.

Skunk currant has a scattered distribution in interior Alaska, most commonly in disturbed areas beside roads and adjacent to cleared fields. In spite of its strong odor, it makes excellent jelly.

Locally abundant in interior Alaska at Fairbanks and Manley Hot Springs, south to Bristol Bay and Kenai Peninsula. Mt. McKinley National Park. Alaska to southern British Columbia and east across Canada to Hudson Bay, Labrador, and Newfoundland, south in mountains to North Carolina and to Wisconsin and Minnesota.

60. TRAILING BLACK CURRANT

(*Ribes laxiflorum* Pursh)

Usually a low spreading shrub with branches running along the ground but sometimes vinelike and climbing on erect shrubs. **Leaf** blades 2½–3 in. (6–8 cm.) long and 3–4 in. (7–10 cm.) across, divided into 5 deep, triangular lobes doubly toothed along edge with sharp or rounded teeth, lower surface light green with small yellow glands near base. Petiole 2–3 in. (5–7.5 cm.) long. **Twigs** yellow brown and hairy when young, stout, ⅛–³⁄₁₆ (3–5 mm.) in diameter, becoming dark brown and

155

slightly fissured. **Buds** $\frac{1}{4}$–$\frac{5}{16}$ in. (6–8 mm.) long, light to dark red, hairy on surface and edges.

Flowers 10–20 in a raceme 4–6 in. (10–14 cm.) long; sepals $\frac{1}{8}$ in. (3 mm.) long, greenish white, red or dark purple, broadly triangular and rounded at tip; with gland-tipped hairs on ovary and pedicel $\frac{1}{4}$ in. (6–8 mm.) long. **Fruits** black berries $\frac{1}{2}$–$\frac{5}{8}$ in. (12–15 mm.) in diameter with bluish bloom and gland-tipped hairs on surface, with fetid odor when crushed. Flowering in early to late May at the time of leafing, fruits ripening in late July to early August.

Trailing black currant is primarily a low spreading shrub of disturbed ground, open meadows, cutover forest land, and dense spruce-hemlock forests of coastal Alaska. In Oregon and Washington, this shrub may become vinelike and reach heights of 20 ft. (6 m.), but in Alaska it is seldom more than 4 ft. (1.2 m.) high.

From Susitna Valley and Kenai Peninsula southwest along coast. South Tongass, North Tongass, and Chugach National Forests, Glacier Bay National Monument, Kenai National Moose Range. East to Alberta and Idaho and south to California.

61. AMERICAN RED CURRANT

(*Ribes triste* Pall.)

Other name: northern red currant.

Low spreading shrub with bright red berries, branches prostrate and frequently rooting at nodes, sometimes erect to 2–3 ft. (6–9 dm.) high. **Leaf** blades 4 in. (10 cm.) long and 2–3 in. (5–8 cm.) broad but along coast becoming somewhat larger (10 x 4 in. or 25 x 10 cm.), usually 3-lobed but often with pair of small lobes near base, lobes broadly triangular and coarsely toothed along edges. Petiole $\frac{1}{2}$–$\frac{2}{3}$ as long as blade. Young **twigs** smooth and light brown but soon becoming shredded and reddish brown, a characteristic feature in winter. **Buds** dark red, $\frac{3}{16}$–$\frac{1}{4}$ in. (5–6 mm.) long.

Flowers 6–20 on a drooping raceme 2–4 in. (5–10 cm.) long; sepals rounded, $\frac{1}{16}$ in. (2 mm.) long, purplish, inconspicuous. **Fruit** a translucent red berry $\frac{1}{4}$–$\frac{3}{8}$ in. (6–10 mm.) in diameter, smooth, sour. Flowering in May and early June before or with the leaves, fruit ripening in August.

American red currant is a rather common shrub in the white spruce and paper birch forests of the interior of Alaska. North and west of the treeline, it is found in willow and alder thickets in protected ravines. In southeast Alaska, it grows only at the heads of some of the fiords usually in association with alder thickets. American red currant closely resembles the commercially grown currants and is widely used in Alaska for jellies and jams as well as eaten raw.

Mostly within the boreal forests of Alaska but occasionally growing beyond the treeline as at Umiat on the north slope of the Brooks Range, extending to the Bering Sea at Norton Sound. In southeast Alaska at head of Lynn Canal in the vicinity of Haines and Skagway. Chugach National Forest, Katmai National Monument, Mt. McKinley National Park, Kenai National Moose Range. East across Canada to Labrador and Newfoundland, south to West Virginia, Minnesota, South Dakota, and Oregon. Also in northeastern Asia.

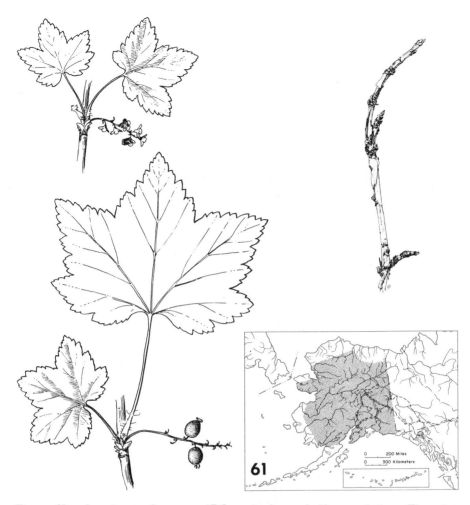

Figure 61.—American red currant (*Ribes triste*), one-half natural size. Flowering twig at upper left; winter twig at right.

ROSE FAMILY

(Rosaceae)

The rose family (Rosaceae) is well represented in Alaska by 22 species and 10 genera of woody plants among the State's 65 native species. Distinguishing characters are as follows: (1) leaves alternate, simple or pinnately or palmately compound, with paired stipules; (2) flowers regular, often large and showy or small and many, with cuplike base, 5 sepals mostly persistent, 5 petals mostly white or less commonly pink, purple, or yellow, many stamens, and usually 1 pistil with 2–5—celled ovary (often inferior) and 2–5 styles (sometimes many simple pistils); and (3) fruit variable, like an apple (pome) or plum (drupe), aggregate of many 1-seeded fruits ("berry"), or many separate fruits. Numerous wild and cultivated fruits and ornamental plants belong to this family. Several native genera produce fruits edible to mankind as well as

157

wildlife, for example, serviceberry (*Amelanchier*), crab apple (*Malus*), raspberry (*Rubus*), and strawberry (*Fragaria*). Others, such as mountain-ash (*Sorbus*), mountain-avens (*Dryas*), and spirea (*Spiraea*) are ornamentals. Rose (*Rosa*) is both ornamental and edible, rose hips being a good source of vitamin C.

Four native species of the rose family and another naturalized species become small trees in Alaska. All belong to the apple sub-family and have juicy or mealy fruits resembling small apples. These species are Pacific serviceberry (*Amelanchier florida*), Oregon crab apple (*Malus diversifolia*), Greene mountain-ash (*Sorbus scopulina*), Sitka mountain-ash (*Sorbus sitchensis*), and the naturalized European mountain-ash (*Sorbus aucuparia*).

62. PACIFIC NINEBARK

(*Physocarpus capitatus* (Pursh) Kuntze)

Other name: *Physocarpus opulifolius* (L.) Maxim. var. *tomentellus* (Ser.) Boivin.
Spreading to erect deciduous shrub 3–16 ft. (1–5 m.) high. **Leaves** alternate, with narrow paired stipules less than ¼ in. (6 mm.) long, shedding early, and slender petioles ½–1¼ in. (1.2–3 cm.) long. Blades ovate to heart-shaped, 1¼–3 in. (3–7.5 cm.) long and wide, palmately 3–5 lobed about half to midrib, the lobes short-pointed and irregularly or double toothed, above dark green with sparse star-shaped hairs or hairless, beneath paler and often with star-shaped hairs. **Twigs** angled, hairless or with minute star-shaped hairs. **Bark** peeling and shedding in long strips (hence the common name), exposing the orange-brown inner bark.

Flower clusters (corymbs) terminal, much-branched, flattened, 1½–2 in. (4–5 cm.) across. **Flowers** white, nearly ½ in. (12 mm.) across, composed of greenish cup-shaped base (hypanthium), 5 long-pointed light green persistent sepals ⅛ in. (3 mm.) long, with star-shaped hairs, 5 white rounded petals about ³⁄₁₆ in. (5 mm.) long, about 30 stamens as long as petals or longer and 3–5 pistils slightly united at base with 1-celled ovary hairless or nearly so, 2–4 ovules, and slender style. **Fruits** 3–5 pod-like (follicles), ¼–⅜ in. (6–10 mm.) long, egg-shaped, swollen, ending in long-pointed style, light brown, opening on 2 lines, persistent in winter. **Seeds** 2–4, more than ¹⁄₁₆ in. (2 mm.) long, pear-shaped, shiny, light brown. Collected with flowers and fruit in July and August.

Moist soil, streambanks, near coast, probably uncommon and local. Extreme southeast Alaska, collected at Kazan, Nawashy, and Le Conte Bay. South Tongass National Forest. Southeast Alaska south in lower mountain slopes to western Washington, western Oregon, and central and southern California, also in northern Idaho.

Plants of related species are grown as ornamentals.

SPIREA (*Spiraea*)

Deciduous shrubs with alternate simple small **leaves**, short petioles, and blades with toothed edges, without stipules. **Flowers** many in much-branched terminal clusters, small, with cup-shaped base (hypanthium), 5 persistent sepals, 5 rounded white or pink petals, many stamens, and mostly 5 distinct pistils composed of 1-celled ovary, 2–several ovules, and slender persistent style. **Fruits** mostly 5 podlike (follicles), splitting open on 1 line, containing 2–several minute seeds.

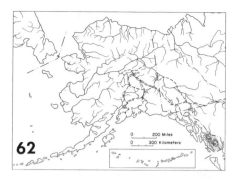

62

Figure 62.—Pacific ninebark (*Physo-carpus capitatus*), one-half natural size.

Key to the 2 Alaska Species

Flower clusters flat-topped to half round, petals white; leaves rounded at both ends, with edges mostly toothed nearly to base _____ _____ 63. Beauverd spirea (*Spiraea beauverdiana*)
Flower clusters conic, much longer than broad, petals pink to rose; leaves short-pointed to rounded at both ends, with edges toothed in upper half _____ 64. Douglas spirea (*Spiraea douglasii*)

63. BEAUVERD SPIREA

(*Spiraea beauverdiana* Schneid.)

Other name: Alaska spirea.

Small much-branched deciduous shrub 1–2 (4) ft. (3–6 (12) dm.) high. **Leaves** with short petioles $\frac{1}{16}$ in. (2 mm.) long. Blades elliptic to ovate, $\frac{5}{8}$–2 in. (1.5–5 cm.) long, $\frac{3}{8}$–1$\frac{1}{4}$ in. (1–3 cm.) wide, rounded at both ends, edges sharply toothed nearly to base (sometimes almost without teeth), above dull green and hairless or nearly so, beneath paler and often finely hairy. **Twigs** slender, purplish brown, hairy when young, afterwards outer bark shedding in long thin strips. **Buds** about $\frac{1}{16}$ in. (2 mm.) long, of few slightly hairy scales.

Flower clusters (corymbs or headlike) terminal, flattened to half round, $\frac{3}{4}$–1$\frac{1}{2}$ in. (2–4 cm.) across.

Flowers many, crowded, short-stalked, small, about $\frac{1}{4}$ in. (6 mm.) across, with 5 triangular sepals bent down, 5 white petals (or rose-tinged in center, pink in bud) $\frac{1}{16}$ in. (2 mm.) long, many white stamens more than twice as long as petals, and 5 pistils. **Fruits** usually 5 podlike (follicles) less than $\frac{1}{8}$ in. (3 mm.) long, shiny brown, finely hairy, containing 2–several narrow seeds, persistent in winter. Flowering June–August, with mature fruits July–September.

A variable species. Plants at high altitudes are dwarfed (often less than 8 in. (2 dm.) high) with small leaves and were named a separate variety (var. *stevenii* Schneid.; *S. stevenii* (Schneid.) Rydb.) This species honors Gustave Beauverd (1867–1942), Swiss botanist.

Common in tundra, swamps, black spruce muskegs, and forests, from lowland to alpine. Almost

159

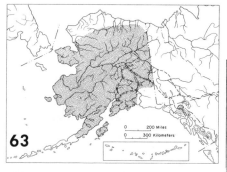

Figure 63.—Beauverd spirea (*Spiraea beauverdiana*), natural size. Winter twig with old fruits at right.

tional Moose Range, Kodiak National Wildlife Refuge, Arctic National Wildlife Range. Also Yukon Territory, District of Mackenzie, and northeastern Asia.

64. DOUGLAS SPIREA

(*Spiraea douglasii* Hook.)

Other names: Menzies spirea; *Spiraea menziesii* Hook., *S. douglasii* var. *menziesii* (Hook.) Presl and ssp. *menziesii* (Hook.) Calder & Taylor.

throughout Alaska except extreme north, Aleutian Islands, and southeast part. Chugach and North Tongass National Forests, Mt. McKinley National Park, Katmai National Monument, Kenai Na-

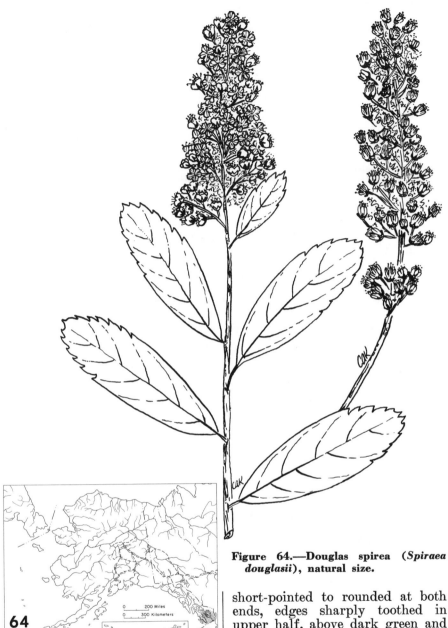

64

0 200 Miles
0 300 Kilometers

Figure 64.—Douglas spirea (*Spiraea douglasii*), natural size.

Erect deciduous shrub 3–5 ft. (1–1.5 m.) high. **Leaves** with short hairy petioles about ⅛ in. (3 mm.) long. Blades elliptic to oblong, 1¼–3 in. (3–7.5 cm.) long and ⅜–1¼ in. (1–3 cm.) wide, short-pointed to rounded at both ends, edges sharply toothed in upper half, above dark green and usually hairless, beneath pale green and sometimes hairy. **Twigs** slender, reddish brown, with fine soft hairs when young, sometimes nearly hairless, becoming dark brown and hairless. **Buds** 1/16 in. (2 mm.) long, scaly, white hairy toward apex.

161

Flower clusters (panicles) terminal, 1½–6 in. (4–15 cm.) long, conic, several times as long as broad, mostly finely hairy. Flowers many, crowded, short-stalked, small, ¼ in. (6 mm.) across, with 5 triangular sepals bent down, 5 pink to rose petals, round to obovate, 1⁄16 in. (2 mm.) long, many pink to rose stamens, and 5 pistils. Fruits 5 podlike (follicles) ⅛ in. (3 mm.) long, shiny brown, hairless or nearly so, containing 2 to several narrow seeds, persistent in winter. Collected in flower in July and August, with mature fruits in September.

Moist soil, especially borders of streams and lakes. Ketchikan and elsewhere in extreme southeastern Alaska. South Tongass National Forest. Southeast Alaska along coast and inland to northern California, eastern Oregon, and central Idaho.

Named for the discoverer, David Douglas (1798–1834), Scotch botanical explorer. Plants of Alaska and adjacent coast of British Columbia have been accepted also as a separate species, Menzies spirea (*Spiraea menziesii* Hook.), later reduced to a variety.

stalked flowers 5⁄16 in. (8 mm.) across. Flowers composed of half-round base, 5 pointed sepals, 5 rounded spreading white petals, about 20 stamens united at base, and usually 5 pistils. Fruits 5 podlike (follicles) with several minute seeds. Flowering June–September, fruit maturing July–September.

Common, forming mats or carpets in alpine meadows near snow in mountains. On rocky peaks to 4,900 ft. (1,500 m.) altitude in Juneau Ice Field. Reported to be suitable for planting in rock gardens.

Through southeast and southern Alaska west to Kodiak Island and Alaska Peninsula and north to Alaska Range. South Tongass, North Tongass, and Chugach National Forests, Glacier Bay and Katmai National Monuments. Alaska and Yukon Territory south in mountains to Alberta, Idaho, and California.

This genus of a single species was dedicated to Friedrich P. Lütke (1797–1882), Russian admiral and geographer who visited Alaska in 1827 on his voyage around the world.

65. LUETKEA

(*Luetkea pectinata* (Pursh) Kuntze)

Other names: partridge-foot, meadow-spirea.

Creeping and mat-forming herbaceous undershrub with prostrate stems and erect leafy stems 2–6 in. (5–15 cm.) high. Leaves crowded at base, alternate above, bright green, hairless, less than 1 in. (2.5 cm.) long, twice divided into 3 narrow pointed divisions.

Flower clusters (racemes) at top of erect leafy stems, to 2 in. (5 cm.) long, bearing many small short-

66. OREGON CRAB APPLE

(*Malus diversifolia* (Bong.) Roem.)

Other names: western crab apple, wild crab apple, *Malus fusca* (Raf.) Schneid., *M. rivularis* (Dougl.) Roem., *Pyrus diversifolia* Bong., *Pyrus fusca* Raf.

Deciduous small tree to 25 ft. (7.5 m.) high, with usually several trunks to 5 in. (12.5 cm.) in diameter, much branched, or a shrub forming thickets. Leaves with slender petioles 1–2 in. (2.5–5 cm.) long, ovate, elliptic, or lance-shaped, 1½–4 in. (4–10 cm.) long, short-

162

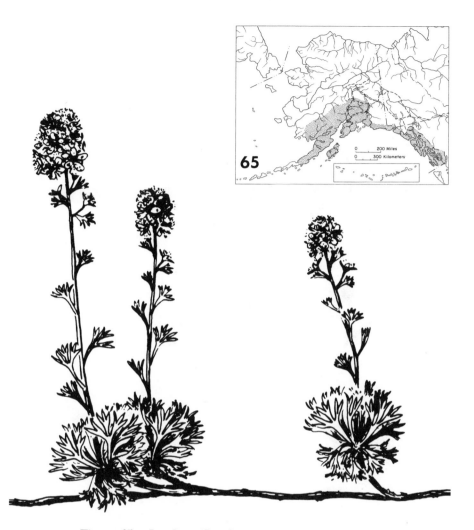

Figure 65.—Luetkea (*Luetkea pectinata*), natural size.

pointed, sharply toothed and sometimes slightly 3-lobed toward apex,
shiny green and becoming hairless
above, beneath pale and usually
slightly hairy. **Twigs** hairy when
young, becoming red and shiny and
later brown or gray, the side twigs
or spurs short and spinelike. **Winter buds** very small, ¹⁄₁₆ in. (1.5
mm.) long, rounded, brown, composed of many scales. **Bark** gray,
smooth to slightly scaly, thin.
Wood light brown, heavy, hard,
fine-textured.

Flower clusters (cymes) with
slender stalks bearing several to
many **flowers** ¾ inch (2 cm.) broad,
composed of 5 pointed hairy sepals,
5 rounded white or pink petals, 20
stamens, and pistil with inferior
2–4-celled ovary and 2–4 styles.
Fruit oblong, like a small apple
(pome), ½–¾ in. (12–20 mm.)
long, yellow or red, with thin sour
flesh and 2–4 papery lined cells,
each with 1 or 2 large seeds. Flowering in June, fruit maturing
August–October.

163

Figure 66.—Oregon crab apple (*Malus diversifolia*), natural size. Winter twigs at right.

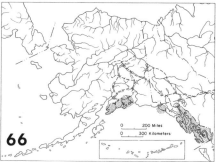

Where the trees are sufficiently large, the wood is suitable for tool handles. It is also used for smoking salmon but less commonly than alder wood. The crab apples were eaten by the Indians and are used in jellies and preserves.

Commonly a shrub forming thickets or a slow-growing small tree scattered to plentiful on beach meadow and muskeg fringes, river bottoms, low slopes, and heavy wet soils along the Pacific coast of southeast and southern Alaska. From southern end north to Haines and Skagway at Lynn Canal, also

164

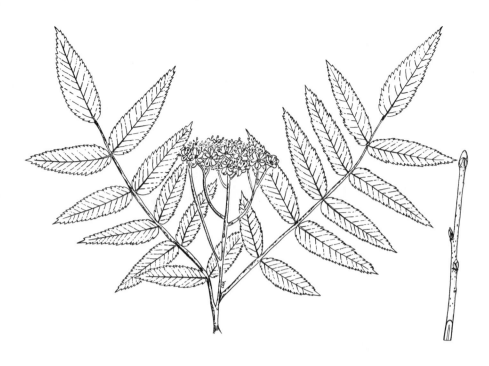

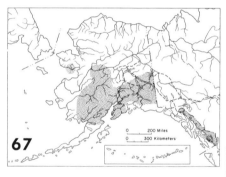

Figure 67.—Greene mountain-ash (*Sorbus scopulina*), one-half natural size. Winter twig at right.

at Yakutat and from Prince William Sound southwest to end of Kenai Peninsula. South Tongass, North Tongass, and Chugach National Forests. Alaska and southward near coast to Washington, Oregon, and northwestern California.

MOUNTAIN-ASH (*Sorbus*)

Deciduous shrubs and small trees with stout twigs and large buds with overlapping scales. **Leaves** alternate, with paired stipules attached to petiole, pinnate with 7–17 toothed leaflets paired except at end. **Flower clusters** (corymbs) terminal, much branched, showy. **Flowers** many, small, white, composed of calyx of 5 triangular persistent sepals, 5 white mostly rounded petals, 15–20 stamens, and pistil with inferior 2–5-celled ovary, 2 ovules in each cell, and 2–5 styles. **Fruits** like a small red apple (pome) with calyx at apex, 2–4-celled with 1–2 flattened seeds in each cell. Alaska has 3 native species, 2 of which become small trees, and 1 introduced and naturalized tree species.

165

Key to the 4 Alaska Species

Leaflets 9 or 11 or more, oblong or elliptic, short-pointed or rounded at apex.
    Leaflets mostly 11–15, oblong, short-pointed, edges toothed nearly to base.
        Leaflets becoming hairless; shrub or rarely small tree _____ 67. Greene mountain-ash (*Sorbus scopulina*)
        Leaflets white-hairy beneath; naturalized tree _____ 68. European mountain-ash (*Sorbus aucuparia*)
    Leaflets mostly 9 or 11, elliptic, rounded or short-pointed at apex, edges not toothed in lowest third _____ 69. Sitka mountain-ash (*Sorbus sitchensis*)
Leaflets mostly 7 or 9, lance-shaped, long-pointed (westernmost Aleutian Islands) _____ 70. Siberian mountain-ash (*Sorbus sambucifolia*)

67. GREENE MOUNTAIN-ASH

(*Sorbus scopulina* Greene)

Other names: western mountain-ash; *Sorbus alaskana* G. N. Jones not Hollick, *S. andersonii* G. N. Jones, *Pyrus scopulina* (Greene) Longyear.

Deciduous shrub 3–13 ft. (1–4 m.) high, rarely becoming a small tree to 20 ft. (6 m.) high and 4 in. (10 cm.) d.b.h. **Leaves** pinnate, 4–9 in. (10–23 cm.) long, with paired, very narrow hairless stipules ¼–⅜ in. (6–10 mm.) long. Leaflets 11–15, stalkless, oblong-lanceolate, 1¼–2½ in. (3–6 cm.) long and ⅜–¾ in. (1–2 cm.) wide, unequal and rounded at base, short- or long-pointed at apex, edges sharply toothed almost to base, becoming hairless, above shiny dark green, beneath slightly paler. **Twigs** with whitish hairs when young, with scattered elliptic dots (lenticels). **Buds** conical, dark reddish brown, inner scales with whitish hairs. **Bark** gray, smooth.

Flower clusters (corymbs) ter-minal, rounded, 1¼–3 in. (3–7.5 cm.) broad, bearing on whitish hairy stalks many fragrant **flowers** ⅜ in. (1 cm.) across, composed of 5 minute triangular sepals, 5 elliptic petals ³⁄₁₆ in. (5 mm.) long, many stamens, and pistil with inferior hairy 3–4-celled ovary and 3–4 styles. **Fruits** fewer than 25, like a small apple (pome), round, less than ⅜ in. (10 mm.) in diameter, bright shiny red, bitter, with few elliptic brown seeds more than ⅛ in. (3 mm.) long, persistent in winter. Flowering June–July, maturing fruits in July.

Openings and clearings in forests. Central interior Alaska from central Yukon River and Bering Sea south to Katmai, southern, and southeast Alaska. South Tongass, North Tongass, and Chugach National Forests, Katmai National Monument. Alaska and British Columbia southeast to Alberta, South Dakota, New Mexico, and California.

This shrubby species was observed at Haines as a small tree 20 ft. (6 m.) high and can be added to Alaska's list of trees.

Figure 68.—European mountain-ash (*Sorbus aucuparia*), one-half natural size. Fruits at upper left; winter twigs at right.

68. EUROPEAN MOUNTAIN-ASH

(*Sorbus aucuparia* L.)

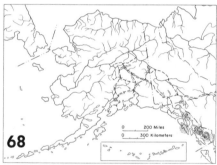

Other name: Rowan-tree.

Deciduous small to medium tree planted as an ornamental in southeast Alaska and sparingly naturalized, 20–40 ft. (6–12 m.) tall and 1 ft. (30 cm.) in trunk diameter, with symmetrical rounded crown. **Leaves** pinnate, 4–8 in. (10–20 cm.) long, with paired 3-angled stipules. Leaflets 9–17, oblong or lance-shaped, 1–2 in. (2.5–5 cm.) long, short-pointed, with edges coarsely toothed except near unequal rounded base, dull green and becoming hairless above, pale and white-hairy beneath. Young **twigs** and **winter buds** densely white-hairy or woolly, winter buds conical, ³⁄₁₆–³⁄₈ in. (5–10 mm.) long. **Bark** dark gray, smooth, with horizontal lines (lenticels), aromatic.

Flower clusters (corymbs) terminal rounded, 4–6 in. (10–15 cm.) across, bearing 75–100 flowers on densely white-hairy stalks. **Flowers** ³⁄₈ in. (10 mm.) across, composed of 5 triangular white-hairy sepals, 5 white rounded petals ³⁄₁₆ in. (4 mm.) long, many stamens, and pistil with inferior hairy ovary and 3–4 styles. **Fruits** many, like a small apple (pome), round, ³⁄₈ in. (10 mm.) in diameter, bright red;

167

seeds elliptic, light brown, $\frac{3}{16}$ in. (4 mm.) long. Fruits maturing in August–September.

Planted as an ornamental tree at Wrangell, Ketchikan, Sitka, Juneau, and probably other towns along the coast of southeast Alaska, where it spreads rapidly from cultivation. Sparingly naturalized along roads and forming thickets. The fruits persist into late fall and early winter and provide food for birds, such as crossbills, grosbeaks, and cedar waxwings, which probably spread the seeds. Numerous crows can be seen eating the fruits in trees of southeastern towns also.

Not a true ash, European mountain-ash is the only introduced or exotic tree to become established in Alaska and grow as if wild. Its specific name, meaning to catch birds, refers to the use of the mucilaginous fruits by fowlers in making birdlime.

Naturalized in southeast Alaska. Native of Europe and Asia but widely planted and naturalized in many places across Canada and northern contiguous United States.

69. SITKA MOUNTAIN-ASH

(*Sorbus sitchensis* Roem.)

Other names: western mountain-ash, Pacific mountain-ash.

Deciduous shrub 4–8 ft. (1.2–2.5 m.) high, or a small tree to 15–20 ft. (4.5–6 m.) high and 6 in. (15 cm.) in trunk diameter, with handsome, round-topped head. In rocky alpine situations at higher altitudes it is a low shrub often only 1–2 ft. (30–61 cm.) high. **Leaves** pinnate, 4–8 in. (10–20 cm.) long, with paired narrow rusty-hairy stipules. Leaflets usually 9 or 11 (sometimes 7 to 13), elliptic or oblong, 1¼–2½ in. (3–6 cm.) long, rounded or blunt-pointed at apex, with edges coarsely and sharply toothed above the middle, dull blue green and

hairless above, pale and hairless or nearly so beneath. **Twigs** stout, rusty hairy when young, becoming gray, with few elliptic dots (lenticels), with odor and bitter taste of cherry. **Buds** oblong, to ½ in. (12 mm.) long, dull reddish brown, densely rusty hairy. **Bark** gray, smooth. **Wood** pale brown, lightweight, fine-textured.

Flower clusters (corymbs) terminal, rounded, 2–4 in. (5–10 cm.) across, bearing 15–60 flowers on rusty-hairy stalks. **Flowers** small, ¼ in. (6 mm.) across, fragrant, composed of 5 broadly triangular hairless sepals, 5 white rounded petals ¼ in. (5 mm.) long, many stamens, and pistil with inferior hairy ovary and 3–4 styles. **Fruits** several to many, like a small apple (pome), round, ⅜–½ in. (10–12 mm.) in diameter, red but becoming orange and purple, with few elliptic brown seeds ⅛ in. (3 mm.) long. Flowering June–August, fruits maturing in August–September.

Uncommon to rare in forests from sea level to timberline, Pacific coast of southeast and southern Alaska. Throughout southeast Alaska from Ketchikan and Hyder north to head of Lynn Canal at Skagway, west along coast to Glacier Bay, Yakutat, Prince William Sound, Cook Inlet, Katmai Region at base of Alaska Peninsula, and Afognak and Kodiak Islands. South Tongass, North Tongass, and Chugach National Forests. Glacier Bay and Katmai National Monuments. Kenai National Moose Range. Alaska southeast along coast to southern British Columbia and in mountains to Washington, central California, Nevada, and northwestern Montana. Reported from Yukon Territory.

Often cultivated as an ornamental north to Anchorage but with less regular form than European mountain-ash. Birds eat the fruits. Sitka mountain-ash is named for

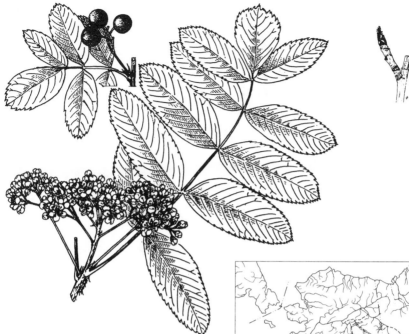

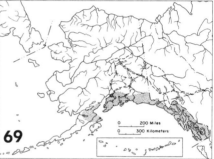

Figure 69.—Sitka mountain-ash (*Sorbus sitchensis*), one-half natural size. Fruits at upper left; winter twig at upper right.

69

Sitka, Alaska, where it was discovered. Hybrids with Greene mountain-ash (*Sorbus scopulina* Greene) have been reported.

70. SIBERIAN MOUNTAIN-ASH

(*Sorbus sambucifolia* (Cham. & Schlecht.) Roem.)

Other names: elder-leaf mountain-ash; *Pyrus sambucifolia* Cham. & Schlecht.

Deciduous shrub 2–5 ft. (0.6–1.5 m.) high. **Leaves** pinnate, 2½–5 in. (6–12.5 cm.) long, with paired rusty hairy lance-shaped stipules ⅛ in. (3 mm.) long. **Leaflets** 7 or 9 (11), lance-shaped, 1–1¾ in. (2.5–4.5 cm.) long and ⅜–¾ in. (1–2

cm.) wide, usually broadest near unequal rounded base, gradually narrowed to long-pointed apex, edges sharply toothed almost to base, becoming hairless, above shiny green, beneath dull and paler. **Twigs** rusty hairy when young, becoming gray, with few elliptic whitish dots (lenticels). **Buds** shiny reddish brown, sticky, slightly rusty hairy.

Flower clusters (corymbs) terminal, rounded, 1¼–2 in. (3–5 cm.) wide, bearing 8–15 flowers on slightly rusty hairy stalks. **Flowers** ⅜–⅝ in. (1–1.5 cm.) across, composed of 5 triangular sepals hairy on edges, 5 white rounded petals ³⁄₁₆ in. (5 mm.) long, many stamens, and pistil with inferior hairy 5-celled ovary and 5 styles. **Fruits** few, like a small

169

Figure 70.—Siberian mountain-ash (*Sorbus sambucifolia*), one-half natural size. Fruits at upper left.

apple (pome), elliptic, 3/8–5/8 in. (10–15 mm.) in diameter, reddish with a bloom, with calyx at apex, containing few dark brown seeds more than 1/8 in. (3 mm.) long. Flowering in July, fruits maturing in August.

The fruits are described as not very acid and suitable for jam.

In Alaska only in 4 of westernmost Aleutian Islands (Attu, Buldir, Alaid, Agattu). Aleutian Islands National Wildlife Refuge. Asia from Kamchatka to Korea and Japan.

SERVICEBERRY

(*Amelanchier*)

Deciduous shrubs or small trees. **Leaves** alternate, simple, with paired narrow stipules soon shedding, short petioles, and mostly small elliptic to oblong blades mostly rounded at both ends and coarsely toothed on edges. **Buds** oblong or conical, long and narrow, covered by several overlapping scales. **Flowers** several in small terminal clusters (racemes) appearing with or before the leaves, composed of bell-shaped base (hypanthium), calyx of 5 persistent lobes or sepals, 5 showy narrow white petals, 10–20 stamens, and pistil with inferior 2–5-celled ovary with 2 ovules in each cell and 2–5 styles mostly united at base. **Fruit** like a small apple (pome), round, dark blue or purple, with calyx at apex, juicy and sweet, containing 4–10 seeds and cells.

Key to the 2 Alaska Species

Leaves nearly round, thick, about as broad as long, hairy beneath when young; calyx densely hairy when young ----------------------- -------------- 71. saskatoon serviceberry (*Amelanchier alnifolia*)
Leaves elliptic, longer than broad, thin, hairless or nearly so beneath; calyx hairless or nearly so --------------------------------- ------------------ 72. Pacific serviceberry (*Amelanchier florida*)

170

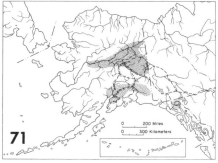

71

Figure 71.—Saskatoon serviceberry (*Amelanchier alnifolia*), one-half natural size. Winter twig at left.

71. SASKATOON SERVICEBERRY

(*Amelanchier alnifolia* (Nutt.) Nutt.)

Other name: northwestern serviceberry.

Shrub 3–6 ft. (1–2 m.) high (small tree to 13 ft. (4 m.) southward). **Leaves** with slender petioles ⅜–¾ in. (1–2 cm.) long, hairy when young. Blades nearly round, ¾–1½ in. (1–4 cm.) long, ⅝–1¼ in. (1.5–3 cm.) wide, rounded at both ends with teeth toward apex, thick and firm, above dark green and hairless, beneath paler and hairy when young.

Flower clusters (racemes) 1¼–2½ in. (3–6 cm.) long. **Flowers** 5–15, fragrant, ½–¾ in. (1.2–2 cm.) broad, composed of calyx of 5 narrow lobes, densely woolly when young, 5 white oblong petals ⅜ in.

171

(1 cm.) long, about 20 short stamens, and pistil with inferior hairy 5-celled ovary and 5 styles. **Fruit** like an apple (pome), rounded, ⅜–⅝ in. (1–1.5 cm.) in diameter, purple or nearly black and covered with a bloom, sweet, juicy, and edible, containing several elliptic flattened brown seeds 3/16 in. (5 mm.) long. Flowering in June, maturing fruit in July.

A rare shrub in Alaska, growing on steep dry south-facing bluffs, usually with aspen and common juniper. Not abundant enough to be significant as a wildlife food. Listed as suitable for ornamental planting in interior Alaska for the white flowers and attractive fruits, spreading freely and forming thickets.

Interior Alaska along Chitina and Copper Rivers and the head of Cook Inlet. Also along Tanana and central Yukon Rivers as far west as Galena and at Chilkat River at northern end of southeast Alaska. Alaska and Yukon Territory east to western Ontario and Minnesota, south to Iowa, Nebraska, Colorado, Utah, and Oregon.

72. PACIFIC SERVICEBERRY

(*Amelanchier florida* Lindl.)

Other names: western serviceberry, juneberry.

Deciduous shrub or small tree to 16 ft. (5 m.) high and 5 in. (12.5 cm.) in trunk diameter. **Leaves** longer than broad, elliptic or oblong, 1–2 in. (2.5–5 cm.) long, ¾–1¼ in. (2–3 cm.) wide, rounded at both ends, coarsely toothed above middle, thin, dark green and becoming hairless above, pale green and hairless or nearly so beneath, petioles slender, ⅜–1 in. (1–2.5 cm.) long. Young **twigs** reddish brown, becoming hairless. **Winter buds** narrow, purplish, of several scales.

Bark gray or brown, thin, smooth or slightly fissured. **Wood** light brown, heavy hard, fine-textured.

Flower clusters (racemes) 1½–3 in. (4–7.5 cm.) long, erect. **Flowers** several, fragrant, about 1 in. (2.5 cm.) across, composed of 5 pointed persistent sepals hairless or nearly so, 5 white oblong petals ½–⅝ in. (12–15 mm.) long, about 20 stamens, and pistil with inferior hairy ovary and 5 styles. **Fruit** like an apple (pome), rounded, ⅜–½ in. (10–12 mm.) in diameter, purple and covered with a bloom, sweet, juicy, and edible, with few dark brown seeds ¼ in. (5 mm.) long. Flowering June–July, maturing fruit August–September.

The fruits of the 2 native species of serviceberry are eaten fresh or prepared in puddings, pies, and muffins. The dried berries are used like raisins and currants. Birds are fond of the fruits.

Forests and openings, Pacific coast of southeast and southern Alaska in four separate areas: Extreme southeastern Alaska north to Wrangell; northern part of southeast Alaska from Taku River to Haines and Skagway at head of Lynn Canal; Kenai Peninsula and Cook Inlet area; and base of Alaska Peninsula to Wood River Lakes area north of Dillingham. South Tongass, North Tongass, and Chugach National Forests, Katmai National Monument, Kenai National Moose Range. Alaska and western British Columbia and south along coast from western Washington to northwestern California.

73. BLACK HAWTHORN

(*Crataegus douglasii* Lindl.)

Deciduous shrub collected in Alaska only at Hyder at southeast border, and in the Prince William Sound area, southward becoming a

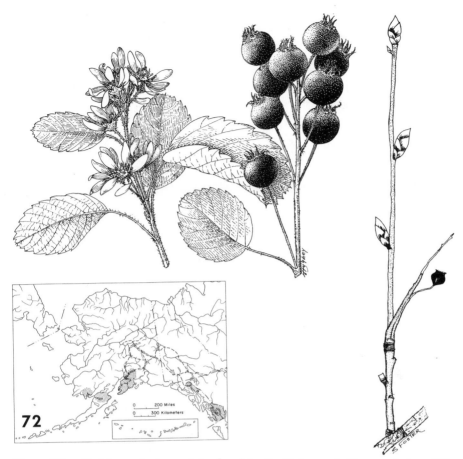

Figure 72.—Pacific serviceberry (*Amelanchier florida*), one-half natural size. Winter twig at right.

small spreading tree 25–40 ft. (7.5–12 m.) high and 1½ ft. (45 cm.) d.b.h. **Leaves** alternate, with paired broad, toothed stipules, slender petioles ½–¾ in. (1.2–2 cm.) long, and obovate to ovate thin blades 1–3 in. (2.5–7.5 cm.) long and ⅝–2 in. (1.5–5 cm.) wide, broadest toward the short-pointed apex, base short-pointed sharply toothed and often slightly lobed, becoming hairless, above shiny dark green, paler beneath. **Twigs** slender hairless shiny reddish, often with straight or slightly curved stout red to gray spines ⅜–1 in. (1–2.5 cm.) long. **Bark** gray, smoothish.

Flower clusters (corymbs) terminal, broad with several **flowers** ½ in. (1.2 cm.) across on slender stalks, composed of greenish base (hypanthium), 5 long-pointed sepals reddish at end, 5 white rounded spreading petals ¼ in. (6 mm.) long, 10–20 stamens, and pistil with inferior 2–5-celled ovary and 2–5 styles. **Fruits** like small apple (pome), many in drooping clusters on long stalks, rounded, ½ in. (12 mm.) in diameter, shiny black with calyx persistent at apex, thick light yellow flesh, sweetish and mealy but somewhat insipid and usually 5 nutlets ¼ in. (6 mm.) long.

Rare and very local in Alaska,

173

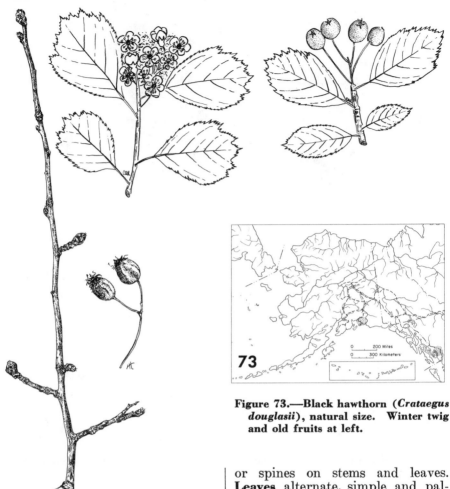

73

Figure 73.—**Black hawthorn (*Crataegus douglasii*), natural size. Winter twig and old fruits at left.**

collected only at Hyder at southeast border and in the Prince William Sound area. Southern and southeast Alaska and British Columbia and south to Montana, Wyoming, Nevada, and California; also in southwestern Ontario and Michigan.

RASPBERRY (*Rubus*)

Shrubs with perennial or biennial stems, perennial herbs, and trailing vines, mostly with prickles or spines on stems and leaves. **Leaves** alternate, simple and palmately lobed or pinnately or palmately compound with 3–5 toothed leaflets, with paired stipules attached to base of petiole. **Flowers** clustered, often large, composed of saucerlike to conic base (hypanthium), calyx of 5 persistent sepals, 5 white to red petals, many stamens, and many pistils with 1-celled ovary, 2 ovules, and style. **Fruits** aggregate, composed of usually many separate drupelets, fleshy, mostly edible, 1-seeded. Represented in Alaska by 4 species of shrubs 2–7 ft. (0.3–2.2 m.) high and by 3 species of low herbs less than 1 ft. (0.3 m.), which are described briefly.

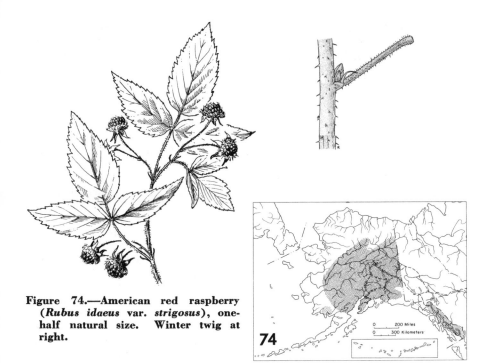

Figure 74.—American red raspberry (*Rubus idaeus* var. *strigosus*), one-half natural size. Winter twig at right.

74

Key to the 4 Alaska Shrub Species

Leaves compound, with 3 or 5 leaflets; stems often spreading, spiny or prickly; fruit rounded.
  Twigs covered with bristles and prickles; fruit a red raspberry _____
  _____ 74. American red raspberry (*Rubus idaeus* var. *strigosus*)
  Twigs with spines or prickles.
    Twigs light brown, zigzag, with weak straight rounded prickles; petals pink to purple; fruit yellow to dark red, edible, almost tasteless _____ 75. salmonberry (*Rubus spectabilis*)
    Twigs whitish, with stout hooked flattened prickles or spines; petals white; fruit reddish to black raspberry _____
    _____ 76. western black raspberry (*Rubus leucodermis*)
Leaves simple, palmately 3–7 lobed; stems erect, without spines or prickles; fruit red, half round, edible _____
_____ 77. western thimbleberry (*Rubus parviflorus*)

74. AMERICAN RED RASPBERRY

(*Rubus idaeus* L. var. *strigosus* (Michx.) Maxim.)

Other names: red raspberry, raspberry; *Rubus idaeus* ssp. *melanolasius* (Dieck) Focke, *R. idaeus* var. *canadensis* Richards., *R. strigosus* Michx.

Deciduous bristly shrub 2–4 ft. (0.6–1.2 m.) high with biennial stems. **Leaves** pinnately compound, 2½–7 in. (6–18 cm.) long, with very narrow paired stipules less than ⅜ in. (1 cm.) long. Leaflets 3 or 5, paired except at end, ovate, 1½–3½ in. (4–9 cm.) long, ¾–2 in. (2–

175

5 cm.) wide, long-pointed at apex, rounded at base, irregularly toothed and shallowly lobed, above green and mostly hairless, beneath gray green and usually hairy. **Twigs** reddish brown, covered with bristles and prickles, often hairy. **Bark** yellow brown, shreddy.

Flowers 1–4 lateral, small, ⅜–½ in. (10–12 mm.) across, composed of calyx of 5 narrow hairy sepals about ¼ in. (6 mm.) long, 5 white oblong petals about ¼ in. (6 mm.) long erect or slightly spreading, many (75–100) stamens, and many pistils. **Fruit** aggregate, a red raspberry, rounded, ¾ in. (2 cm.) long and broad, of many hairy drupelets, separating from base. Flowering June–July, fruits maturing July–September.

Red raspberries are eaten fresh or in jams and jellies.

Common to abundant in openings and borders of forests, forming thickets, also a roadside weed. Across Alaska from interior to southeast, but not in far north, Alaska Peninsula, or Aleutian Islands. Chugach, North Tongass, and South Tongass National Forests. Mt. McKinley National Park, Kenai National Moose Range. Alaska across Canada to Newfoundland, south to North Carolina, Iowa, Arizona, California, and northern Mexico.

A variable species with geographical varieties, this one also in northern Asia. The typical variety extends across northern Europe to northwestern Asia.

75. SALMONBERRY

(*Rubus spectabilis* Pursh)

Large or small thicket-forming deciduous shrub 2–7 ft. (0.6–2 m.) high, with erect and curved biennial stems. **Leaves** compound, 2–5 in. (5–12 cm.) long, slender hairy axis and paired very narrow needlelike hairy persistent stipules ¼–⅜ in.

(6–10 mm.) long. Leaflets 3, ovate, mostly 1–2½ in. (2.5–6 cm.) long and ⅝–2 in. (1.5–2.5 cm.) wide, the terminal one larger than the lateral pair, thin, long-pointed at apex and short-pointed at base, sharply and irregularly toothed and shallowly lobed, above green and nearly hairless, beneath paler and slightly hairy. **Twigs** zigzag, light brown, becoming hairless, often with scattered sharp weak spines or prickles 1/16–⅛ in. (2–3 mm.) which break off easily. **Buds** ⅛–⅜ in. (3–10 mm.) long, light brown, of overlapping scales, white hairy at pointed apex with 2 needlelike stipules at base. **Bark** light brown, becoming shreddy.

Flowers 1 or 2 lateral on long slender stalks, large and showy, 1½ in. (4 cm.) across, composed of calyx of 5 spreading long-pointed hairy greenish sepals ⅜–⅝ in. (10–15 mm.) long, 5 spreading elliptic pink to reddish purple petals ⅝–⅞ in. (15–22 mm.) long, many (75–100) purplish stamens, and many (20–40) pistils. **Fruit** aggregate, separating from base and persistent calyx like a raspberry, orange to dark red, conelike, ⅝–1 in. (1.5–2.5 cm.) long and broad, juicy, of many small drupes, edible, taste mild. Flowering April–July, maturing fruit by early July near Ketchikan but not until August on Kodiak and Afognak Islands and at higher altitudes.

The fruits make good jelly but are rather seedy for jam. They are eaten by bears in the fall. New leaves and twigs are browsed in the spring by deer, moose, and mountain goats.

Salmonberry is scattered to common or abundant in moist soil, forming dense thickets in openings in lowland forests, clearings, and along streams. It spreads quickly after clearcutting and can be a serious competitor of conifer regeneration on moist valley bottom sites.

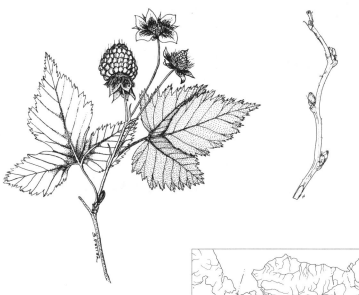

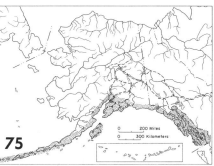

Figure 75.—Salmonberry (*Rubus spectabilis*), one-half natural size. Winter twig at right.

Southeast and southern Alaska to Aleutian Islands. South Tongass, North Tongass, and Chugach National Forests, Glacier Bay and Katmai National Monuments, Kenai National Moose Range, Kodiak Island and Aleutian Islands National Wildlife Refuges. Alaska south to northwestern California. Also a variety in Japan. Hybrids with nagoon-berry (*Rubus arcticus* L.), a herbaceous species, have been recorded from southern and southeast Alaska (Alaska bramble, *R.* ×*alaskensis* Bailey).

76. WESTERN BLACK RASPBERRY

(*Rubus leucodermis* Dougl.)

Other name: whitebark raspberry.

Deciduous spiny shrub 3–6 ft. (1–2 m.) high, with biennial stems. **Leaves** compound, 3–5 in. (7.5–12.5 cm.) long, with very narrow paired stipules less than ¼ in. (6 mm.) long. Leaflets 3, ovate, ¾–3 in. (2–7.5 cm.) long, ⅜–2 in. (1–5 cm.) wide, short to long-pointed at apex, rounded at base, edges irregularly toothed to shallowly lobed, above green and hairless or nearly so, beneath whitish hairy. **Twigs** whitish, with many stout hooked flattened prickles or spines to ¼ in. (6 mm.) long.

Flower clusters (racemes) of 2–7 **flowers** close together at leaf base, less than ½ in. (12 mm.) across, composed of calyx of 5 narrow hairy sepals ¼–½ in. (6–12 mm.) long and bent downward, 5 white petals shorter than sepals, many (70–100) stamens, and many pistils. **Fruit** aggregate, a reddish to black raspberry with whitish bloom, rounded, to ½ in. (12 mm.) broad, of many hairy drupes, edible, sep-

177

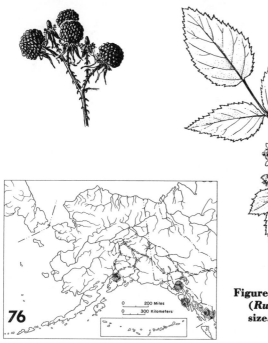

Figure 76.—Western black raspberry (*Rubus leucodermis*) one-half natural size. Fruits at upper left.

arating from base. Collected with fruit in August and September.

Rare in southeast Alaska, possibly introduced. Recorded from abandoned Tongass Village, Sitka, and Haines, also along railroad at Indian Creek southeast of Anchorage. South Tongass and North Tongass National Forests. Alaska and British Columbia south to southern California, east to Utah, Wyoming, and Montana.

77. WESTERN THIMBLEBERRY

(*Rubus parviflorus* Nutt.)

Other names: thimbleberry; *R. nutkanus* Moc.

Deciduous erect shrub 2–5 ft. (0.6–1.5 m.) high, with erect perennial stems, without spines. **Leaves** simple, with paired lance-shaped stipules ¼–½ in. (6–12 mm.) long and slender petioles 1–4 in. (2.5–10 cm.) long with stalked gland

hairs. Blades rounded or 5-angled, 2½–6 in. (6–15 cm.) long and broad, thin, palmately lobed with mostly 5 (sometimes 3 or 7) shallow short-pointed lobes, heart-shaped at base, edges sharply doubly toothed with gland teeth, with 5 main veins from base, above dull green and nearly hairless, beneath paler, slightly hairy and with stalked gland hairs along veins. **Twigs** greenish, finely hairy and with stalked gland hairs. **Bark** gray, shreddy or flaky.

Flower clusters (corymbs or panicles) terminal and flat-topped. **Flowers** mostly 3–7, 1½–2 in. (4–5 cm.) across, composed of calyx of 5 spreading narrow hairy greenish sepals ⅜–⅝ in. (10–15 mm.) long, 5 white obovate spreading petals ⅝–1 in. (20–25 mm.) long, many stamens, and many pistils. **Fruit** aggregate, thimblelike, half round and flattened, ½ in. (12 mm.) across, juicy and edible, composed of many small hairy red drupelets 1/16 in. (2 mm.) long. Flowering

77

Figure 77.—Winter thimbleberry (*Rubus parviflorus*), one-half natural
  size. Winter twig at right.

179

June–July, with mature fruits August–September.

The fruits are excellent for jelly but too seedy for jam.

Common in moist soil in thickets and openings of forests, along roadsides, and on cutover land, southeast Alaska north to Lynn Canal and Yakutat. South Tongass and North Tongass National Forests. Southeast Alaska east to Ontario and Minnesota, south in mountains to New Mexico, California, and northern Mexico.

Besides the 4 shrubby species with woody stems described here, 3 additional native species of this genus are herbs with creeping stems or erect herbaceous stems usually less than 1 ft. (30 cm.) high. These are summarized below.

Five-leaf bramble (*Rubus pedatus* Sm.). Slender trailing herbaceous vine rooting at nodes and forming mats, flowering twigs less than 1 in. (2.5 cm.) high. **Leaves** 2–4, palmately compound, with slender petiole 1–3 in. (2.5–7.5 cm.) long and 5 nearly stalkless obovate irregularly toothed leaflets ⅜–1¼ in. (1–3 cm.) long. **Flower** 1, erect white, ½–⅝ in. (1.2–1.5 cm.) across, with petals and sepals about equal. **Fruit** of 1–6 red drupelets ⅜ in. long (1 cm.), juicy, edible, used for jam. Forests in southern and southeast Alaska, southeast to Alberta, Montana, and Oregon. Also in Japan.

Cloudberry (*Rubus chamaemorus* L.; baked-apple berry). Erect herb 2–8 in. (5–20 cm.) high from creeping rootstock. **Leaves** 2 or 3 with slender petioles ½–1 in. (1.2–2.5 cm.) long and rounded blades 1–2 in. (2.5–5 cm.) across, with 3 or 5 rounded lobes and finely toothed border. **Flower** 1 erect white, ½–1 in. (1.2–2.5 cm.) across. **Fruit** ½–¾ in. (1.2–2 cm.) in diameter, edible, composed of 6–18 large pink drupelets the color of a baked apple. In bogs almost

throughout Alaska, across Canada to Labrador and Greenland, south to New York. Also across northern Eurasia. The edible berries are collected in quantities in late August and early September and are stored frozen by the Eskimos for winter use. Rich in vitamin C, even when frozen soon after picking, the berries are eaten fresh and in jam, shortcake, and pie.

Nagoon-berry (*Rubus arcticus* L.; other names: wineberry, Arctic bramble, kneshenada; *R. acaulis* Michx., *R. stellatus* Sm., *R. arcticus* ssp. *acaulis* (Michx.) Focke, *R. arcticus* ssp. *stellatus* (Sm.) Boivin). Herbs 2–10 in. (5–25 cm.) high from spreading rootstock. **Leaves** with slender petioles 1–2 in. (2.5–5 cm.) long and 3 almost stalkless elliptic toothed leaflets ⅝–1¼ in. (1.5–3 cm.) long; a variation with simple rounded leaves 1–2 in. (2.5–5 cm.) long and broad, deeply 3-lobed. **Flowers** 1–3, pink or red, ¾–1¼ in. (2–3 cm.) across. **Fruit** red, ½–¾ in. (1.2–2 cm.) across, of 15–40 drupelets not separating from calyx, edible. The berries are a favorite for jam, jelly, and wine, because of their excellent flavor. Common in sedge meadows and bogs, interior, western, southern, and southeast Alaska and through Aleutian Islands. This widespread variable species has intergrades and hybrids among its races. Across Canada to Labrador and Newfoundland, south to Minnesota and Colorado. Also across northern Eurasia.

78. BUSH CINQUEFOIL

(*Potentilla fruticosa* L.)

Other names: shrubby cinquefoil, yellow-rose; *Dasiphora fruticosa* (L.) Rydb.

Much branched deciduous shrub 1–5½ ft. (0.3–1.7 m.) high. **Leaves** alternate, pinnate, ¾–1½ in. (2–3.5 cm.) long, with paired clasping,

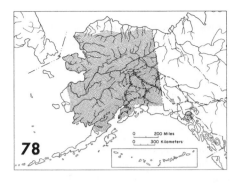

Figure 78.—Bush cinquefoil (*Potentilla fruticosa*), natural size. Winter twig at right.

ovate, light brown membranous hairy persistent stipules ¼–½ in. (6–12 mm.) long, with very slender light brown hairy axis. Leaflets 5, stalkless, close together near end of axis and paired except at end, narrowly oblong or oblanceolate, ¼–¾ in. (6–20 mm.) long and ¹⁄₁₆–¼ in. (2–6 mm.) wide, short-pointed at both ends, edges turned under, above dull green with inconspicuous pressed hairs, beneath whitish green with silky hairs. **Twigs** slender, light brown, with long silky hairs, becoming hairless. **Bark** brown gray, shreddy.

Flowers borne singly at leaf bases or 3–7 in small terminal clusters (cymes), erect on slender silky hairy stalks, large and showy ¾–1¼ in. (2–3 cm.) across, composed of saucer-shaped hairy base (hypanthium), 5 narrow green bracts ¼ in. (6 mm.) long, 5 spreading ovate hairy sepals ¼ in. (6 mm.) long, 5 rounded spreading yellow petals ⅜–⅝ in. (10–15 mm.) long, 20–30 short stamens, and many pistils with very hairy 1-celled ovary, 1 ovule, and short persistent style attached on side. **Fruits** (akenes) many, egg-shaped, ¹⁄₁₆ in. (2 mm.) long, light brown and covered with whitish hairs, 1-seeded. Flowering June – August, fruits maturing July – September and persistent.

Wild plants tested in interior Alaska as ornamentals have scraggly growth. Several horticultural varieties including dwarf and large-flowered are cultivated elsewhere. It is reported that the leaves have been used for tea by the Eskimos at Nome.

Common to abundant in moist soil of swamps and borders of streams and lakes and on dry rocky hillsides. Almost throughout Alaska except western Alaska Peninsula, Aleutian Islands, and most of southeast. Chugach National Forest, Mt. McKinley National Park, Katmai National Monument, Kenai National Moose Range, Arctic National Wildlife Range. Alaska across Canada to Labrador, Newfoundland, and Greenland, south to New Jersey, Iowa, New Mexico, and California. Also across northern Eurasia.

181

MOUNTAIN-AVENS (Dryas)

Evergreen densely tufted, herbaceous dwarf shrubs with prostrate stems woody at base, branching, rooting, often forming large rounded mats or clumps. **Leaves** crowded but alternate, with 2 narrow long-pointed stipules attached to slender petiole. Blade mostly oblong, leathery, with wavy toothed or straight edges, dark green above and densely white-hairy beneath. **Flowers** many and showy, solitary on erect stalks, ¾–1 in. (2–2.5 cm.)

across, composed of saucerlike or convex base (hypanthium), calyx of 8–10 persistent sepals, 8–10 widely spreading white petals (pale yellow and slightly spreading in Drummond mountain-avens, *Dryas drummondii*), many stamens, and many pistils with 1-celled ovary with 1 ovule and slender hairy styles forming feathery plumes.

Besides the 3 species generally accepted and illustrated here, variations and hybrids have been described. Also 2–5 additional species or subdivisions listed under other names are sometimes accepted in Alaska.

Key to the 3 Alaska Species

Leaves short-pointed (wedge-shaped) at base; flowers nodding with pale yellow, slightly spreading petals _____ _____ 79. Drummond mountain-avens (*Dryas drummondii*)
Leaves straight or notched (heart-shaped) at base; flowers erect with white, widely spreading petals.
  Leaves with edges wavy-toothed from apex to base, very rough on upper surface, with glands and scales on midvein beneath _____ _____ 80. white mountain-avens (*Dryas octopetala*)
  Leaves with edges straight (entire) or slightly wavy in lower half, not rough or slightly rough on upper surface, without glands and scales on midvein beneath _____ _____ 81. entire-leaf mountain-avens (*Dryas integrifolia*)

79. DRUMMOND MOUNTAIN-AVENS

(*Dryas drummondii* Richards.)

Other name: yellow dryas.
Evergreen herbaceous dwarf shrub with prostrate stems, forming large mats. **Leaves** crowded, with long slender petiole. Blades elliptic, ⅝–1¼ in. (1.5–3 cm.) long, ⅜–¾ in. (1–2 cm.) wide, thick, rounded at apex and short-pointed at base, edges wavy-toothed and turned under, above dark green and usually slightly hairy with sunken veins, beneath densely white hairy.

Flowers solitary, nodding on whitish hairy stalks 2–8 in. (5–20 cm.) high, yellow, ¾–1 in. (2–2.5 cm.) across, with saucer-like base, 8–10 ovate short-pointed, blackish, gland hairy sepals nearly ¼ in. (6 mm.) long, and 8–10 yellow petals nearly ½ in. (12 mm.) long. **Fruits** headlike of many akenes 3⁄16 in. (4 mm.) long with persistent long hairy styles forming feathery plumes 1–1½ in. (2.5–3.5 cm.) long in mass 1–2½ in. (2.5–6 cm.) in diameter. Flowering June–July, fruits maturing July–August.

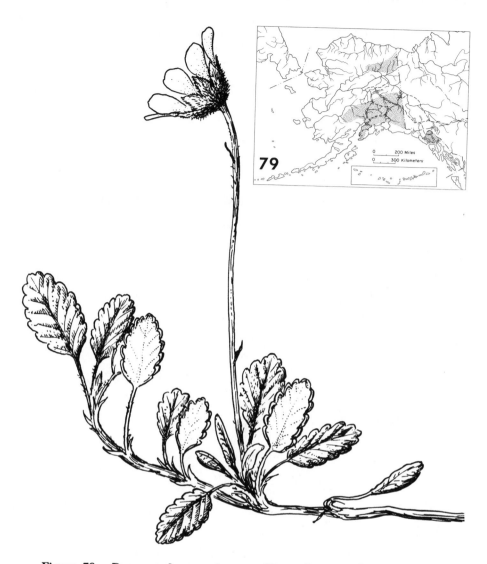

Figure. 79.—Drummond mountain-avens (*Dryas drummondii*), natural size.

Arctic-alpine to lowland areas especially as a pioneer on gravel bars of flood plains. Interior Alaska in eastern Brooks Range and from Alaska Range south to Kenai Peninsula and to north end of southeast Alaska. North Tongass National Forest, Mt. McKinley National Park, Glacier Bay National Monument, Kenai National Moose Range, Arctic National Wildlife Range. Alaska and Yukon Territory east to Great Slave Lake, south to Montana, and local in Washington and Oregon; local on north shore of Lake Superior and in Gaspé Peninsula region.

The scientific name honors the discoverer, Thomas Drummond (1780–1835), Scotch botanical explorer in North America.

183

80. WHITE MOUNTAIN-AVENS

(*Dryas octopetala* L.)

Other names: eight-petal mountain-avens; *Dryas octopetala* ssp. *alaskensis* (Porsild) Hult. ssp. *hookeriana* (Juz.) Hult., var. *hookeriana* (Juz.) Breit., var. *kamtschatica* (Juz.) Hult., var. *viscida* Hult.; *D. alaskensis* Porsild, *D. crenulata* Juz., *D. kamtschatica* Juz., *D. punctata* Juz.

Evergreen tufted herbaceous dwarf shrub with prostrate stems. **Leaves** crowded, with slender petiole. Blades oblong, ⅜–1¼ in. (1–3 cm.) long, ³⁄₁₆–⅜ in. (0.5–1 cm.) wide, rounded at apex and short-pointed, rounded, or notched at base, edges coarsely wavy toothed and turned under, above shiny green, hairless and rough with veins deeply sunken, beneath densely white hairy and with glands and scales on midvein. **Flowers** solitary on erect hairy stalks 1–5 in. (2.5–12.5 cm.) high, white, 1–1¼ in. (2.5–3 cm.) across, with convex base, 8–10 narrow, gland hairy sepals ¼ in. (6 mm.) long, and 8–10 widely spreading white petals ⅜–½ in. (10–12 mm.) long. **Fruits** headlike, of many akenes ⅛ in. (3 mm.) long with persistent elongate hairy styles forming feathery plumes more than 1 in. (2.5 cm.) long. Flowering May–June, fruits maturing July–August.

Arctic-alpine areas through most of Alaska except northern coastal plain, Aleutian and Kodiak Islands, and south central and southeastern coastal areas. Southeast to Glacier Bay and head of Lynn Canal. Chugach National Forest, Mt. McKinley National Park, Glacier Bay and Katmai National Monuments, Kenai National Moose Range, Arctic National Wildlife Range Alaska and Yukon Territory east to Mackenzie Delta and south in Rocky Mountains to Colorado, Utah, and Oregon. Also Greenland and Iceland and across northern Eurasia.

One variation (*Dryas octopetala* ssp. *alaskensis* (Porsild) Hult.) has the leaves broadest above middle and more numerous teeth deeply divided nearly half way to midvein. Interior Alaska, especially above tree line, except far north, southwest, and southeast, also in Yukon Territory and Mackenzie Delta.

This species is widely grown in rock gardens and is rated as excellent for interior Alaska. Plants of this and the other Alaska species can be propagated by layering or by cuttings.

81. ENTIRE-LEAF MOUNTAIN-AVENS

(*Dryas integrifolia* Vahl)

Other names: *Dryas chamissonis* Spreng. ex Juz., *D. integrifolia* var. *sylvatica* Hult. and ssp. *sylvatica* (Hult.) Hult., *D. sylvatica* (Hult.) Porsild).

Evergreen herbaceous dwarf shrub with prostrate stems. **Leaves** crowded with slender hairy petiole ¼ in. (6 mm.) long. Blades narrowly oblong or lanceolate, ⅜–1 (1½) in. (1–2.5 (3.5) cm.) long, ⅛–⅜ in. (0.3–1 cm.) wide, thick with blunt apex, broadest near rounded or notched base, edges mostly turned under and without teeth or with few wavy teeth toward base, above shiny dark green, smooth, and usually hairless, beneath densely white hairy. **Flowers** solitary on erect stalks 1–4 (8) in. (2.5–10 (20) cm.) high, hairy, and usually with blackish

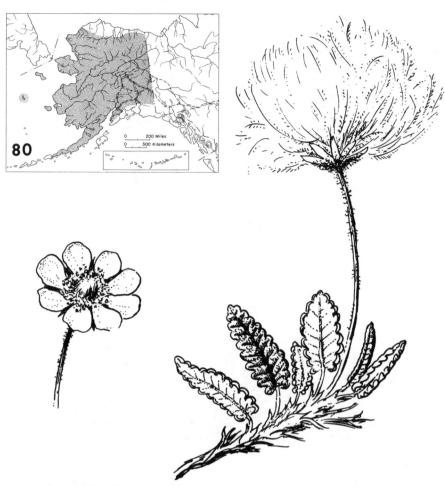

Figure 80.—White mountain-avens (*Dryas octopetala*), natural size.

gland hairs, ¾–1 in. (2–2.5 cm.) across with convex base, 8–9 narrow, gland hairy sepals nearly ¼ in. (5 mm.) long, and 8–9 spreading white petals ⅜–½ in. (10–12 mm.) long. **Fruits** headlike, of many akenes ⅛ in. (3 mm.) long with persistent long hairy styles forming whitish feathery twisted plumes ¾–1¼ in. (2–3 cm.) long in mass 1–1½ in. (2.5–3.5 cm.) in diameter. Flowering May–August, fruits maturing June–August.

Common and widespread in lowland and alpine tundra, on gravel bars and rocky slopes, in muskegs, also in open spruce stands near timberline. Arctic-alpine areas nearly throughout Alaska from Bering Strait to Canadian border but not found in the Aleutians, southwest, and extreme southeast. Chugach and North Tongass National Forests, Mt. McKinley National Park, Glacier Bay National Monument, Kenai National Moose Range, Arctic National Wildlife Range. Alaska across northern Canada to Greenland, Labrador, and Newfoundland, and south to Gaspé Peninsula, north of Lake Superior, and southeastern British

185

81

Figure 81.—Entire-leaf mountain-avens
(*Dryas integrifolia*), natural size.

Columbia (reported from Montana and long ago from New Hampshire).

A variation at low altitudes in interior Alaska (*Dryas integrifolia* var. *sylvatica* Hult.) has leaves long-stalked, long, thin, flat, with round apex, base rounded or short-pointed, and edges mostly without teeth, and taller flower stalks. It is found in bogs and spruce forests on gravel and limestone in interior Alaska except far north, southwest, and southeast, also in Yukon Territory and northwest District of Mackenzie.

186

ROSE (Rosa)

Deciduous shrubs, sometimes climbing, with prickly or spiny twigs. **Leaves** alternate, with paired stipules attached to base of petiole, pinnate with leaflets paired except at end, toothed on edges. **Flowers** few or single, large, fragrant, composed of rounded base (hypanthium) narrowed at apex, 5 narrow sepals mostly persistent, 5 large spreading commonly pink petals broad and notched at apex, many stamens, and within the hairy base many pistils with 1-celled hairy ovary, 1 ovule, and style. **Fruit** berrylike, a rounded reddish fleshy hip containing several to many "seeds" (akenes).

Key to the 3 Alaska Species

Leaflets simply toothed; stipules long-pointed, not toothed; twigs with slender round prickles or spines, many or scattered (interior Alaska).
Leaflets pale green and slightly hairy beneath; stipules mostly broad; prickles many; flowers 1 to few, about 2 in. (5 cm.) across _____ _____ 82. prickly rose (*Rosa acicularis*)
Leaflets whitish green and mostly hairless beneath; stipules narrow; prickles few, scattered; flowers several in clusters, about 1 in. (2.5 cm.) across _____ 83. Woods rose (*Rosa woodsii*)
Leaflets mostly doubly toothed with teeth of 2 sizes; stipules short-pointed, with gland teeth; twigs with few flattened prickles or spines paired at base of leaves or twigs (nodes); flowers mostly 1, more than 2 in. (5 cm.) across (southeast and southern Alaska) _____ _____ 84. Nutka rose (*Rosa nutkana*)

82. PRICKLY ROSE

(*Rosa acicularis* Lindl.)

Other name: wild rose.

Spiny much branched shrub 1–4 (7) ft. (0.3–2.2 m.) high. **Leaves** alternate, pinnate, 2–3½ in. (5–9 cm.) long, with hairy glandular axis and paired broad pointed stipules ⅜–1 in. (1–2.5 cm.) long. Leaflets mostly 5 (3–9), paired except at end, stalkless, elliptic, mostly ⅝–2¼ in. (1.5–6 cm.) long and ¼–1¼ in. (0.5–3 cm.) wide, rounded at both ends, edges toothed, the teeth often gland-tipped, above dull green and usually hairless, beneath pale green and slightly hairy. **Twigs** light green when young, becoming dark red purple to gray, bristly with many straight slender gray sharp spines or prickles ⅛–¼ in. (3–6 mm.) long, unequal and round (not flattened). **Buds** ¹⁄₁₆–⅛ in. (2–3 mm.) long, blunt, dark red, with few hairless scales.

Flowers 1, sometimes 2 or 3, at end of short mostly lateral twigs, on slender curved hairless stalk 1–1½ in. (2.5–4 cm.) long, large, 1½–2¼ in. (4–6 cm.) across, with hairless greenish base (hypanthium) pear-shaped, elliptic or rounded and narrowed into neck at apex, 5 narrow leaflike greenish sepals ⅝–1¼ in. (1.5–3 cm.) long, narrowest in middle, hairy and with gland hairs, and 5 pink to rose petals ¾–1¼ in. (2–3 cm.) long. **Fruit**

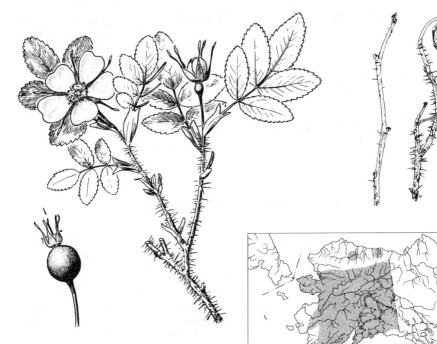

Figure 82.—**Prickly rose (*Rosa acicularis*), one-half natural size. Winter twigs at right.**

82

berrylike, pearlike, elliptic or rounded hip ⅝–¾ in. (15–20 mm.) long and ¼–⅝ in. (6–15 mm.) in diameter, dark red or purplish, fleshy and edible, becoming shrunken and wrinkled, curved downward and bearing at apex the persistent long sepals mostly pressed together, containing few light brown hairy "seeds" (akenes) nearly ³⁄₁₆ in. (5 mm.) long, persistent through winter. Flowering June–July, fruits turning red in August.

The reddish edible fruits of this and related species, known as rose hips or rose haws, are very rich in vitamin C (ascorbic acid) and serve as a winter source. They are gathered in the fall when hard but persist through the winter, becoming soft. The juice extracted by boiling is mixed with other fruit juices or used in jellies or syrups. Jams, marmalades, and catchup are prepared from the pulp after seeds and skins are removed by sieving. Flavor is improved by combining with a tart fruit or juice such as cranberry or high bushcranberry. It is reported that a tea has been made from the leaves. Rose hips are eaten by grouse and other birds during fall and winter.

Wild rose bushes make attractive ornamentals when transplanted in interior Alaska but need careful pruning.

Locally common in shaded undergrowth of deciduous and spruce forests, with aspen on old burns, also thickets, roadsides, and bogs. Almost throughout central Alaska except extreme north, southwest, Aleutian and Kodiak Islands, and southeast. Collected north of Brooks Range at Umiat and Sadlerochit Hot Springs. Chugach National Forest, Mt. McKinley National Park, Kenai National Moose

188

Figure 83.—Woods rose (*Rosa woodsii*), one-half natural size. Winter twig at right.

Nootka rose (*Rosa nutkana* Presl) intermediate between the parents occur in southern Alaska where the ranges meet.

83. WOODS ROSE
(*Rosa woodsii* Lindl.)

Spiny deciduous shrub 2–5 ft. (0.6–1.5 m.) high. **Leaves** alternate, pinnate, 2–4 in. (5–10 cm.) long, with paired narrow pointed stipules ⅜–¾ in. (1–2 cm.) long. Leaflets 5–9, paired except at end, rounded at apex, short-pointed at

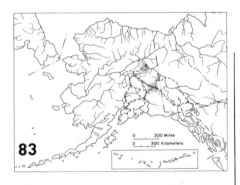

Range, Arctic National Wildlife Range. Alaska east across Canada to Labrador and Anticosti south to West Virginia, Minnesota, New Mexico, Idaho, and British Columbia. Also widespread across northern Eurasia.

A variable species. Hybrids with

189

base, edges toothed, above green and hairless, beneath whitish green and hairless or finely hairy. **Twigs** greenish, becoming reddish brown, hairless, with few scattered straight or curved spines or prickles $\frac{1}{8}$–$\frac{1}{4}$ in. (3–6 mm.) long.

Flowers mostly several in lateral clusters (cymes), sometimes few or 1, 1–1$\frac{1}{2}$ in. (2.5–4 cm.) across, with rounded base (hypanthium) $\frac{3}{16}$ in. (5 mm.) wide, 5 narrow persistent sepals $\frac{3}{8}$–$\frac{3}{4}$ in. (10–20 mm.) long, mostly not glandular, and 5 light pink to rose petals $\frac{1}{2}$–$\frac{3}{4}$ in. (12–20 mm.) long. **Fruit** berrylike, rounded or elliptic hip $\frac{1}{4}$–$\frac{1}{2}$ in. (6–12 mm.) long and wide, containing many hairy "seeds" (akenes) more than $\frac{1}{8}$ in. (3 mm.) long. Flowering in July.

Apparently rare and local in Alaska, collected only at Circle Hot Springs and Tok. Yukon Territory and District of Mackenzie east to Saskatchewan and Wisconsin, and south to Kansas and Colorado.

Named for Joseph Woods (1776–1864), English botanist and specialist on roses.

84. NOOTKA ROSE

(*Rosa nutkana* Presl)

Spiny deciduous shrub 5–8 ft. (1.5–2.5 m.) high, sometimes only 2 ft. (0.6 m.). **Leaves** alternate, pinnate, 2$\frac{1}{2}$–4 in. (6–10 cm.) long, with hairy glandular axis and paired short-pointed stipules $\frac{3}{8}$–$\frac{3}{4}$ in. (1–2 cm.) long with gland teeth. Leaflets mostly 5–7 (9), paired except at end, stalkless, elliptic or ovate, $\frac{1}{2}$–2 in. (1.2–5 cm.) long, $\frac{1}{4}$–1$\frac{1}{2}$ in. (0.6–4 cm.) wide, rounded at both ends, edges mostly doubly toothed with gland teeth, above dull green and hairless, beneath paler and mostly hairy along viens. **Twigs** pink brown, hairless, with few mostly paired stout flattened whitish spines $\frac{1}{8}$–$\frac{1}{4}$

in. (3–6 mm.) long, straight or slightly curved at base of leaves or twigs (nodes) or nearly spineless. **Buds** $\frac{1}{8}$ in. (3 mm.) long, blunt, dark red, with few hairless scales.

Flowers mostly 1, sometimes 2 or more, at end of short lateral twigs, on stout erect stalk $\frac{3}{4}$–1 in. (2–2.5 cm.) long, large, 2–2$\frac{1}{2}$ in. (5–6 cm.) across, with rounded mostly hairless base (hypanthium) $\frac{1}{4}$–$\frac{3}{8}$ in. (6–10 mm.) broad, 5 narrow leaflike persistent sepals $\frac{5}{8}$–1$\frac{1}{4}$ in. (15–30 mm.) long, narrowest in middle, hairy and with gland hairs, and 5 pink to rose petals $\frac{3}{4}$–1$\frac{1}{4}$ in. (20–30 mm.) long. **Fruit** berrylike, rounded red or purplish hip $\frac{1}{2}$–$\frac{3}{4}$ in. (12–20 mm.) in diameter, without neck, with long sepals at apex, hairless, fleshy, containing several to many hairy shiny brown "seeds" (akenes) $\frac{3}{16}$–$\frac{1}{4}$ in. (5–6 mm.) long, becoming wrinkled and persistent through winter. Flowering June–August, with mature fruits in August.

Rose hips of this species are utilized for jelly, preserves, and catchup and as a source of vitamin C as noted under prickly rose.

Forming thickets along beaches, coastal areas of southeastern and southern Alaska, Kodiak Island, and Aleutian Islands (collected only at Unalaska). Common around Haines and Skagway at head of Lynn Canal and on Kodiak Island but uncommon elsewhere. South Tongass, North Tongass, and Chugach National Forests, Kenai National Moose Range, Kodiak National Wildlife Refuge, Aleutian Islands National Wildlife Refuge. Southeast along coast from Aleutian and Kodiak Islands to northwestern California and inland in mountains to eastern Oregon, Utah, and Colorado.

As indicated by the names, this species was discovered at Nootka Sound, Vancouver Island, British Columbia.

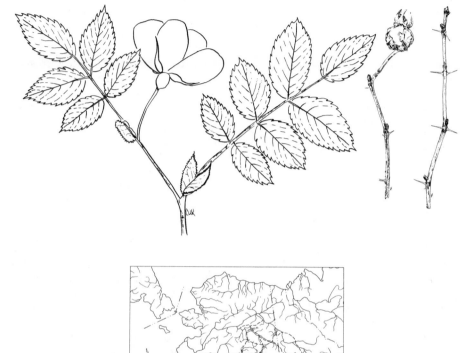

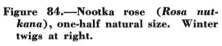

84

Figure 84.—Nootka rose (*Rosa nut-*
kana), one-half natural size. Winter
twigs at right.

191

MAPLE FAMILY

(Aceraceae)

The maple family composed of deciduous trees is represented in Alaska by Douglas maple in the southeast part. Maples have the following characteristics for recognition: (1) leaves paired (opposite), long-stalked, broad, 3-lobed or 5-lobed and toothed; (2) flowers male and female on the same or different trees, small, in clusters appearing with the leaves; and (3) fruits, distinctive paired winged, 1-seeded keys. In winter the paired (opposite) U-shaped leaf-scars aid in recognition.

85. DOUGLAS MAPLE

(*Acer glabrum* Torr. var. *douglasii* (Hook.) Dipp.)

Other names: dwarf maple, Douglas Rocky Mountain maple; *Acer glabrum* ssp. *douglasii* (Hook.) Wesmael, *A. douglasii* Hook.; variety of Rocky Mountain maple, *A. glabrum* Torr.

Deciduous small tree of southeast Alaska becoming 20–30 ft. (6–9 m.) tall and 6–12 in. (15–30 cm.) in trunk diameter but often a several-stemmed shrub 4–6 ft. (1.2–1.8 m.) high. **Leaves** paired (opposite), ovate, 2–4 in. (5–10 cm.) long and broad, slightly heart-shaped at base, shallowly 3-lobed with the lobes long-pointed, deeply, sharply, and irregularly or doubly toothed, hairless, shiny dark green above, pale beneath with yellowish veins. Petioles 1½–4 in. (4–10 cm.) long, slender, reddish tinged. **Twigs** paired (opposite), reddish, hairless, with U-shaped leaf scars. **Winter buds**

short-pointed, ⅛–¼ in. (3–6 mm.) long, dark red, the side buds paired (opposite). **Bark** gray, smooth. **Wood** light brown, heavy, hard, fine-textured.

Flower clusters (corymbs) terminal, appearing with the leaves, with several flowers on slender spreading or drooping stalks. **Flowers** mostly male and female on different trees (dioecious), about ⅛ in. (3 mm.) long, composed of 4 narrow yellow green sepals as long as the narrow yellow green petals, 7–8 stamens, and in female flowers very short stamens and pistil with 2-celled ovary and 2 styles. **Fruit** of paired, winged, 1-seeded keys (samaras) ¾–1 in. (2–2.5 cm.) long, usually red until shed, then turning to light brown. Flowering in May, fruit maturing July–August.

Common along shores in southeast Alaska, sometimes fringing tidal meadows or bogs. Occasional in rich moist soils on forested slopes. The trees are seldom large enough for commercial purposes.

Southeast Alaska, common along the coast north to the head of Lynn Canal at Skagway. South Tongass and North Tongass National Forests. Southeast Alaska, southeast to western and southern British Columbia, southern Alberta, western Montana, and northwestern Wyoming, and west to Idaho, Washington, and Oregon. Rocky Mountain maple (*Acer glabrum* Torr., including this and other varieties) extends southward to northwestern Nebraska and in mountains to southern New Mexico and southern California.

Douglas maple is the only member of the maple family (Aceraceae) native in Alaska. Named for its discoverer, David Douglas (1798–1834), Scotch botanical explorer, who introduced many trees from western North America to Europe.

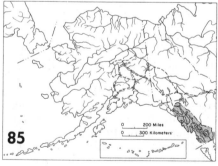

Figure 85.—Douglas maple (*Acer glabrum* var. *douglasii*), one-half natural size. Winter twigs at left.

Bigleaf maple (*Acer macrophyllum* Pursh) has been reported from the southern end of southeastern Alaska, apparently in error. It was not found in a special search along Portland Canal at the border with British Columbia. However, it extends northward nearly to the boundary (not to Queen Charlotte Islands) and southward in the Pacific coast region to southern California. Bigleaf maple is readily distinguished by the paired (opposite) long-stalked, very large leaves 5–14 in. (12.5–35.5 cm.) long and broad, which are heart-shaped, deeply 5-lobed with additional smaller lobes, and with few teeth. The clustered fruits are paired, winged 1-seeded keys 1¼–2 in. (3–5 cm.) long and ½ in. (1.2 cm.) wide, bristly hairy at base.

193

ELAEAGNUS FAMILY

(Elaeagnaceae)

Deciduous shrubs (elsewhere also small trees and also evergreen), covered with scurfy or star-shaped silvery or brown scales. **Leaves** alternate or opposite, simple, without stipules, not toothed on edges. **Flowers** small, lateral, single or few with both stamens and pistil (bisexual) or male and female, without petals, composed of tube (hypanthium), 4-lobed calyx, 4 or 8 stamens, and pistil with 1-celled ovary, 1 ovule, and style. **Fruit** drupelike, consisting of fleshy tube and 1-seeded nutlet.

Key to the 2 Alaska Species

Leaves opposite, green above and brownish scaly beneath; flowers male and female on different plants ----------------------------------- ----------------------- 86. buffaloberry (*Shepherdia canadensis*)
Leaves alternate, silvery scaly on both surfaces; flowers bisexual ------ ----------------------- 87. silverberry (*Elaeagnus commutata*)

86. BUFFALOBERRY

(*Shepherdia canadensis* (L.) Nutt.)

Other names: soapberry, soopolallie; *Lepargyraea canadensis* (L.) Greene, *Elaeagnus canadensis* (L.) A. Nels.

Deciduous shrub 2–6 ft. (0.6–2 m.) high, with silvery or reddish brown minute scales. **Leaves** opposite, wth short scaly petioles less than ⅛ in. (3 mm.) long, without stipules. Blades ovate, ½–2 in. (1.2–5 cm.) long, ¼–1 in. (0.6–2.5 cm.) wide, rounded or blunt at both ends, not toothed on edges, above green and slightly hairy with scattered star-shaped hairs, beneath densely covered with reddish brown scales and silvery star-shaped hairs. **Twigs** gray, scaly, with paired branches, young twigs and buds covered with reddish brown scales. **Buds** flattened, composed of pair of small leaves (scales).

Flowers small, about 3/16 in. (5 mm.) wide, yellowish or brownish, male and female on different plants (dioecious), in short lateral spikes in spring before the leaves, from round buds 1/16 in. (1.5 mm.) in diameter formed in previous summer. Male flowers with calyx of 4 spreading scaly lobes and 8 stamens alternate with lobes of disk. Female flowers with scaly cup bearing at apex 8-lobed disk with 4 lobed calyx, and pistil with 1-celled ovary, 1 ovule, and short style. **Fruit** elliptic, red or yellowish, ¼ in. (6 mm.) long, nearly transparent, drupelike with calyx at apex, fleshy and edible but almost tasteless or bitter, and 1 nutlet. One of the earliest flowering

194

Figure 86.—Buffaloberry (*Sherpherdia canadensis*), natural size. Flowering twig at upper right; winter twig at left.

plants in the interior, blooming in early May as soon as the snow has melted; fruits maturing in July.

The fruits were gathered in quantities and eaten by the Indians. Fruits were pressed into cakes, which were smoked and eaten, the taste sweet at first then replaced by a bitter taste (saponin) like quinine. Also the fruits were mixed with sugar and water and beat into an edible foam or froth, which was used on deserts like whipped cream. The berries are eaten in the fall by grouse and bears. Plants are sometimes grown for ornament.

Uncommon or locally common in openings and forests of dry uplands and in aspen forests on old burns. Forming dense thickets on gravel bars of rivers near tree line. Widespread across eastern interior Alaska to north slope Brooks Range and Firth River, south to Skagway and Homer. Reaching the Chukchi Sea coast at Kotzebue. North Tongass National Forest, Mt. McKinley National Park, Glacier Bay National Monument. Kenai National Moose Range, Arctic National Wildlife Range. Arctic America from Alaska and Yukon Territory to Great Bear Lake, James Bay and Newfoundland, south in mountains to Maine, New York, Michigan, New Mexico, and Oregon.

87. SILVERBERRY

(*Elaeagnus commutata* Bernh.)

Other name: *E. argentea* Pursh, not Calla.

Deciduous shrub 3–12 ft. (1–3.7 m.) high, sometimes treelike, spreading from rootstocks, much branched. **Leaves** alternate, with short petiole less than ¼ in. (6 mm.) long, without stipules. Blades elliptic to ovate, 1–2½ in. (2.5–6 cm.) long, ⅜–1 in. (1–2.5 cm.) wide, blunt or short-pointed at both ends, not toothed on edges, densely silvery scaly on both surfaces, paler beneath. **Twigs** covered with rusty brown scales when young becoming silvery. **Buds** ⅛–¼ in. (3–6 cm.) long, covered by 2 long scales or small leaves.

Flowers 1–3 at base of leaves, short-stalked and turned down, ½–⅝ in. (12–15 mm.) long, exceptionally fragrant, silvery, funnel-shaped, composed of tube with calyx of 4 yellow lobes at apex, 4 short stamens alternate and inserted in tube which is yellowish within, and pistil with 1-celled ovary, 1 ovule, and long style. **Fruit** elliptic, ½–⅝ in. (12–15 mm.) long, silvery, drupelike, composed of dry mealy, edible tube and 1 narrow slightly 8-angled nutlet. Flowering mid-June, fruit ripening in August.

The fruits are eaten raw or cooked in moosefat, especially by the Indians. Plants are grown as ornamentals in interior Alaska, spreading from roots. Elsewhere the plants are used sometimes as a windbreak.

Common locally on rocky south-facing slopes and forming thickets on sandbars of major rivers in the interior. Central Alaska from Yukon and Porcupine Rivers south to Matanuska and west to upper Kuskokwim River. Mt. McKinley National Park. Alaska and Yukon Territory east to Great Slave Lake, James Bay and Gaspé Peninsula, south to Minnesota, South Dakota, Colorado, and Utah.

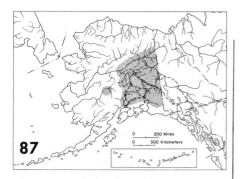

87

Figure 87.—**Silverberry** (*Elaeagnus commutata*), one-half natural size. Winter twigs at right.

GINSENG FAMILY

(Araliaceae)

Mostly tropical trees and shrubs, represented in Alaska by 1 species of herb and the following spiny shrub. Leaves various but often palmately lobed or compound and large, with stipules often forming sheathlike base. Flowers small, in-conspicuous, greenish, in spreading rounded clusters (umbels), 5-parted, with inferior ovary. Fruit a berry; often flattened and 2-celled.

88. DEVILSCLUB

(*Oplopanax horridus* (Sm.) Miq.)

Other names: *Echinopanax horridus* (Sm.) Decne. & Planch., *Fatsia horrida* (Sm.) Benth. & Hook. f.

Large deciduous spiny shrub 3–10 ft. (1–3 m.) high, with few or several thick stems and very few branches. **Leaves** few, alternate, very large, with long stout spiny hairy petiole 6–12 in. (15–30 cm.) long. Blades rounded, 6–14 in. (15–35 cm.) or more in diameter, thin, palmately 5–9-lobed, lobes sharp pointed and irregularly

197

sharply toothed, heart-shaped at base, with spines along veins, above dull green and hairless, beneath light green and slightly hairy. Stems, petioles, and veins densely covered with many sharp slender yellowish spines or bristly prickles ¼–⅜ in. (6–10 mm.) long. **Stems** thick, ½–1 in. (1.2–2.5 cm.) in diameter, light brown, with very large white pith. **Buds** large, ½ in. (12 mm.) long, elliptic, blunt pointed, brownish tinged, of large, nearly hairless, overlapping scales.

Flower clusters (umbels in a raceme or panicle) terminal, erect, 4–12 in. (10–30 cm.) long, nearly stalkless. **Flowers** many, greenish white, ¼ in. (6 mm.) long, fragrant, composed of calyx of 5 teeth, 5 petals ⅛ in. (3 mm.) long, 5 alternate stamens longer than petals, and pistil with inferior 2-celled ovary and 2 spreading styles. **Fruits** numerous bright red berries ¼–⅜ in. (6–10 mm.) long, rounded but slightly flattened, with 2 styles at apex, 2-seeded, not edible. Flowering in June, fruits persistent over winter.

Common in ravines and openings, moist well-drained soil, characteristic of undergrowth and forming impenetrable thickets in coastal and flood plain forests, especially under alder and on good Sitka spruce sites. Plants grow best under partial shade and decline in vigor after clearcutting and exposure to full sunlight.

In spite of their spiny nature, the young shoots are browsed by deer and elk in spring and early summer. The Indians sometimes brew tea from the very bitter bark as a tonic or may strip off the thorns and eat the green bark as a tonic. Years ago the stalks were used by Indians for beating suspected witches to obtain confessions. Even today old people will nail the devilsclub stalk over their door or window to protect the house from witches, evil influences, and bad luck.

The numerous sharp spines are painful and fester when imbedded in the skin, making this shrub dangerous and to be avoided. However, the plants are handsome because of the bright red berries and beautiful mosaic of large leaves arranged to catch the maximum amount of filtered sunlight at the forest edge.

Devilsclub is sometimes used as an ornamental in southeast Alaska and southward. It can be planted where seen but not touched, such as in corners and fences. In the fall the foliage provides a prominent splash of yellow.

Southeast Alaska north to south central Alaska, eastern part of Alaska Peninusla, and Kodiak Island. South Tongass, North Tongass, and Chugach National Forests, Glacier Bay National Monument, Kenai National Moose Range, Kodiak National Wildlife Refuge. South central Alaska east to Manitoba, Montana, southern Oregon, and Idaho; also local in Isle Royale, Mich., and Ontario. A closely related species or variety is found in Japan.

DOGWOOD FAMILY

(Cornaceae)

Shrubs and trees but represented in Alaska by 1 species of shrubs and 2 of low herbs. Leaves in the Alaska species paired, elliptic, without teeth or lobes, with long curved side veins, without stipules. Flowers small but often crowded and bordered by showy petallike bracts, 4- or 5-parted, with inferior ovary. Fruit a drupe.

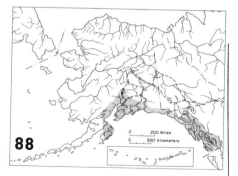

88

Figure 88.—Devilsclub (*Oplopanax horridus*), one-half natural size. Winter twig at right.

89. RED-OSIER DOGWOOD

(*Cornus stolonifera* Michx.)

Other names: American dogwood; *Cornus stolonifera* f. *interior* (Rydb.) Rickett, var. *baileyi* (Coult. & Evans) Drescher; *C. instolonea* A. Nels.

Deciduous shrub 3–12 ft. (1–3.5 m.) high, with several stems, reported to become 15 ft. (4.5 m.) high and treelike. **Leaves** paired (opposite), with hairy petioles ¼–½ in. (6–12 mm.) long, without stipules. Blades elliptic to ovate,

199

1½–3½ in. (4–9 cm.) long and ⅝–2 in. (1.5–5 cm.) broad, short- or long-pointed at apex, short-pointed or rounded at base, edges not toothed, 5–7 long curved, sunken veins on each side of midrib, dull green and nearly hairless above, finely hairy and whitish green beneath. **Twigs** dark red, mostly finely hairy when young, with rings at nodes, whitish dots (lenticels), and large white pith. **Bark** gray, smooth to slightly furrowed into flat thick plates.

Flower clusters (cymes) terminal, flat, 1¼–2¼ in. (3–5.5 cm.) across, the branches persistent in winter. **Flowers** many, crowded, short-stalked, about ¼ in. (6 mm.) long and broad, finely hairy, composed of calyx of 4 minute sepals united at base, 4 white petals ⅛ in. (3 mm.) long, 4 alternate stamens, and pistil with inferior 2-celled ovary and short style. **Fruit** (drupe) round, ¼–⅜ in. (6–10 mm.) in diameter, whitish or light blue, with 1 nutlet 3⁄16 in. (5 mm.) long. Flowering June–July, fruits maturing July–September.

Native plants are often used as ornamentals and are easily propagated by stem cuttings. Young twigs are a preferred browse of moose during fall and winter. The lower branches root at tip, as indicated by the scientific name, at least in some parts of the broad range.

Common in moist soil in clearings and in open understory of forests, especially on flood plains of major rivers. Central interior Alaska from lower and central Yukon River to southeast Alaska. South Tongass and North Tongass National Forests. Alaska and Yukon Territory east to Labrador and Newfoundland, south in the east to Virginia and Kansas and in the west to New Mexico, California, and northern Mexico.

Two related species of dwarf dogwoods are low herbs from creeping woody stems, with flowers in showy heads bordered by 4 white petallike bracts. They hybridize where their ranges overlap.

Bunchberry (*Cornus canadensis* L., dwarf cornel, Jacob-berry, Canadian dwarf cornel) has erect stems 4–8 in. (10–20 cm.) high, **leaves** 1 pair small and at summit 4–6 large leaves (whorled), short-stalked, elliptic, 1½–2½ in. (4–6 cm.) long and ¾–1½ in. (2–4 cm.) wide. **Flowers** many, minute, whitish or yellowish, in a head ¾–1¼ in. (2–3 cm.) across the 4 white elliptic petallike bracts. **Fruit** a cluster of 10 or fewer orange-red round drupes 5⁄16 in. (8 mm.) in diameter. Very common in Alaska except extreme north and to Unalaska Island in Aleutian Islands. Forming ground cover in interior spruce forests. Alaska across Canada to Labrador and Greenland, south in mountains to Kentucky and New Mexico; also in northeastern Asia. In southeast Alaska utilized during all seasons as browse by blacktail deer. Propagated as an ornamental ground cover in interior Alaska for its showy flowers and fruits and fall coloring. It is reported that the berries are sometimes used for jelly and pies.

Lapland cornel (*Cornus suecica* L., Swedish dwarf cornel) has erect stems 2–8 in. (5–20 cm.) high, bearing 2–8 paired **leaves** (opposite), ¾–1¼ in. (2–3 cm.) long and ⅝–1 in. (1.5–2.5 cm.) wide, stalkless, lanceolate to elliptic. **Flowers** many, minute, dark purple, in a head ¾–1 in. (2–2.5 cm.) across the 4 white elliptic petallike bracts. **Fruit** a cluster of 3–10 rose-red round drupes 5⁄16 in. (8 mm.) in diameter. Western, south central, southern, and southeast Alaska and Aleutian Islands. Alaska, also Labrador and Newfoundland to Greenland and in northern Europe and northeastern Asia.

Figure 89.—Red-osier dogwood (*Cornus stolonifera*), one-half natural size. Winter twigs at left; fruits at upper right.

89

CROWBERRY FAMILY
(Empetraceae)

Evergreen small heathlike shrubs with crowded narrow leaves grooved beneath, without stipules. Flowers small, mostly 3-parted, partly male and female; fruit berrylike, containing few nutlets. This small family has a single species in Alaska.

90. CROWBERRY
(*Empetrum nigrum* L.)

Other names: mossberry, blackberry, curlewberry; *Empetrum hermaphroditum* (Lange) Hagerup, *E. nigrum* ssp. *hermaphroditum* (Lange) Böcher.

Low, creeping or spreading evergreen heatherlike shrub to 6 in. (15 cm.) high, forming dense mats, with horizontal, much branched stems. **Leaves** crowded, 4 in a whorl or sometimes alternate,

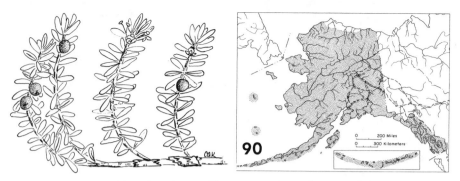

90

Figure 90.—Crowberry (*Empetrum nigrum*), natural size.

without stipules, with minute petiole, linear or needlelike, ⅛–¼ in. (3–6 mm.) long, shiny yellow green, with groove on lower surface formed by curved margins, hairless. **Twigs** curving upward 2–6 in. (5–15 cm.) long, very slender, brown, finely hairy, becoming shreddy.

Flowers single, inconspicuous, stalkless at base of leaves, small, ⅛–¼ in. (3–6 mm.) long, purplish, composed of 3 bracts, 3 sepals, 3 spreading petals, 3 stamens much longer than petals, and pistil with 6–9–celled ovary and flat stigma with 6–9 narrow lobes; also some plants with male flowers and others with female flowers. **Fruit** round, berrylike, 3⁄16–⅜ in. (5–10 mm.) or more in diameter, shiny dark blue black or purple, very juicy and sweet, containing 6–9 reddish brown nutlets. Flowering in June, fruits ripening in August and persisting under the snow throughout the winter.

The edible berries are consumed in quantities locally, usually mixed with other berries and reported to be excellent in pies. In winter Eskimos gather the fruits under the snow. The berries serve also as fall and winter food of grouse, ptarmigan, and bear. Some plants bear fruits in abundance, but male plants have none.

Crowberry is used as a ground cover in rough low areas in interior Alaska. Plants can be grown from cuttings.

Common and widespread in arctic-alpine tundra, moist rocky slopes, and muskegs, also in spruce forests, almost throughout Alaska including Aleutian Islands. One of the commonest species in heath mats to 5,600 ft. (1,700 m.) altitude on the rocky cliffs or nunataks of the Juneau Ice Field. In interior mostly in mountains, also along southern coast. South Tongass, North Tongass, and Chugach National Forests, Mt. McKinley National Park, Glacier Bay National Monument, Kenai National Moose Range, Kodiak National Wildlife Refuge, Arctic National Wildlife Range. Alaska east across northern Canada to northern Greenland, south to Labrador and Newfoundland, and south along coast and in high mountains to Maine, New York, Michigan, and California. Also widespread across Eurasia.

PYROLA FAMILY
(Pyrolaceae)

Low evergreen perennials, mostly herbs, but occasionally shrubs. **Leaves** thick and leathery, usually

202

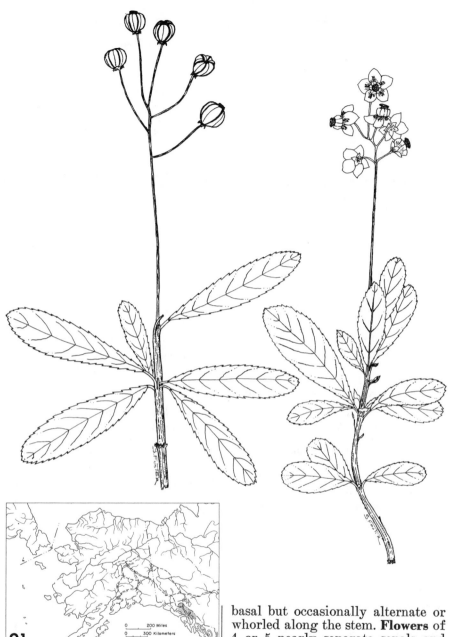

Figure 91.—Pipsissewa (*Chimaphila umbellata*), natural size. Flowers at right; fruits at left.

basal but occasionally alternate or whorled along the stem. **Flowers** of 4 or 5 nearly separate sepals and petals, usually pink to white; stamens twice as many as the petals. **Fruit** a 5-parted dry capsule with many small seeds. In Alaska, the family includes the herbaceous wintergreens (*Pyrola*) and one half-shrub.

203

91. PIPSISSEWA

(*Chimaphila umbellata* (L.) Barton)

Other names: princes–pine, wintergreen, waxflower; *Chimaphila umbellata* ssp. *occidentalis* (Rydb.) Hult. and var. *occidentalis* (Rydb.) Blake; *C. occidentalis* Rydb.

A low evergreen half-shrub, clumped or matlike, with creeping branches that ascend to 4–12 in. (10–30 cm.). **Leaves** thick, shiny, ¾–2½ in. (3–7 cm.) long, ³⁄₁₆–1 in. (0.5–2.5 cm.) wide, broadest near tip, tapering toward base into a short petiole ⅛–⁵⁄₁₆ in. (3–8 mm.) long, sharply toothed, alternate or whorled on the stem. **Twigs** slender, only semiwoody, yellow or green.

Flowers 4 to 15, nodding in a cluster at the end of the twigs, on a stalk 2–4 in. (5–10 cm.) long, saucer shaped; petals separate, reddish to pink, ³⁄₁₆–⁵⁄₁₆ in. (5–8 cm.) long, sepals hairy, fringed at tip. **Fruit** a spherical dry, 5-parted, many seeded capsule ¼–⁵⁄₁₆ in. (6–8 mm.) in diameter.

Pipsessewa is a rare shrub in southeastern Alaska growing under Sitka spruce and hemlock.

Northern part of southeastern Alaska from Juneau north to Haines and Skagway at the head of Lynn Canal. North Tongass National Forest. With a gap of several hundred miles between the Alaska location and southern British Columbia; from British Columbia south in the Rocky Mountains to Colorado and along the coast to southern California. Also in Eastern Canada and United States south in mountains to Georgia and with a scattered distribution in northern Europe and Asia.

HEATH FAMILY

(Ericaceae)

A large family of shrubs in Alaska, elsewhere also trees and herbs, usually growing in wet, acid soil. **Leaves** mostly alternate, simple, leathery, evergreen or occasionally deciduous. **Flowers** usually with funnel-shaped or urn-shaped corolla with 4 or 5 lobes, occasionally with 5 spreading distinct petals; sepals 4 or 5, partly united at base; stamens equal to or twice as many as petals; and pistil with ovary usually 5-celled, superior (except in *Vaccinium*) and 1 style. **Fruit** a capsule, berry, or drupe.

This family is well represented in Alaska by 13 genera and 30 species, all shrubs. It includes the blueberries, huckleberries, cranberries, and such beautiful showy shrubs as Labrador-tea, rhododendrons, and mountain-heaths. It also has a number of less conspicuous forest and bog shrubs, such as rusty menziesia, leatherleaf, and bog rosemary. Some examples, such as mountain-heaths, Labrador-teas, and mountain-cranberries, are evergreen, but many are deciduous. The foliage of several species is reported to be poisonous to grazing animals.

92. COPPERBUSH

(*Cladothamnus pyrolaeflorus* Bong.)

Other name: copper-flower.

Erect shrub 1½–4½ ft. (0.5–1.5 m.) tall, with clustered long leaves and showy copper-colored

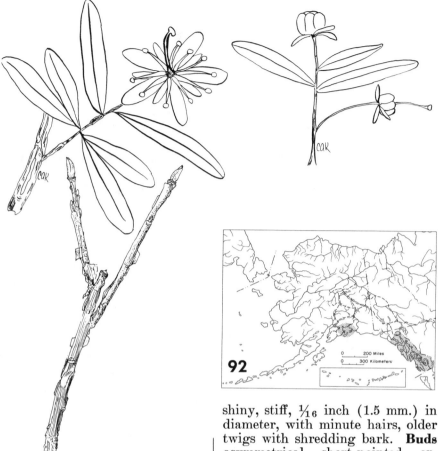

Figure 92.—Copperbush (*Cladothamnus pyrolaeflorus*), natural size. Winter twig at lower left.

flowers. **Leaves** ovate to oblanceolate, ¾–1½ in. (20–40 mm.) long, ³⁄₁₆–½ in. (5–12 mm.) wide, with rounded to abruptly pointed (mucronate) tip, pale green and somewhat whitish (glaucous) on underside, appearing in whorls. First year **twigs** light brown and shiny, stiff, ¹⁄₁₆ inch (1.5 mm.) in diameter, with minute hairs, older twigs with shredding bark. **Buds** asymmetrical, short-pointed, orange, shiny, of 2 keeled scales.

Flowers 1 to several at ends of twigs, about 1 in. (25 mm.) across; sepals 5, narrow; 5 spreading oval copper-colored petals ⅜–⅝ in. (10–15 mm.) long; stamens 10, ⅜ inch (10 mm.) long, hooked near tip; style long, curved. **Fruit** a round capsule ⅛–¼ in. (3–6 mm.) in diameter, dark reddish brown. Flowering from late June through middle of August, fruits ripening August and September.

Copperbush forms dense clumps several yards (meters) across in meadows at and just above treeline and in openings and along streambanks within the coastal forests. The unusual color of the flowers makes this shrub desirable for cultivation. It is often planted in southeastern Alaskan towns.

Along the coast from Prince William Sound to southern tip of Alaska. South Tongass, North Tongass, and Chugach National Forests, Glacier Bay National Monument. Coastal Alaska south to northwestern Oregon.

LABRADOR-TEA (*Ledum*)

Low, much branched, resinous, evergreen shrubs. **Leaves** alternate, thick and leathery, densely woolly beneath and with margins rolled under. **Flowers** white, with 5 spreading petals and 5-lobed calyx, 5–10 stamens, and 5-celled ovary with 5-lobed stigma. **Fruit** a 5-parted capsule, opening from base.

Key to the 2 Alaska Species

Leaves nearly linear, tightly rolled under, $\frac{1}{32}$–$\frac{1}{16}$ in. (0.8–1.5 mm.) wide; stalks of flower and fruit abruptly bent just below apex _____ _____ 93. narrow-leaf Labrador-tea (*Ledum decumbens*)
Leaves wider, $\frac{3}{16}$–$\frac{1}{2}$ in. (5–12 mm.), edges slightly rolled under, flower stalks evenly curved ____ 94. Labrador-tea (*Ledum groenlandicum*)

93. NARROW-LEAF LABRADOR-TEA

(*Ledum decumbens* (Ait.) Small)

Other names: Hudson-Bay-tea, *Ledum palustre* L. ssp. *decumbens* (Ait.) Hult. and var. *decumbens* Ait.

Evergreen shrub 1–2 ft. (3–6 dm.) tall, similar to the more common Labrador-tea but smaller and with narrower leaves rolled under at edges. **Leaves** linear, $\frac{5}{16}$–$\frac{5}{8}$ in. (8–15 mm.) long, $\frac{1}{16}$–$\frac{1}{8}$ in. (1.5–3 mm.) wide, leathery, rolled under at edges, upper surface shiny, dark green, lower surface with reddish-brown woolly hairs. Young **twigs** hairy, light brown, older twigs gray.

Flowers numerous, in clusters at tips of twigs, about $\frac{1}{2}$ in. (12 mm.) broad; petals 5, white, spreading $\frac{3}{16}$–$\frac{5}{16}$ in. (5–8 mm.) long; stamens mostly 10; flower stalks $\frac{1}{2}$–

$\frac{3}{4}$ in. (12–20 mm.) long, sharply and abruptly bent just below apex. **Fruit** a capsule $\frac{1}{8}$–$\frac{1}{4}$ in. (3–6 mm.) long, oval, finely hairy, maturing in July and August, opening from base in autumn and persistent most of winter.

Narrow-leaf Labrador-tea is a common shrub in arctic and alpine tundra in sedge tussocks and wet depressions. In the boreal forest it is common in sphagnum bogs and wet black spruce types. Its large white, fragrant flower clusters are conspicuous during June and early July.

A palatable tea can be made by boiling the aromatic leaves of either species of Labrador-tea. However, if used in large quantities, it may have a carthartic effect.

From mountains at head of Lynn Canal northward across most of Alaska except Aleutian Islands. Chugach National Forest, Katmai National Monument, Mt. McKinley National Park, Kenai National

Figure 93.—Narrow-leaf Labrador-tea (*Ledum decumbens*), natural size.

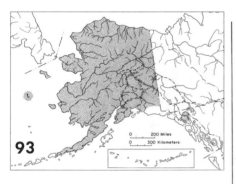

93

Moose Range, Kodiak National Wildlife Refuge, Arctic National Wildlife Range. Eastward across the Canadian Arctic to Labrador and Greenland, south to Hudson Bay and Lake Athabaska District. Also in northern Europe and Asia.

94. LABRADOR-TEA

(*Ledum groenlandicum* Oeder)

Other names: *Ledum palustre*

L. ssp. *groenlandicum* (Oeder) Hult., *L. pacificum* Small.

Evergreen shrub 3 feet (1 m.) tall, with upright or prostrate branches. **Leaves** narrowly oblong, 1–2 in. (25–50 mm.) long, $\frac{3}{16}$–$\frac{1}{2}$ in. (5–12 mm.) wide, with fragrant odor, leathery, margins strongly rolled under, underside covered with reddish brown woolly hairs, upper surface dark green and roughened. Young **twigs** hairy, light brown, older twigs gray.

Flowers numerous, conspicuous, white, fragrant, in clusters at end of twigs, $\frac{5}{8}$ in. (15 mm.) across; petals 5, spreading $\frac{3}{16}$–$\frac{5}{16}$ in. (5–8 mm.) long; stamens mostly 8; flower stalks $\frac{3}{8}$–$\frac{3}{4}$ in. (10–20 mm.) long, evenly curved. **Fruit** a hairy, oblong capsule $\frac{1}{4}$ in. (6 mm.) long, opening from base in autumn and persistent most of winter.

Labrador-tea is a common shrub of black spruce and birch forests

207

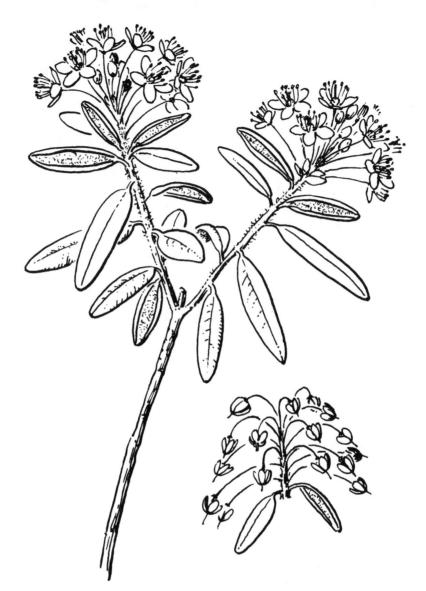

Figure 94.—Labrador-tea (*Ledum groenlandicum*), natural size. Fruits at lower right.

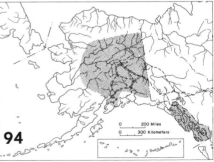

94

and bogs. It comes in abundantly after fire in the black spruce type. It is also abundant near treeline in open white spruce stands where it blooms profusely from mid-June

208

to mid-July. In southeast Alaska it grows in open bogs at low elevations. As with narrow-leaf Labrador-tea, a tea can be made by boiling the aromatic dried leaves, though seldom used today.

Southeast Alaska northward throughout most of the boreal forest but not in the extreme northern or western parts. South Tongass, North Tongass, and Chugach National Forests, Glacier Bay National Monument, Mt. McKinley National Park, Kenai National Moose Range. East across Canada to Newfoundland and Greenland, south to New Jersey, Ohio, Minnesota, and Washington.

Closely related to *Ledum palustre* L. of Europe and Asia, to which both Alaskan species have been united as subspecies.

RHODODENDRON

(*Rhododendron*)

Low evergreen shrubs or subshrubs in Alaska (elsewhere also tall shrubs and small trees). **Leaves** alternate, entire on margins, with short petioles. **Flowers** with showy corolla with 5 large spreading lobes, calyx 5-parted and small, stamens 10, and long slender persistent style. **Fruit** an oblong capsule mostly 5-parted.

Key to the 2 Alaska Species

Leaves oval, mostly less than ½ in. (12 mm.) in length, with resin dots on both sides, not hairy on the margins; flowers several in terminal cluster; corolla less than ¾ in. (20 mm.) across _____ _____ 95. Lapland rosebay (*Rhododendron lapponicum*)
Leaves spatula-shaped to obovate, mostly more than ½ in. (12 mm.) long, without resin dots, hairy on margins; flowers 1–3 at tips of twigs, corolla more than 1¼ in. (32 mm.) across _____ ____ 96. Kamchatka rhododendron (*Rhododendron camtschaticum*)

95. LAPLAND ROSEBAY

(*Rhododendron lapponicum* (L.) Wahlenb.)

Other name: alpine rhododendron.

Matted to erect, much branched evergreen shrub, 4–16 in. (1–4 dm.) tall, with showy purple flowers. **Leaves** oval, ³/₁₆–⁹/₁₆ in. (5–15 mm.) long, ⅛–¼ in. (3–6 mm.) wide, blunt at apex, somewhat rolled down on margins, leathery, crowded at ends of twigs, both surfaces with greenish to brown resin dots, new leaves light green, old leaves dark green to brown. **Twigs** stout, much branched, scurfy with resin dots.

Flowers 1 to several in terminal clusters, fragrant, corolla spreading and slightly irregular, pinkish to deep purple, ⅝–¾ in. (15–20 mm.) across; stalks ¼–½ in. (6–12 mm.) long, scurfy, curved or straight. **Fruit** a dry capsule ³/₁₆–¼ in. (5–6 mm.) long, opening from tip, persisting through most of winter.

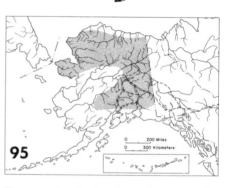

Figure 95.—Lapland rosebay (*Rhododendron lapponicum*), natural size.

Lapland rosebay is an occasional to rare, early-flowering shrub of tundra and open spruce forests at treeline. Its fragrance becomes noticeable in late May to mid-June, the period of flowering. Individual shrubs and flowers are showy, but the shrub is rarely abundant enough to become conspicuous.

From mountains of south-central Alaska northward and westward to the Arctic coast and north slope of Brooks Range but absent on northern coastal plain. Mt. McKinley National Park, Arctic National Wildlife Range. Eastward across the Canadian Arctic to Ellesmere Island, Baffin Island and Labrador, south in the mountains to New York and British Columbia. Also in northern Europe and Asia.

96. KAMCHATKA RHODODENDRON

(*Rhododendron camtschaticum* Pall.)

Evergreen subshrub 2–6 in. (5–15 cm.) tall with large showy flowers. **Leaves** obovate, ½–1¾ in. (12–45 mm.) long and ⅜–¾ in. (10–20 mm.) wide, tapering to base, with conspicuous stiff hairs

Figure 96.—Kamchatka rhododendron (*Rhododendron camtschaticum*), natural size.

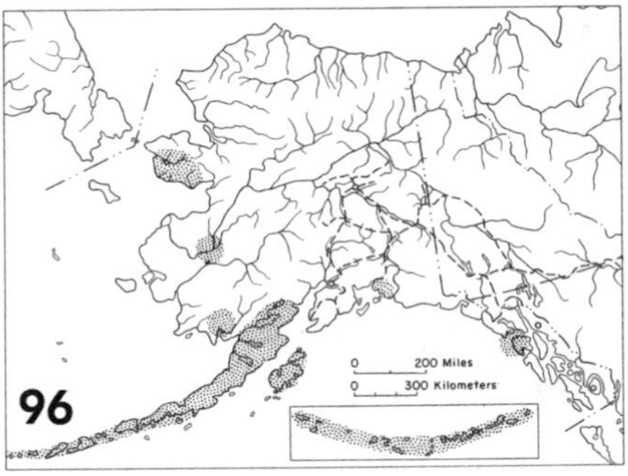

96

This low, showy shrub is common in some areas of the Aleutian Islands on dry rocky tundra characterized by the heath family. In forested regions it is a low shrub of the alpine zone.

There are 2 distinct forms in Alaska. The typical subspecies (*Rhododendron camtschaticum* ssp. *camtschaticum*) has the corolla hairy on outside and on margins of lobes and the leaf margins mostly with nonglandular hairs. The other subspecies (*R. camtschaticum* ssp. *glandulosum* (Standl.) Hult.) has the corolla without hairs on outside and margins and the leaf margins with glandular hairs.

on margins and prominent network of veins on underside; petiole lacking. **Twigs** coarse, much-branched, gray brown to reddish, with shredding bark.

Flowers 1 to several on erect leafy stalks ¾–1¼ in. (2–3 cm.) long at ends of twigs; corolla rose-purple to deep red, spreading, 1¼–1¾ in. (32–45 mm.) across, style conspicuous, ½–¾ in. (12–20 mm.) long, curved. **Fruit** a capsule ¼–⅜ in. (6–10 mm.) long on a long stalk.

211

The typical form or subspecies is found from Prince William Sound westward along the coast to western tip of Aleutians. It has been collected also near the northern end of southeast Alaska. Subspecies *glandulosum* is on Seward Peninsula and lower Yukon River. Chugach National Forest, Kodiak and Aleutian Islands National Wildlife Refuges. Also in eastern Asia and Japan.

97. RUSTY MENZIESIA

(*Menziesia ferruginea* Sm.)

Other names: skunkbrush, foolshuckleberry.

Loose-spreading, odorous, deciduous shrub to 6–10 ft. (2–3 m.) high, with slender, widely forking paired branches and small yellowish red flowers. **Leaves** obovate to elliptic, 1¼–2½ in. (3–6 cm.) long and ½–¾ in. (1.2–2 cm.) wide, short-pointed usually with abrupt (mucronate) tip, edges minutely toothed with gland-tipped hairs, upper side gray green with scattered brown hairs, under side whitish (glaucous) with glandular ("sticky") hairs; petioles ⅛ in. (3 mm.) with gland-tipped hairs. Young **twigs** glandular, with odor when crushed, older twigs reddish brown to gray, smooth to peeling in thin layers. **Buds** of 2 sizes, the larger with many scales developing into flower cluster.

Flowers several to many at ends of twigs on glandular stalks ⅜–¾ in. (1–2 cm.) long; corolla urn-shaped, yellowish red (sometimes described as coppery-pink), ¼–½ in. (6–12 mm.) long, with 4 shallow lobes; calyx 4-lobed, with long glandular hairs; stamens 8; stigma 4-lobed. **Fruit** an ovid 4-parted capsule ³⁄₁₆–⁵⁄₁₆ in. (5–8 mm.)

long, green to reddish brown, often persistent through the winter. Flowering from late May through July, capsules maturing July and August.

Rusty menziesia is a common shrub in undergrowth of the coastal spruce-hemlock forest, often under a dense canopy, also in openings, and on cutover forest land, especially on well drained slopes in association with blueberries. It also grows in the southern part of the boreal forest in white spruce and white spruce-paper birch stands. Because of the leaf and flower size and shape, menziesia is sometimes confused with the huckleberries, but its fruit is not a berry.

Coastal forests of southeast Alaska and the Cook Inlet area and reaching inland along the Susitna River to the south slope of the Alaska Range. South Tongass, North Tongass, and Chugach National Forests, Glacier Bay National Monument, Kenai National Moose Range. Coastal Alaska south to northern California and eastward to eastern Washington.

This genus was dedicated to Archibald Menzies (1754–1842), Scotch physician and naturalist with Vancouver's voyage of 1793–94 to the Northwest coast.

98. ALPINE-AZALEA

(*Loiseleuria procumbens* (L.) Desv.)

Matted or trailing evergreen subshrub 1–2 in. (25–50 mm.) tall. **Leaves** opposite, elliptic, small, ⅛–¼ in. (3–6 mm.) long and ¹⁄₁₆ in. (1.5 mm.) wide, leathery, with margins rolled under, upper side hairless, lower side with dense short

Figure 97.—Rusty menziesia (*Menziesia ferruginea*), natural size. Winter twig with fruits at lower left.

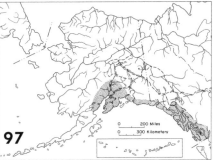

white hairs and a prominent ridge. **Twigs** much branched, nearly totally concealed by the persistent leaves.

Flowers 1 to several at ends of twigs, erect on stalks $\frac{1}{8}$–$\frac{1}{4}$ in. (3–6 mm.) long; corolla bell-shaped, pink or sometimes white, $\frac{1}{8}$–$\frac{3}{16}$ in. (3–5 mm.) long, divided nearly to the middle into 5 lobes; calyx deeply divided into 5 reddish-purple lanceolate lobes; stamens 5. **Fruit** an erect, round 2–3-parted dark red capsule $\frac{1}{8}$–$\frac{3}{16}$ in. (3–5 mm.) in diameter. Flowering from late May through July, fruits maturing in July and August.

Alpine-azalea is occasional to common on well drained rocky sites in arctic and alpine tundra. It frequently forms pure mats, usually 4–12 in. (1–3 dm.) in diameter,

213

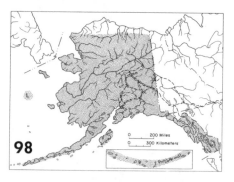

Figure 98.—Alpine-azalea (*Loiseleuria procumbens*), natural size.

but as wide as 1 yard (1 m.) with a large number of flowers for the size of the plant.

In mountains and arctic tundra throughout Alaska except northern coastal plain. To 5,000 ft. (1,524 m.) altitude on rocky cliffs or nunataks of Juneau Ice Field. South Tongass, North Tongass, and Chugach National Forests, Glacier Bay and Katmai National Monuments, Mt. McKinley National Park, Kenai National Moose Range, Kodiak and Aleutian Islands National Wildlife Refuges, Arctic National Wildlife Range. Eastward across the Canadian Arctic to Baffin Island, Labrador, and Newfoundland, south to New England, Hudson Bay, and Alberta. Also in northern Europe and Asia.

99. BOG KALMIA

(*Kalmia polifolia* Wang.)

Other names: swamp-laurel, bog-laurel, pale-laurel.

Evergreen spreading shrub of bogs and mountain meadows, 4–20 in. (1–5 dm.) tall, with showy rose to purple flowers. **Leaves** opposite, stalkless, oblong to linear ¾–1½ in. (2–4 cm.) long, ⅛–⁵⁄₁₆ in. (3–8 mm.) wide, flat or with edges rolled under, dark green above and whitish (glaucous) beneath; petioles short, ¹⁄₁₆–³⁄₁₆ in. (1.5–5 mm.) long. **Twigs** slightly 2-angled.

Flowers several in cymes at ends of twigs on stalks ⅜–1¼ in. (1–3 cm.) long; corolla saucer-shaped, ⅜–¾ in. (1–2 cm.) across, with 5 lobes and 10 ridges (keels), rose to purple; sepals 5, thick; stamens 10. **Fruit** a 5-parted capsule about ³⁄₁₆ in. (5 mm.) long. Flowering from late May to early July, fruits maturing in August.

Bog kalmia occurs occasionally in wet open habitats of mountains and lowlands throughout southeast Alaska.

Along the coast of southeast Alaska as far north as head of Lynn Canal. South Tongass and North Tongass National Forests. From Alaska east to Hudson Bay and Newfoundland, south to New Jersey, Minnesota, and California.

214

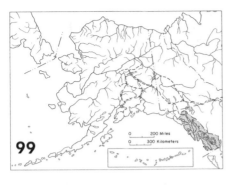

Figure 99.—Bog kalmia (*Kalmia poli-folia*), three-fourths natural size.

MOUNTAIN-HEATH
(*Phyllodoce*)

Low clump or mat-forming evergreen shrubs of alpine tundra. **Leaves** crowded, small, needlelike, linear, blunt-pointed. **Twigs** with conspicuous peglike leaf-scars. **Flowers** in terminal clusters (corymbs); corolla bell-shaped or urn-shaped with 5 small lobes; sepals 5, persistent; stamens 10, short. **Fruit** a 5-parted rounded capsule.

Key to the 3 Alaska Species

Corolla bell-shaped, flowers pink to red _____ _____ 100. red mountain-heath (*Phyllodoce empetriformis*)
Corolla urn-shaped, flowers yellow or blue.
    Corolla purple to blue _____
    _____ 101. blue mountain-heath (*Phyllodoce coerulea*)
    Corolla yellow __ 102. Aleutian mountain-heath (*Phyllodoce aleutica*)

100. RED MOUNTAIN-HEATH
(*Phyllodoce empetriformis* (Sm.) D. Don)

Other names: red mountain-heather, red heather, purple heather.

Low matted evergreen shrub 4–8 in. (1–2 dm.) tall, with pink to red flowers. **Leaves** needlelike, linear, ¼–½ in. (6–12 mm.) long and ¹⁄₁₆ in. (1.5 mm.) wide, crowded on the upper 2–4 inches (5–10 cm.) of stem, edges with minute glandular teeth, with 2 deep grooves on lower surface. **Stems** slender, gray, with conspicuous peglike leaf-scars.

Flowers 5–15 at tips of stems on slightly nodding to upright

215

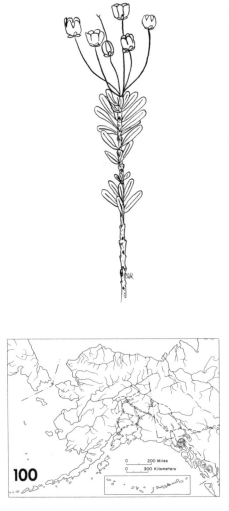

Figure 100.—Red mountain - heath (*Phyllodoce empetriformis*), natural size.

Red mountain-heath is a rare alpine or subalpine shrub of protected snow deposition areas where it usually occurs with one or more of the other mountain-heaths. In Alaska only in mountains at head of Lynn Canal. Eastward to Yukon Territory, south in mountains to California and Wyoming.

101. BLUE MOUNTAIN-HEATH

(*Phyllodoce coerulea* (L.) Bab.)

Other name: blue mountain-heather.

Low matted evergreen shrub 2–6 in. (5–15 cm.) high, with purple or blue flowers. **Leaves** scattered, needlelike, linear, 1/8–1/4 in. (3–6 mm.) long, 1/16–3/16 in. (1.5–5 mm.) wide, rounded at tip, shiny dark green, hairless, grooved on under surface. **Stems** much branched, slender, with conspicuous peglike leaf-scars and shredded bark.

Flowers 3–4 at tips of stems on erect to curved glandular stalks 3/8–5/8 in. (1–1.5 cm.) long; corolla urn-shaped with 5 small lobes, 5/16–3/8 in. (8–10 mm.) long, purple to blue. **Fruit** an oval capsule, 1/16–1/8 in (1.5–3 mm.) long, erect on stalk elongating in fruit to 1 in. (2.5 cm.). Flowering in July and August, fruits maturing in August and September.

Blue mountain-heath is a rare shrub of the coastal and mountain tundra of central and western Alaska, usually in depressions where the snow remains late in the spring. Western Alaska Range and mountains of the western coast of Alaska from the Kuskokwim River to the Seward Peninsula. Common in the southern parts of the Canadian Arctic but absent

glandular-haired stalks 5/8–3/4 in. (15–20 mm.) long; corolla pink to red, bell-shaped, 3/16–1/4 in. (5–6 mm.) long, divided 1/4 into 5 lobes which are rolled outwards; sepals 5, divided nearly to base, dark red, persistent. **Fruit** an erect capsule, 3/16–1/4 in. (5–6 mm.) long. Collected in flower in early and late August.

216

Figure 101.—Blue mountain-heath (*Phyllodoce coerulea*), natural size.

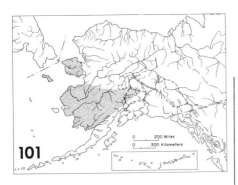

101

from western Alaska to Great Slave Lake. Eastward to Hudson Bay, Labrador, Newfoundland, and Greenland, south to mountains of New England. Also in northern Europe and Asia.

102. ALEUTIAN MOUNTAIN-HEATH

(*Phyllodoce aleutica* (Spreng.) Heller)

Other names: Aleutian mountain-heather, Aleutian heather, cream mountain-heather, yellow mountain-heather, yellow heather.

Low much branched, yellow-flowered evergreen shrub, 2–6 in. (5–15 cm.) tall. **Leaves** needlelike, linear, thick, ¼–½ in. (6–12 mm.) long, ¹⁄₁₆ in. (1.5 mm.) wide, with minute glandular teeth on edge, yellow green, grooved, hairy on lower surface, crowded in upper 2–4 in. (5–10 cm.) of stem. **Stems** much branched, slender, with conspicuous peglike leaf-scars.

Flowers 5–15 at tips of erect or nodding stems, glandular hairy stalks, ½–⅝ in. (12–15 mm.) long; corolla yellow-green, urn-shaped, ¼ in. (6 mm.) long, with 5 small lobes, hairless or with glandular hairs (ssp. *glanduliflora*), calyx with short-pointed lobes divided nearly to base, hairless or glandular hairy. **Fruit** a capsule ⁵⁄₁₆–⅜ in. (8–10 mm.) long, oval, splitting into 5 parts.

Aleutian mountain-heath can commonly be found blooming from early June until late August in protected depressions and adjacent to snow fields in the mountains of

217

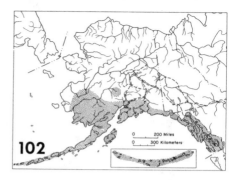

Figure 102.—Aleutian mountain-heath
(*Phyllodoce aleutica*), natural size.

as Prince William Sound. South Tongass, North Tongass, and Chugach National Forests, Katmai National Monument, Kenai National Moose Range, Kodiak and Aleutian Islands National Wildlife Refuges. Eastward in Canada to Yukon Territory and south in mountains to Wyoming and Oregon. Also in eastern Asia.

southeastern and western Alaska, both above and below timberline. It forms pure mats several yards (meters) in diameter, especially at the head of snow field slopes. In the mountains near Juneau, it forms extensive heath mats to elevations of 5,400 ft. (1,646 m.), also on fresh moraine and outwash at sea level.

Mountains along coast of southeastern Alaska westward to western Aleutians, and along the west coast as far north as Yukon River. One collection in Alaska Range in mountains near Tonzona River. A subspecies (*Phyllodoce aleutica* ssp. *glanduliflora* (Hook.) Hult., formerly also a species, *P. glanduliflora* (Hook.) Cov.), characterized by glandular corolla and filaments hairy at base, is found in southeast Alaska and as far west

CASSIOPE (*Cassiope*)

The members of the genus *Cassiope* are often called mountain-heathers, but to distinguish them from the mountain-heaths or mountain-heathers of the genus *Phyllodoce*, it is preferable to refer to them as cassiopes.

The cassiopes are a group of white-flowered, low, prostrate, mosslike evergreen shrubs of the alpine and arctic tundra. **Leaves** scalelike or needlelike, closely pressed to stem (spreading in 1 species). **Flowers** with pink to white bell-shaped corolla with usually 5 (sometimes 4) short lobes; sepals usually 5 (sometimes 4), nearly separate, persistent; stamens usually 10, short. **Fruit** a 5-parted round capsule. There are

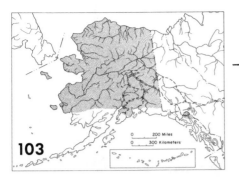

103

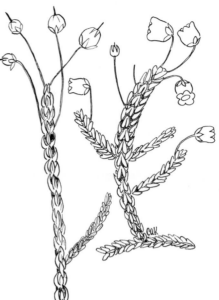

Figure 103.—Four-angled cassiope (*Cassiope tetragona*), natural size.

4 species in Alaska. Four-angled cassiope is primarily of northern and central Alaska, but the other 3 are restricted to mountains of Alaska Range and southward.

Key to the 4 Alaska Species

Leaves alternate, spreading; flower 1 on short stout stalk at end of stem ---------------------- 105. starry cassiope (*Cassiope stelleriana*)
Leaves opposite, pressed to stem, flowers usually 2 or more on long stalks from sides of stem.
    Leaves deeply grooved on back ----------------------------------- ----------------- 103. four-angled cassiope (*Cassiope tetragona*)
    Leaves not grooved on back.
        Leafy stems ⅛ in. (3 mm.) or more in diameter ------------------ ---------------- 104. Mertens cassiope (*Cassiope mertensiana*)
        Leafy stems about ¹⁄₁₆ in. (1.5–2 mm.) in diameter -------------- --------------106. Alaska cassiope (*Cassiope lycopodioides*)

103. FOUR-ANGLED CASSIOPE

(*Cassiope tetragona* (L.) D. Don)

Other names: firemoss cassiope, four-angled mountain-heather, Lapland cassiope.

Low, creeping, evergreen, moss-like mat-forming shrub with stems 4–8 in. (1–2 dm.) tall. **Leaves** opposite in 4 rows, thick, lance-shaped, ⅛–³⁄₁₆ in. (3–5 mm.) long, deeply grooved, with short fine hairs along edge. **Stems** covered by leaves except at base, 4-angled, including leaves nearly ³⁄₁₆ in. (5 mm.) in diameter.

Flowers about ¼ in. (6 mm.) long, nodding on slender stalks ½–1 in. (12–25 mm.) from sides of upper 1½ in. (4 cm.) of stem; corolla bell-shaped, white, with lobes about half as long as tube; sepals separate nearly to base, rounded and reddish. **Fruit** an erect round capsule ⅛ in. (3 mm.) long. Flowering from late May

219

through August, fruit maturing August and September.

Four-angled cassiope is one of the prettiest and most common of the cassiopes on the alpine and arctic tundra of central and northern Alaska. It forms rather dense mats in protected areas that are snow covered during the winter and that have snow remaining into the summer. It is sometimes called firemoss because even in the green condition it burns rather well and has been used by mountain climbers and arctic travelers as a source of fuel in areas where no larger woody plants are available.

In mountains in the northern end of southeastern Alaska, north and west across central and northern Alaska, but lacking in southwestern part and Aleutian Islands. To 5,400 ft. (1,650 m.) on rocky cliffs or nunataks of Juneau Ice Field. Chugach National Forest, Mt. McKinley National Park, Arctic National Wildlife Range. East across northern Canada to Ellesmere Island, Baffin Islands, and Greenland and south in mountains to New England, Montana, and Washington. Northern Europe and Asia.

104. MERTENS CASSIOPE

(*Cassiope mertensiana* (Bong.) D. Don)

Other names: Mertens mountain-heather, white heather.

Prostrate, mosslike, evergreen, mat-forming shrub with upturned branches 2–12 in. (5–30 cm.) tall. **Leaves** opposite in 4 rows and pressed to stem, scalelike, ovate-lanceolate, $\frac{1}{16}$–$\frac{1}{8}$ in. (1.5–3 mm.) long, rounded on back and grooved at base, hairless or with small glandular hairs along edge. **Stems** covered by leaves except at base,

including leaves about $\frac{1}{16}$–$\frac{1}{8}$ in. (1.5–3 mm.) in diameter, 4-angled or square in cross section.

Flowers several about $\frac{1}{4}$ in. (6 mm.) long on slender erect stalks $\frac{1}{4}$–1 in. (6–25 mm.) long, from sides of stems; corolla bell-shaped, white to pink, with 5 lobes about half as long as tube; sepals 5, rounded, reddish. **Fruit** an erect round capsule $\frac{1}{8}$ in. (3 mm.) in diameter. Flowering from late June through August, fruits maturing August and September.

Mertens cassiope is a common mat-forming shrub in seepage areas, protected slopes, mountain meadows, and slopes adjacent to snowfields in southeastern Alaska to 5,000 ft. (1,525 m.) altitude, where it is usually associated with related species.

Mountains of southeastern Alaska as far west as Glacier Bay. South Tongass and North Tongass National Forests, Glacier Bay National Monument. East to southern Yukon Territory and south to western Montana, Nevada, and California.

This species honors Carl Heinrich Mertens (1796–1830), German naturalist, who discovered it at Sitka in 1827.

105. STARRY CASSIOPE

(*Cassiope stelleriana* (Pall.) DC.)

Other names: moss heather, Alaska heather, Alaska moss heath; *Harrimanella stelleriana* (Pall.) Cov.

Low spreading, mat-forming evergreen shrub, the upright stems from 2–4 in. (5–10 cm.) tall. **Leaves** alternate, spreading, linear-lanceolate, $\frac{1}{8}$–$\frac{3}{16}$ in. (3–5 mm.) long, keeled on lower surface, hairless or with hairs along edge.

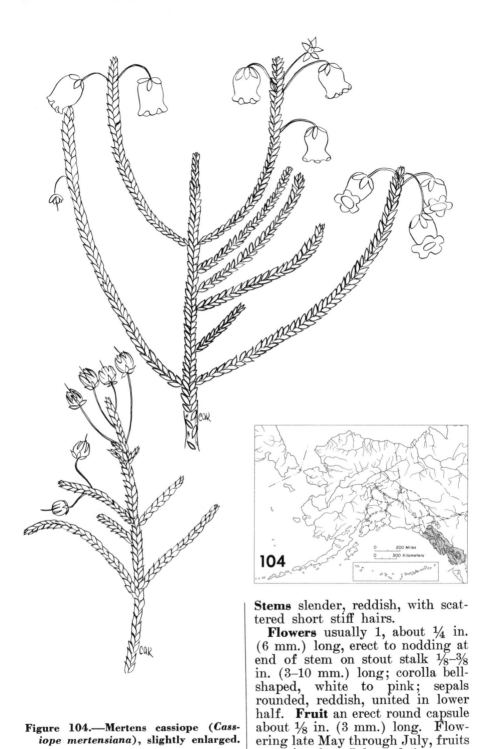

Figure 104.—Mertens cassiope (*Cassiope mertensiana*), slightly enlarged.

Stems slender, reddish, with scattered short stiff hairs.

Flowers usually 1, about ¼ in. (6 mm.) long, erect to nodding at end of stem on stout stalk ⅛–⅜ in. (3–10 mm.) long; corolla bell-shaped, white to pink; sepals rounded, reddish, united in lower half. **Fruit** an erect round capsule about ⅛ in. (3 mm.) long. Flowering late May through July, fruits maturing late July and August.

221

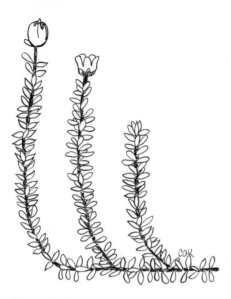

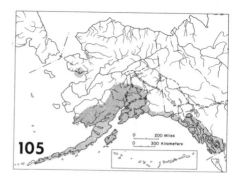

105

Figure 105.—Starry cassiope (*Cassiope stelleriana*), natural size.

The scientific name commemorates Georg Wilhelm Steller (1708–46), German naturalist with Bering's expedition, who in 1741 made the first plant collections in Alaska.

Starry cassiope is a trailing mat-forming shrub of protected slopes, snow deposition areas, and moist seepage areas in the alpine area of southeastern and south central Alaska. It is common in southeastern Alaskan mountains, usually associated with mountain-heaths, to 5,400 ft. (1,650 m.) on rocky cliffs of Juneau Ice Field. It is rare in the Alaska Range, growing with four-angled cassiope.

Coastal mountains of Alaska from southeastern tip north and westward to the Aleutians, in Alaska Range on both north and south slopes as far west as Tonzona River. Also one isolated collection from the Seward Peninsula. South Tongass, North Tongass, and Chugach National Forests, Glacier Bay and Katmai National Monuments, Mt. McKinley National Park, Kenai National Moose Range, Kodiak and Aleutian Islands National Wildlife Ranges. South in coastal mountains to Washington. Also in eastern Asia.

106. ALASKA CASSIOPE

(*Cassiope lycopodioides* (Pall.) D. Don)

Other name: clubmoss mountain-heather.

Delicate low creeping mosslike evergreen shrub with erect branches only 1–2 in. (2.5–5 cm.) tall. **Leaves** tiny, pressed to stem, scale-like, 1/16–1/8 in. (1.5–3 mm.) long, edges with short fine hairs. **Stems** completely obscured by leaves, about 1/16 in. (1.5–2 mm.) in diameter, including leaves.

Flowers nodding on long slender stalks 1/2–3/4 in. (12–20 mm.) back from tip of stem, about 1/4 in. (6 mm.) long; corolla bell-shaped, white, with usually 5 lobes nearly as long as tube; sepals rounded, reddish, transparent at edges. **Fruit** an erect round capsule about 1/8 in. (3 mm.) long. Flowering in June and July, fruit ripening in August.

222

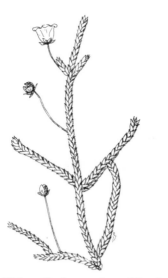

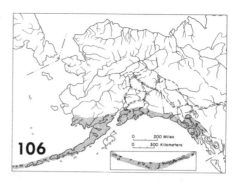

106

Figure 106.—Alaska cassiope (*Cassiope lycopodioides*), natural size.

Alaska cassiope, the smallest of the 4 cassiopes in Alaska, is more creeping than the others and does not form extensive mats. It occurs at edges of exposed ridges in mountains of the southern coast, to 5,400 ft. (1,650 m.) altitude in Juneau Ice Field.

From the mountains of northern half of southeast Alaska west along the coast to western end of Aleutians and north along western coast to Kuskokwim River. North Tongass and Chugach National Forests, Kodiak National Wildlife Range. Aleutian Islands National Wildlife Refuge. Also in northwestern British Columbia and northeastern Asia.

107. BOG-ROSEMARY

(*Andromeda polifolia* L.)

Small delicate, spreading, evergreen shrub, usually 1–2 ft. (30–60 cm.) tall, occasionally to 3 ft. (1 m.) often prostrate and rooting along nodes. **Leaves** narrowly elliptic to nearly linear, ½–1 in. (12–25 mm.) long, ⅛–¼ in. (3–6 mm.) wide, thick, strongly inrolled along edges, with small projection at tip, hairless; upper surface dark green with sunken veins, lower surface whitish (glaucous); petioles short.

Flowers 1–4 at ends of twigs, nodding on thin reddish-purple stalks ¼–½ in. (6–12 mm.) long; sepals 5, short, bluntly triangular, reddish-purple; corolla pink, broadly urn-shaped, with 5 lobes; stamens 10. **Fruit** a spherical, 5-parted capsule, ⅛–¼ in. (3–6 mm.) in diameter, becoming erect, often persisting into winter. Flowering in June and early July, fruits maturing July and August.

Bog-rosemary is an early flowering shrub, common in bogs of the coastal and boreal forests of Alaska and in the wet sedge tundra of the northern and western parts of the State.

The plants contain a strong poison, andromedotoxin (from the generic name), which causes vomiting, dizziness, low blood pressure, breathing difficulty, diarrhea, and cramps. However, it is unlikely that the bitter leaves would be eaten by humans or browsed in quantity by wildlife.

Throughout southeastern Alaska, northward nearly to the Arctic Ocean near Point Barrow, westward throughout western Alaska except tip of Alaska Peninsula and Aleutian Islands. South Tongass, North Tongass, and Chugach

223

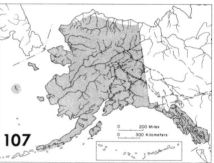

107

Figure 107.—Bog-rosemary (*Andromeda polifolia*), natural size.

National Forests, Glacier Bay and Katmai National Monuments, Mt. McKinley National Park, Kenai National Moose Range, Kodiak National Wildlife Refuge, Arctic National Wildlife Range. East across Canada to northern Labrador and south Greenland, south to New Jersey, Minnesota, and Washington. Northern Europe and Asia.

108. LEATHERLEAF

(*Chamaedaphne calyculata* (L.) Moench)

Other names: cassandra, *Cassandra calyculata* (L.) D. Don.

Prostrate to erect evergreen shrub, rooting at nodes, usually 2–3 ft. (6–10 dm.) tall. **Leaves** alternate, oblong to elliptic, ½–1¼ in. (12–30 mm.) long and ¼–½ in. (6–12 mm.) wide, thick, leathery, and slightly rolled downward on edges, surfaces dark green with scurfy scales often appearing as white dots; petioles short. **Twigs** with fine short white hairs when young but becoming hairless with age, light to dark brown.

Flowers several to many in a row on short stalks, hanging down from lower side of stem (a leafy raceme) about ¼ in. (6 mm.) long,

224

108

Figure 108.—Leatherleaf (*Chamaeda-phne calyculata*), natural size.

corolla white, cylindrical and slightly constricted just below the 5 short triangular lobes; sepals 5, thick, green ovate to lanceolate, with dense hairs on margins; stamens 10, short. **Fruit** a round 5-parted capsule about ⅛ in. (3 mm.) in diameter, longer than sepals with slender style persistent.

Leatherleaf is one of the earliest flowering plants in the interior of Alaska, flowering in early to late May, usually before leaves of most plants have developed. In fall, winter, and spring the leaves have a reddish color, giving many bogs this hue when viewed from a distance. Leatherleaf is an abundant shrub in bogs and open black spruce stands throughout the boreal forest. North of the treeline, it is rare and occurs primarily in wet sites along river terraces.

Lowlands of central Alaska from Cook inlet area to south slope of Brooks Range, also local on north slope including Umiat. Along the western coast, it occurs primarily where the spruce forests reach the coast. Mt. McKinley National Park. Eastward to southern Hudson Bay and Newfoundland, south to Georgia, Minnesota, and northern British Columbia. Northern Europe and Asia.

WINTERGREEN

(*Gaultheria*)

Low evergreen shrubs. **Leaves** alternate, evergreen, ovate to ellip-tic, toothed on edges. **Flowers** with urn- to bell-shaped pink corolla with 5 short lobes; calyx with 5 short glandular hairy lobes; stamens 10, short. **Fruit** a berrylike fleshy 5-celled capsule surrounded by the enlarged fleshy calyx.

Key to the 2 Alaska Species

Leaves 2–4 in. (5–10 cm.) long, sharply toothed; flowers many; fruit purplish; low shrub of southeast Alaska _____ _____ 109. salal (*Gaultheria shallon*)
Leaves ⅝–1⅜ in. (15–35 mm.) long, finely wavy toothed; flowers 1–6; fruit white; prostrate shrub of Kiska Island in eastern Aleutians _____ 110. Miquel wintergreen (*Gaultheria miqueliana*)

109. SALAL

(*Gaultheria shallon* Pursh)

Stiff, creeping to erect evergreen shrub, 2–3 ft. (0.6–1 m.) tall. **Leaves** alternate, short-stalked, large, thick, ovate to elliptic, 2–4 in. (5–10 cm.) long, 1–2 in. (2.5–5 cm.) wide, stiff and leathery, short-pointed at apex, sharply toothed on edges, with occasional long reddish hairs, upper surface shiny green with raised veins, lower surface lighter green. **Twigs** with scattered long, often gland-tipped hairs, hairless with age, reddish-brown, with shredding bark.
Flowers 5–15 in long glandular hairy racemes, usually at tips of twigs, ⅜ in. (1 cm.) long; corolla urn- to bell-shaped, 5/16–⅜ in. (8–10 mm.) long, pink, with stiff reddish brown hairs, and 5 short triangular lobes; calyx lobes reddish-brown, glandular haired, about ⅓ as long as corolla; stamens 10 short. **Fruit** a round capsule enclosed by fleshy calyx, berrylike, purplish, ¼–½ in. (6–12 mm.) in diameter. Collected in flower in May and June.

Salal is a common undershrub of poor scrub timber sites of western redcedar, Alaska-cedar, spruce and hemlock forests in the southern parts of southeastern Alaska where it forms a nearly continuous cover in some stands. The stiff evergreen leaves and densely hairy flowers and twigs make this shrub easily recognized. The spicy berries are eaten by grouse and other birds but seldom by humans. It is reported that Indians in the Northwest gathered the fruits.
Southeast Alaska as far north as Sitka. South Tongass and North Tongass National Forests. South along coast to California.

110. MIQUEL WINTERGREEN

(*Gaultheria miqueliana* Takeda)

Low, prostrate evergreen shrub to 16 in. (41 cm.) high. **Leaves** oval, ⅝–1⅜ in. (15–35 mm.) long, and ⅜–⅝ in. (10–15 mm.) wide, wavy toothed, rounded at tip.

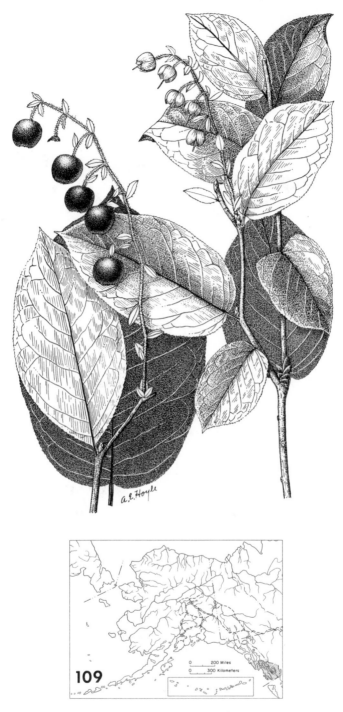

Figure 109.—Salal (*Gaultheria shallon*), natural size.

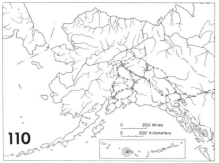

Figure 110.—Miquel wintergreen (*Gaultheria miqueliana*), natural size.

Flowers 1–6, about ¼ in. (6 mm.) long, in glandular hairy racemes; corolla urn-shaped, pink; calyx lobes triangular, glandular hairy on back. **Fruit** a fleshy white berrylike capsule.

Miquel wintergreen, a small Asiatic shrub, has been collected only on Kiska Island in the western Aleutians. It illustrates the close relationship between the flora of eastern Asia and western Alaska.

Kiska Island. Aleutian Islands National Wildlife Refuge. Eastern Asia and Japan.

Named for Frederick Anton Willem Miquel (1811–71), Dutch botanist.

BEARBERRY

(*Arctostaphylos*)

In Alaska low prostrate trailing or matted shrubs, although in California becoming tall shrubs and an important element in the chaparral vegetation. **Leaves** alternate, evergreen or deciduous, usually thick and leathery. **Flowers** in few-flowered racemes at the tip of stems, sepals 4 or 5 nearly separate, corolla white to pink, urn-shaped, with 4 or 5 recurved lobes, stamens 10 (sometimes 8), ovary superior, mostly 4–5-celled. **Fruit** a mealy or juicy "berry" (drupe) containing 4–5 stony nutlets.

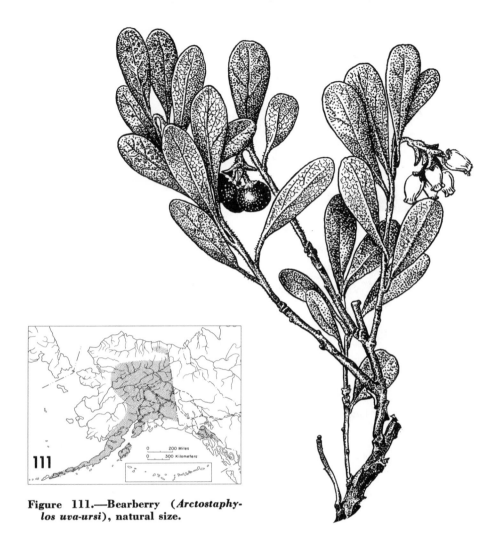

Figure 111.—Bearberry (_Arctostaphylos uva-ursi_), natural size.

Key to the 3 Alaska Species

Leaves evergreen, margin entire; twigs hairy; berries red and mealy
_____ 111. bearberry (_Arctostaphylos uva-ursi_)
Leaves turning red in fall, margin toothed; twigs hairless; berries
red or blue-black, juicy.
    Leaves or partly skeletonized leaves persistent several years, leathery;
    berries blue-black __ 112. alpine bearberry (_Arctostaphylos alpina_)
    Leaves dropping the first winter, thinner; berries red _____
    _____ 113. red-fruit bearberry (_Arctostaphylos rubra_)

229

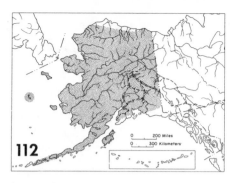

Figure 112.—Alpine bearberry (*Arctostaphylos alpina*), natural size.

111. BEARBERRY

(*Arctostaphylos uva-ursi* (L.) Spreng.)

Other names: kinnikinnik, mealberry.

Prostrate evergreen shrub 3–4 in. (7.5–10 cm.) tall, forming mats by rooting along the stems. **Leaves** obovate, ½–¾ in. (15–20 mm.) long, persistent, leathery, light green, prominently net-veined, tapering to petiole ⅛ in. (3 mm.) long. **Twigs** slender and creeping, brown, with shredding bark.

Flowers, 1 to several in a raceme at ends of twigs, nodding; corolla urn-shaped, ⅛–¼ in. (3–6 mm.) long, white to pink; stalks short, ¹⁄₁₆–⅛ inch (1.5–3 mm.). **Fruit** a red berry ¼–⅝ in. (6–15 mm.) in diameter, dry and seedy, persistent in winter. Flowering in May and June, fruits ripening in August.

Bearberry is a common shrub of dry sites in the boreal forest, usually under aspen but sometimes in open spruce stands or on open dry rocky bluffs. It often forms pure mats several yards (meters) in diameter. The mealy and dry berries are rather tasteless when raw but palatable when cooked.

According to reports, the dry leaves were occasionally used as a substitute for tobacco. As the name indicates, the berries are commonly eaten by bears.

Common in the boreal forest region of Alaska and occasional on the north slope of the Brooks Range and Aleutian and Kodiak Islands, in southeast Alaska, in the vicinity of Glacier Bay and Lynn Canal. North Tongass and Chugach National Forests, Glacier Bay and Katmai National Monuments, Mt. McKinley National Park, Kodiak and Aleutian Islands National Wildlife Refuges, Arctic National Wildlife Range. Alaska to Newfoundland, south in mountains to Georgia and California. Also in northern Europe and Asia.

112. ALPINE BEARBERRY

(*Arctostaphylos alpina* (L.) Spreng.)

Other names: ptarmiganberry, alpine ptarmiganberry, *Arctous alpinus* (L.) Niedenzu.

Matted or trailing shrub 2½–4 in. (6–10 cm.) tall. **Leaves** obovate or oblanceolate, ⅝–1½ in. (15–40 mm.) long and ⅜–¾ in. (10–

230

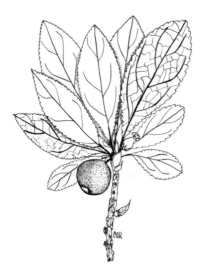

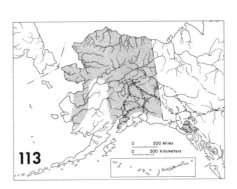

Figure 113.—Red-fruit bearberry (*Arctostaphylos rubra*), natural size.

20 mm.) wide tapering to short petiole, leathery, prominently net-veined on both sides, upper side dark green, under side light green, whitish (glaucous), edges with fine teeth, skeletonized leaves remaining several years. **Twigs** prostrate, brown, hairless, with shredding bark.

Flowers few clustered at tips of branches, nodding; corolla ¼–⁵⁄₁₆ in. (6–8 mm.) long, yellowish green, white, or tinged with pink. **Fruit** a juicy berry, ⅜–½ in. (10–12 mm.) in diameter, black when ripe. Flowering mid-May and and June before the leaves develop, fruit ripening in August.

Alpine bearberry is a common matted shrub of dry, wind exposed sites of the arctic and alpine tundra, and the treeless regions of Kodiak Island and the Aleutians. It also occurs in open black spruce stands and dry sites in bogs at lower elevations. In the fall the leaves turn a deep red and add conspicuously to the color of the tundra landscape.

The berries are edible but seedy and of a rather poor taste. In poor berry years, they are often picked and mixed with blueberries. Large quantities are eaten by both bears and ptarmigan.

Through most of central, western, and northern Alaska, but absent along the coast from Cook Inlet southeastward. Katmai National Monument, Mt. McKinley National Park, Kodiak and Aleutian Islands National Wildlife Refuges, Arctic National Wildlife Range. Eastward across the Canadian Arctic to Greenland. South to Newfoundland, New Hampshire, James Bay, and northern British Columbia. Also in tundra and mountains of Europe and Asia.

113. RED-FRUIT BEARBERRY

(*Arctostaphylos rubra* (Rehd. & Wilson) Fern.)

Other names: ptarmiganberry, *Arctostaphylos alpina* ssp. *ruber* (Rehd. & Wilson) Hult., *Arctous rubra* (Rehd. & Wilson) Nakal.

Similar to alpine bearberry in general appearance but somewhat taller, to 6 in. (15 cm.) with red fruits, and growing more commonly at lower elevations in spruce forests and bogs. **Leaves** thinner and not as deeply wrinkled as in

231

alpine bearberry, dropping the first winter. **Fruit** bright red when ripe, edible but seedy, with insipid taste.

Throughout northern Alaska and in southeastern Alaska at the head of the Lynn Canal and in Glacier Bay, not in southwestern Alaska and Aleutian Islands. Chugach National Forest, Mt. McKinley National Park, Glacier Bay National Monument, Kenai National Moose Range, Arctic National Wildlife Range. Across North America to Baffin Island and south to St. Lawrence Bay, James Bay, and southern British Columbia. Also eastern Asia.

BLUEBERRY (*Vaccinium*)

Other names: huckleberry, mountain-cranberry, cranberry.

Low creeping or tall ascending shrubs, mostly deciduous but sometimes evergreen. **Leaves** alternate, often leathery.

Flowers 1 to several at base of leaves or at ends of twigs; corolla urn-shaped or bell-shaped with 4–5 lobes or of 4 petals bent backward; calyx of 4–5 persistent teeth or lobes on inferior ovary; stamens 8–10, within corolla. **Fruit** a blue or red round juicy berry.

All 6 species in this genus in Alaska are sources of edible fruit. Only 3, bog blueberry, mountain-cranberry, and bog cranberry, reach northern Alaska, the rest are primarily species of the coastal forest. This genus is often separated in the blueberry family (Vacciniaceae), and true cranberry is also placed in its own genus (*Oxycoccus*).

Key to the Alaska Species

A. Leaves evergreen, thick; low trailing shrubs.
 B. Leaves oval; corolla bell-shaped _____
 _____ 114. mountain-cranberry (*Vaccinium vitis-idaea*)
 BB. Leaves lance-shaped; corolla of 4 petals bent backward _____
 _____ 120. bog cranberry (*Vaccinium oxycoccos*)
AA. Leaves deciduous, corolla urn-shaped; usually upright shrubs, though occasionally rooting at nodes.
 C. Twigs round; plants usually less than 16 in. (40 cm.) tall.
 D. Leaves entire on margins; flowers 1–4 from scaly buds on old twigs _____ 119. bog blueberry (*Vaccinium uliginosum*)
 DD. Leaves finely toothed on margins; flower 1 on new twig ____
 _____ 115. dwarf blueberry (*Vaccinium caespitosum*)
 CC. Twigs angled; plants usually more than 2 ft. (6 cm.) tall.
 E. Fruit red; leaves usually less than 1 in. (2.5 cm.) long; twigs green, strongly angled _____
 _____ 116. huckleberry (*Vaccinium parvifolium*)
 EE. Fruit blue or black; leaves commonly more than 1 in. (2.5 cm.) long; twigs reddish to brown, weakly angled.
 F. Flowering with or before the leaves; corolla longer than broad; stalk not enlarged below fruit; leaves without hairs on midrib beneath _____
 _____ 117. early blueberry (*Vaccinium ovalifolium*)
 FF. Flowering after the leaves; corolla as broad or broader than long; stalk enlarged just below fruit; leaves with fine hairs on midrib beneath _____
 _____ 118. Alaska blueberry (*Vaccinium alaskaense*)

232

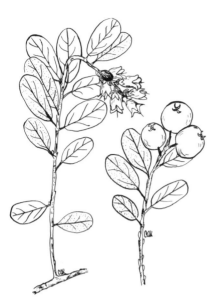

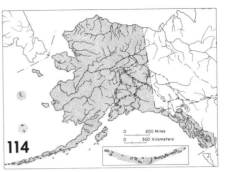

Figure 114.—Mountain-cranberry (*Vaccinium vitis-idaea*), natural size.

114. MOUNTAIN-CRANBERRY

(*Vaccinium vitis-idaea* L.)

Other names: lingenberry, lingberry, lowbush cranberry, partridgeberry, cowberry.

Evergreen creeping, mat-forming subshrub 2–6 in. (5–15 cm.) tall, with shiny leaves and bright red berries. **Leaves** oval, ⅜–¾ in. (10–20 mm.) long and ¼–⅜ in. (6–10 mm.) wide, thick, green, and shiny above, light green beneath and spotted with short stiff brown hairs, edges slightly rolled under. **Stems** slender and trailing, rooting at nodes, light brown to yellow.

Flowers 1 to several, nodding on short stalks ¹⁄₁₆ in. (1–2 mm.) long at ends of twigs, corolla pink, bell-shaped, about ³⁄₁₆ in. (5 mm.) long, with 4 short lobes. **Fruit** a bright red, sour berry, ¼–⁵⁄₁₆ in. (6–8 mm.) in diameter. Flowering in mid- to late June and July, berries ripening in August.

Mountain-cranberry is common in spruce and birch woods of the boreal forest, in bogs and alpine types in most of Alaska, and in the tundra of the north and western sections. It usually forms a loose mat in moist mossy situations but also forms dense mats in dry rocky slopes in arctic and alpine areas.

The berries are abundant and usually picked in the fall after the first frost but may remain under the snow during the winter and become available in the spring when the snow melts. They are commonly used for jams, jellies, relishes, and beverages. Although sour, they have a better flavor than the commercial cranberry. The berries also provide a source of food for ptarmigan, grouse, and bears. The foliage is reported to be of some value as winter browse for reindeer and caribou.

North American plants are smaller in leaf and berry size than those in the Old World and have been named a variety (*Vaccinium vitis-idaea* var. *minus* Lodd. or ssp. *minus* (Lodd.) Hult.).

Throughout Alaska. South Tongass, North Tongass, and Chugach National Forests, Glacier Bay and Katmai National Monuments, Mt. McKinley National Park, Kenai National Moose Range, Kodiak and Aleutian Islands National Wildlife Refuges,

233

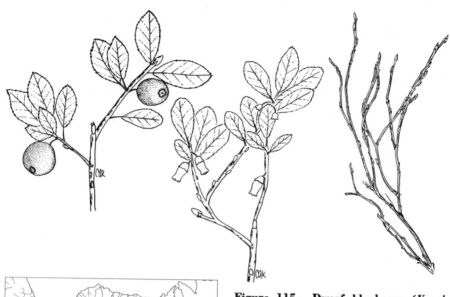

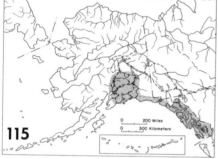

115

Figure 115.—Dwarf blueberry (*Vaccinium caespitosum*), natural size. Winter twig at right.

Arctic National Wildlife Range. Eastward across the Canadian Arctic to Baffin Island and western Greenland, south to Massachusetts, Great Lakes, and Vancouver Island. Also in northern Europe and Asia.

115. DWARF BLUEBERRY

(*Vaccinium caespitosum* Michx.)

Other names: swamp blueberry, dwarf bilberry, dwarf huckleberry, *Vaccinium caespitosum* var. *paludicolum* (Camp) Hult., *V. paludicolum* Camp, *V. arbusculum* Gorman.

Low spreading shrub forming mats to 16 in. (40 cm.) high. **Leaves** elliptic to oblanceolate, ⅜–1 in. (10–25 mm.) long and ³⁄₁₆–⅜ in. (5–10 mm.) wide, rounded to short-pointed at apex, edges with fine teeth usually gland-tipped, netted veins conspicuous in some leaves but obscure on others; upper surface green, lower surface lighter; both hairless or with scattered short stiff hairs. **Twigs** much branched, often rooting at nodes, young twigs slender, green, with short hairs, round or sometimes angled, older twigs brown to gray, bark usually shredding. **Buds** small, red or green with 2 even scales, which meet at the edge.

Flowers single, at base of leaves, nodding on stalks ⅛ in. (3 mm.) long, corolla white or pink, urn-shaped ¼–⁵⁄₁₆ in. (6–8 mm.) long, with 5 small rolled lobes. **Fruit** a blue berry ¼–⁵⁄₁₆ in. (6–8 mm.) in diameter, with a bluish bloom,

234

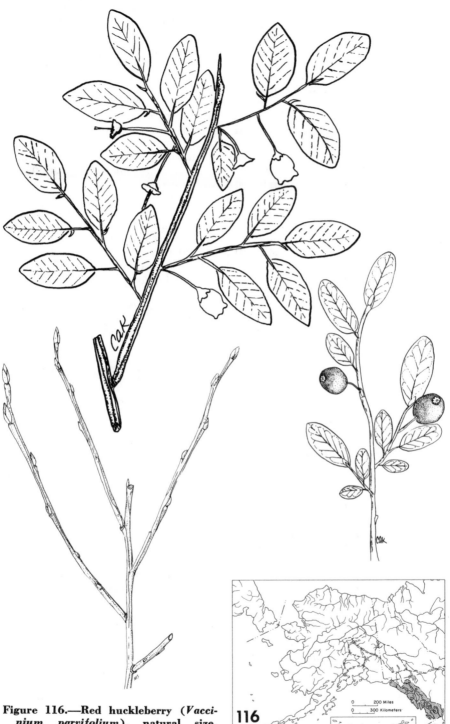

Figure 116.—Red huckleberry (*Vaccinium parvifolium*), natural size.
Winter twig at lower left.

235

sweet. Flowering from late May through mid-July, fruit ripening in August.

Dwarf blueberry is a common shrub of bogs, subalpine meadows, and open spruce-hemlock stands in the coastal forest and is occasional in white spruce and paper birch stands in the southern parts of the boreal forest. It also occurs above tree-line in the coastal mountains to elevations of 3,800 feet (1200 m.). The fruits, which ripen early in August, are eaten raw or made into jams and jellies.

From the south slopes of the Alaska Range to the Kenai Peninsula and southward throughout all of southeastern Alaska. South Tongass, North Tongass, and Chugach National Forests, Glacier Bay National Monument, Kenai National Moose Range. East to Newfoundland and south in mountains to New England, New York, Minnesota, Colorado, and California.

116. RED HUCKLEBERRY

(*Vaccinium parvifolium* Sm.)

Other name: red whortleberry. Erect shrub 3–10 ft. (1–3 m.) tall, with small leaves and red berries. **Leaves** deciduous, often persisting on twigs into early winter, oval to elliptic, ⅜–1¼ in. (1–3 cm.) long and ¼–⅜ in. (6–10 mm.) wide, entire, green on upper surface and grayish beneath; petioles short, ¹⁄₃₂ in. (1 mm.) long. **Twigs** slender, green, shiny, strongly angled or ridged, ending in narrow stub. **Buds** light green, ⅛–³⁄₁₆ in. (3–5 mm.) long, covered by 2 scales, end bud lacking.

Flowers single at base of leaves on stalks ¼–⅜ in. (6–10 mm.), nodding, corolla broadly urn-shaped with 5 small lobes, waxy,

yellowish pink to red, ⅛–¼ in. (3–6 mm.) long. **Fruit** a bright red round berry, ¼–⅜ in. (6–10 mm.) in diameter. Flowering in May and June, berries ripening mid- to late August.

Red huckleberry is an occasional to common shrub in openings along roadsides, and in cut-over forest land, in the coastal spruce-hemlock forests. The berries are sour but with good flavor and are used for jelly. The green twigs are commonly browsed by deer, elk, and goats in fall and winter, and the berries are eaten by blue grouse and bears.

Southeastern Alaska north to Yakutat Bay. South Tongass and North Tongass National Forests, Glacier Bay National Monument. South along coast to central California.

117. EARLY BLUEBERRY

(*Vaccinium ovalifolium* Sm.)

Other names: blue huckleberry, ovalleaf whortleberry, blue whortleberry.

Early flowering, spreading shrub to 5 ft. (1.5 m.) tall. **Leaves** oval, rounded at tip and base, ¾–2 in. (2–5 cm.) long and ⅜–1 in. (1–2.5 cm.) wide, thin, entire to shallowly toothed on edges, hairless, green on upper surfaces, whitish (glaucous) beneath, leaves at tips of twigs usually largest. **Twigs** slender, ¹⁄₁₆ in. (1.5–2 mm.) in diameter, yellowish green to reddish, shiny, weakly angled, becoming gray the 2d or 3d year, ending in narrow stub. **Buds** green or red, ⅛ in. (3 mm.) long, with 2 even scales, end bud lacking.

Flowers in spring before the leaves, single on sides of twig, nodding on stalks ³⁄₁₆–¼ in. (5–6 mm.) long; corolla pink, urn-shaped,

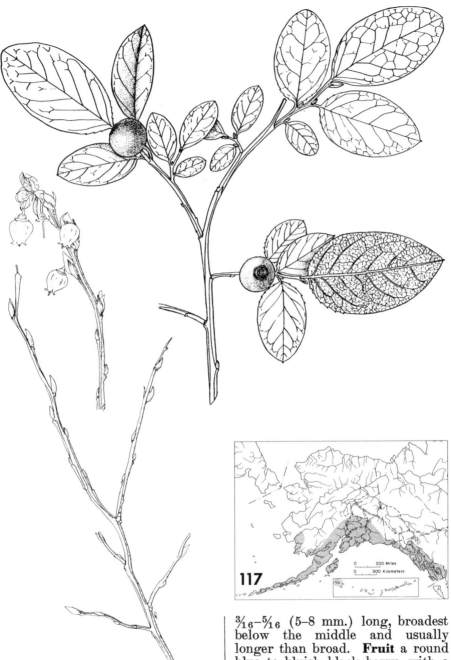

Figure 117.—**Early blueberry** (*Vaccinium ovalifolium*), natural size. Winter twig at lower left; flowering twig at left.

³⁄₁₆–⁵⁄₁₆ (5–8 mm.) long, broadest below the middle and usually longer than broad. **Fruit** a round blue to bluish black berry, with a bluish bloom; stalk usually less than ³⁄₈ in. (1 cm.) long, curved, not enlarged below fruit. Flowering in April and May, berries ripening in mid-July to August.

Early blueberry is the most common blueberry of the coastal forest, where it may form a nearly continuous shrub layer under an open tree canopy and on cutover forest land. This species and Alaska blueberry (*Vaccinium alaskaense*) provide most of the blueberries picked in coastal Alaska where they are made into jellies and jams and frozen for use in winter. The shrub is also used as winter browse by deer, mountaingoat, and elk.

Early blueberry and Alaska blueberry are very similar in appearance and upon detailed study might be united. The following may help to differentiate between the two during various stages of development.

Early blueberry
(*Vaccinium ovalifolium*)

Leaves hairless.

Flowering before or with the leaves.

Corolla usually longer than broad, pink, style included.

Berry bluish or blue-black, with whitish bloom.

Fruit stalks usually less than ⅜ in. (1 cm.), curved, not enlarged just below the fruit.

Alaska blueberry
(*Vaccinium alaskaense*)

Leaves with few short glandular hairs along midvein on lower surface.

Flowering after the leaves are half developed.

Corolla usually broader than long, bronzy pink, style exserted.

Berry blue-black, without whitish bloom.

Fruit stalks often more than ⅜ in. (1 cm.), straight or nearly so, somewhat enlarged just below fruit.

Southeastern Alaska north to south slopes of Alaska Range and west to tip of Aleutians but absent between Attu and Unalaska, also 2 collections along Kuskokwim

River. South Tongass, North Tongass and Chugach National Forests, Glacier Bay and Katmai National Monuments, Kenai National Moose Range, Kodiak and Aleutian Islands National Wildlife Refuges. East to British Columbia and south to southern Oregon. Isolated populations at Lake Superior, Gaspé Peninsula, Labrador, and Newfoundland. A closely related species occurs in eastern Asia.

118. ALASKA BLUEBERRY

(*Vaccinium alaskaense* Howell)

Spreading to erect shrub to 6 ft. (2 m.) high. **Leaves** ¾–2 in. (2–5 cm.) long and ⅜–1 in. (1–2.5 cm.) wide, thin, entire or shallowly toothed on edges, upper surface green, lower surface whitish (glaucous), with few short glandular hairs on midvein. **Twigs** thin, 1/32 in. (1–1.5 mm.) in diameter, weakly angled, yellow green, becoming gray with age, ending in narrow stub. **Buds** green or red, ⅛ in. (3–4 mm.) long, with 2 even scales, end bud lacking.

Flowers single at base of leaves after leaves are partially developed, on straight stalks ¼–⅜ in. (6–10 mm.) long; corolla bronzy pink, rounded urn-shaped, ¼–5/16 in. (6–8 mm.) long, widest just above base, usually broader than long. **Fruit** a berry, bluish black to purple, variable in shape, usually without a bloom, 5/16–⅝ in. (8–15 mm.) in diameter, on a stalk often more than ⅜ in. (1 cm.) long, straight, or nearly so, enlarged just below fruit. Flowering in April and May, berries ripening from mid-July to mid-August.

Alaska blueberry is common in

238

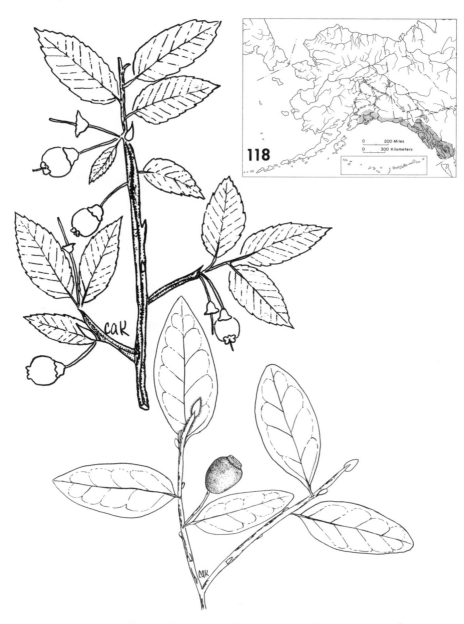

Figure 118.—Alaska blueberry (*Vaccinium alaskaense*), natural size.

the spruce-hemlock forests of the coast (especially in forest openings and cutover land). The berries of this species and of early blueberry are usually picked together, as the shrubs occur in similar habitats. Used widely for jam and jelly and frozen for winter use. The berries are eaten by bears; the twigs are browsed by goat, elk, and deer. For differences between Alaska blueberry (*Vaccinium alaskaense*)

239

and early blueberry (*V. ovalifolium*), see the latter.

Coastal Alaska from Prince William Sound south to southern tip of the State. South Tongass, North Tongass, and Chugach National Forests, Glacier Bay National Monument. From Alaska south along coast to northern Oregon.

119. BOG BLUEBERRY

(*Vaccinium uliginosum* L.)

Other names: bog bilberry, great bilberry, whortleberry.

Much branched low shrub, erect or prostrate, 8–16 in. (20–40 cm.) high, often rooting along branches. **Leaves** oval (obovate) to elliptic, 3/8–3/4 in. (1–2 cm.) long, dark green on upper surface, lighter below, with conspicuous veins. **Twigs** slender, round, 1/32 in. (1 mm.) in diameter, brown, minutely hairy, older twigs much branched, yellow-brown to gray with shredding bark. **Buds** small, 1/32 in. (1 mm.) long, several scales with scattered short hairs.

Flowers 1–4 from ends or side branches, nodding on stalk 1/16–1/8 in. (1.5–3 mm.) long; corolla pink, urn-shaped, 1/8–3/16 in. (3–5 mm.) long with 4 short lobes. **Fruit** a blue to black berry with bluish bloom, ovoid 3/16–3/8 in. (5–10 mm.) in diameter. Flowering in June, berries ripening in late July and August.

Bog blueberry is a very common shrub of bog, open forest, and tundra of all of Alaska except for the extreme northern coastal plain. In southeastern Alaska it grows in the alpine tundra to elevations of 5,600 ft. (1,710 m). The berries are picked in large quantities in north, central, and western Alaska,

but not used extensively in southeastern Alaska where other blueberries are more readily available. The berries are also eaten by bears, grouse, and ptarmigan. Blueberries of this and related species are eaten raw or cooked in pies, puddings, and muffins and may be frozen or canned. They are a fair source of vitamin C.

Throughout Alaska except extreme northern coastal plain. South Tongass, North Tongass, and Chugach National Forests, Glacier Bay and Katmai National Monuments, Mt. McKinley National Park, Kenai National Moose Range, Kodiak and Aleutian Islands National Wildlife Refuges, Arctic National Wildlife Range. Alaska, across Canada to Labrador and Greenland, south to New England, New York, and Minnesota. Also across Europe and Asia. The New World plants belong to a variety (*Vaccinium uliginosum* var. *alpinum* Bigel. or ssp. *alpinum* (Bigel.) Hult.).

120. BOG CRANBERRY

(*Vaccinium oxycoccos* L.)

Other names: swamp cranberry, wild cranberry, small cranberry, *Vaccinium oxycoccos* L. var. *microcarpus* (Turcz.) Fedtsch. & Flerov. *Oxycoccus microcarpus* Turcz.

Evergreen shrub with very slender stems, creeping vinelike through moss and rooting at nodes. **Leaves** persistent, small, lance-shaped, 1/8–3/8 in. (3–10 mm.) long, 1/32–1/8 in. (1–3 mm.) wide, short-pointed, leathery, edges strongly rolled under; shiny dark green on upper surface, gray or whitish beneath with conspicuous midrib. **Stems** yellow to reddish brown, trailing, very slender, 1/32–1/16 in.

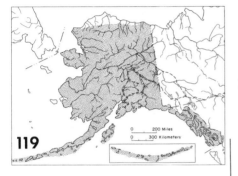

119

Figure 119.—Bog blueberry (*Vaccinium uliginosum*), natural size. Winter twig at right.

(1–1.5 mm.) in diameter, hairless when young.

Flowers 1–4 at ends of stems, nodding on erect slender stalks ¾–1½ in. (2–4 cm.) long with 2 tiny bractlets below middle; petals 4, red to pink, bent backward, ¼ in. (6 mm.) long; 8 stamens ⅛ in. (3 mm.) long, yellow, pointing forward. Because the petals are bent backward, the cranberry flower resembles that of a miniature shootingstar. **Fruit** a red, juicy, round berry ¼–⅜ in. (6–10 mm.) in diameter. Flowering in June, berries ripening in August.

Bog cranberry occurs in most sphagnum bogs and peat hummocks in the coastal and boreal forests but is seldom abundant. Because it is so tiny, the plant is often overlooked until the berries turn red in the fall. The berries are good tasting and can be eaten raw or prepared as jelly or jam in the same manner as the closely related commercial cranberries. However, the bog cranberry seldom is abundant enough to be gathered in large quantities.

Coastal forests north to south slopes of Brooks Range, with 2 collections from Umiat area on north slope, westward to Bering Strait and tip of Aleutians, though absent from many of those islands. South Tongass, North Tongass, and Chugach National Forests, Glacier Bay and Katmai National Monuments, Mt. McKinley National Park, Kenai National Moose Range, Kodiak and Aleutian Islands National Wildlife Refuges.

241

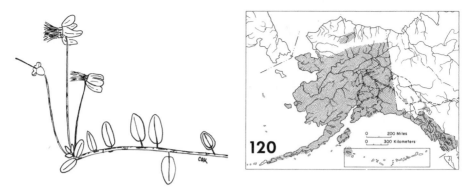

Figure 120.—Bog cranberry (*Vaccinium oxycoccos*), natural size.

Eastward to Hudson Bay and south to southern British Columbia and Alberta. Also in northern Europe and Asia.

The closely related small **cranberry** (*Vaccinium palustre* Salisb.; *Oxycoccus palustris* Pers., *O. quadripetalus* Gilib.) has been reported from Prince of Wales Island. It has thicker stems hairy when young, slightly larger oblong leaves, and larger flowers and fruits.

DIAPENSIA FAMILY

(Diapensiaceae)

Evergreen low shrubs with crowded or alternate leaves without stipules. Flowers with 5-lobed corolla and 5 stamens; fruit a 3-parted capsule. This small family related to the heath family has a single species in Alaska.

121. DIAPENSIA

(*Diapensia lapponica* L.)

Other names: arctic diapensia, *Diapensia lapponica* ssp. *obovata*

(Fr. Schm.) Hult. and var. *obovata* Fr. Schm.

Low, creeping, cushionlike evergreen shrub with stems horizontal or 1–3 in. (2.5–7.5 cm.) high, much branched, with dense mat of dead leaves beneath. **Leaves** densely crowded and overlapping like rosettes or alternate, without stipules, narrowly oblong or spoon-shaped, ⅛–⅜ in. (3–10 mm.) long, ¹⁄₁₆ in. (1.5 mm.) wide, rounded at apex, edges turned under, thick and fleshy, stiff, hairless, dark green on upper surface, light green beneath. **Twigs** slender, hairless, concealed by leaves.

Flowers single, erect on stalks 1–2 in. (2.5–5 cm.) high, ⅝–¾ in. (15–20 mm.) across, composed of 1–3 bracts, 5 persistent yellow green sepals, bell-shaped corolla with 5 rounded spreading lobes white or rarely pink to red, 5 alternate stamens inserted in notches of corolla, and pistil with 3-celled ovary, long slender style, and 3-lobed stigma. **Fruit** an erect elliptic or egg-shaped capsule nearly ¼ in. (6 mm.) long, 3-celled, with several seeds. Flowering from late May often into July.

The many large flowers make diapensia showy and suitable for alpine rock gardens in spite of its small size. Compact mats to 2 ft.

242

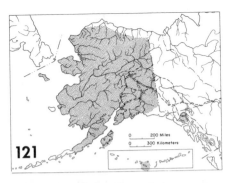

Figure 121.—Diapensia (*Diapensia lapponica*), natural size.

(60 cm.) in diameter are common in dry rocky and gravelly upland slopes in arctic and alpine tundra.

Arctic-alpine nearly throughout interior Alaska except on arctic coastal plain near Pt. Barrow, south to Kodiak Island and Alaska Peninsula. Also Amchitka Island in southwestern Aleutian Islands. In southeast Alaska only in mountains above Haines and Skagway. Chugach National Forest, Mt. McKinley National Park, Katmai National Monument, Kenai National Moose Range, Kodiak Island and Aleutian Islands National Wildlife Refuges, Arctic National Wildlife Range. Alaska, east across northern Canada to Hudson Bay, Greenland, Labrador, and Newfoundland, south in mountains to New England and New York. Also in northern Eurasia.

HONEYSUCKLE FAMILY

(Caprifoliaceae)

Deciduous or evergreen shrubs, sometimes small trees, woody vines, and herbs. **Leaves** opposite, simple or pinnately compound, without stipules (present in *Sambucus*).

Flowers mostly small, regular or irregular, composed of calyx of 4–5 teeth, tubular corolla with 4–5 lobes, 4–5 stamens inserted on tube and alternate with lobes, and pistil with inferior ovary of 2–5 cells and usually 1 ovule in each and 1 style or none. **Fruit** mostly a berry or berrylike drupe. Five genera in Alaska, each with a single native species.

122. PACIFIC RED ELDER

(*Sambucus callicarpa* Greene)

Other names: scarlet elder, redberry elder, stinking elder, elderberry; *Sambucus racemosa* L. var. *arborescens* (Torr. & Gray) Gray.

Deciduous clump-forming shrub 6–12 ft. (2–3.5 m.) high, sometimes large and treelike, with several stems to 2–4 in. (5–10 cm.) d.b.h., rarely a small tree to 20 ft. (6 m.) high and 5 in. (12.5 cm.) d.b.h. **Leaves** opposite, compound, pinnate, 5–10 in. (12.5–25 cm.) long, with small narrow stipules about ⅛ in. (3 mm.) long soon shedding and leaving ring scar on twig, with

243

unpleasant odor. Leaflets 5 or 7, paired except at end, short-stalked. Blades lanceolate or elliptic, 2–5 in. (5–12.5 cm.) long and 1–2 in. (2.5–5 cm.) wide, long-pointed at apex and short-pointed and often unequal at base, finely and sharply toothed on edges, thin, above green and nearly hairless, beneath paler and hairy. **Twigs** stout, finely hairy when young, gray, with raised brown dots (lenticels), with rings at nodes. **Buds** paired, large, egg-shaped, ¼–½ in. (6–12 mm.) long, gray, covered by several slightly hairy overlapping scales often persistent around twig. **Bark** light to dark gray or brown, smoothish, becoming cracked or furrowed into small scaly or shaggy plates. Pith thick, whitish on youngest twigs, becoming deep yellow-orange or brown. **Wood** soft, whitish.

Flower clusters (compound cymes) terminal, erect, longer than broad, 2–4 in. (5–10 cm.) long and 1½–2 in. (4–5 cm.) wide, with many small whitish flowers with unpleasant odor, turning brown on drying. **Flower** composed of minute 5-toothed calyx, white spreading 5-lobed corolla ³⁄₁₆–¼ in. (5–6 mm.) across, 5 stamens inserted at base of corolla and alternate with lobes, and pistil with inferior 3-celled ovary with 1 ovule in each cell, short style, and 3 stigmas. **Fruit** many berrylike drupes about ³⁄₁₆ in. (5 mm.) in diameter with calyx persistent at apex, bright red or scarlet, sometimes orange, containing 3 1-seeded poisonous nutlets. Flowering May–July, fruit maturing July–August.

Elders are easily detected by a strong odor when leaves or stems are crushed. The red fruits are classed as not edible, at least when raw, but are sometimes made into wine. They are eaten by some birds, especially robins and thrushes. The "seeds" (nutlets) are reported to be poisonous, causing diarrhea and vomiting. Plants can be grown as ornamentals but in the interior only in moist situations.

Common locally in moist soil, especially open areas and recently cutover land in coastal forests. Unimak Island in Aleutians, and Pacific coast regions of southwestern, southern, and southeast Alaska. Chugach, North Tongass, and South Tongass National Forests, Katmai and Glacier Bay National Monuments, Kenai National Moose Range, Kodiak and Aleutian Islands National Wildlife Refuges. Pacific coast region from southwest Alaska southeast to western Oregon and mountains of central and southern California.

This elder is added here to the list of native trees in Alaska, rarely reaching the minimum size. Small trees were observed to 20 ft. in height and 5 in. in trunk diameter at Myers Chuck on Cleveland Peninsula northwest of Ketchikan. Southward in the Pacific States heights of 25–30 ft. and trunk diameters to 1 ft. have been recorded.

The plants of northwestern North America from Alaska to California have been treated also as a variety of European red elder (*S. racemosa* L.)

123. HIGH BUSHCRANBERRY

(*Viburnum edule* (Michx.) Raf.)

Other names: squashberry, mooseberry, *Viburnum pauciflorum* La Pylaie.

Deciduous shrub 2–12 ft. (0.6–3.5 m.) high with several to many stems to 1½ in. (4 cm.) d.b.h., sometimes larger and treelike. **Leaves** opposite, with petioles

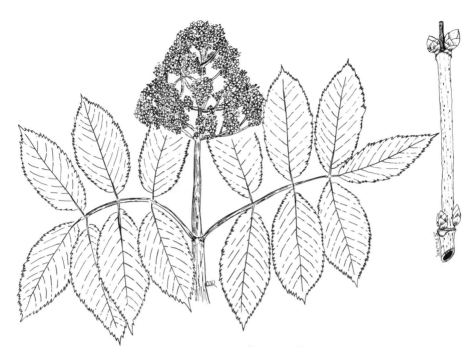

Figure 122.—Pacific red elder (*Sambucus callicarpa*), one-half natural size. Winter twig at right.

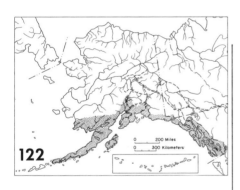

122

¼–¾ in. (6–20 mm.) long, slightly hairy when young, without stipules. Blades rounded, thin, mostly shallowly and palmately 3-lobed, 1–4 in. (2.5–10 cm.) long and wide, with 3 main veins from rounded base which usually has 2 glands, edges sharply toothed and lobes short-pointed, above dull green and hairless, beneath light green and often hairy, especially on veins. **Twigs** light gray, hairless, stout, with rings at nodes and thick white pith. **Buds** narrowly elliptic, ⅛–½ in. (3–12 mm.) long, covered by 2 dark red brown, partly united hairless scales, the side buds paired. **Bark** gray, smooth.

Flower clusters (cymes) terminal on short lateral twigs bearing only 2 leaves, with persistent stalks ½–1 in. (1.2–2.5 cm.) long, small, ½–1 in. (1.2–2.5 cm.) wide, with many or several short-stalked whitish flowers ¼ in. (6 mm.) long and wide. Flower buds white or tinged with pink. **Flowers** composed of short 5-toothed calyx, whitish corolla ¼ in. (6 mm.) across the 5 nearly equal spreading lobes, 5 short stamens inserted on corolla and alternate with lobes, and pistil with inferior 3-celled ovary, 1 ovule, and minute stigma. **Fruit** an elliptic red or orange drupe ⅜–½ in. (10–12 mm.) long, with calyx at apex, sour and edible, containing 1 rounded flat stone ³⁄₁₆ in. (5 mm.) long. Flowering May–July, fruit maturing July–September.

245

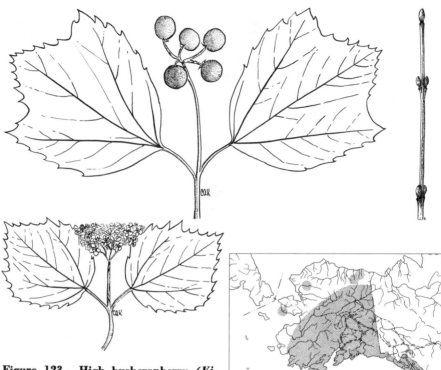

Figure 123.—High bushcranberry (*Vi-burnum edule*), one-half natural size. Winter twig at upper right.

123

The fruits are edible, as the scientific name indicates. They make excellent jelly or juice, especially if picked before mature. Later the flavor may be musty. The flavor of the jelly is improved if the juice is mixed with rose hip puree. The overripe berries give a musty odor to many areas of interior Alaska in late fall. Wildlife browse the foliage, and numerous birds eat the berries. This species has been recommended for cultivation for its brilliant red autumnal foliage.

Scattered to common, sometimes abundant, in thickets, forest openings, and along streams. Through most of Alaska except northern border, western Alaska Peninsula, and Aleutian Islands. South Tongass, North Tongass, and Chugach National Forests, Mt. McKinley National Park, Katmai and Glacier Bay National Monuments, Kodiak National Wildlife Refuge. Alaska and Yukon Territory to mouth of Mackenzie River, Great Bear Lake, Hudson Bay, Ungava Bay, and Newfoundland, south to Pennsylvania, Michigan, Minnesota, Colorado, and Oregon.

124. SNOWBERRY

(*Symphoricarpos albus* (L.) Blake)

Other names: *Symphoricarpos rivularis* Suksd., *S. albus* ssp. *laevigatus* (Fern.) Hult. and var. *laevigatus* (Fern.) Blake.

Deciduous, much branched shrub 1–4 ft. (3–12 dm.) high sometimes

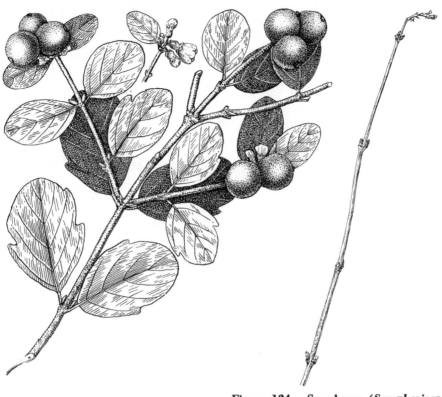

Figure 124.—Snowberry (*Symphoricarpos albus*), natural size. Winter twig at right.

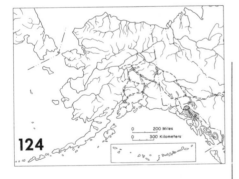

124

taller. **Leaves** opposite, with slender petioles about ⅛ in. (3 mm.) long, without stipules. Blades elliptic to ovate, ⅝–1½ in. (1.5–4 cm.) long, ½–1 in. (1.2–2.5 cm.) wide, blunt at both ends, on vigorous twigs larger and often with a few irregular teeth or lobes, thin, above dark green and hairless or nearly so, beneath often whitish green and hairy. **Twigs** slender,

reddish brown, hairless or minutely hairy, ringed at nodes, older twigs gray with shreddy bark. **Buds** 1⁄16 in. (1.5 mm.) long, scaly.

Flowers mostly few in short clusters (racemes) at ends of twigs or also at bases of upper leaves, about ¼ in. (6 mm.) long, pink, composed of 5-toothed calyx, pink tubular bell-shaped corolla ¼ in. (6 mm.) long and nearly as wide, 5-lobed, hairy within, with 5 stamens inserted in tube alternate with lobes, and pistil with elliptic inferior 4-celled ovary with 2 ovules and short hairless style. **Fruits** 1 to few, round white berry-like drupes ¼–⅝ in. (6–15 mm.) long, with calyx at apex, containing 2 light brown nutlets or stones

247

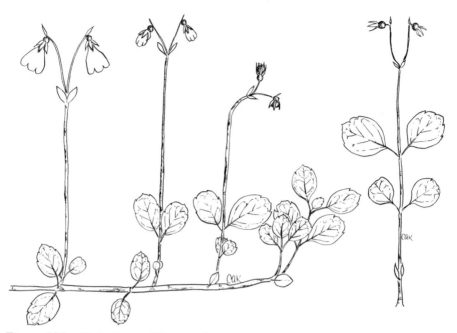

Figure 125.—Twin-flower (*Linnaea borealis*), natural size.

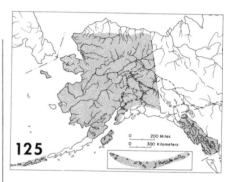

125

³⁄₁₆ in. (5 mm.) long. Collected in flower in July.

Local in southeast Alaska, known only from Haines and Chilkat Valley, and the vicinity of Juneau. North Tongass National Forest. Southeast Alaska, Queen Charlotte Islands, and British Columbia, across Canada to Quebec, south to Virginia, Michigan, Nebraska, Colorado, and California.

Cultivated elsewhere as an ornamental.

125. TWIN-FLOWER

(*Linnaea borealis* L.)

Other names: *Linnaea americana* Forbes, *L. borealis* ssp. *borealis*, ssp. *americana* (Forbes) Hult. and var. *americana* (Forbes) Rehd., *L. borealis* ssp. *longiflora* (Torr.) Hult.

Creeping evergreen dwarf shrub or herbaceous, forming loose mats, with long slender, slightly hairy, woody horizontal stems rooting at nodes and many erect twigs to 4 in. (10 cm.) high. **Leaves** opposite, with slender petioles less than ⅛ in. (3 mm.) long, with stipules. Blades elliptic or rounded, ¼–⅝ in. (6–15 mm.) long and wide, thick with few wavy teeth above middle, hairless or nearly so, above dull green, beneath whitish green.

Flowers paired at apex of very slender erect stalks 1½–3 in. (4–7.5 cm.) long, nodding, fragrant,

248

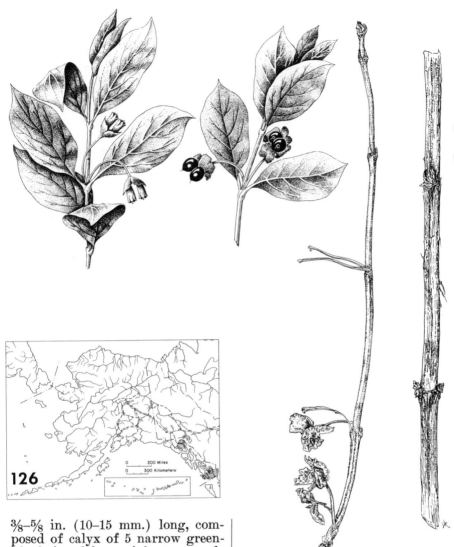

Figure 126.—Bearberry honeysuckle (*Lonicera involucrata*), one-half natural size. Winter twigs at right, natural size.

⅜–⅝ in. (10–15 mm.) long, composed of calyx of 5 narrow greenish hairy lobes, pink to purple funnel-shaped or bell-shaped tubular corolla with 5 nearly equal lobes, 4 stamens in pairs inserted near base of tube and enclosed, and pistil with inferior greenish 3-celled ovary, 1 ovule, and slender style. **Fruit** small, dry, round, ¹⁄₁₆ in. (1.5 mm.) in diameter, with calyx at apex and enclosed by bracts, 1-seeded. Flowering June–August, fruits maturing July–August.

Twin-flower can be transplanted into cultivation as a spreading evergreen ground cover in shady places.

Scattered in open forests and tundra. Widespread almost throughout Alaska (except Arctic coastal plain) from Aleutian Islands through interior to southeast Alaska. South Tongass, North Tongass, and Chugach National Forests, Mt. McKinley National Park, Glacier Bay and Katmai National Monuments, Kenai National Moose Range, Kodiak National Wildlife Refuge, Aleutian Islands National Wildlife Refuge, Arctic National Wildlife Range. Alaska across Canada to Labrador and Newfoundland, south especially in mountains to New Jersey, West Virginia, Indiana, South Dakota, New Mexico, and California. Also widespread across Eurasia.

Three varieties differing slightly in shape of leaves and flowers have been distinguished in Alaska. The generic name honors Carolus Linnaeus (1707–78), Swedish botanist.

126. BEARBERRY HONEYSUCKLE

(*Lonicera involucrata* (Richards.) Banks)

Other names: honeysuckle, black twinberry.

Deciduous shrub 3–10 ft. (1–3 m.) high. **Leaves** opposite, with petioles less than ¼ in. (6 mm.) long, without stipules. Blades elliptic, 2–5 in. (5–12.5 cm.) long, 1–3 in. (2.5–7.5 cm.) wide, long-pointed or short-pointed at both ends, edges hairy and not toothed, above dull green and hairless or nearly so, beneath pale green and hairy on veins. **Twigs** 4-angled when young, hairless, ringed at nodes. **Bark** becoming gray and shreddy.

Flowers paired above 4 leaflike green or purple bracts on stalk 1–2 in. (2.5–5 cm.) long at base of leaves, ½–⅝ in. (12–15 mm.) long, composed of short tubular

calyx, yellow funnel-shaped corolla swollen on one side at base and with 5 nearly equal short lobes, 5 glandular hairy stamens inserted within tube, and pistil with inferior 3-celled ovary, many ovules, and slender style. **Fruits** paired above 4 dark red bracts, 3-celled, few-seeded black berries, round, ⅜ in. (10 mm.) in diameter.

The bitter fruits are said to be poisonous.

Rare and local in wet soil. Restricted in Alaska to vicinity of Portland Canal at extreme southern end of southeast Alaska and at head of Lynn Canal, at northern end of southeast Alaska. South Tongass National Forest. Widespread across northern North America from southeast Alaska and British Columbia to Hudson Bay, James Bay, Quebec, and New Brunswick, south to Michigan and Wisconsin, and in western mountains to New Mexico, California, and Chihuahua, Mexico.

COMPOSITE FAMILY

(Compositae)

This very large family is well represented in Alaska by numerous species of herbs and 1 genus with 2 species woody near base. Leaves in this family are various, often toothed or lobed, without stipules. Flowers small, crowded and stalkless in heads bordered by greenish scales (bracts), with tubular corolla 5-toothed or strap-shaped (ray flowers), calyx of hairs (pappus) or minute scales or none, and inferior ovary. Fruit dry, 1-seeded (akene).

Sagebrush or wormwood (*Artemisia*) is the only genus of this family with woody plants in Alaska. Of about 20 Alaskan

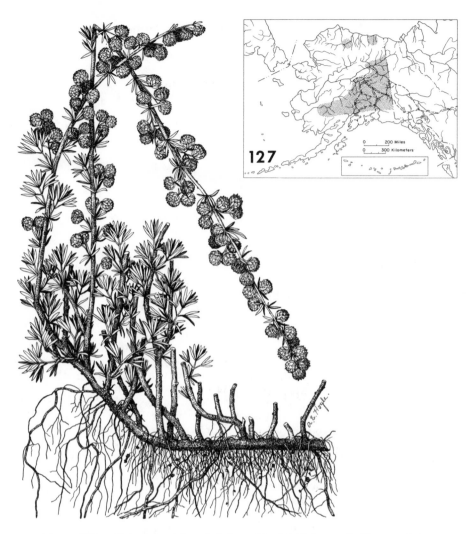

127

200 Miles
300 Kilometers

Figure 127.—Fringed sagebrush (*Artemisia frigida*), one-half natural size.

species, only 2, fringed sagebrush and Alaska sagebrush, can be considered as shrubs, though primarily herbaceous and woody only near base. Both grow on the driest, warmest sites in central and northern Alaska, the steep rocky south-facing river bluffs.

Key to the 2 Alaska Shrub Species

Basal leaves 2 to 3 times divided into linear segments $\frac{1}{32}$ in. (1 mm.) wide, leaf blade $\frac{1}{4}$–$\frac{1}{2}$ in. (6–12 mm.) long _____ 127. fringed sagebrush (*Artemisia frigida*)

Basal leaves 2–3 times divided into spatula-shaped (spatulate or oblanceolate) segments $\frac{1}{16}$–$\frac{1}{8}$ in. (2–3 mm.) wide, leaf blade 1–2 in. (2.5–5 cm.) long _____ 128. Alaska sagebrush (*Artemisia alaskana*)

127. FRINGED SAGEBRUSH

(*Artemisia frigida* Willd.)

Other name: prairie sagewort.

Shrubby spreading perennial, much branched from woody base, 12–18 in. (30–45 cm.) high, fragrant, and silvery in appearance. **Leaves** densely crowded at base and along stem, small and divided 2 or 3 times into linear segments less than $\frac{1}{32}$ in. (1 mm.) wide, total length of blade $\frac{3}{16}$–$\frac{1}{2}$ in. (5–12 mm.), densely silky hairy throughout. **Stems** of current year herbaceous, silvery from dense white hairs, dying back each winter to a few short woody stems, older woody stems covered with dead gray leaves, silvery in some parts but becoming brown with age.

Flowers in small compact heads about $\frac{1}{8}$ in. (3–4 mm.) in diameter, on a narrow erect leafy branch (raceme), yellow without ray flowers, the underlying bracts with dense silvery hairs. **Fruits** many tiny hairless seeds (akenes). Flowering in July–August, seeds maturing August–September.

Fringed sagebrush is a common shrub on sunny, south facing, well drained river bluffs in central Alaska, too dry or unstable for trees. In the summer it may be confused with other herbaceous species of *Artemisia*, which have much larger, less dissected leaves.

Along river bluffs of Matanuska, Copper, Kuskokwim, Tanana, and Yukon rivers of central Alaska. Collected on a bluff on the Saddlerochit River and along the Colville River, both north of the Brooks Range. Mt. McKinley National Park, Arctic National Wildlife Range. Southeast across Canada to Minnesota and south to Texas and Arizona. Also in northern Asia.

128. ALASKA SAGEBRUSH

(*Artemisia alaskana* Rydb.)

Other name: *Artemisia tyrellii* Rydb.

Silvery spreading shrub, 18–24 in. (45–60 cm.) high, much branched from woody base, fragrant. Basal **leaves** 1–2 in. (2.5–5 cm.) long, divided into 3–5 segments, each again divided into spatula-shaped (spatulate), oblong, or linear segments $\frac{1}{16}$ in. (2 mm.) wide; stem leaves becoming less divided so that upper leaves may be

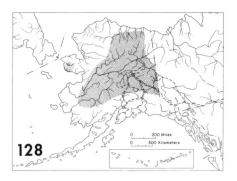

128

undivided and linear-shaped; present year's leaves densely silky hairy, past year's basal leaves usually persisting, gray brown in color. **Stems** herbaceous, silvery from dense hairs, dying back each winter to a few short basal woody stems; older stems brown and covered with old dead gray leaves.

Flowers in compact heads ¼–⁵⁄₁₆ in. (6–8 mm.) in diameter, often nodding, on a branched, narrow, erect leafy twig (raceme), yellow, and lacking ray flowers, the bracts with dense silvery hairs. **Fruits** many tiny hairless seeds (akenes). Flowering in July and August, seeds maturing August and September.

Alaska sagebrush grows on steep south-facing, usually rocky, dry slopes, commonly with fringed sagebrush. The two may form a nearly complete cover on many river bluffs and steep south-facing road cuts.

Common along the river bluffs of central Alaska and occasionally along rivers north of the Brooks Range. One locality on the Seward Peninsula near Nome. Mt. McKinley National Park, Arctic National Wildlife Range. Southeast in Canada only to the headwaters of Tanana and Yukon Rivers and to Lake Kluane region. Closely related to *Artemisia krushiana* Bess., of Asia.

Figure 128.—Alaska sagebrush (*Artemisia alaskana*), one-half natural size.

SELECTED REFERENCES

Additional information about the trees and shrubs of Alaska, also the forests and other vegetation, is available in many articles and books. A selected list of these references is included here. Some that were especially helpful in the preparation of this handbook were cited in the introduction by author and year of publication. Comprehensive bibliographies on Alaska plants have been prepared by Hultén (1941–50, 1967, 1968).

Anderson, H. E.
1953. Range of western redcedar (*Thuja plicata*) in Alaska. USDA Forest Serv. Alaska Forest Res. Center Tech. Note 22, 1 p. and map.

——.
1959. Silvical characteritsics of Alaska-cedar (*Chamaecyparis nootkatensis*). USDA Forest Serv. Alaska Forest Res. Center Sta. Pap. 11, 10 p.

Anderson, J. P.
1939. Plants used by the Eskimo in the northern Bering Sea and Arctic regions of Alaska. Amer. J. Bot. 26: 714–716.

——.
1943–52. Flora of Alaska and adjacent parts of Canada. Iowa State Col. J. Sci. 18: 137–175, 381–445; 19: 133–205; 20: 213–257, 297–347; 21: 363–423; 23: 137–187; 24: 219–271; 26: 387–453.

——.
1959. Flora of Alaska and adjacent parts of Canada. 543 p. Ames, Iowa: Iowa State Univ. Press.

Anderson, James R.
1925. Trees and shrubs, food, medicinal, and poisonous plants of British Columbia. 165 p. Victoria, B.C.

Argus, George W.
1965. The taxonomy of the *Salix glauca* complex in North America. Contrib. Gray Herb. Harvard Univ. 196, 142 p.

——.
1969. New combinations in the *Salix* of Alaska and Yukon. Can. J. Bot. 47: 795–801.

——.
1972. The systematics of the genus *Salix* in Alaska and Yukon. Nat. Mus. Can. Publ. Bot. No 2. (In press)

Babb, M. F.
1959. Ornamental trees and shrubs for Alaska. Univ. Alaska Agr. Exp. Sta. Bull. 24, 39 p.

Ball, Carleton, R.
1940. Dr. W. A. Setchell and Alaska willows. Proc. Nat. Acad. Sci. 21: 181–186.

Bank, T. P.
1951. Botanical and ethnobotanical studies in the Aleutian Islands. I. Aleutian vegetation and Aleut culture. Mich. Acad. Sci. Arts Lett. Pap. 37: 13–30.

Barney, Richard J.
1967. Buildup indexes for interior Alaska 1956–65. USDA Forest Serv. Pacific Northwest Forest and Range Exp. Sta. Inst. of Northern Forest. Misc. Publ. 49 p.

——.
1968. Fire danger rating spread index and buildup index frequencies for interior Alaska. USDA Forest Serv. Pacific Northwest Forest and Range Exp. Sta. Inst. of Northern Forest. 8 p.

——.
1969a. Interior Alaska wildfires, 1956–65. USDA Forest Serv. Pacific Northwest Forest and Range Exp. Sta. Inst. of Northern Forest. Misc. Publ. 47 p.

——.
1969b. National fire-danger rating system fine fuel moisture content tables—an Alaskan adaptation. USDA Forest Serv. Res. Note PNW–109, 12 p.

Baxter, Dow V., and Wadsworth, Frank H.
1939. Forest and fungus succession in the lower Yukon Valley. Univ. Mich. Sch. Forest. Conserv. Bull. 9, 52 p.

Benninghoff, W. S.
1952. Interaction of vegetation and soil frost phenomena. Arctic 5: 34–44.

Berger, Alwin.
1924. A taxonomic review of currants and gooseberries. N.Y. Agri. Exp. Sta. Tech. Bull. 109: 1–118.

Bliss, L. C., and Cantlon, J. E.
1957. Succession on river alluvium in northern Alaska. Amer. Midland Natur. 52: 452–469.

Bones, James T.
1963. Wood processing in Alaska—1961. USDA Forest Serv. Res. Bull. NOR–1, 14 p.

Brayshaw, T. C.
1965. The status of the black cottonwood (*Populus trichocarpa* Torrey and Gray). Can. Field-Natur. 79: 91–95.

Briggs, W. R.
1953. Some plants of Mount McKinley National Park, McGonegall Mountain Area. Rhodora 55: 245–252.

Britton, M. E.
1958. Vegetation of the arctic tundra. 18th Annu. Biol. Colloq. Oregon State Coll. p. 26–61.

Bruce, David, and Court, Arnold
1945. Trees for the Aleutians. Geogr. Rev. 35: 418–423.

Bruce, Mason, B.
1960. National forests in Alaska, J. Forest. 58: 437–442.

Buckley, John L., and Libby, Wilbur L.
1959. The distribution in Alaska of plant and animal life available for survival. Arctic Aeromedical Lab. Tech. Rep. 58–10, 43 p.

Burns, John J.
1964. Pingos in the Yukon-Kuskokwim Delta, Alaska: Their plant succession and use by mink. Arctic 17: 203–210.

Cahalaney, Victor H.
1959. A biological survey of Katmai National Monument. Smithsonian Misc. Collect. 138(5), 246 p.

Calder, James A., and Taylor, Roy L.
1965. New taxa and nomenclature changes with respect to the flora of the Queen Charlotte Islands, British Columbia. Can. J. Bot. 43: 1,387–1,400.

——————, and Mulligan, Gerald A.
1968. Flora of the Queen Charlotte Islands. Can. Dep. Agr. Res. Monogr. 4, Parts 1–2.

254

Camp, W. H.
1942. A survey of the American species of *Vaccinium*, subgenus *Euvaccinium*. Brittonia: 205–247.

———.
1944. A preliminary consideration of the biosystematy of *Oxycoccus*. Bull. Torr. Bot. Club 71: 426–437.

———.
1945. The North American blueberries with notes on other groups of Vacciniaceae. Brittonia 5: 203–275.

Canada, Department of Forestry.
1961. Native trees of Canada. Bull. 61, ed. 6, 291 p. Ottawa.

Churchill, E. D.
1955. Phytosociological and environmental characteristics of plant communities in the Umiat region of Alaska. Ecology 36: 606–627.

Cooper, W. S.
1924. The forests of Glacier Bay (Alaska), present, past, and yet unborn. J. Forest. 22(1): 16–23.

———.
1930. The seed plants and ferns of the Glacier Bay National Monument, Alaska. Bull. Torr. Bot. Club 57: 327–338.

———.
1931. The layering habit in Sitka spruce and the two western hemlocks. Bot. Gaz. 91: 441–451.

———.
1939. Additions to the flora of Glacier Bay National Monument, Alaska, 1935–36. Bull. Torr. Bot. Club 66: 453–456.

———.
1942a. An isolated colony of plants on a glacier-clad mountain. Bull. Torr. Bot. Club 69: 429–433.

———.
1942b. Vegetation of the Prince William Sound Region, Alaska; with a brief excursion into post-Pleistocene climatic history. Ecol. Monogr. 12: 1–22.

Coville, F. V.
1900. The tree willows of Alaska. Proc. Wash. Acad. Sci. 2: 275–286.

———.
1901. The willows of Alaska. Proc. Wash. Acad. Sci. 3: 297–362.

———, and Funston, F.
1895. Botany of Yakutat Bay, Alaska, with a field report by F. Funston. Contrib. U.S. Nat. Herb. 3: 325–350.

Daubenmire, R. F.
1953. Notes on the vegetation of forested regions of the far northern Rockies and Alaska. Northwest Sci. 27: 125–138.

1968. Some geographic variations in *Picea sitchensis* and their ecological interpretation. Can. J. Bot. 46: 787–798.

Davidson, John.
1927. Conifers, junipers, and yew: gymnosperms of British Columbia. 72 p. London.

Dayton, William A.
1931. Important western browse plants. U.S. Dep. Agr. Misc. Pub. 101, 214 p.

Drew, J. V., and Shanks, R. E.
1965. Landscape relationships of soils and vegetation in frost-tundra ecotone, Upper Firth River Valley, Alaska—Canada. Ecol. Monogr. 35: 285–306.

Drury, William H., Jr.
1956. Bog flats and physiographic processes in the upper Kuskokwim River regions, Alaska. Contrib. Gray Herb. Harvard Univ. 178, 130 p.

Dugle, Janet R.
1966. A taxonomic study of western Canadian species in the genus *Betula*. Can. J. Bot. 44: 929–1,007.

Eastwood, Alice.
1947. A collection of plants from the Aleutian Islands. Leafl. Western Bot. 5: 9–13.

———.
1957. A list of plants from Dall and Annette Islands, Alaska. Leafl. Western Bot. 7: 102.

Eliot, Willard Ayres, and McLean, G. B.
1938. Forest trees of the Pacific coast. 565 p. New York.

Evans, W. H.
1899. An undescribed birch from Alaska. Bot. Gaz. 27: 481–482.

———.
1900. Notes on the edible berries of Alaska. Plant World 3: 17–19.

Farr, Wilbur A.
1967a. Board-foot tree volume tables and equations for white spruce in interior Alaska. USDA Forest Serv. Res. Note PNW–59, 4 p.

———.
1967b. Growth and yield of well-stocked white spruce stands in Alaska. USDA Forest Serv. Res. Pap., PNW–53, 30 p.

Fernow, B. C.
1902. Forests of Alaska. Harriman Alaska Exped. Rep. 3: 235–256.

Fowells, H. A., compiler.
1965. Silvics of forest trees of the United States. U.S. Dep. Agr., Agr. Handb. 271, 762 p.

Funsch, Robert W.
1964. A summary of seasonal temperature and precipitation data for the interior forested area of Alaska. USDA Forest Serv. Res. Note NOR–9, 50 p.

Garman, E. H.
1963. Pocket guide to the trees and shrubs of British Columbia. British Columbia Forest Serv. Publ. B. 28, 137 p.

Gjaervoll, O.
1958–67. Botanical investigations in central Alaska, especially in the White Mountains. Parts I–III. K. Norske Vidensk. Selsk. Skr. (Trondheim) 5, 74 p.; 4, 115 p.; 10, 63 p.

Gregory, Robert A.
1957. Some silvicultural characteristics of western redcedar in Alaska. Ecology 38: 646–649.

———.
1960. Identification of spruce seedlings in interior Alaska. USDA Forest Serv. Alaska Forest. Res. Center Tech. Note 45, 4 p.

———.
1966. The effect of leaf litter upon establishment of white spruce beneath paper birch. Forest. Chron. 42: 251–255.

———, and Haack, Paul M.
1964. Equations and tables for estimating cubic-foot volume of interior Alaska tree species. USDA Forest Serv. Res. Note, NOR–6, 21 p.

———.
1965. Growth and yield of well-stocked aspen and birch stands in Alaska. USDA Forest Serv. Res. Pap. NOR–2, 28 p.

——— and Wilson, Brayton F.
1967. A comparison of cambial activity of white spruce in Alaska and New England. Can. J. Bot. 46: 733–734.

Griggs, R. F.
1914. Observations on the edge of the forest in the Kodiak region of Alaska. Bull. Torr. Bot. Club 41: 381–385.

———.
1915. The effect of the eruption of Katmai on land vegetation. Bull. Amer. Geogr. Soc. 47: 193–203.

———.
1918. The recovery of vegetation at Kodiak. Ohio J. Sci. 19: 1–57.

———.
1919. The beginnings of revegetation in Katmai Valley. Ohio J. Sci. 19: 318–342.

Griggs, R. F.
1934. The edge of forest in Alaska and the reasons for its position. Ecology 15: 80–96.

———.
1936. The vegetation of the Katmai district. Ecology 17: 380–417.

Guthrie, John D.
1922. Alaska's interior forests. J. Forest. 20: 363–373.

Haack, Paul M.
1963a. Aerial photo volume tables for interior Alaska tree species. USDA Forest Serv. Res. Note NOR–2, 8 p.

———.
1963b. Volume tables for trees of interior Alaska. USDA Forest Serv. Res. Note NOR–5, 11 p.

Hanks, Leland F., and Swanson, Carl W.
1967. Lumber grade yields from paper birch and balsam poplar logs in the Susitna River Valley. USDA Forest Serv. Res. Pap. PNW–51, 30 p.

Hanson, H. C.
1950. Vegetation and soil profiles in some solifluction and mound areas in Alaska. Ecology 31: 606–630.

———.
1953. Vegetation types in northwestern Alaska and comparisons with communities in other Arctic regions. Ecology 34: 111–140.

Hardy, Charles E., and Franks, James W.
1963. Forest fires in Alaska. USDA Forest Serv. Res. Pap. INT–5, 163 p.

Harris, Arland S.
1964. Sitka spruce; Alaska's new State tree. Amer. Forest. 70(8): 33–35.

———.
1965. Subalpine fir on Harris Ridge near Hollis, Prince of Wales Island, Alaska. Northwest Sci. 39: 123–128.

———.
1967. Natural reforestation on a mile-square clearcut in southeast Alaska. USDA Forest Serv. Res. Pap. PNW–52, 16 p.

———.
1969a. Alaska cedar, a bibliography with abstracts. USDA Forest Serv. Res. Pap. PNW–73, 47 p.

———.
1969b. Ripening and dispersal of a bumper western hemlock-Sitka spruce seed crop in southeast Alaska. USDA Forest Serv. Res. Note PNW–105, 11 p.

———.
1970. The loners of Alaska. Amer. Forest. 76(5): 20–22, 55–56.

Harshberger, J. W.
1928. Tundra vegetation of central Alaska directly under the Arctic Circle. Proc. Amer. Phil. Soc. Phila. 67: 215–234.

———.
1929. The forests of the Pacific coasts of British Columbia and southeastern Alaska. Acta Forest. Fennica 34: 1–5.

Hayes, Doris W., and Garrison, George A.
1960. Important woody plants of eastern Oregon and Washington. U.S. Dep. Agr. Handb. 148, 227 p.

Hegg, Karl M.
1966. A photo identification guide for the land and forest types of interior Alaska. USDA Forest Serv. Res. Pap. NOR–3, 55 p.

Heintzleman, B. F.
1928. Pulp-timber resources of southeastern Alaska. U.S. Dep. Agr. Misc. Publ. 41, 34 p. (Reprinted and slightly rev. 28 p. 1937.)

———.
1949. Forests of Alaska. Trees, U.S. Dep. Agr. Yearb. 1949, 361–372.

Heller, Christine A.
1953. Wild edible and poisonous plants of Alaska. Univ. Alaska Ext. Bull. F–40, 87 p.

———.
1966. Wild flowers of Alaska. 104 p. Portland, Oreg.

Henry, Joseph Kaye.
1915. Flora of southern British Columbia and Vancouver Island, with many references to Alaska and northern species. 363 p. Toronto.

Heusser, C. J.
1954a. Alpine fir at Taku Glacier with notes on its postglacial migration to the Territory. Bull. Torr. Bot. Club 81: 83–86.

———.
1954b. Nunatak flora of the Juneau Ice Field, Alaska. Bull. Torr. Bot. Club 81: 236–250.

———.
1960. Late Pleistocene environments of Pacific North America. 308 p. New York: Amer. Geogr. Soc.

Hitchcock, C. Leo, Cronquist, Arthur, Ownbey, Marion, and Thompson, J. W.
1955–69. Vascular plants of the Pacific Northwest. 5 parts. Seattle and London: Univ. Wash. Press.

Hultén, Eric.
1936. New or notable species from Alaska. Contributions for the flora of Alaska I. Svensk Bot. Tidskr. 30: 515–528.

———.
1940a. History of botanical exploration in Alaska and Yukon Territories from the time of their discovery to 1940. Bot. Notiser 1940: 289–346.

———.
1940b. Two new species of Salix from Alaska. Svensk Bot. Tidskr. 34: 373–376.

———.
1941–50. Flora of Alaska and Yukon, 1–10. Lunds Univ. Arsskr., N. F., Avd. 2, v. 37–46, 1,902 p.

———.
1958. The Amphi-Atlantic plants and their phytogeographical connections. Svensk Vetenskapskad. Handl. 7(71), 340 p.

———.
1959. Studies in the genus Dryas. Svensk Bot. Tidskr. 53: 507–542.

———.
1960a. Contribution to the knowledge of flora and vegetation of the southwestern Alaska mainland. Svensk Bot. Tidskr. 60: 177–189.

———.
1960b. Flora of the Aleutian Islands. Ed. 2, 376 p. Weinheim/Bergstr.

———.
1962a. Flora and vegetation of Scammon Bay, Bering Sea Coast, Alaska. Svensk Bot. Tidskr. 56: 36–54.

———.
1962b. The circumpolar plants. I. Vascular cryptograms, conifers, monocotyledons. Svensk Vetenskapsakad. Handl. 8(5), 275 p.

———.
1967. Comments on the flora of Alaska and Yukon. Svensk Vetenskapsakad. Handl. Ser. 2, 7(1), 147 p.

———.
1968. Flora of Alaska and neighboring territories; a manual of the vascular plants. 1,008 p. Stanford, Calif.: Stanford Univ. Press.

Hutchison, O. Keith.
1967. Alaska's forest resource. USDA Forest Serv. Res. Bull. PNW–19, 74 p.

Johnson, A. W., and Viereck, Leslie A.
1962. Some new records and range extensions of Arctic plants from Alaska. Univ. Alaska Biol. Pap. 6, 32 p.

Johnson, A. W., Viereck, Leslie A., Johnson, E. R., and Melchior, H.
1966. Vegetation and flora. p. 277–354. *In* Willomovsky, N. J., and Wolfe, J. N., eds. Environment of the Cape Thompson region, Alaska. U.S. Atomic Energy Comm. Div. Tech. Inform. 1,250 p.

Johnson, Phillip, and Vogel, Theodore C.
1966. Vegetation of the Yukon Flats region, Alaska. U.S. Army Cold Reg. Res. Eng. Lab., Hanover, N.H., Res. Rep. 209, 53 p.

Johnson, Von J.
1964. The chronology and analysis of the Hughes Fire, 1962. USDA Forest Serv. Res. Note NOR–8, 12 p.

Jones, George Neville.
1939. A synopsis of the North American species of *Sorbus*. J. Arnold Arboretum 20: 1–43.

———.
1940. A monograph of the genus *Symphoricarpos*. J. Arnold Arboretum 21: 201–252.

———.
1946. American species of *Amelanchier*. Ill. Biol. Monogr. 20(2), 126 p.

Jordal, L. H.
1951. Plants from the vicinity of Fairbanks, Alaska. Rhodora 53: 156–159.

———.
1952. Some new entities in the flora of the Brooks Range region, Alaska. Rhodora 54: 35–39.

Kellogg, R. S.
1910. The forests of Alaska. USDA Forest Serv. Bull. 81, 24 p.

La Roi, George H.
1967. Ecological studies in the boreal spruce-fir forests of the North American taiga. I. Analysis of the vascular flora. Ecol. Monogr. 37: 229–253.

Laurent, T. H.
1966. Dwarfmistletoe on Sitka spruce—a new host record. Plant Dis. Rep. 50: 921.

Lepage, Ernest.
1951. New and noteworthy plants in the flora of Alaska. Amer. Midland Natur. 46: 574–759.

Little, Elbert L., Jr.
1953a. Check list of native and naturalized trees of the United States (including Alaska). U.S. Dep. Agr., Agr. Handb. 41, 472 p.

———.
1953b. A natural hybrid spruce in Alaska. J. Forest. 51: 745–747.

Lotspeich, Frederick B., Mueller, Ernst W., and Frey, Paul J.
1970. Effects of large scale forest fires on water quality in interior Alaska. U.S. Dep. Interior, Fed. Water Pollut. Contr. Admin., Alaska Water Lab., College, Alaska, 115 p.

Löve, Doris, and Freedman, N. J.
1956. A plant collection from southwest Yukon. Bot. Notiser 109: 153–211.

Lutz, H. J.
1951. Damage to trees by black bears in Alaska. J. Forest. 49: 522–523.

———.
1952. Occurrence of clefts in the wood of living white spruce in Alaska. J. Forest. 50: 99–102.

———.
1956a. Damage to paper birch by red squirrels in Alaska. J. Forest. 54: 31–33.

———.
1956b. Ecological effects of forest fires in the interior of Alaska. U.S. Dep. Agr. Tech. Bull. 1,133, 121 p.

———.
1958a. Effect of red squirrels on crown form of black spruce in Alaska. USDA Forest Serv. Tech. Notes NO–42, 3 p.

———.
1958b. Observations on "diamond willow" with particular reference to its occurrence in Alaska. Amer. Midland Natur. 60: 176–185.

———.
1959. Aboriginal man and white man as historical causes of fires in the boreal forest with particular reference to Alaska. Yale Univ. Sch. Forest. Bull. 65, 49 p.

———.
1963a. Early forest conditions in the Alaska interior, an historical account with original sources. USDA Forest Serv. Northern Forest Exp. Sta. 74 p.

———.
1963b. Sitka spruce planted in 1805 at Unalaska Island by the Russians. USDA Forest Serv. Northern Forest Exp. Sta. 25 p.

———, and Caporaso, A. P.
1958. Indication of forest land classes in airphoto interpretation of the Alaska Interior. USDA Forest Serv. Sta. Pap. NO–10, 31 p.

McMinn, Howard E., and Maino, Evelyn.
1937. An illustrated manual of Pacific coast trees. 409 p. Berkeley, Calif. (Reprinted 1946.)

Markwardt, L. J.
1931. The distribution and the mechanical properties of Alaska woods. U.S. Dep. Agr. Tech. Bull. 226, 79 p.

Massie, Michael R.
1966. Marketing hardwoods from Alaska's Susitna Valley. Univ. Alaska, Inst. of Social, Economic and Government Res. SEG Rep. 9, 162 p.

———.
1967. Forest resource utilization in Alaska. Rev. Bus. Econ. Cond. 4(5): 1–8.

Mitchell, William W.
1968. On the ecology of Sitka alder in the subalpine zone of south-central Alaska. p. 45–56. *In* Trappe, J. M., Franklin, J. F., Tarrant, R. F., and Hansen, G. M., editors. Biology of alder. Proc. Symp. Northwest Sci. Assn. 40th Annu. Meeting, Pullman, Wash. USDA Forest Serv. Pacific Northwest Forest and Range Exp. Sta. 292 p.

Noste, Nonan V.
1969. Analysis and summary of forest fires in coastal Alaska. USDA Forest Serv. Pacific Northwest Forest and Range Exp. Sta. Inst. North. Forest. Misc. Publ. 12 p.

Orth, Donald J.
1967. Dictionary of Alaska place names. U.S. Geol. Surv. Prof. Pap. 567, 1,084 p.

Ostenfeld, C. H., and Larsen, C. Syrach.
1930. The species of the genus Larix and their geographical distribution. Kgl. Dansk. Vid. Selsk. Biol. Meddel. 9(2), 107 p.

Polunin, N.
1959. Circumpolar Arctic flora. 514 p. Oxford Univ. Press.

Porsild, A. E.
1938a. Flora of Little Diomede Island in Bering Strait. Trans. Roy. Soc. Can. Ser. 3, Sect. 5, 32: 21–38.

———.
1939. Contributions to the flora of Alaska. Rhodora 41: 141–183, 199–254, 262–301.

———.
1944. Vascular plants collected on Kiska and Great Sitkin Islands in the Aleutians by Lt. H. R. McCarthy and Capt. N. Kellas, August, September, and October 1943. Can. Field Natur. 58: 130–131.

Porsild, A. E.
1947. The genus *Dryas* in North America. Can. Field Natur. 61: 175–192.

———.
1951a. Botany of southeastern Yukon adjacent to the Canol Road. Nat. Mus. Can. Bull. 121, 400 p.

———.
1951b. Plant life in the Arctic. Can. Geogr. J. March 1951, 27 p.

———.
1953. Edible plants of the Arctic. Arctic 6: 15–34.

———.
1964. Illustrated flora of the Canadian Arctic Archipelago. Ed. 2. Nat. Mus. Can. Bull. 146: 1–218.

———.
1965. Some new or critical vascular plants of Alaska and Yukon. Can. Field Natur. 79: 79–90.

Potter, Louise.
1962. Roadside flowers of Alaska. 590 p. Thetford Center, Vermont: Publ. by author.

Raunkiaer, C.
1934. The life forms of plants and statistical plant geography. 632 p. Oxford: Claredon Press.

Raup, Hugh M.
1945a. Forests and gardens along the Alaska Highway. Geog. Rev. 35: 22–48.

———.
1945b. Vegetation along the Alaska Highway and the north Pacific coast. J. N.Y. Bot. Gard. 46: 177–191.

———.
1947. The botany of southwestern Mackenzie. Sargentia 6, 275 p.

———.
1959. The willows of boreal western America. Contrib. Gray Herb. Harvard Univ. 185, 95 p.

Rigg, G. B.
1914. Notes on the flora of some Alaskan sphagnum bogs. Plant World 17: 167–182.

———.
1937. Some raised bogs of southeastern Alaska with notes on flat bogs and muskegs. Amer. J. Bot. 24: 194–198.

Rowe, J. S.
1959. Forest regions of Canada. Can. Dep. North. Aff. Natur. Res., Forest. Branch Bull. 123, 71 p.

Sargent, Charles Sprague.
1926. Manual of the trees of North America (exclusive of Mexico). Ed. 2, reprinted with corrections. 910 p. Boston and New New York: Houghton Mifflin Co. (Reprinted 1933, 1961.)

Saville, D. B. O.
1969. Interrelationships of *Ledum* species and their rust parasites in Western Canada and Alaska. Can. J. Bot. 47: 1085–1100.

Scamman, Edith.
1940. A list of plants from interior Alaska. Rhodora 42: 309–349.

Shacklette, Hansford T., et al.
1969. Vegetation of Amchitka Island, Aleutian Islands, Alaska. U.S. Geol. Surv. Prof. Pap. 648, 66 p.

Sharples, Ada White.
1938. Alaska wild flowers. 156 p. Stanford Univ. Press.

Shetler, Stanwyn.
1963. An annotated list of vascular plants from Cape Sabine, Alaska. Rhodora 65: 208–224.

Sigafoos, Robert S.
1958. Vegetation of northwestern North America, as an aid in interpretation of geological data. U.S. Geol. Surv. Bull. 1061–E: 165–185.

Spetzman, Lloyd A.
1959. Vegetation of the Arctic slope of Alaska. U.S. Geol. Surv. Prof. Pap. 302–B: 19–58.

———.
1963. Terrain study of Alaska, Part V: vegetation [folded map, 1:2,500,000]. *In* Engineer Intelligence Study EIS 301. U.S. Dep. Army, Office Chief Eng. Wash., D.C.

Standley, Paul C.
1943. Edible plants of the Arctic region. U.S. Dep. Navy, Bur. Medicine and Surgery, Navmed 119, 49 p.

Stoeckler, E. G.
1952. Trees of interior Alaska, their significance as soil and permafrost indicators. U.S. Dep. Army, Corps Eng. 25 p.

Suda, Y., and Argus, George W.
1969. Chromosome numbers of some North American Arctic and Boreal *Salix*. Can. J. Bot. 47: 859–862.

Sudworth, George B.
1908. Forest trees of the Pacific slope. USDA Forest Serv. 441 p. Wash., D.C. (Reprinted 1967.)

Tatewaki, M.
1930–31. Notes on plants of the western Aleutian Islands collected in 1929. Parts 1–2. Trans. Sapporo Natur. Hist. Soc. 11: 152–156; 12: 200–209.

———, and Kobayashi, Y.
1934. A contribution to the flora of the Aleutian Islands. J. Fac. Agr. Hokkaido Imp. Univ. 36, 119 p.

Taylor, Raymond F.
1929. Pocket guide to Alaska trees. U.S. Dep. Agr. Misc. Publ. 55, 39 p.

———.
1932. The successional trend and its relation to second-growth forests in southeastern Alaska. Ecology 13: 381–391.

———.
1934. Yield of second-growth western hemlock-Sitka spruce stands in southeastern Alaska. U.S. Dep. Agr. Tech. Bull. 412, 30 p.

———, and Little, Elbert L., Jr.
1950. Pocket guide to Alaska trees. U.S. Dep. Agr., Agr. Handb. 5, 63 p.

Thomas, John H.
1951. A collection of plants from Point Lay, Alaska. Contrib. Dudley Herb. Stanford Univ. 4: 53–56.

———.
1957. The vascular flora of Middleton Island, Alaska. Contrib. Dudley Herb. Stanford Univ. 5: 39–56.

Trigg, William M., and Noste, Nonan V.
1969. Summary and analysis of fire danger indexes for selected coastal Alaska stations. USDA Forest Serv. Pacific Northwest Forest and Range Exp. Sta. Inst. Northern Forest. Misc. Publ. 21 p.

USDA Forest Products Laboratory.
1963. Characteristics of Alaska woods. USDA Forest Serv. Res. Pap. FPL–1, 64 p.

USDA Forest Service.
1940. Tongass National Forest, Alaska. 46 p. Wash., D.C.

Viereck, Leslie A.
1966. Succession and soil development on gravel outwash of the Muldrow Glacier, Alaska. Ecol. Monogr. 36: 181–199.

———.
1970. Forest succession and soil development adjacent to the Chena River in interior Alaska. Arctic and Alpine Res. 2: 1–26.

Viereck, Leslie A., and Foote, Joan M.
1970. The status of *Populus balsamifera* and *P. trichocarpa* in Alaska. Can. Field Natur. 84: 169–173.

Wahrhftig, Clyde.
1965. Physiographic divisions of Alaska. U.S. Geol. Surv. Prof. Pap. 482, 52 p.

Whitford, H. N., and Craig, R. D.
1918. Forests of British Columbia. 409 p. Ottawa.

Wiggins, Ira L., and MacVicar, D. G.
1958. Notes on the plants in the vicinity of Chandler Lake, Alaska. Contrib. Dudley Herb. Stanford Univ. 5: 69–95.

————, and Thomas, J. H.
1962. A flora of the Alaskan Arctic slope. Arct. Inst. N. Amer. Spec. Publ. 4, 425 p.

Wight, W. F.
1908. A new larch from Alaska. Smithsonian Institution Misc. Collect. 50: 174.

Williams, M. M.
1952. Alaska wild flower glimpses. 52 p. Juneau, Alaska: The Totem Press.

Zasada, John C., and Gregory, Robert A.
1969. Regeneration of white spruce (*Picea glauca* (Moench) Voss) with reference to interior Alaska: a literature review. USDA Forest Service Res. Pap. PNW–79, 37 p.

INDEX OF COMMON AND SCIENTIFIC NAMES

The preferred common names adopted in headings and the page numbers where the descriptions begin are in heavy (boldface) type. Other common names appear in ordinary (roman) type. English common names are indexed under the last word.

Scientific names accepted in headings are shown in heavy (boldface) italics, and the page numbers where the descriptions begin are in heavy (boldface) type. Other scientific names, including synonyms, are in italics. Family names, common and scientific, are shown in capitals. Scientific names of varieties and subspecies, with few exceptions, are not indexed.

261

262

264

willow, low blueberry, 18, 19, **99**
willow, mountain, 120
willow, netleaf, 19, 21, 22, 23, **86**
willow, ovalleaf, 22, 23, **94**
willow, Pacific, 20, **126**
willow, park, 16, 20, **108**
willow, planeleaf, 120
willow, polar, 22, 23, **88**
willow, reticulate, 86
willow, Richardson, 16, 20, 21, 22, **110**
willow, sage, 115
willow, sandbar, 9, 20, **126**
willow, Scouler, 15, 16, 17, 18, 20, **120**

willow, serviceberry, 108
willow, Setchell, 10, 21, **87**
willow, silky, 122
willow, silver, 11, **115**
willow, Sitka, 15, 20, 21, **122**
willow, skeletonleaf, 23, **89**
willow, sprouting, 94
willow, tall blueberry, 16, 18, 20, **101**
willow, thickleaf, 86
willow, undergreen, 19, 20, 21, 22, **106**
willow, wedgeleaf, 11, **92**
willow, western black, 126
willow, woolly, 110

willow, Yakutat, 10, 106
willow, yellow, 126
WILLOW FAMILY, 6, 8, **70**
wineberry, 180
wintergreen, 204, **226**
wintergreen, Miquel, 11, **226**
wormwood, 250

yellow-cedar, 66
yellow-cedar, Alaska, 66
yellow-rose, 180
Yew, Pacific, 8, 11, **44**
yew, western, 44
YEW FAMILY, **43**

☆ U.S. GOVERNMENT PRINTING OFFICE : 1978 O—276-137